T0198135

CompTIA CTT+™ Certified Technical Trainer

EXAM GUIDE

CompTIA CTT+™
Certified Technical Trainer

EXAM GUIDE

Joseph Phillips

New York • Chicago • San Francisco • Athens
London • Madrid • Mexico City • Milan
New Delhi • Singapore • Sydney • Toronto

Library of Congress Cataloging-in-Publication Data

Phillips, Joseph.
  CompTIA CTT+TM certified technical trainer all in one exam guide / Joseph Phillips.
     p. cm. — (All-in-one)
  Includes bibliographical references and index.
  ISBN 978-0-07-177116-0
  1. Technical education—Examinations—Study guides.   2. Vocational teachers—Certification.   I. Title.
  T65.P56 2012
  607.1—dc23

2012002295

McGraw-Hill Education books are available at special quantity discounts to use as premiums and sales promotions or for use in corporate training programs. To contact a representative, please visit the Contact Us pages at www.mhprofessional.com.

CompTIA CTT+™ Certified Technical Trainer All-in-One Exam Guide

11 12 13 LKV 23

ISBN: Book p/n 978-0-07-177114-6 and CD p/n 978-0-07-177115-3 of set 978-0-07-177116-0

MHID: Book p/n 0-07-177114-X and CD p/n 0-07-177115-8 of set 0-07-177116-6

Sponsoring Editor
Timothy Green

Editorial Supervisor
Jody McKenzie

Project Editor
Howie Severson, Fortuitous Publishing Services

Acquisitions Coordinator
Stephanie Evans

Technical Editor
James A. Ward

Copy Editors
Jan Jue, Lisa McCoy

Proofreader
Paul Tyler

Indexer
Jack Lewis

Production Supervisor
James Kussow

Composition
Apollo Publishing Services

Art Director, Cover
Jeff Weeks

For Andrea.

ABOUT THE AUTHOR

Joseph Phillips, PMP, Project+, CTT+, is the Director of Education for Project Seminars. He has taught technical courses since 1995 for various industries, including health care, information sciences, pharmaceutical, manufacturing, and architectural. Phillips has served as a project management consultant for organizations creating project offices, maturity models, and best-practice standardization.

As a leader in adult education, Phillips has taught organizations how to successfully implement project management methodologies, information technology project management, risk management, and other courses. He has taught for Columbia College, University of Chicago, and Ball State University. He is a certified technical trainer and has taught over 10,000 professionals in the United States and Europe. Phillips has contributed as an author or editor to more than 35 books on technology, careers, education, and project management.

When not writing, teaching, or consulting, Phillips can be found behind a camera or on the working end of a fly rod. You can contact him through www.instructing.com.

About the Technical Editor

James A. Ward, principal consultant with James A. Ward & Associates, Inc., manages a practice specializing in information technology project management, business systems analysis, technical writing, and PMO (Project Management Office) implementation. His services are highly sought for interim IT management and implementation of quality and process improvement initiatives. Mr. Ward's seminars and workshops in project management, PMP exam prep, quality improvement, requirements definition, project risk management, and Microsoft Project are always well attended and highly recommended by his clients. He is a frequent speaker at IT and project management conferences and has written numerous articles for professional journals.

Mr. Ward holds an MBA in finance from the University of Chicago and a bachelor's degree in economics and mathematics from the University of Minnesota. He is a PMP Certified Project Manager. He resides in Richmond, Virginia, and can be reached via e-mail at soozward@earthlink.net. Further information is available on his website at www.JamesAWard.com.

CompTIA.

CompTIA Approved Quality Curriculum

It Pays to Get Certified

In a digital world, digital literacy is an essential survival skill. Certification proves you have the knowledge and skill to solve business problems in virtually any business environment. Certifications are highly valued credentials that qualify you for jobs, increased compensation, and promotion.

CompTIA CTT+ certification is an international, vendor-neutral certification that covers core instructor skills, including preparation, presentation, communication, facilitation, and evaluation in both a classroom and virtual classroom environment.

- Certified Technical Trainers personify excellence in preparation, presentation, communication, facilitation, and evaluation in a classroom environment.

- CompTIA CTT+ (Certified Technical Trainer) provides a globally recognized measure of core skills, actions, and behaviors required of competent technical instructors.

- Starting salary—the average salary for CompTIA CTT+ certification holders is $52,000. Average salaries can vary greatly due to company, location, industry, experience, and benefits.

- Mandated/recommended by organizations worldwide—Adobe, Dell, Microsoft, Novell, and Ricoh recommend that their trainers be CompTIA CTT+ certified. The Training Associates also look for CompTIA CTT+ certification when hiring trainers.

- More than 17,000 people have become CompTIA CTT+ certified.

How Certification Helps Your Career

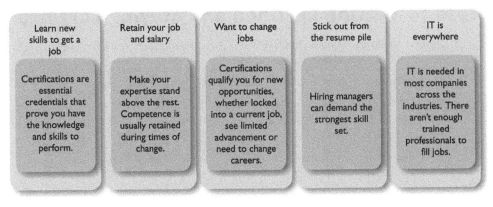

Learn new skills to get a job	Retain your job and salary	Want to change jobs	Stick out from the resume pile	IT is everywhere
Certifications are essential credentials that prove you have the knowledge and skills to perform.	Make your expertise stand above the rest. Competence is usually retained during times of change.	Certifications qualify you for new opportunities, whether locked into a current job, see limited advancement or need to change careers.	Hiring managers can demand the strongest skill set.	IT is needed in most companies across the industries. There aren't enough trained professionals to fill jobs.

CompTIA Career Pathway

CompTIA offers a number of credentials that form a foundation for your career in technology and that allow you to pursue specific areas of concentration. Depending on the path you choose, CompTIA certifications help you build upon your skills and knowledge, supporting learning throughout your career.

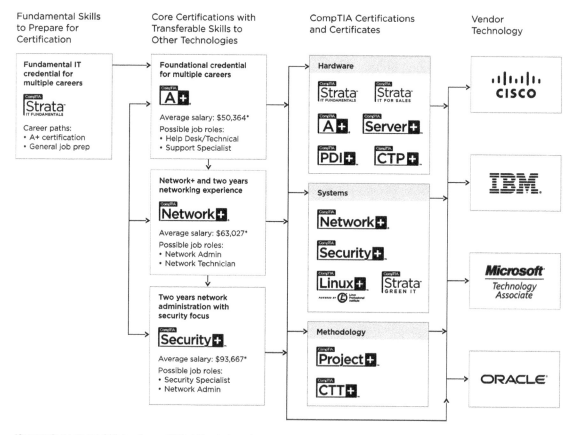

*Source: Computerworld Salary Survey 2010—U.S. salaries only

Steps to Getting Certified and Staying Certified

1. **Review exam objectives.** Review the certification objectives to make sure you know what is covered in the exam:

   www.comptia.org/certifications/testprep/examobjectives.aspx

2. **Practice for the exam.** After you have studied for the certification, take a free assessment and sample test to get an idea of what types of questions might be on the exam:

   www.comptia.org/certifications/testprep/practicetests.aspx

3. **Purchase an exam voucher.** Purchase exam vouchers on the CompTIA Marketplace, which is located at:

   www.comptiastore.com

4. **Take the test!** Select a certification exam provider, and schedule a time to take your exam. You can find exam providers at the following link:

   www.comptia.org/certifications/testprep/testingcenters.aspx

Join the Professional Community

The free online IT Pro Community provides valuable content to students and professionals.

Career IT job resources include

- Where to start in IT
- Career assessments
- Salary trends
- U.S. job board

Join the IT Pro Community and get access to

- Forums on networking, security, computing, and cutting-edge technologies
- Blogs written by industry experts
- Current information on cutting-edge technologies
- Various industry resource links and articles related to IT and IT careers

Content Seal of Quality

This courseware bears the seal of CompTIA Approved Quality Content. This seal signifies this content covers 100 percent of the exam objectives and implements important instructional design principles. CompTIA recommends multiple learning tools to help increase coverage of the learning objectives.

Why CompTIA?

- **Global recognition** CompTIA is recognized globally as the leading IT nonprofit trade association and has enormous credibility. Plus, CompTIA's certifications are vendor-neutral and offer proof of foundational knowledge that translates across technologies.

- **Valued by hiring managers**   Hiring managers value CompTIA certification because it is vendor- and technology-independent validation of your technical skills.
- **Recommended or required by government and businesses**   Many government organizations and corporations (for example, Dell, Sharp, Ricoh, the U.S. Department of Defense, and many more) either recommend or require technical staff to be CompTIA certified.
- **Three CompTIA certifications ranked in the top 10**   In a study by DICE of 17,000 technology professionals, certifications helped command higher salaries at all experience levels.

How to Obtain More Information

- **Visit CompTIA online**   Go to www.comptia.org to learn more about getting CompTIA certified.
- **Contact CompTIA**   Please call 866-835-8020, ext. 5, or e-mail questions@comptia.org.
- **Join the IT Pro Community**   Go to http://itpro.comptia.org to join the IT community to get relevant career information.
- **Connect with CompTIA**   Find us on Facebook, LinkedIn, Twitter, and YouTube.

CAQC Disclaimer

The logo of the CompTIA Approved Quality Curriculum (CAQC) program and the status of this or other training material as "Approved" under the CompTIA Approved Quality Curriculum program signifies that, in CompTIA's opinion, such training material covers the content of CompTIA's related certification exam.

The contents of this training material were created for the CompTIA Certified Technical Trainer+ examinations covering CompTIA certification objectives that were current as of the date of publication.

CompTIA has not reviewed or approved the accuracy of the contents of this training material and specifically disclaims any warranties of merchantability or fitness for a particular purpose. CompTIA makes no guarantee concerning the success of persons using any such "Approved" or other training material in order to prepare for any CompTIA certification exam.

CONTENTS AT A GLANCE

Part I	Planning Prior to the Course	. . . .	I
Chapter 1	Preparing for the Exam	. . . .	3
Chapter 2	Evaluating Learners' Needs	. . . .	43
Chapter 3	Managing the Technical Classroom	. . . .	81
Part II	Methods for Effective Instruction	. . . .	III
Chapter 4	Engaging Learners Through Instructional Methods	. . . .	II3
Chapter 5	Managing Instructional Materials	. . . .	I47
Part III	Establishing Instructor Credibility and Maintaining Communications	. . . .	I75
Chapter 6	Instructing with Confidence	. . . .	I77
Chapter 7	Leading a Successful Class	. . . .	205
Part IV	Leading Group Facilitation	. . . .	231
Chapter 8	Managing Learner-Centered Instruction	. . . .	233
Chapter 9	Promoting Learner Engagement	. . . .	261
Chapter 10	Motivating Adult Learners	. . . .	285
Part V	Evaluating the Training Event	. . . .	309
Chapter 11	Evaluating Learner Competencies	. . . .	311
Chapter 12	Evaluating Instructor and Course Performance	. . . .	333
Part VI	Appendices	. . . .	353
Appendix A	Certified Technical Trainer+ Exam Objectives	. . . .	355
Appendix B	About the CD	. . . .	369
	Glossary	. . . .	371
	Index	. . . .	391

CONTENTS

Preface xix
Acknowledgments xxi
Introduction xxiii

Part I   Planning Prior to the Course I

Chapter I   Preparing for the Exam 3
About the CompTIA CTT+ Essentials Exam 4
    Domain 1: Planning Prior to the Course 5
    Domain 2: Methods and Media for Instructional Delivery . . 6
    Domain 3: Instructor Credibility and Communications 7
    Domain 4: Group Facilitation 8
    Domain 5: Evaluate the Training Event 9
Passing the CompTIA CTT+ Essentials Exam 10
Passing the Trainer Performance Exam 13
    Recording Your Presentation 14
    Understanding the Classroom Trainer Scoring 16
    Scoring the Virtual Classroom Trainer Exam 21
Chapter Summary 27
    Key Terms 28
    Questions 31
    Questions and Answers 34

Chapter 2   Evaluating Learners' Needs 43
Determining the Learning Needs 44
    Defining Instructional Goals for Participants 44
    Developing the Learning Objectives 46
Measuring Learner Competencies 52
    Creating Course Prerequisites 53
    Administering Assessment Exams 54
Introducing the ADDIE Model 56
    Analyzing the Learning Need 57
    Designing the Technical Training 57
    Developing the Course Material 59
    Implementing the Technical Course 60
    Evaluating the Technical Course 62
Chapter Summary 64
    Key Terms 66
    Questions 68
    Questions and Answers 72

Chapter 3 Managing the Technical Classroom 81
   Configuring the Learning Environment 82
      Preparing the Physical Space 83
      Planning the Course Logistics 86
   Teaching the Perfect Class 88
      Managing the Learning Environment 89
      Adding Presentation Software 90
   Adding Classroom Features 92
      Creating Learning Handouts for Participants 93
      Considering the Room Color 94
      Adding Music to Your Classroom 95
   Chapter Summary 96
      Key Terms 97
      Questions 98
      Questions and Answers 102

Part II Methods for Effective Instruction 111

Chapter 4 Engaging Learners Through Instructional Methods 113
   Training the Technical Participant 114
      Facilitating a Technical Class 115
      Teaching Technology for Different Learning Styles 116
   Exploring Learning Theories 121
      Understanding Gagné's Theory of Instruction 122
      Exploring the Cognitive Learning Theory 124
      Using the Constructivist Learning Theory 125
   Facilitating Technical Content 126
      Creating Group Exercises 127
      Teaching with Games and Simulations 128
      Demonstrating the Technology 128
   Chapter Summary 129
      Key Terms 130
      Questions 133
      Questions and Answers 138

Chapter 5 Managing Instructional Materials 147
   Determining the Make-or-Buy Decision 148
      Considering Financial Impact of Course Materials 148
      Considering Internal Development Solutions 150
   Designing Effective Technical Classes 151
      Preparing for Effective Technical Training 152
      Ensuring Quality Course Design 153
   Controlling Materials in the Virtual Classroom 155
      Managing Virtual Classroom Material Challenges 156
      Selecting Media Visuals for Learners' Needs 157

Chapter Summary 159
    Key Terms 160
    Questions 162
    Questions and Answers 166

Part III   Establishing Instructor Credibility and
Maintaining Communications 175

Chapter 6   Instructing with Confidence 177
Establishing Instructor Fundamentals 178
    Preparing to Train 179
    Maintaining a Positive Learning Environment 181
Managing Learners in the Classroom 182
    Involving Learners in the Training 183
    Dealing with Learner Behavior 186
Chapter Summary 189
    Key Terms 190
    Questions 190
    Questions and Answers 195

Chapter 7   Leading a Successful Class 205
Training like a Professional 206
    Speaking with Clarity 206
    Speaking with Your Voice 208
    Connecting with Your Audience 209
Managing Learning Momentum 210
    Maintaining Learner Interest 211
    Presenting with Charm 212
    Reviewing and Summarizing Content 214
Chapter Summary 216
    Key Terms 217
    Questions 218
    Questions and Answers 222

Part IV   Leading Group Facilitation 231

Chapter 8   Managing Learner-Centered Instruction 233
Establishing Learner-Centered Instruction 234
    Delivering Performance-Based Training 234
    Analyzing Learner Tasks 236
Exploring Bloom's Taxonomy 238
    Reviewing the Psychomotor Domain 239
    Reviewing the Affective Domain 240
    Reviewing the Cognitive Domain 242

Chapter Summary 245
    Key Terms 246
    Questions 249
    Questions and Answers 253

Chapter 9   Promoting Learner Engagement 261
    Engaging Technical Learners 262
        Teaching Through Listening 262
        Creating Quizzes for Technical Classes 265
    Utilizing Social Learning Theory 267
        Training with Group Participation 268
        Offering Learning Games and Activities 269
    Chapter Summary 271
        Key Terms 272
        Questions 274
        Questions and Answers 278

Chapter 10   Motivating Adult Learners 285
    Understanding Adult Learners 286
        Adapting Adult Learning Characteristics 287
        Facilitating Adult Education 289
    Motivating Adult Learners 291
        Finding Learner Motivation 292
        Motivating Adults to Learn 293
    Chapter Summary 295
        Key Terms 296
        Questions 297
        Questions and Answers 301

Part V   Evaluating the Training Event 309

Chapter 11   Evaluating Learner Competencies 311
    Determining Learner Competence 311
        Creating a Course Examination 312
        Utilizing Embedded Assessments 314
    Exploring Authentic Assessment 315
        Meeting Learning Goals 316
        Changing Learner Behavior 317
    Chapter Summary 319
        Key Terms 320
        Questions 320
        Questions and Answers 324

Chapter 12   Evaluating Instructor and Course Performance   333
Understanding Trainer Evaluations   333
Utilizing a Summative Evaluation   334
Offering Formative Assessment   335
Applying Effective Instructor Evaluations   336
Reviewing the Kirkpatrick Evaluation Model   336
Considering E-based Evaluations   337
Chapter Summary   338
Key Terms   339
Questions   340
Questions and Answers   345

Part VI   Appendices   353

Appendix A   Certified Technical Trainer+ Exam Objectives   355
Planning Prior to the Course   356
Review of Organizational Needs and Learners' Backgrounds
in Relationship to Course Objectives   356
Instructional Environment in Relationship
to Learning Objectives   357
Utilizing Methods and Media for Instructional Delivery   359
Selection and Implementation of Instructional Methods   . . .   359
Use of Presentation and Instructional Media   360
Maintaining Instructor Credibility and Communications   361
Instructor Delivery Competence and Content Expertise   361
Instructor Communication and Presentation Skills   362
Facilitating Adult Education   363
Establishment and Management of a Learner-Centered
Environment   363
Promotion of Learner Engagement and Participation   364
Assessment of Learners' Needs for Additional Explanation
and Encouragement   365
Motivation and Positive Reinforcement of Learners   366
Evaluating the Training Event   366
Evaluation of Learner Performance During and at Close
of Instruction   367
Evaluation of Instructor and Course   368

Appendix B   About the CD   369
System Requirements   369
Installing and Running MasterExam   369
MasterExam   369

Video Training 370
PDF Copy of the Book 370
Help 370
Removing Installations 370
Technical Support 370
    LearnKey Technical Support 370

Glossary 371

Index 391

PREFACE

The first technical class I taught was in Chicago in 1995—an ancient version of Microsoft Windows on computers that Moses once owned. I was nervous, sweating like I ran a marathon, and convinced everyone in the room hated me and the class content. Then something magical happened. I found a rhythm to all that I had prepared to deliver, and the people in the class followed along like a good dance partner. My nerves settled, I quit sweating, and people were actually learning. My confidence began to creep up and things were tolerable, then good, then actually fun! It was a successful class, and I loved the feeling of helping people learn something new.

I still love that feeling—as I bet you do, too. In this book I've tried to write in a conversational, down-to-earth tone. I've imagined you and I have a coffee and are just talking about training, about the CompTIA Certified Technical Trainer+ exam, and about all the things you'll have to know and do to earn the certification. There are lots of terms, philosophies, and theories about learning discussed in this book, but there's really just one important message: The learner is the most important person in the classroom, not the trainer. If you keep that as your focus you'll be a great trainer.

The CompTIA CTT+ certification is a great accomplishment for any trainer. Earning this certification demonstrates that you understand more than just the fundamentals of technical training and have a proficiency in leading learner-centered classrooms. As a traditional classroom trainer or a virtual classroom trainer, the principles in this book will help you to not only pass the CTT+ certification, but to become more aware of your training style, more flexible to learners' preferences, and will serve as a guide to focus on the classroom participants rather than the classroom trainer.

ACKNOWLEDGMENTS

Books, projects, and successful training endeavors are rarely a solo act. So many people contribute to the final deliverable, the final product. Thank you to my editor, Stephanie Evans, for her incredible patience during this book creation. Thank you also to my friend and editor, Tim Green, for his guidance and support over the years. Thank you to Jan Jue and Lisa McCoy for helping my writing shine. And kudos to Howie Severson for his organization through the book's final stages.

I'm so fortunate to have so many friends and colleagues who have cheered me on in my businesses, my writing, and in my life. Thank you to Jo, Andy, and Mike Diaczyk for your friendship, business talks, and lots of good wine. A big thanks for my friends that have cheered me on during the writing of this book: Curt Farris, Angela and Carl Richter, Duane Schoon, Fred and Carin McBroom, Greg and Mary Huebner, Lamont Hatcher, Jonathan Acosta, Jennifer Real, Jennifer Hatfield, Greg Kirkland, John and Cara Sutherland, Don Kuhnle, Norm and Paulette Tarantola, and many more than what's reasonable to include here. As always, thank you to my parents, Don and Virginia Phillips, and my son Kyle. Finally, thanks for my brothers Steve, Mark, Sam, and Ben for listening, reading, and being fairly good brothers.

INTRODUCTION

Of course, this book also has a goal of you earning your CTT+ certification. In each chapter I've addressed the CompTIA objectives as per their website (www.comptia.org) and I've offered some practice questions for your review on each topic. You'll also find key terms at the end of each chapter. I highly recommend you get a stack of index cards and create flashcards based on the key terms in each chapter. Keep these with you and buzz through the terms at every chance you get—if you understand the terminology, you'll be better prepared to answer questions dealing with the terms.

On the CD there are 12 videos I've created for you. These videos will coach you through some of the more complex topics in this book. You can watch these all at once or watch one per chapter—with a few extras at the end of the book. You'll also find a practice exam on the CD and a link to download another practice exam from the Internet. My hope for you is that you become a better trainer than you already are, that you pass the CTT+ examination, and that you continue to positively influence people's lives in your roles as a technical trainer.

Exam Objective Reference

Exam Domain and Percentage	Chapter #	Page #
Domain 1: Planning Prior to the Course 13%		
1A: Review of Organizational Needs and Learners' Backgrounds in Relationship to Course Objectives	2, 3, 4, 5, 6, 7, 8, 9, 10, 11	44, 45, 59, 88–90, 119, 126, 150–152, 179, 181, 211–212, 234, 236–238, 262–263, 286–288, 315
1B: Instructional Environment in Relationship to Learning Objectives	2, 3, 5, 6, 12	59–62, 82–86, 154–158, 181–183, 334–336
Domain 2: Methods and Media for Instructional Delivery 14%		
2A: Selection and Implementation of Instructional Methods	2, 4, 5, 6, 7, 9	57–58, 115–119, 155, 183–189, 206–210, 267–269
2B: Use of Presentation and Instructional Media	1, 3, 5, 7, 9	6, 90–92, 95, 157–158, 210–212, 262–264
Domain 3: Instructor Credibility and Communications 10%		
3A: Instructor Delivery Competence and Content Expertise	1, 5, 6, 10, 11	7, 151–152, 183–189, 206–210, 267–269
3B: Instructor Communication and Presentation Skills	3, 4, 5, 6, 7, 9	7, 89, 126, 151, 154, 179–183, 206–213, 263–265

Exam Domain and Percentage	Chapter #	Page #
Domain 4: Group Facilitation 45%		
4A: Establishment and Management of a Learner-Centered Environment	1, 3, 4, 5, 6, 7, 8, 9, 11, 12	8, 89, 121, 152, 156, 181–183, 212–213, 234–236, 268–270, 311–314, 335
4B: Promotion of Learner Engagement and Participation	4, 6, 8, 9	8, 122, 124, 182–185, 234–235, 267–269
4C: Assessment of Learners' Needs for Additional Explanation and Encouragement	4, 6, 7, 8, 9, 10	8, 123–125, 183–184, 214–215, 237–238, 265–266, 291
4D: Motivation and Positive Reinforcement of Learners	4, 8, 9, 10, 11	8, 125–126, 238–245, 267–268, 291–295, 317–318
Domain 5: Evaluate the Training Event 18%		
5A: Evaluation of Learner Performance During and at Close of Instruction	2, 11, 12	9, 62–64, 311–312, 314–315
5B: Evaluation of Instructor and Course	2, 11, 12	9, 62–64, 334–335, 336–338

PART I

Planning Prior to the Course

- **Chapter 1**   Preparing for the Exam
- **Chapter 2**   Evaluating Learners' Needs
- **Chapter 3**   Managing the Technical Classroom

Preparing for the Exam

In this chapter you will:

- Learn about the CompTIA Certified Technical Trainer+ certification
- Review the objectives for the CTT+ TK0-201 computer-based examination
- Understand the objectives for the CTT+ TK0-202 classroom performance-based examination
- Examine the objectives for the CTT+ TK0-203 virtual classroom performance-based examination
- Know the testing and evaluation process to earn the CTT+ certification
- Review the costs of the examinations and CompTIA membership

If you are a technical trainer and you want to prove your experience and training abilities, and set yourself apart from other trainers, you'll be interested in the CompTIA Certified Technical Trainer+ certification. This is a certification that can show employers, clients, and students that you have experience training technical topics, that you understand how to teach, and that you've passed at least two rigorous exams testing your competence.

If you're like me, you really enjoy teaching complex topics to other people. It's rewarding to take a complicated topic, break it down to simple terms, and see people's expressions when they learn. Technology, from custom software to servers and bleeding-edge hardware, can be a demanding topic to present. But this isn't a book about presenting, and it's really not even a book about training. This is a book about how you, the expert trainer that you are, can help people learn technical topics.

While there is a connection between training and learning, there's also a distinct difference between lecturing, telling, and teaching. As a CompTIA CTT+ candidate you'll need to recognize the characteristics of a good instructor, how people learn when you teach, and how to overcome challenges of the classroom and teaching over the Internet.

 VIDEO   See the video *Earning your CTT+ Certification.*

Like training, this book has goals for you. This book will:

- Cover the exam objectives in detail for the computer-based CompTIA CTT+ examination

- Help you prepare for the classroom-performance and the virtual-performance review for the CompTIA CTT+ certification process
- Offer videos to reinforce the concepts of each chapter
- Focus your efforts on passing the CompTIA CTT+ examination
- Help you become a better instructor
- Provide a review of each chapter's terminology
- Test your exam readiness with chapter exams and practice exams on the CD
- Not be boring

This first chapter details the exam objectives and the complete certification process.

While it's true that anyone can pay for and take the CompTIA CTT+ examination, not just anyone can pass the exam. This test requires that you understand how to train others, manage the classroom, engage learners, and recognize different learning styles. While you can learn many of these techniques from this book, the real knowledge, the understanding of the materials, is proven through your performance-based examination. In other words, you might be good at taking tests, but if you can't teach—and prove it—you'll score poorly on the practical examination for the classroom- or web-based trainer exam.

This book will help you prepare to pass the CTT+ examination—not just take the test. You'll learn the meaty stuff the exam will test you on, how to best prepare for the exam, and how to remember loads of terms. As an instructor you might already be familiar with some of the concepts in this book, though you'll also need to be familiar with the terminology associated with the concepts of technical training.

About the CompTIA CTT+ Essentials Exam

CompTIA is the Computing Technology Industry Association, and they're the certifying body for vendor-neutral certifications like the Project+ Professional, A+ Technician, and your next certification, the Certified Technical Trainer+. You can usually spot the CompTIA certifications because they have the "+" symbol after the designation. CompTIA certifications aren't easy, but they don't have the same prerequisites to take the exam such as proven experience or education.

The CompTIA CTT+ Essentials exam will test your knowledge of how to train adults on technical topics. This examination will challenge your knowledge of adult learning styles, classroom management techniques, and how to teach—not lecture. You'll need to be familiar with learning theories, how to create a learner-centered environment, and how to engage your learners in the materials you present. This exam will also test your instructional design comprehension to some extent and your ability to adapt, shift, and overcome challenges in the materials you're teaching from. You'll also need to be familiar with how to utilize effective class and instructor evaluations. In this book I'll coach you through all of the exam objectives. You'll be prepared to pass this exam and get back to teaching with more confidence and with your shiny, new certification.

The CompTIA CTT+ Essentials examination has 95 questions, and you'll have 90 minutes to complete the exam. The CompTIA CTT+ Essentials exam will cost you $246, and you'll have to pay an additional $266 for either the classroom-based or virtual classroom performance exam, depending on which recording you choose to submit. You'll register for the exam through www.comptia.org—where you can choose your local testing center and schedule the exam date. You'll need to be familiar with the five domains on the CompTIA CTT+ examination. This book will help you prepare for each of the exam objectives.

Domain 1: Planning Prior to the Course

This domain accounts for 13 percent of the exam (roughly 12 questions of the 95 test questions). You'll be tested on your experience and knowledge of how you can assess organizational needs and learners' backgrounds, and how these needs relate to the course objectives you're about to create. You'll also be tested on the modality of the training session—how you'll accomplish the goals of the training in a classroom environment, via the Web, or even in smaller coaching sessions.

Instructors need to anticipate the sections of the course material that are likely to cause confusion and questions in the classroom. By anticipating the questions, you can adjust your lecture, allow learners to learn through participation, and encourage peer learning. Instructors also will use this opportunity to plan for topics where learners may understand the material but may be resistant to the topic at hand. For example, new applications, organizational change, and new work procedures using technology are often resisted before being adopted by learners. This domain will test your ability to involve learners, overcome challenges, and to promote the needs of the organization.

Your course objectives may be determined through surveys and needs analysis, but how you teach the objectives may be adapted to each scenario. You'll need to adjust your teaching approach and learning materials to the identified learning styles, the learners' reception to the messages, and the group or situation you're training within. This includes adjusting your instructional activities to the organization, the audience, and the needs of your organization. The goal is to keep a learner-centered environment, classroom or virtual, to satisfy the needs of the organization you're teaching for.

As a CompTIA CTT+ you should also be familiar with managing the environment you're about to teach in. You'll need to coordinate with colleagues and vendors the logistics of every class: course materials, classroom computers' setup, classroom configuration, pre-course work for learners, and login information for the systems—and even physical access to the training room. Once you're done teaching, you'll need to know how you are expected to return extra materials, reset the classroom, and secure the computers and equipment. Managing the instructional environment also includes collecting and recording enrollment and following up with the correct personnel with regard to any technical problems.

Just as you'll manage the physical environment for the promotion of learning, you'll need to do the same with a virtual environment. You'll prepare the virtual classroom by confirming the reliability and usability of the software, audio, connectivity, and learner interaction. Part of your virtual classroom management is to create and communicate a contingency plan for how you'll react when things don't go as planned. You don't want to abandon remote learners when they can't connect or when software fails in the virtual classroom.

 NOTE I'll address this domain in detail in Chapters 2 and 3. Successful training events don't happen by accident; it's the preparation, planning, and understanding of what learners need from you, the trainer, that make a successful event.

Domain 2: Methods and Media for Instructional Delivery

This domain accounts for 14 percent of the exam (approximately 13 questions). As a trainer you'll need to be experienced and versed in choosing the correct instruction methods. This means understanding the pros and cons of instructor-led training in the classroom versus web-based training for distance learning. You'll also be tested on how you should present the material to the different learning styles.

Technical courses typically follow a logical learning workflow: the instructor lectures, provides a demo of the work, and then allows the learners to complete a lab. The designers of the courses, however, may have instructional methods incorporated into the coursework that are different from what you're used to. When delivering courses, you'll always be prepared for the learners' acceptance of the delivery by understanding the pros and cons of the instructional method—and adapting the method as appropriate.

As a CompTIA CTT+ you'll know that people, in particular adults, learn in different styles. You'll need to be able to recognize the different learning styles, such as auditory versus visual, and adapt your teaching style to bolster learners' retention and understanding. Depending on what you're teaching, either technical or nontechnical content, you'll adapt your delivery technique for what's best for the learners. This is part of keeping the training learner-centric rather than trainer-centric. You'll do this approach in the classroom and in the virtual classroom environment.

Technical trainers can also use different tools and techniques to organize the material in a classroom. This can be through comparing and contrasting different solutions, creating a demo to complete with the learners, or walking the learners through a complex activity as a group one step at a time. Your experience as a CompTIA CTT+, classroom observance, and insight into the learners' needs will help you determine what the best approach is for each scenario. Technical and nontechnical content can be taught in many different ways, but it's important to see the nonverbal communications of the learners to adapt your delivery of and approach to the message.

One of the best attributes of a trainer is the ability to "read your audience." This is based on the learners' involvement with the activities, participation in class discussions, and even their interactions with other people in the classroom. You can monitor how learners are engaged—and promote their engagement—through questions, demonstrations, and activities in the classroom. Promoting interactions isn't all just technical know-how; anecdotes, media clips, and even humor can all be leveraged to get people involved in the classroom.

> **NOTE** You'll learn all of the details, methods, and media for good, solid instructional delivery in Chapters 3, 4, and 5.

Domain 3: Instructor Credibility and Communications

The Instructor Credibility and Communications domain accounts for 10 percent of the exam, about 9 or 10 questions. (I'm not sure how CompTIA finds 10 percent of 95 questions. You won't see any "half-questions," but they could map a question to more than one objective if they wanted.) In this domain you'll be tested on your *delivery competence*—that's how well you present the material. You can expect scenario-driven questions where you'll need to respond to the question on how you'd manage a particular scenario in the classroom.

Credibility as an instructor is often based on first impressions. This is why it's important for the instructor to be clean, look professional, and wear appropriate clothing for the classroom. Instructors are often judged by their appearances, and a sloppy, late, and poorly groomed instructor may have a challenge to gain credibility with learners. Credibility also comes from how the trainer speaks, the type of jokes and humor they introduce, and in their overall behavior in different classroom scenarios.

Learners want the instructor to be in charge of the classroom environment. Learners don't want the instructor to blame others for problems rather than finding solutions. Blaming includes being critical of the training materials, the organization hosting the trainer, or even the topic the CompTIA CTT+ is teaching. When the instructor is critical of others, the learning environment can shift from a positive atmosphere to a negative focus on the learning objectives. The learners' goal and requirement are to learn what the trainer is to teach. When the trainer is critical or encourages blame for errors, the focus is removed from the learners and solutions.

One of the strongest methods to show delivery competence is to demonstrate the depth of knowledge of the course material. One of the most effective methods to do that is to clearly demonstrate how the information in the course will be applicable to the learners in their day-to-day functions after the class. If there's a disconnect between how the technology is used in the classroom and how learners are expected to use the material outside of the classroom, then the objective of the learners and organization has not been achieved. It's important for the trainer to involve the learners in the conversation of how they'll use the technology in their work roles.

When most people think of training, they think of the mechanics of training: how you teach and use public-speaking tools, and what speech patterns you have. The mechanics of training are part of your communication and presentation skills. Technical terms, acronyms, jargon, and even your grammar and syntax affect your credibility as a trainer. You need to adjust your speech to the learners' so that what you're discussing is in synch with what they're learning. In other words, you don't want to speak below or above the competence level of your audience.

Presentation skills describe how to present a topic to an audience. You will be tested on the proper techniques for speaking to your audience. Good trainers speak clearly, at an appropriate pace, and use voice inflection, pauses, and emphasis on key points to help convey their messages. Verbal and nonverbal communications are part of presentation skills because they help the learners understand the message and help the trainer understand the reception of the learners.

 NOTE Throughout this book having *instructor credibility* is implied as being a good, confident instructor. I'll specifically address this topic in Chapters 6 and 7.

Domain 4: Group Facilitation

Group facilitation accounts for nearly half of your exam score at a whopping 45 percent of the passing score (that's about 43 questions). First, you'll need to prove your expertise and experience in establishing and managing the learner-centered environment. This means you'll be tested on how the instructor manages the classroom and the learners, and helps address different learning styles. This objective will test your experience on the promotion of learner engagement and participation—how you get your learners involved in the classroom. You'll also be tested on the methods you can use to quickly assess learners' needs—and how you respond to those needs. Finally, this hefty objective covers how you motivate learners and reinforce learning objectives.

This is the portion of the CompTIA CTT+ examination where you'll be tested on learning methodologies. You'll need to understand how groups and teams work together—called *group dynamics* and *group development phases*. By understanding how people interact in a learning environment, you can better facilitate the event, engage learners, and involve them more in the learning opportunity. Group facilitation actually starts before the class even begins—and then continues through your introduction, course overview, and interactions with the learners throughout the course. In a virtual environment you'll need to manage technical disruptions, virtual class tools, and polling to promote learner involvement.

This domain on the CompTIA CTT+ examination also includes the promotion of learner engagement and participation. You'll need to be familiar with active listening, questioning learners, and understanding how learners question the instructor. This domain also will test your approach to managing students of different learning styles and social learning, and creating opportunities for students to converse on a topic rather than just telling learners about the topic. This is the concept that learners can gain from the entire classroom experience, not just through the lecture and labs.

As a trainer you probably already know when your participants aren't understanding the material you're sharing. You can see their body language, hear their questions and comments, and through virtual classes you can see their feedback to what you're sharing. This assessment of learner needs happens throughout the course—not just before your training and intermittently. You're persistently looking for feedback and clues from your learners to confirm their involvement and understanding of the course materials.

As a trainer you always hope that learners will be prepared and motivated to learn what you have to offer them. The reality is that learners often need reinforcement for learning. They need praise, rewards, and of course, access to the technology you're teaching. Personalities and learning styles can also affect the learning environment, so you have to monitor all learners to see how one person's contributions, or lack thereof, may affect the rest of the participants. You'll do this in the formal classroom environment by reading nonverbal clues, determining how learners are engaged, and promoting conversations and involvement with all of the learners. In a web-based classroom you'll use chat, polling, and exercises to involve learners.

 NOTE As a CompTIA CTT+ trainer, group facilitation is the bulk of your job. You'll learn different aspects of group facilitation throughout this book, but this specific exam objective is addressed in Chapters 8, 9, and 10.

Domain 5: Evaluate the Training Event

The evaluation of the training event accounts for 18 percent of the CompTIA CTT+ exam (roughly 17 questions). It's important to evaluate the training so you can learn what did, and did not, work in the learning environment. You'll need to review learner performance throughout the course so you can adjust your training style. Evaluations also happen at the close of instruction so learners can review the course, but mainly so you, the technical trainer, can prepare to teach more effectively in the future. This objective addresses both the evaluation of the instructor and the course itself. It's always possible that the instructor did well, but a poorly designed course could cause the learner to be frustrated.

You can use different methods to evaluate your training event—and you'll learn about all of them in this book. You'll be tested on the types of evaluations you can use, legal requirements related to your evaluation of learners, and adhering to your company's requirements for end of course reporting. You may have to, for example, collect information about your attendees, their successful participation in the course, and their involvement in the course throughout the event. While you'll always adhere to your organization's policies, you'll be tested on what you should do as the instructor in different exam scenario-based questions. Of course, the right answer is to always follow the rules and policies of your company.

Evaluating the course also includes the evaluation of the course design—your organization needs feedback on errors or mistakes in the course so that other trainers and learners can anticipate these mistakes. For example, if you modified the course at all during the training to accommodate a better approach to learning, then you'd need to document and report this modification of the course materials—for most scenarios. Reporting and evaluation also include the critique of your own performance of the course delivery, preparedness for the course, and how you think the training event was received by the participants.

When a trainer receives evaluations from the learners, the evaluations don't judge the trainer, but provide insight into what worked, and didn't work, in the training event. You'll use these evaluations to identify trends, topics, and activities that need improvement, and to become a better trainer. Evaluations from learners will also help you prepare an end-of-training report if it's required by your organization. The end-of-training report is a formal assessment of the training event, your performance, and the participation of the learners.

 NOTE   You'll learn the specific exam objectives for the evaluation exam domain in Chapters 11 and 12.

Passing the CompTIA CTT+ Essentials Exam

You are not preparing to take the CompTIA CTT+ Essentials exam—you are preparing to pass this exam. I firmly believe there's a big difference between just taking an exam and preparing to pass the exam. You'll need to have a positive mindset as you study, learn the CompTIA objectives, and reinforce your learning for the exam. Your goal, starting right now, is to pass the exam. Ideally, you'll schedule this exam today—or at least choose a date to work toward. You need a deadline so you don't keep studying forever and never get to the testing center.

The CompTIA CTT+ examination uses multiple-choice questions. Each question has four possible answers, and you'll have to choose the best possible answer. Only one answer to each question may be selected, only one answer is actually correct, and blank answers are incorrect. You can move forwards and backwards in the exam, mark questions for later review, and you can change answers if you need to. Once you're finished with this exam, you'll end the test, and the exam software will calculate your score. You'll know within just a few moments if you've passed or failed the CompTIA CTT+ Essentials examination.

As you now know, five knowledge domains are on the exam. This book has been divided to match these five domains by parts:

- Part 1: Planning Prior to the Course includes Chapters 1, 2, and 3
- Part 2: Methods for Effective Instruction includes Chapters 4 and 5
- Part 3: Establishing Instructor Credibility and Maintaining Communications includes Chapters 6 and 7
- Part 4: Leading a Group Facilitation includes Chapters 8, 9, and 10
- Part 5: Evaluating the Training Event includes Chapters 11 and 12

These five parts cover the specifics you'll need to know to pass your CompTIA CTT+ examination. You can move from part to part, or even chapter to chapter, if you want to focus on specific exam objectives. While I think you should read this book in the order I've written it, there's nothing wrong with first focusing on your favorite (or weakest) attribute of training.

At the end of each chapter is a practice exam that focuses just on that chapter's topics. The practice exams are tricky, picky, and sometimes you'll see that I've included two answers where either answer may be a good choice, but one answer is the better choice. In other words, these exam questions will be tricky, and you may be influenced by distractors to choose the wrong answer. So slow down, take your time, read the question carefully, and make certain you understand the question's intent before answering the question.

 NOTE On the CD there's a file called Score Tracker—it's a Microsoft Excel document that will help you track your chapter-by-chapter scores. After you complete a chapter quiz, record your score in this document to help you track which topics you need to review, which exam topics you're passing. The Score Tracker will help you predict your readiness for passing the CompTIA CTT+ Essentials exam with a 655 on a scale of 100 to 900.

Now that you're working toward passing this exam, you need to create an exam study strategy. This means you'll want to create a plan of attack for how you'll learn the exam objectives, confirm your understanding of training methodologies, and retain all that you've learned. I've created a nifty study chart (Table 1-1) as an ideal example of how long it'll take you to pass the exam. I've included the exam objectives, the specifics of each objective, the chapter where you can find this information, and the expected number of questions so you can study accordingly.

The Study Day column reflects the day of your strategy that you'll study the related exam objective. This doesn't mean you have to study every day for the CompTIA CTT+ examination, but if you take time away from your studying efforts, you can pick up with the studying where you last left off. You'll note that I've predicted 24 days of preparation for the examination just to thoroughly understand the objectives and the content of this book. Based on your experience you may need more or less than that predicted amount.

The 24 days that you invest in preparing to pass the CompTIA CTT+ examination does not include time you'll need for reviewing terms and completing the two practice exams on the CD. You could safely prepare and pass the CompTIA CTT+ examination, on average, within 30 days from now if you have daily time to study, work through the materials, and maintain your regular job duties. More realistically, when you consider your obligations to work and family, you may need more like 60 actual days of studying efforts. The challenge, of course, is that the longer you take to prepare, the more you may have the sense of dread of taking the exam. I encourage you to find an aggressive and feasible schedule for the work that you're about to commence.

As part of your preparations I strongly encourage you to create flashcards. You'll see loads of terms in every chapter. In fact, at the end of each chapter I'll help you by listing all of the key terms you need to know for your CompTIA CTT+ examination. Get yourself a big stack of index cards, and make your flashcards by hand. On one side of the card write the term, and on the opposite side of the card write the explanation. Yes, do this by hand—not with software or on the computer. In my experience, the actual writing of the terms helps people to remember the term and definition more clearly than using computer-generated flashcards. Every day whip through your flashcards, take your cards with you to review as you travel, and be persistent in your studying.

Domain 1: Planning Prior to the Course			
Exam Objective	**Related Chapter(s)**	**Expected Number of Questions**	**Study Day**
Review of Organizational Needs and Learners' Backgrounds in Relationship to Course Objectives	Chapter 2	6 questions	Days 1–2
Instructional Environment in Relationship to Learning Objectives	Chapter 3	6 questions	Days 3–4
Domain 2: Methods and Media for Instructional Delivery			
Exam Objective	**Related Chapter(s)**	**Expected Number of Questions**	**Study Day**
Selection and Implementation of Instructional Methods	Chapter 4	6 questions	Days 5–6
Use of Presentation and Instructional Media	Chapters 4, 5	7 questions	Days 7–8
Domain 3: Instructor Credibility and Communications			
Exam Objective	**Related Chapter(s)**	**Expected Number of Questions**	**Study Day**
Instructor Delivery Competence and Content Expertise	Chapters 6, 7	5 questions	Days 9–10
Instructor Communication and Presentation Skills	Chapters 7	5 questions	Days 11–12
Domain 4: Group Facilitation			
Exam Objective	**Related Chapter(s)**	**Expected Number of Questions**	**Study Day**
Establishment and Management of a Learner-Centered Environment	Chapter 8	11 questions	Days 13–14
Promotion of Learner Engagement and Participation	Chapters 8, 9	11 questions	Days 15–16
Assessment of Learners' Needs for Additional Explanation and Encouragement	Chapters 9, 10	11 questions	Days 17–18
Motivation and Positive Reinforcement of Learners	Chapter 10	10 questions	Days 19–20
Domain 5: Evaluate the Training Event			
Exam Objective	**Related Chapter(s)**	**Expected Number of Questions**	**Study Day**
Evaluation of Learner Performance During and at Close of Instruction	Chapter 11	9 questions	Days 21–22
Evaluation of Instructor and Course	Chapter 12	8 questions	Days 23–24

Table 1-1 A Study Strategy to Pass the CompTIA CTT+ Essentials Examination

NOTE Once you successfully pass the CompTIA CTT+ Essentials exam—and you will pass the CompTIA CTT+ Essentials exam—you'll need to complete one of two performance-based examinations: the Classroom Trainer exam or the Virtual Classroom Trainer exam. If you already know which exam you're preparing to pass, you can skip ahead to that section in this chapter—or be studious and read 'em both.

Passing the Trainer Performance Exam

In this CompTIA certification program you'll be certified as either a CTT+ Classroom Trainer or as a CTT+ Virtual Classroom Trainer. Each designation requires that you pass a corresponding performance examination that will show your abilities as a trainer, your understanding of the training competencies, and how you manage and engage the learners. The CompTIA CTT+ Classroom Trainer performance exam is, as of this writing, TK0-202, while the CompTIA CTT+ Virtual Classroom Trainer performance exam is TK0-203. You must designate which performance exam you're submitting your recording to because the exams are scored slightly differently by CompTIA judges.

Both performance-based exams allow you to show your teaching prowess, but how you demonstrate your expertise depends on good planning, your comfort level with the topic, and on an adherence to the exam objectives. The performance-based examination is a video recording of you teaching a technical topic to at least five people. The recording must be between 17 and 22 minutes and clearly show and record you teaching, interacting with your audience, and giving real training. This isn't acting or a contrived infomercial—this is you really teaching your participants about something you're an expert at. If your recording is longer than 22 minutes, the judges will watch and score only to minute 22 of your recording.

The topic of the video is up to you—CompTIA gives much leeway on what's covered in the presentation, but you want the topic to be technical in nature to show your expertise conveying information and teaching. In other words, don't make this too easy, as you are becoming a technical trainer—not just a trainer. Choose a technical topic you're skilled in and have taught many times, and create exercises, interactions, and lectures to engage the learners and to showcase your talents.

You also have some requirements as to how you'll teach your materials. You can't just set up the old video camera or screen capture software and record 22 minutes of you doing your thing. You'll need to sketch out what you're going to teach, how you'll interact with your participants, and how you'll demonstrate all of the exam objectives in your presentation. This means you'll likely plan on how you'll cover the topics, the types of exercises you'll complete in the training, and what you're going to say to map to all 12 exam objectives. You should practice your class a few times before the recording—you don't want to stammer, lose your focus, or wreck your chances of passing the performance examination.

NOTE In some "train-the-trainer" seminars, participants may have the opportunity to record their technical training in front of colleagues for this portion of the examination. That approach is perfectly acceptable, but the video of you that you'll submit to CompTIA must be only of you. You can't have more than one instructor teaching in the video or it'll be rejected.

Recording Your Presentation

When you set the stage for your training, think of how the training event will look to the CompTIA CTT+ judges that will review your presentation. For the classroom presentation, set the camera off to the side so your video technician can easily pan the room as you interact with your audience. Yes, you'll want the camera on a tripod to eliminate shakes and bumps. Consider the lighting of the room—more lighting usually means a better recording, but beware of glare on the camera and on the whiteboards. In fact, you may want to neatly tape paper over your whiteboard to write and draw on to eliminate glare. Be aware of your movement in the classroom and how that will convey to the movement of the camera and to the people watching the video.

You don't have to create a Hollywood set to record a good video, and you may use only one camera in the recording—not multiple cameras. Chances are your consumer-grade video camera will work just fine, but you should test the camera a few times—move around the room and speak, and see how the camera focuses on and records your movements, and what you sound like in the recording. Test the battery, digital memory, the zoom features, and all the mechanics of the camera before your training event. You don't want your head sliced off, your face out of focus, or the camera battery to die during your presentation—that won't work for CompTIA's review.

For the virtual classroom recording choose a topic you're familiar with, practice with the conferencing software, and plan how you'll show evidence of each objective. Most virtual classrooms record audio and video, but if your software doesn't, you'll need to acquire screen recording software to record your presentation. Be sure to use wired access to the Internet because wireless can sometimes be choppy and unreliable for audio. Your video and audio must be in synch with what's happening on your screen, or your submission will be rejected. Be sure to set your virtual stage too: shut down unneeded applications, close windows, and turn off any distracting sounds on your PC.

One of the most important factors of the video recording session is the audio. What your learners hear in the classroom isn't always the same as what's recorded—it's easy to sound muffled and distant, and this will hurt your chances of scoring well on the exam. When you're preparing for the room, listen to the noise level of the room—fans, computer blips and beeps, noise from nearby street traffic, and people strolling by in the hallway can all degrade your performance. Do all that you can to minimize the excess noise—choose a quiet room, mute the computers, switch off unneeded electrical devices, make sure cell phones are off, and put a sign on your door warning bystanders: "Silence! Video Recording in Progress!"

If possible, use a lapel microphone or a boom microphone to make certain your voice is easily heard and recorded. Give your participants some instruction to just be natural—but to speak up when asking questions and during the interaction. If the judges reviewing your video can't hear what you're saying and how you're interacting with your audience, they may assume that the people in the training session can't hear you either. While it's true that the learners in the classroom need to learn what you're offering, your teaching and presentation is for the judges that will be reviewing your teaching and training. Do everything you can to make certain the judges can hear and see clear evidence of your training abilities.

Once you're done with the recording session—remember, no more than 22 minutes—you'll prep the video for submission. First, no editing of the video is allowed at all; no splices, fancy effects, or cuts and fades. You are allowed to stop the recording one time during your presentation, but even this needs to fit into your class—such as stopping the tape for a class exercise, not to redo a portion of the recording. Only in the classroom certification recording will CompTIA allow you to stop the recording twice, for moving the class to a different locale and for an exercise. If you choose to stop the presentation, you'll want the recording to begin right after the exercise is complete—there shouldn't be an impression that the judge has missed any information because of the stop in the recording. Your video must also be submitted in the order the information was delivered to your participants.

You'll then need to take your video recording and choose how you'll get it to CompTIA. Ideally, you'll convert the video to digital format as MPEG, MPEG4, or FLV formats. You'll submit your video when you pay for the assessment online. While these links are valid as of today, always check with www.comptia.org to confirm the assessment and uploading of your videos:

- If you pay by PayPal or credit card, you'll use http://CTTSubmission.com.
- If you're not a CompTIA member and you pay by voucher, you'll use http://CTTSubmission.com/profile/register.php?q_paypal=1.
- If you are a CompTIA member and you pay by voucher, you'll use http://CTTSubmission.com/profile/register.php?q_paypal=0.

You can, if you really want to, choose to mail your video presentation to CompTIA for their review. There is, however, a $35 fee for submitting your video via the mail or courier. There's an additional $35 fee if you submit your recording on a CD via courier and it's not in the MPEG, MPEG4, or FLV formats. Basically, it's much more cost effective to just convert your videos to the correct format and upload them through the CTTSubmission.com web site. Also note that if you send your video presentation to CompTIA via the mail or courier, CompTIA won't review videos on cassette tapes. You have to put the recording on a CD in the correct format or send them a DVD-R format using the region-free or Region-1 formatting. CompTIA will not return any CDs or DVDs to you if you choose to submit them by mail or courier service.

 NOTE Being a technical trainer, you're probably also a technical person. Be a good technical person and make a backup of your recording. Always, always back up your work, right? That's the message here too—while it's unlikely CompTIA will lose your recording, things happen, files get corrupted, and tears are shed. Immediately back up and keep your recording in a safe and secure locale. Better safe than way sorry.

When you're ready to submit your recording to CompTIA CTT+ for their review, you'll need to complete either the Classroom Trainer exam or the Virtual Classroom Trainer exam submission forms. These are simply titled CompTIA CTT+ Forms A, B, and C, but you must choose the correct form for the type of performance-based exam you're applying for, or your scoring will be delayed. These forms are available through www.comptia.org, and you'll be instructed to submit the form as part of your recording upload. The forms for both exams ensure that your recording is ready to be submitted to CompTIA. The form will require documentation of:

- Proof of payment for the examination
- Photocopy of government-issued ID
- Verification of passed CompTIA CTT+ Essentials exam including a photocopy of the score report
- Proof by two witnesses that you are the trainer in the recording
- Name, signature, and contact information for participants in the recording
- Details about the course you've presented and its subject matter
- Information on how you planned prior to the course and how you prepared the learning environment
- Explanation for why the recording may have been stopped, if applicable to your recording
- Evaluation of your performance, the success of the presentation, and any additional remarks

If you do not complete and submit these forms, you'll fail your performance exam! It's extremely important to complete the forms, because the pre- and post-class exam objectives are documented in the forms. On several of the exam objectives CompTIA clearly states that failure to complete the "necessary paperwork" will result in a failure in that objective. These forms are the necessary paperwork.

Understanding the Classroom Trainer Scoring

Just like with the CompTIA CTT+ examination, it's important to understand the objectives you'll be tested on during the review of your Classroom Trainer performance-based exam. By understanding what the judges will be reviewing and how you'll be scored, you're more apt to prepare accordingly for your classroom recording. The domains on the classroom training examination are the same domains you'll be tested on during the CompTIA CTT+ examination. The difference, of course, is that during the review of your performance-based exam, you'll need to show your understanding of these objectives by actually performing the objectives. And you'll have no more than 22 minutes to show your expertise in all of these objectives.

You can do this, however, because many of the things you do in the classroom recording can map to more than one objective. You'll be scored on each of the objectives on a scale of 4 down to 1. Here's the breakdown:

- 4—Outstanding performance
- 3—Successful performance
- 2—Limited performance
- 1—Seriously deficient performance

A score of 1, seriously deficient performance, on any of the objectives means that you'll fail the performance portion of the examination. Should you fail the performance exam, there's no waiting period between your first and second attempt. If you fail any attempts after the second examination, however, you'll have to wait at least 30 days before you can try again. Of course, your goal is to pass this exam and get on with your life, get back to training. Here are the sections you'll need to gear your training efforts toward in your classroom trainer presentation.

Review of Organizational Needs and Learners' Backgrounds in Relationship to Course Objectives

To score well on this objective, you'll need to show that you've mastered the material to the point of relating the content to the learner's role or use of the product. You'll want to clearly and accurately convey points about your topic that may be confusing to the learner or where the learner may bristle at the information you're sharing. You'll also need the skill set to assess where learners are now with the technology and how their competency level relates to the course prerequisites. CompTIA also stresses that this objective allows you to modify learning materials to meet the needs of your organization without changing the original course design.

If you want to score an outstanding performance, you'll need to address individual learners and show that you've made an assessment of learners' skills. Based on the assessments you've made, you'll adapt your teaching approach, the course content, and the approach in your delivery. Also find a way to connect the activities of the classroom to the real-world application of how the participants will use what you're sharing. If you ramble or offer irrelevant or inappropriate statements in your presentation, you'll likely fail this portion of the exam.

Instructional Environment in Relationship to Learning Objectives

The goal of this objective is to communicate how you, the instructor, understand the learning environment and how the learners will participate in the classroom environment. For example, you might be teaching a network operating system and want to give the details of the network, TCP/IP information, and server names for the classroom. You'll explain how the computers are connected so that the learners can then anticipate and relate to the learning objectives of the session. Your explanation of the room setup must clearly relate to how the configuration meets the learners' needs. In other words, you don't need to record information that's not relevant to your presentation.

You want to explain the configuration of the room, but also the configuration of the class. Explain when breaks will happen, the duration of the course, a course agenda or topics to be covered, and any post-class information, such as helpdesk information or a web site for additional support. Instructors that don't offer information about the learning environment, don't adjust the room for learners' needs, and don't communicate how the course will help the learners in their roles won't score well on this objective.

Selection and Implementation of Instructional Methods

If you want to score well in this objective, you'll create logical and seamless transitions between topics in your presentation. In your presentation you'll address different learning styles through your instruction, such as lecture, demonstrations, and hands-on exercises. It's also a good idea to show that you're knowledgeable in the subject through stories, experiences, and even humor to set the class at ease. Of course, you'll want to interact with the participants and keep them involved in the exercises and lectures. This is a portion of the Classroom Trainer exam where you can show your style as a trainer—use humor, ask questions, and create discussion with your participants.

Instructors that don't adapt their presentation to different learning styles score poorly in this objective. In other words, if you just drone on and on about a topic, you're not adapting your teaching to allow for different learning styles. However, exercises, activities, stories, and jokes that don't support the material and point of the presentation also will cause a low score in this objective.

Use of Presentation and Instructional Media

Instructors are to teach the course materials in the manner that the materials were designed. The course materials help guide you and the participants through the topics, organize information, and set the expectations for the course. The course materials are not a script, however. The instructor is to use the materials as a portion of the training, to adapt the presentation for the learning styles in the room and the questions of the participants, and to encourage interest and participation in the topic being presented.

You'll score well on this topic if you can utilize more than one media for learning—don't get bogged down in slideshows. You'll want to use the whiteboard, demonstrate the technical component for the learners, and even host a lab. Ideally, you'll utilize at least two different forms of media—though three would be good. This means you'll use the whiteboard, overhead presenter, handouts, and other visual aids to help with the learning process. If you don't use any learning media at all, you'll fail this portion of the exam.

Instructor Delivery Competence and Content Expertise

Learners will see you, the technical trainer, as the expert on the material to be presented. After all, if you're teaching the topic, you should be the expert. But being the expert means that you have to establish and maintain your expert status in the presentation. You'll demonstrate your confidence level with the material—and practicing the presentation several times will help you be more confident on the recorded presentation. You'll also show your expertise by linking the knowledge transfer in the classroom to how the learners will use the technology in their roles in the organization. You should not fictionalize answers, overstep your boundaries, or criticize other trainers, the training materials, or the technology you're presenting.

One way to score high on this portion of the CompTIA CTT+ classroom exam is to take the content of the course and the technology at hand, and use these resources to answer learner questions. If you know your audience, through pre-course assessments and the course dialogue, you should address the participants by name when you need to highlight certain attributes and features of the technology that are relevant to the learner. Never read from the training materials—people can read at home. Do this in your recorded training and you'll fail.

Instructor Communication and Presentation Skills

A portion of being an effective instructor is being an effective public speaker. You know how to speak clearly, at a good pace for your audience, and you can use the inflection, pitch, and tone of your voice to communicate well. In your recorded presentation you'll want to be certain to be professional; keep your conversation void of anything obviously offensive or biased. When you present, eliminate distracting habits such as pacing, rocking back and forth, or jingling change in your pocket. Put down markers when you're done using them, and don't go bonkers with laser pointers—commonsense stuff here.

To score high on this objective, you'll need to focus on how you emphasize the key points of the class, how you move from one topic to another, and your body language and eye contact with the learners. Be certain to start and conclude your presentation with an agenda of the course and to summarize the course content as you move along. If you open your presentation without any introduction or course overview, sit at your computer without moving and interacting with the learners, or say something wrong, offensive, or biased, you'll fail this exam objective.

Establishment and Management of a Learner-Centered Environment

A learner-centered environment takes the focus off of you and puts the attention on the goal of the presentation—for the learners to learn. It's always more important that the people in the room learn than it is for you to teach. This exam objective can be accomplished by being positive, interacting with the learners, and addressing issues that learners may have regarding their expectations for the course and the actual content of the course. It's important to engage all of the learners in the class—not just the most eager to participate. You want to avoid favorites, bias, and any criticism in the class. A learner-centered environment also encourages participants to interact with one another, not just the instructor.

During your presentation you should communicate the objectives of the class as to how the learners will use the materials and participate, and how the information is relevant beyond the classroom. Get your participants involved in discussions and conversations among themselves, and facilitate the dynamics of the group to put the focus on the learners, not you, the instructor. Be certain to use an activity where learners are involved in the lesson, such as a lab, a quiz, or a team activity. If you focus on how wonderful you are or you fail to achieve the learning objectives of the presentation, you'll fail this objective.

Promotion of Learner Engagement and Participation

Here's an objective that overlaps with other CompTIA CTT+ Classroom Trainer exam objectives. The "Promotion of Learner Engagement and Participation" can also map to the previous objective of the "Establishment and Management of a Learner-Centered Environment." Both objectives put the focus on learner involvement; this objective, however, concentrates more on how you get learners involved. Your listening skills, the questions you ask of the participants, and how you introduce opportunities for all of the participants to be involved in the conversation are all evidence of being a proficient technical trainer. Be certain to do this in your recording, and you'll score well in this domain.

Technical trainers that will score low on this portion of the exam don't ask questions. If you've ever sat through a lecture with zero interaction from the trainer, you'll know how painful it can be to try to learn. Questions and participation are two key elements of the objectives. Just as you ask questions, you need to make certain you've allowed opportunities for the learners to ask questions too. And, when a participant asks a question, treat the question with respect—don't insult the learner or their question. This is unacceptable in the classroom and certainly not acceptable for a passing CompTIA CTT+ score.

Assessment of Learners' Needs for Additional Explanation and Encouragement

A good technical trainer is in tune with the comprehension of the learners. You can read body language, see how the learners are doing in their labs, and hear their banter with peers about the technology you're teaching. When you see participants who are confused or frustrated, you don't ignore them—you go to the problem and look for a resolution. You identify what the misunderstanding is by asking questions and then, once you clearly understand what the learner needs, you address the issue. Some learners are good at masking their confusion with the course content, but would like an opportunity to ask a question—be certain to encourage questions by pausing and asking the group if anyone has a comment or question.

If you're in tune with your learners' body language and clues of comprehension and you respond to learners' needs, you'll do well on this portion of the exam. Anticipate questions, prompt users to get involved, and then address the learning need. Instructors who ignore learners aren't good instructors, and they won't be CompTIA CTT+ Professionals either. When learners ask questions, don't dismiss the questions—be a professional, be courteous, and care for the learner. These are all components of the learner-centered environment.

Motivation and Positive Reinforcement of Learners

It's important to praise and encourage learners in the class. By paying attention to how learners are completing exercises, their body language, and conversation, you can easily spot opportunities to praise their efforts, encourage progress on shortcomings, and offer positive reinforcements in the classroom. As a CompTIA CTT+ candidate you must demonstrate this objective in your classroom exam recording—if you offer no motivation or if you offer negative reinforcement, you'll fail the exam. In the classroom you should consistently, across all learners, encourage individuals to keep doing the good work, encourage their efforts and praise their successes, and keep the learners from feeling discouraged and overwhelmed.

One method of positive reinforcement is to link the subject matter in your presentation to the learners' work and lives beyond the classroom. Show learners how what you're teaching will be applied in their day-to-day lives, and they'll be motivated to learn and stick with the course objectives. You can also give positive reinforcement through group conversations, questions and answers, and responding to user remarks about the material, the technology, or the class. Don't ignore complaints from participants—these are often an indication that they need a little help or that they disagree with the content.

Evaluation of Learner Performance During and at Close of Instruction

Throughout your presentation you should be monitoring how your learners comprehend the material. Be aware and cognizant of their interactions with your presentation, demonstrations, and the course material. Your observation of the learners is just the first step, because you'll also need to query their involvement, their comprehension, and their remarks through questions, conversations, and activities. Using many different approaches to measure the learners' comprehension is encouraged for your role in the classroom environment and in the trainer recording you'll submit to CompTIA.

If you do nothing to assess how the participants in the room comprehend the subject, you'll fail this objective on the CompTIA CTT+ classroom examination. Ideally, you'll monitor, observe, question, and involve the learners to see how well they understand the topic that you are presenting. Once you've learned the level of comprehension, then you can tailor your dialogue to address their needs more clearly. When you're leading hands-on activities, you should move about the room so you can see how the learners are doing with the material. Don't sit at your desk and wait for the class to declare they're finished. Get out there and see how they're doing, and be available during their exercises.

Evaluation of Instructor and Course

Evaluations aren't to be critical of the instructor or the course materials. Evaluations are an opportunity to identify weaknesses in the course materials, identify how well the materials function and relate to the work, and to see how well the technical trainer was able to facilitate the material. The instructor should also review the course performance, areas that worked well—or didn't work so well—and what modifications may have been made in the class. The evaluation should reflect the success of the course, need for improvements in the course, and evidence of how the learning objectives were achieved.

In the video you should offer an assessment of the course from your perspective as the instructor, the purpose of what you've taught from the organization's point of view, and how learners will use what you've presented. You want to show that you've completed the course learning objectives and what the participants should have learned. Explain how the learning objectives were met in the recording as part of your closing remarks. Define the tools, exercises, and topics that were taught and how the learners will use the knowledge in their roles outside of the classroom.

Scoring the Virtual Classroom Trainer Exam

Once you've passed the CompTIA CTT+ Essentials examination, you can then submit your virtual classroom training session to CompTIA for their review. The objectives of the Virtual Classroom Trainer examination are identical to the Classroom Trainer examination, but the implementation and demonstration of the objectives are different. You'll have to show competency in all 12 of the exam objectives to pass this exam—and you'll be doing this demonstration through a virtual classroom environment.

The good news is that some objectives and activities can map to more than one objective. For each of the exam objectives, you'll be scored on a scale of 4 down to 1. Here's the scoring structure:

- 4—Outstanding performance
- 3—Successful performance
- 2—Limited performance
- 1—Seriously deficient performance

If you score a 1 on any of the exam objectives, you'll fail the entire certification. It's not difficult, however, to score well on this exam if you plan ahead on what you're going to share with the learners. If you fail—and if you prepare for the recording, you won't—you can attempt this portion of the certification again immediately. If you fail the second or any attempts thereafter, you'll have to wait at least 30 days to attempt the exam again. The following are the objectives specific to the virtual classroom recording examination.

Review of Organizational Needs and Learners' Backgrounds in Relationship to Course Objectives

The goal of any training is to help learners learn. You'll do this by first understanding the needs of the organization you're teaching for, the readiness of the people in the class, and the backgrounds of the people attending the training. The background of the learners means that you understand their expectations and their anticipation of how they'll apply what you present to them to their roles and lives. You need to understand the learners' skill levels coming into the class and determine if they've met the prerequisites for the course. You'll need to adapt your presentation for the learners—but don't change the topic beyond the intent and design of the course.

To score well on this objective, you'll document the background of the learners, their needs for the virtual classroom, geographic location, language barriers, and time zone differences. You'll also need to make certain the people in the presentation are familiar with how to interact with you in the presentation—how they'll use the virtual classroom for chat, sidebars, polling, and submitting information to you. In the recording you can ask if the learners have ever taken a virtual class before, and then give them a quick tour of how they can interact with you in the presentation.

Instructional Environment in Relationship to Learning Objectives

A virtual classroom environment can have more challenges to prepare for the training than a classroom environment. You'll need to take extra pre-class steps to confirm that the learners understand how and when to connect to the virtual classroom and to confirm the networking, audio, and system compatibility with your learners. Your goal with this objective is to prepare a learning environment so that the actual training goes smoothly and learners are comfortable with the virtual classroom. You'll need to test the labs and access to network data and applications, and to plan for how you'll manage interruptions in the course, such as disconnected users, software glitches, and password mismatches.

In your recorded presentation explain how the system works and where files for exercises, software, and other materials are located. Be involved with your learners from the start to help them quickly become comfortable with the classroom interface. Be sure to describe how learners will use the information you're teaching back in their workplace. If you fail to have your slides loaded, don't have access to information, or appear generally disorganized and unprepared, you'll likely fail this portion of the exam. You must have a working, functional virtual classroom environment—and be comfortable with the environment—to pass this section. Your comfort with the training tool is part of the formula that will lead the participants to learning.

Selection and Implementation of Instructional Methods

In a virtual classroom you have to choose the best tools and techniques to instruct your remote learners. The course designers may have already identified the procedures to deliver the course, but in some situations you may need to adapt the course to help certain learners comprehend what you're teaching. This can mean offering an analogy or a demonstration, or creating an additional exercise for the learners. Your goal is to choose the most effective learning activities to engage the learners and address different learning styles. Throughout your training don't ignore learners during their exercises, but keep in touch with them to make certain they're completing the work and are fine with their progress.

If you use only one instructional method, such as a slideshow, you'll fail this exam objective. Practice your presentation so that you move between lecture, a demonstration, and perhaps an exercise for the participants. You want to show that you have mastered the different instructional methods that are available to you in the virtual classroom environment. Engage your learners through stories, humor, and demonstrations without criticizing the technology you're teaching or the virtual classroom. If possible, use polling in the course to confirm learner engagement and participation.

Use of Presentation and Instructional Media

In the virtual classroom you must have mastered the interface to use it effectively. You need to know how to interact with participants as a group or one-on-one. Your virtual classroom may allow for chat, polling, quizzes, remote control of users' desktops, and more. The classroom interface is a great tool for promoting learning and engaging learners—this is a topic that can help in many of the exam objectives. Beyond the virtual classroom tool, however, you'll also need to manage the learning by transitioning from topic to topic, have your demonstration prepared, and have access to information so as not to delay the learning.

If you're unprepared to lead in the virtual classroom, it can become more painful for the learners, and you'll likely fail the presentation. You'll definitely fail the presentation if you have no content for and interaction with the learners—a blank screen doesn't facilitate learning (nor does staying on just one slide while you lecture). Use at least two different tools during your presentation—or better yet, three. Plan for how you'll introduce the learning tools, how you'll transition from topics, and how the tools can engage and support learning. Be certain to keep learners posted on where they should be in their materials by stating steps or page numbers in your lecture and demonstrations.

Instructor Delivery Competence and Content Expertise

Your being prepared to teach will help learners comprehend and retain the information you present. A trainer that's unprepared, isn't familiar with the learning environment, and can't show how the subject will help learners in their roles in the workplace is likely to fail this portion of the examination. You need to show your learners and the CompTIA judges that not only have you mastered the virtual classroom software, but also the technology you're presenting. Learners expect trainers to be experts in the subject matter—and this only comes with experience, education, and planning. Being prepared is the key to showing competence and expertise.

At the start of your presentation introduce yourself and the classroom topic, involve the learners, and then share with them what you're about to present. Set the expectations for the learning and the timing of the presentation—and what the learners will get from their time in the classroom. When a learner asks a question, apply the information in the course to the specific learner; don't just repeat what you've already offered. In the recording you'll want to speak with authority and confidence. Should issues happen in the recording, or in any virtual classroom, you can show your expertise by not panicking, but finding and implementing a quick solution. Reading from the materials or slides will ensure that you'll fail this portion of the exam.

Instructor Communication and Presentation Skills

In the virtual classroom environment it's extremely important to speak clearly, at an appropriate pace, and to use your voice to accurately convey the meaning of your presentation. Your pitch, tone, and inflection directly influence the message you're giving to your audience, so you must be aware of your audience composition—consider their background, time zone and language concerns, and varying levels of experience with technology. You can use emoticons, different pointers on your screen, and your virtual classroom software to help convey your message to your audience. Take advantage of private and group chats to address learner concerns and progress. In the virtual classroom you don't have the same advantage of nonverbal communication as you do in a live classroom, so you must take extra steps to communicate accurately with your audience.

Be certain to include introductory and closing remarks about what the participants have learned in your presentation; failure to do so will result in a failure for this exam objective. You'll also need to be professional, courteous, and in control of your interface that you're recording. Don't make offensive or biased remarks, keep dialogue on point, and have a plan of what you'll say and how you'll say it. In your recording be prepared to change your pointer tool quickly to highlight, draw on the presentation, or to use other creative methods to engage the remote learners. As in all presentations, you want to avoid conversation fillers such as "ahs," "ums," and rambling speech.

Establishment and Management of a Learner-Centered Environment

You'll be judged based on your ability to take a virtual environment and transform it to a learner-centered environment. This can be tricky in the virtual environment because the learners are often watching what you're doing. Find a method to quickly and consistently get your learners involved in the course. As you share the agenda and plan for the learning event, you might use a few polling questions to immediately get your audience involved. Your learning environment needs to shift the focus to the learning objectives of the training and how it correlates to the participants' roles in your organization. The focus is on helping the learners learn, not on the trainer doing the training.

If your lesson doesn't involve the learners and it's more of an instructor-centered approach, you'll fail this portion of the CompTIA CTT+ Virtual Classroom Trainer exam. You want to get the learners involved through conversations and exercises where the learners and you can interact, and to engage the learners throughout the training. If you are doing a demonstration, for example, use your mouse pointer to highlight areas of the demonstration without moving the mouse too quickly—smooth, slow movements help learners quickly see what you're doing. In your recording be sure to use your voice, software, and the course materials in combination to engage learners.

Promotion of Learner Engagement and Participation

Because in a virtual classroom environment you'll lose the nonverbal communication aspects of training, you must listen more intently to your participants. You must query their understanding, confirm the participants' understanding through quizzes and challenges, and then clarify any concerns or issues before moving forward. Different class activities can help you promote the learner engagement—your goal is to get the learner participating in the class rather than being a passive member of the group. Understanding your classroom software, being an expert in the technology you're teaching, and planning for activities to get learners involved will help you score well on this section of your exam.

If you don't ask questions and just assume that the learners comprehend your instruction, then you'll automatically fail this portion of the exam. You must ask questions, challenge, and present opportunities for learners to ask questions of you. Your questions, however, should be valuable and related to the course content. Show the learners how to contact you in the course or how to talk with other members of the class. Use your pointer, such as stars and checkmarks, to show approval to classroom involvement of the learners. If you want to score well on this section, create open-ended questions that will get your participants talking with you and their colleagues in the presentation. Don't rush the dialogue, but control the direction of the dialogue with input to keep the focus on track.

Assessment of Learners' Needs for Additional Explanation and Encouragement

As a virtual trainer you must take extra steps to ensure that learners comprehend the information you're presenting—and spend time to explain concepts in detail. You can demonstrate this objective in your recording by keeping users on task with your demonstrations, referring to page numbers in their materials, and pausing frequently to ask and receive questions. You might also, if appropriate, do remote control of a participant's screen to help them through a lab, but use caution that you're helping the user, not doing the assignment for them. Participation and involvement with the remote learners projects encouragement and an openness to entertain questions and provide clarifications on materials you've taught.

To score well on this exam objective, you should repeat the learner's question to make certain you understand their question, provide a clear and direct answer, and if possible, demonstrate the solution for them. Throughout the recording you'll want to gauge and monitor your learners to keep them involved in the course—use polls and private chats to stay in touch with your participants while not distracting from the course. When you're providing a clarification for a user, do more than simply repeat what you've said. Explain the topic in another manner, using an analogy or a demonstration, or involve the group to help answer the question. Never take a private chat message and share with the group in such a way as to identify the person in the private chat. Don't ignore learners; stay in touch with them, and answer their questions in a timely manner.

Motivation and Positive Reinforcement of Learners

In a virtual class you can motivate and reinforce learning by explaining the concept, demonstrating the concept, and then having the learners apply the concept. When learners can link the training to their roles and responsibilities outside of the classroom, they'll be more eager to learn and want to be more involved in what you're presenting. In some cases you can even have a participant take over your screen and coach them through the demonstration for the entire group. Be certain to ask for someone rather than just assign the activity—and thank them for demonstrating the materials for the class. Encouraging learners, recognizing their participation in the class, and keeping them involved all can help reinforce your learning topics.

 NOTE When a participant leads the class by demonstrating the materials, it's sometimes called "driving through" the materials. It's like when you're teaching someone to drive a car you actually let them drive for awhile.

If you don't motivate the learners, if you ignore their presence, and if you don't show that the learners are involved in the presentation, you'll likely fail this portion of the examination. You need to communicate with, not just to, the class participants. Positive reinforcement helps the learners see the connection to their work and the course objectives. Negative reinforcement uses fear and embarrassment to prod the learners along—something you don't want to do in your presentation. Thank the learners for participating, getting involved, and asking questions; this makes them feel comfortable in the class and encourages other participants to get involved too.

Evaluation of Learner Performance During and at Close of Instruction

Your evaluation of the learners doesn't happen just at the end of the course, but throughout the instruction. You can demonstrate this CompTIA CTT+ objective in your virtual classroom in a number of ways: ask and answer questions, challenge learner knowledge, assign exercises, and give quizzes on the information you're teaching. By consistently monitoring the learners' progress, you'll be able to ascertain which participants understand the materials and which learners may need some extra attention.

Don't embarrass the learners, but do interact with them to confirm their understanding and involvement. You can also achieve this objective by observing the students' work and coaching them to a successful completion of the exercises.

Instructors that ramble on, ignore students and their signs of needing additional support, or that don't offer participants the opportunity to ask questions and for clarifications are certain to fail this objective on the CompTIA CTT+ Virtual Classroom Trainer examination. In your recording, clearly monitor students' work and their interactions, and encourage feedback by asking open-ended questions about the information you're presenting. When you're giving a quiz, for example, you can read the question aloud for the participants and have them take turns answering questions, using a poll to signal their responses, or they can keep their answer private between just them and you. At the close of the presentation, you'll want learners to always have an opportunity to review your performance and the course materials.

Evaluation of Instructor and Course

Course evaluations are meant to help you become a better instructor and for the course to be improved for future participants. As a virtual instructor you should review your performance, the performance of the virtual classroom, and the course design. You want to see if the course was successful from your perspective, the participants' perspective, and your organization's perspective. This means you'll need to look at your training, the learners' retention, and how the learning objectives and the course content were in alignment. An end of the course report is always needed to convey your finding. Your participants may also complete an instructor evaluation that may, or may not, be shared with you depending on the rules and policies of your organization.

While you may introduce an evaluation for the participants as part of your recorded presentation, you'll actually complete your evaluation as part of your CompTIA CTT+ Virtual Classroom Trainer documentation. This is Form C that you'll complete and submit. The form will ask you to evaluate the training event and how you met the learning objectives you presented in your recording. You'll also be asked to describe the success of the presentation and what worked well, if you'd change anything in the presentation, and what activities you added to help learners in the presentation. Finally, you'll have an opportunity to provide additional remarks about your presentation and the evaluation of your recording.

Chapter Summary

It's not an easy process to earn the CompTIA CTT+, and preparing for an exam can be frustrating and cause anxiety. Just as you'd ease the concerns and fretting of participants in your class, I hope to do the same for you throughout this book. By now you should have a clear overview of what it will take to earn the CompTIA CTT+ certification. You'll need to pass the computer-based exam (TK0-201) and then either the classroom performance based-exam (TK0-202) or the virtual classroom performance-based exam (TK0-203). The objectives in the computer-based exam apply to all trainers—classroom based or virtual.

The CompTIA CTT+ Essentials examination has 95 questions, and you'll complete the exam within 90 minutes. The passing score for the CompTIA CTT+ Essentials exam is 655. Once you've passed the CompTIA CTT+ Essentials test, you can submit your classroom-based recording or the virtual classroom recording. With your submission you must complete the appropriate CompTIA forms and paperwork documenting your recording, participants, and information on your pre- and post-class work. The total cost for your certification will be $512 ($246 for the CompTIA CTT+ Essentials exam and then $266 for the review of your recording).

In this chapter you also learned about the five learning domains for your testing and performance-based examinations: Planning Prior to the Course, Methods and Media for Instructional Delivery, Instructor Credibility and Communications, Group Facilitation, and Evaluate the Training Event. The five domains are then broken down into the 12 exam objectives you'll be tested on. The 12 exam objectives, completely covered in the upcoming chapters, are applicable to the CompTIA CTT+ Essentials examination, the classroom performance-based examination, and the virtual classroom performance-based examination. You'll need to adapt your training strategy to the objectives that are specific to the performance-based examination you'll be passing.

In this chapter you've learned much information already. The content of this chapter will help you create a study strategy to prepare to pass the certification exam. Create flashcards to help you memorize the terms and definitions, and complete the end-of-chapter quizzes. This first quiz will be a bit different from the upcoming quizzes in the book. You probably won't see questions like those from this chapter on your CompTIA CTT+ examination because the information in this chapter was more of an overview of the exam. Treat this first quiz as a refresher on how to answer questions, identify distractors, and how to refresh your exam-passing abilities. Be sure to record your chapter quiz on the Score Tracker document from the CD.

Key Terms

Assessment of Learners' Needs for Additional Explanation and Encouragement   Exam objective that judges the trainer's ability to quickly assess learners' needs, anticipate and answer questions, and offer encouragement to participants.

classroom-based training   The instructor and the participants are in the same physical space for the learning. The trainer and learners can see one another and interact with verbal and nonverbal communications, and the instructor can quickly assess who's on target with the learning and which learners need encouragement and support.

CompTIA CTT+ Certified Technical Trainer   An individual that has shown competency and skill in teaching technical courses. The CTT+ requires the individual to pass the CompTIA CTT+ Essentials examination and a performance-based examination showcasing the trainer in the classroom environment or in a virtual classroom environment.

CTT+ performance-based exam   The recording of a training professional and corresponding paperwork that will be judged by CompTIA as to the ability of the instructor in the recording to satisfy the requirements of the classroom-based instructor exam or the virtual-based instructor exam. The recorded presentation should be formatted as MPEG, MPEG4, or FLV and should be between 17 and 22 minutes in duration.

CTT+ TK0-201   The CompTIA CTT+ Essentials computer-based examination. A passing score is 655 on a scale of 100 to 900.

CTT+ TK0-202   The CompTIA CTT+ Classroom Trainer performance-based examination.

CTT+ TK0-203   The CompTIA CTT+ Virtual Classroom Trainer performance-based examination.

Domain 1: Planning Prior to the Course   The actions the trainer should take to prepare for a successful training session. This domain accounts for 13 percent of the CompTIA CTT+ Essentials examination.

Domain 2: Methods and Media for Instructional Delivery   This exam domain tests your understanding of utilizing different methods, technology, demonstrations, lecture, handouts, and other media to instruct. This domain accounts for 14 percent of the CompTIA CTT+ Essentials examination.

Domain 3: Instructor Credibility and Communications   This exam domain tests your ability to instruct, to communicate, and to interact with participants. First impressions, speech patterns, organization, and command of the classroom all affect instructor credibility. This domain accounts for 14 percent of the CompTIA CTT+ Essentials examination.

Domain 4: Group Facilitation   This exam domain tests the core skills that an instructor must have to teach, understand learning styles, approach learning, and to manage the classroom. This domain accounts for 45 percent of the CompTIA CTT+ Essentials examination.

Domain 5: Evaluate the Training Event   This exam domain accounts for 18 percent of the CompTIA CTT+ Essentials examination. The domain will test your knowledge of course and instructor evaluations, expectations for the instructor, and how final reports for the course are prepared and delivered to the organization.

Establishment and Management of a Learner-Centered Environment   Exam objective that judges how well the instructor encourages learners, shifts the focus from the trainer to the learner, and promotes learning in the classroom environment.

Evaluation of Instructor and Course   Exam objective that measures the instructor's understanding of course evaluations and instructor evaluations. The instructor must also review the course, define successes and failures, and report outcomes to the organization as needed.

Evaluation of Learner Performance During and at Close of Instruction   Exam objective that tests the trainer's ability to examine, observe, and anticipate learner progress. Instructors can demonstrate their expertise in this exam objective by using different methods to gauge learner comprehension, such as changing the instruction, offering demonstrations, and assigning hands-on activities to engage the learner.

Instructional Environment in Relationship to Learning Objectives   Exam objective that tests how the instructor will convey the details of the classroom to the participants, how the classroom is configured, and how the participants may interact with the technology, the instructor, and colleagues in the room.

Instructor Communication and Presentation Skills   Exam objective that judges the ability of the CompTIA CTT+ candidate to clearly speak to, present to, and train the participants in the room.

Instructor Delivery Competence and Content Expertise   Exam objective that tests and judges the instructor's classroom presence and ability to manage learners, address individual needs, adapt the instruction for learners, and to link class materials to organizational needs.

learner-centered environment   The focus of the training should be encouraging and engaging, and should motivate the abilities of the participants to learn the material being presented.

Motivation and Positive Reinforcement of Learners   Exam objective that judges the trainer's encouragement to participants during interactions, motivation of the learners by linking course material to roles and responsibilities, and promotion of a learner-focused environment.

Promotion of Learner Engagement and Participation   Exam objective that judges the trainer's ability to ask questions of the participants, present challenges, and to give exercises that promote learning and classroom engagement.

Review of Organizational Needs and Learners' Backgrounds in Relationship to Course Objectives   Exam objective to test the trainer's preparation for the course, how the learner will use the information to be taught, and how the participants are confirmed for course prerequisites.

Selection and Implementation of Instructional Methods   Exam objective that will test the trainer's ability to move from topic to topic, select appropriate classroom materials, and adjust the course delivery to promote learner participation.

Use of Presentation and Instructional Media   This exam objective will judge how the trainer utilizes all of the available media in their presentation. The trainer should use the most appropriate media type to engage the learners and to promote different learning styles.

virtual classroom-based training   The instructor and the learners are not in one location, but are utilizing software to meet via a network and to participate in a remote training session. The users and instructor operate through a software interface to convey learning, involve participants, ask questions, chat, share control of desktops, lecture, and complete exercises.

Questions

1. You are preparing for the CompTIA CTT+ Essentials examination. How many questions are on this test?

   A. 90

   B. 95

   C. 120

   D. 200

2. Ryan is preparing to pass his CompTIA CTT+ Essentials examination and then his classroom performance examination. What is the total amount Ryan will have to pay to earn his CompTIA CTT+ Classroom Trainer certification?

   A. $246

   B. $255

   C. $266

   D. $512

3. How many learning domains are covered in the CompTIA CTT+ testing examinations?

   A. Three domains

   B. Four domains

   C. Five domains

   D. Seven domains

4. Which learning domain accounts for the largest percentage of the CompTIA CTT+ certification exam?

   A. Planning Prior to the Course

   B. Methods and Media for Instructional Delivery

   C. Instructor Credibility and Communications

   D. Group Facilitation

5. Which exam domain accounts for the smallest percentage of the exam score?

   A. Planning Prior to the Course

   B. Methods and Media for Instructional Delivery

   C. Instructor Credibility and Communications

   D. Group Facilitation

6. Which one of the following is an example of instructor credibility for a classroom-based recording examination?

   A. The ability to read your audience

   B. The clothing the instructor wears in the classroom

   C. How the instructor answers learner questions

   D. How the instructor manages technical disruptions

7. Beth is preparing for her CompTIA CTT+ Virtual Classroom Trainer examination. What is the primary challenge trainers must manage in the virtual classroom?

   A. Language difference

   B. Nonverbal communications

   C. Time zone differences

   D. Connectivity issues

8. What term describes the way groups and teams work together?

   A. Group breakdown

   B. Leaders and followers

   C. Group dynamics

   D. Group additions

9. You are a CompTIA CTT+ candidate and you're preparing to pass your Essentials examination. Based on your experience, complete this statement: You're persistently looking for feedback and clues from your learners to confirm their _____ in the class and _____ of the course materials.

   A. Interest, commitment

   B. Understanding, application

   C. Presence, understanding

   D. Involvement, understanding

10. Which one of the following is not an applicable tool a virtual classroom trainer would use to engage learners in a virtual classroom environment?

    A. Chat

    B. Polling

    C. Exercises

    D. Helpdesk information

11. Why is it important to review learner performance throughout the course you're teaching?

    A. To adjust your training style to match learning styles

    B. To determine who is falling behind in the course

    C. To evaluate students throughout the entire course

    D. To create grades for the learners

12. What is the minimum passing score on the CompTIA CTT+ Essentials examination?

    A. 655

    B. 512

C. 90

D. 877

13. Gary is preparing to pass the TK0-203 examination. Which examination must Gary pass before passing this exam?

A. TK0-200

B. TK0-201

C. TK0-202

D. Gary doesn't have to pass an exam before passing the TK0-203 examination.

14. Ben is about to submit his CompTIA CTT+ performance-based examination. What is the minimum amount of time that must be recorded of Ben instructing a class?

A. 15 minutes

B. 22 minutes

C. 17 minutes

D. 25 minutes

15. Holly has just finished her recording for the Virtual Classroom Trainer performance-based examination. She notices that her recording time is 27 minutes—too long for the CompTIA CTT+ judges to review. What will happen if Holly submits the recording as is?

A. The judges will stop watching the recording at minute 22.

B. The judges will reject her submission, and she will fail this exam.

C. The judges will request a shorter presentation.

D. The judges will watch the presentation until minute 25.

16. Rex has attended a "Train-the-Trainer" course as part of his preparation to earn the CompTIA CTT+ certification. During the course the training company has provided an opportunity for each participant to record their presentation to submit as part of the trainer performance evaluation. Which one of the following if not met will disqualify a recording submission from this course?

A. The course must be an approved CompTIA class.

B. The course must use approved CompTIA materials.

C. The recording must have only one trainer per recorded session.

D. The recording must be no longer than 20 minutes.

17. When you're preparing your classroom performance recording, where's the best place to position the camera?

A. In the back of the training room.

B. Use at least two cameras, one in the front and one in the back.

C. Directly in front of the trainer.

D. At the side of the classroom.

18. What is the minimum number of participants who must be in the CompTIA CTT+ performance-based exam recording?

   A. Ten

   B. Eight

   C. Five

   D. One

19. Jen is recording her classroom presentation for submission to CompTIA. Jen would like to stop the recording in the presentation to make time for an exercise. How many times is Jen allowed to stop the recording?

   A. Zero

   B. One

   C. Two

   D. Three

20. You have just finished your CompTIA CTT+ virtual classroom recording, and you're preparing the video for submission to CompTIA for their review. Which one of the following file formats is not acceptable for the submission upload?

   A. MPEG

   B. MPEG4

   C. RAR

   D. FLV

Questions and Answers

1. You are preparing for the CompTIA CTT+ Essentials examination. How many questions are on this test?

   A. 90

   B. 95

   C. 120

   D. 200

   B. There are 95 questions on this examination, and you have 90 minutes to pass the test. You'll need to score a 655 on a scale of 100 to 900. A is incorrect, as you have 90 minutes to pass the test, not 90 questions. C and D are incorrect—there are only 95 questions on the certification exam.

2. Ryan is preparing to pass his CompTIA CTT+ Essentials examination and then his classroom performance examination. What is the total amount Ryan will have to pay to earn his CompTIA CTT+ Classroom Trainer certification?

   A. $246

   B. $255

   C. $266

   D. $512

> **D.** The total cost of the certification is $512, as he will have to pay $246 for the computer-based Essentials exam and then $266 for the review of his classroom recording. A is incorrect, as the computer-based Essentials exam costs $246. B is incorrect, as $255 isn't a relevant value. C is incorrect, as $266 is the cost for the review of classroom recording.

3. How many learning domains are covered in the CompTIA CTT+ testing examinations?

   A. Three domains

   B. Four domains

   C. Five domains

   D. Seven domains

> **C.** Five domains are on the CompTIA CTT+ testing examinations: Planning Prior to the Course, Methods and Media for Instructional Delivery, Instructor Credibility and Communications, Group Facilitation, and Evaluate the Training Event. A, B, and D are incorrect choices, as there are exactly five learning domains for the CompTIA CTT+ examinations.

4. Which learning domain accounts for the largest percentage of the CompTIA CTT+ certification exam?

   A. Planning Prior to the Course

   B. Methods and Media for Instructional Delivery

   C. Instructor Credibility and Communications

   D. Group Facilitation

> **D.** Group Facilitation is the largest percentage of the CompTIA CTT+ examination, as it accounts for 45 percent of the exam score. A is incorrect; Planning Prior to the Course accounts for 13 percent of the exam score. B is incorrect; Methods and Media for Instructional Delivery accounts for 14 percent of the exam score. C is incorrect; Instructor Credibility and Communications accounts for just 10 percent of the exam score.

5. Which exam domain accounts for the smallest percentage of the exam score?

   A. Planning Prior to the Course

   B. Methods and Media for Instructional Delivery

   C. Instructor Credibility and Communications

   D. Group Facilitation

   C. While Instructor Credibility and Communications is important to a successful class, this domain only accounts for 10 percent of the overall exam score. A is incorrect; Planning Prior to the Course accounts for 13 percent of the exam score. B is incorrect; Methods and Media for Instructional Delivery accounts for 14 percent of the exam score. D is incorrect, as Group Facilitation accounts for 45 percent of the exam score.

6. Which one of the following is an example of instructor credibility for a classroom-based recording examination?

   A. The ability to read your audience

   B. The clothing the instructor wears in the classroom

   C. How the instructor answers learner questions

   D. How the instructor manages technical disruptions

   B. Often instructor credibility is based on the first impression. This means the clothes the instructor wears, the neatness of the instructor, and how the class materials are organized. A is incorrect, as the ability to read your audience is an example of the Methods and Media for Instructional Delivery. How the instructor answers learner questions, choice C, is an important instructor attribute, but it's also part of the Methods and Media for Instructional Delivery exam domain. Managing technical disruptions, choice D, is part of the Group Facilitation domain.

7. Beth is preparing for her CompTIA CTT+ Virtual Classroom Trainer examination. What is the primary challenge trainers must manage in the virtual classroom?

   A. Language difference

   B. Nonverbal communications

   C. Time zone differences

   D. Connectivity issues

   B. Virtual classroom trainers don't have the advantage of the nonverbal communications that classroom trainers enjoy. Beth will need to overcome this challenge by using polling tools, emoticons, and learner engagement.

A, C, and D are all valid concerns for the virtual classroom, but in a learner-centered environment, as on the CompTIA CTT+ examination, the most pressing challenge is the lack of nonverbal communications.

8. What term describes the way groups and teams work together?

A. Group breakdown

B. Leaders and followers

C. Group dynamics

D. Group additions

C. Group dynamics describe the methods a group uses to work together. Understanding the stages of group development and dynamics can help an instructor engage and interact with learners. A, B, and D are not valid answers, as these choices do not describe how teams and groups work together.

9. You are a CompTIA CTT+ candidate and you're preparing to pass your Essentials examination. Based on your experience, complete this statement: You're persistently looking for feedback and clues from your learners to confirm their _____ in the class and _____ of the course materials.

A. Interest, commitment

B. Understanding, application

C. Presence, understanding

D. Involvement, understanding

D. You're persistently looking for feedback and clues from your learners to confirm their involvement in the class and understanding of the course materials. A, B, and C are not the best answers because trainers are to help learners engage in the class through involvement and confirm their understanding of the materials the course presents.

10. Which one of the following is not an applicable tool a virtual classroom trainer would use to engage learners in a virtual classroom environment?

A. Chat

B. Polling

C. Exercises

D. Helpdesk information

D. Helpdesk information doesn't involve learners, so this is the best answer to the question. A, B, and C are incorrect choices, as chat, polling, and exercises are all tools you can use in a virtual classroom to engage and involve learners.

11. Why is it important to review learner performance throughout the course you're teaching?

   A. To adjust your training style to match learning styles

   B. To determine who is falling behind in the course

   C. To evaluate students throughout the entire course

   D. To create grades for the learners

   A. It's important to evaluate the trainer event throughout your presentation to determine where learners are in their progress and understanding and, if needed, to adjust your training style to the learners' learning style. B is incorrect; the point of constant evaluation is to help learners comprehend the course information. C is incorrect; while it is important to evaluate students throughout the entire course, this isn't the primary reason why instructors should evaluate learners. D is incorrect; not all presentations and training offer grades to learners. In addition, the primary reason is to determine if the instructor's training style should be modified for the learners in the classroom.

12. What is the minimum passing score on the CompTIA CTT+ Essentials examination?

   A. 655

   B. 512

   C. 90

   D. 877

   A. The minimum passing score for the CompTIA CTT+ Essentials examination is 655. You must score a 655 on a scale of 100 to 900. Choices B, C, and D are all incorrect answers, as these scores don't reflect the minimum passing score on the CompTIA CTT+ Essentials examination.

13. Gary is preparing to pass the TK0-203 examination. Which examination must Gary pass before passing this exam?

   A. TK0-200

   B. TK0-201

   C. TK0-202

   D. Gary doesn't have to pass an exam before passing the TK0-203 examination.

   B. Before Gary can pass the TK0-203 examination, which is the CompTIA CTT+ Virtual Classroom Trainer recording, he must pass the TK0-201 examination, which is the CompTIA CTT+ Essentials exam. A is incorrect because there is not an exam titled TK0-200. C is incorrect, as TK0-202 is the Classroom Trainer performance examination, and Gary doesn't have to pass that exam in order to pass the CompTIA CTT+ Virtual Classroom Trainer examination. D is incorrect because Gary has to pass the TK0-201 exam first.

14. Ben is about to submit his CompTIA CTT+ performance-based examination. What is the minimum amount of time that must be recorded of Ben instructing a class?

    A. 15 minutes

    B. 22 minutes

    C. 17 minutes

    D. 25 minutes

    C. The presentation that Ben submits must be at least 17 minutes in duration. A is incorrect, as 15 minutes is too short a presentation to be judged. B is incorrect, as 22 minutes is the longest amount of time that Ben can submit for evaluation. D is incorrect; 25 minutes is too long for the presentation.

15. Holly has just finished her recording for the Virtual Classroom Trainer performance-based examination. She notices that her recording time is 27 minutes—too long for the CompTIA CTT+ judges to review. What will happen if Holly submits the recording as is?

    A. The judges will stop watching the recording at minute 22.

    B. The judges will reject her submission, and she will fail this exam.

    C. The judges will request a shorter presentation.

    D. The judges will watch the presentation until minute 25.

    A. The maximum amount of time for a recording is 22 minutes for the CompTIA CTT+ performance-based exams. If Holly submits a recording longer than this, the judges will watch the video until minute 22 and then stop. Holly will be judged on the content until this point of the recording. B and C are incorrect, as the recording won't be rejected or returned; the judges will just watch the video until minute 22 and then judge accordingly. Choice D is incorrect, as the maximum time for the video is 22 minutes, not 25.

16. Rex has attended a "Train-the-Trainer" course as part of his preparation to earn the CompTIA CTT+ certification. During the course the training company has provided an opportunity for each participant to record their presentation to submit as part of the trainer performance evaluation. Which one of the following if not met will disqualify a recording submission from this course?

    A. The course must be an approved CompTIA class.

    B. The course must use approved CompTIA materials.

    C. The recording must have only one trainer per recorded session.

    D. The recording must be no longer than 20 minutes.

    C. The recorded presentation can have only one trainer per submission. If Rex or other trainers submit their video with more than one trainer teaching a topic at a time, CompTIA will reject the video. A is incorrect, as CompTIA does not approve courses to qualify for preparation of the examination. B is incorrect, as CompTIA does not require the course provider to use only approved CompTIA training materials. D is incorrect, as the recording can actually be up to 22 minutes in duration.

17. When you're preparing your classroom performance recording, where's the best place to position the camera?

A. In the back of the training room.

B. Use at least two cameras, one in the front and one in the back.

C. Directly in front of the trainer.

D. At the side of the classroom.

D. CompTIA recommends that the video camera be positioned at the side of the training room so the camera operator can pan the room to show the participants and the trainer interactions. Answer option A is incorrect, as CompTIA recommends the side of the training room. B is incorrect; only one camera is allowed in the recording. C is incorrect, as a camera directly in front of the trainer won't allow the judges to see the people in the training event.

18. What is the minimum number of participants that must be in the CompTIA CTT+ performance-based exam recording?

A. Ten

B. Eight

C. Five

D. One

C. There must be at least five people in the CompTIA CTT+ performance-based exam recording. This is true for the classroom trainer and the virtual classroom trainer recording. Choices A, B, and D are incorrect, as the minimum number of participants is five, not ten, eight, or one.

19. Jen is recording her classroom presentation for submission to CompTIA. Jen would like to stop the recording in the presentation to make time for an exercise. How many times is Jen allowed to stop the recording?

A. Zero

B. One

C. Two

D. Three

C. While CompTIA recommends a maximum of one stop per recording, Jen is allowed to stop the recording two times in extreme circumstances. A, B, and D are all incorrect, as Jen can stop the recording up to two times.

20. You have just finished your CompTIA CTT+ virtual classroom recording, and you're preparing the video for submission to CompTIA for their review. Which one of the following file formats is not acceptable for the submission upload?

    A. MPEG

    B. MPEG4

    C. RAR

    D. FLV

    C. You are not allowed to submit your recording to CompTIA in any other format than MPEG, MPEG4, or FLV. RAR is a compression format that is not acceptable to CompTIA. Choices A, B, and D are incorrect, as these are acceptable file types to CompTIA.

Evaluating Learners' Needs

In this chapter you will:
- Define the learner needs
- Create instructional goals and learning objectives
- Learn how learning outcomes are designed
- Measure learner competencies
- Explore the ADDIE model for instructional design
- Understand the Kirkpatrick model of evaluation

Every trainer needs to start with one simple thought when it comes to teaching a technical class: why the training is needed. The goal of the training must be defined as early as possible in the preparation for the seminar. Once you understand why the training is to happen, that is, once you understand what the organization and the learners expect to receive from the training, it becomes much easier to prepare for a successful class. If you know the learners' needs, it's easier to satisfy those needs. Always start with the end result in mind.

Sometimes the learning objectives are clearly evident, such as teaching a class to help learners pass an examination, like the CompTIA A+ certification or a MOUS (Microsoft Office User Specialist) certification. While the primary class purpose may be obvious, ancillary purposes attached to the class enrollment may not be as obvious. For example, while the A+ seminar goal may seem apparent, that the learners want to learn the exam objectives and be able to pass the A+ certification exams, you may need to dig deeper into the class goals. The participants likely want to also gain practical knowledge from your seminar that they can immediately apply to their work. The general intent of the class may be obvious, but the constituent goals of the class will require deeper analysis.

To define the learning objectives for the seminar you're about to present, you need to ask questions. Keep the end of the seminar in mind: how will the learners take the information you're presenting and apply it to their role in the organization? Chances are the classes you teach will have learners with multiple goals; participants may have goals for passing the certification exams, learning correct technical procedures, understanding the components of the hardware and software, and many more possible objectives. Rarely is there a technical seminar where the learning objective is shallow and direct. More likely you'll encounter multiple learning objectives, multiple classroom goals, and prioritized objectives among the participants in your class.

The secret to identifying learning objectives is communication. You need to speak with the managers, participants, and organizational leaders who are calling for the class. You need to understand each of these stakeholders' interests in the class and what they expect you to deliver. If you don't know what your learners, managers, and organizational leaders want from the class you are preparing, it will be difficult to meet the client objectives. This is true even if you're using off-the-shelf solutions where the learning objectives, classroom books, exercises, and demonstrations are predefined. It's essential to review the course objectives with your learning stakeholders to confirm what the course will and will not cover. This also gives you an opportunity to strike or add objectives to completely satisfy the identified learning objectives.

Determining the Learning Needs

When there is a skills gap, a desired competency, or there are new organizational goals involving technology, organizations almost always gravitate toward training. Training has long been seen as the panacea for increased productivity, higher profits, and happiness among all employees. The truth is, however, throwing money and time at training doesn't ensure anything if the learning needs are not properly identified. For too long companies have pushed their employees into standardized, uniform, beginning-intermediate-advanced seminars for everything from Microsoft Word to Adobe Photoshop and assumed the instructors would return participants as bright as Einstein. While standardized training may be just fine for many organizations, if the learning needs aren't properly identified, then it's just a waste of time and money, an investment in false hopes.

The learning needs describe what the learner needs to know to operate within the organization. Specific learning objectives must be defined based on the roles and responsibilities of the learners. There's no need for a five-day seminar on Microsoft Word if all that the learner really needs is to understand how to do mail merges and to create labels. To define learner needs you'll have to play the role of business analyst to define the requirements for the training. Certainly you'll need to speak with managers, but your best bet for identifying the learning objectives is to meet with the learners. You'll need to see how they'll use the technology you're about to teach in their day-to-day lives. When you can make the connection between the technical topics you're about to teach and how the learners will be using the information, the path to learning and teaching becomes clear.

Defining Instructional Goals for Participants

When a learner enrolls in a course, they expect that the course content will satisfy an expectation. The expectation is the learner need—the outcome of the seminar that will allow the learner to apply what they've learned. *Knowledge transfer* is when information is transferred from the instructor to the learner. *Knowledge application* is the evidence that knowledge transfer has actually occurred—the application of the skills, the fulfillment of the course expectations, and the return on the training investment. The end result of the course shouldn't be just an evaluation, a learning certificate, and "goodbye"; it should be the application and ongoing usage of what the course promised to provide.

"Learner needs" is a way of labeling what a person needs to know to do the tasks required of their role in an organization. Classes for network engineers, programmers, and database administrators aren't going to have the same learner needs because the audience for each class is different—the learners in each class have different goals, different work activities, and different disciplines. However, if the topic is how to use a word processing program, then the learner needs may begin to align because network engineers, programmers, and database administrators may all need to know how to use the word processing program to better serve in their work role. The software developer, network engineer, and database administrator aren't necessarily all going to use the word processing program the same way, but they can all learn how to use the software program and then apply the knowledge in their roles within the organization.

As a trainer it's important for you to know the difference between training and education. While there's plenty of overlap between the concepts of training and education, there is a distinction between the two. *Education* includes the broad goals of transferring knowledge from one individual to another, with the intent to direct and influence the course of an individual's life. Education, from primary school to college, helps the person identify strengths and weaknesses and exposes interests that will influence the direction of the person's career and motivations. *Training*, where you and I operate, focuses on the skills, tools, and competencies to help people complete their roles in an organization. Basically, education is the direction of knowledge and competency, while training provides the techniques to operate within the competency. Training is the gritty, hands-on, get-it-done transfer of skills. Technical training helps people build the framework to operate and apply technology to their lives and careers.

The framework of training is built upon what the learner needs to know. For example, consider a group of people that have worked with spreadsheet applications for years. This group has a need to understand formulas and functions to a level that would allow them to create reports, link spreadsheets together, and forecast profits for their organization. Based on the high-level needs, there's not a compelling reason to spend hours of training on how to enter data, print, and to make macros. While this information may be important to some people, it's not what these learners need to know. Learner needs are linked to the application of the technology after class.

Every course should have a clearly defined *instructional goal*. An instructional goal is a statement that defines the high-level objectives for the course. It's a statement that communicates the broad learning objectives and expected outcomes of the course. Instructional goals might be labeled as "course overview," "course descriptions," or even "learner expectations." Examples of course goals for technical seminars include:

- **Microsoft Word fundamental seminar**   Participants will be able to create new word processing documents, define page layouts, format text, configure tabs and indents, insert artwork, manipulate text, and configure print options.

- **CompTIA Network+ seminar**   With an emphasis on the CompTIA Network+ exam objectives, participants in this seminar will explore networking fundamentals, create network cables, install and configure network interface cards, understand how TCP/IP protocols communicate, and work with routers, switches, and hubs.

- **Adobe Photoshop seminar**   Using a photographer's approach to the Adobe Photoshop environment, participants will learn how to configure photographs for hue, saturation, contrast, dodge, burn, and other traditional darkroom techniques. Participants will be able to implement preconfigured filters, create layers and masks, and complete industry-standard prepress work for photographic images.

Instructional goals communicate the intent of the seminar for the participants. The actual fulfillment of the instructional goal empowers the participants by providing the knowledge to do their jobs more effectively. When employees are better equipped to complete their roles in the organization, they can operate more efficiently, be more productive, and boost the profitability of the entity. It's no secret that when employees are empowered with knowledge, they are happier, fulfilled, and more confident about doing the work with fewer mistakes and errors. Empowerment through training is dependent on the ability of the learners to actually use what they've learned. If the user doesn't have an opportunity to apply the instructional goal in their lives, then knowledge fades and the learner's confidence wanes. Consequently, the value of the training fades, the instructional goal isn't met, and the value of training diminishes.

Developing the Learning Objectives

Learning objectives define the increased knowledge that learners will have as a result of the specifics of the training. Learning objectives are the specific goals of the specific content of the training course. Learning objectives define the exact application of the knowledge, not how the knowledge will be transferred from the instructor to the participants. All learning objectives must support their broader, higher-level instructional goal and provide specific information about how the application of the course content will change behavior in the learner's performance with the technology.

Technical training in any organization must encourage users to actually apply what they've learned. It's a waste of time, money, and energy to teach employees how to complete a task the correct way, only to have the employees continue to do the work incorrectly in production. The application of competencies gained through training is evident in behavior change. In the classroom or virtual learning environment learners may have a chance to practice the learning objectives, but until they actually apply the information in production, the knowledge is stagnant. Application of what's been learned post-training is the clearest evidence of knowledge gained.

Identifying the Topical Units

Because learning objectives are based on the specific outcomes of the learning content, there are several steps to create the learning objectives for a seminar. The first step to define the learning objectives is to break down the instructional goal into topical units. This is basically an outline of what the course will include for the learners. Here's an example using the Microsoft Word instructional goal:

- **Microsoft Word fundamental seminar**   Participants will be able to create new word processing documents, define page layouts, format text, configure tabs and indents, insert artwork, manipulate text, and configure print options.
  - Unit 1, Getting Started with Microsoft Word
    - Defining the Microsoft Word interface
    - Entering text
    - Accessing menus and buttons
    - Saving, printing, and accessing documents
  - Unit 2, Editing Text in Microsoft Word
    - Selecting text
    - Copying, cutting, pasting, and moving text
    - Finding and replacing text
    - Accessing the dictionary, thesaurus, and autocorrect options
  - Unit 3, Formatting Text
    - Changing fonts and styles
    - Formatting pages, columns, and borders
    - Applying predefined paragraph styles
    - Creating and saving paragraph styles
  - Unit 4, Designing Documents
    - Working with headers and footers
    - Inserting tables and graphics
    - Adding sections and page breaks
    - Creating a table of contents

In this example, note how each of the units begins with a verbal noun (or gerund, ending in *-ing*) that describes the goal for the unit. Just as there is an instructional goal for the entire course, so too should each unit have an active goal for the learners. In addition, each of the bullet points also uses a verbal noun to communicate the actions the participants will do; this helps set expectations for the course and conveys a sense of learning by doing, as opposed to seminars where the content is lecture-driven.

Defining the Learning Outcomes

Now that the instructional goal has been broken down into topical units, the next step is to define the learning outcomes for each portion of the topical units. The learning outcomes elaborate on the components of the topical units. The learning outcomes are basically more precise goals that support the content of the learning outcomes, which in turn support the broader, high-level instructional goals. In this example the Microsoft Word seminar is broken down into the precise learning outcomes for each of the topical units:

- **Microsoft Word fundamental seminar**   Participants will be able to create new word processing documents, define page layouts, format text, configure tabs and indents, insert artwork, manipulate text, and configure print options.
- Unit 1, Getting Started with Microsoft Word
  - Defining the Microsoft Word interface
    - Defining what Microsoft Word is and is not
    - Interacting with Microsoft Word as a word processor, not as a typewriter
  - Entering text
    - Typing text
    - Using the keyboard to navigate through the text, and using the mouse to move to new positions in your document
  - Accessing menus and buttons
    - Touring the menus
    - Experimenting with common buttons
    - Hiding and showing toolbars
  - Saving, printing, and accessing documents
    - Saving a document to different computer locations
    - Accessing saved documents
    - Printing a document to various printers
- Unit 2, Editing Text in Microsoft Word
  - Selecting text
    - Understanding why text needs to be selected
    - Using the mouse to select text
    - Using the keyboard to select text
  - Copying, cutting, pasting, and moving text
    - Copying text within a document and between documents
    - Cutting text instead of copying text
    - Pasting text that's been cut or copied
    - Using the mouse and keyboard to cut, copy, and move text
  - Finding and replacing text
    - Finding keywords and phrases
    - Replacing words with new words
    - Finding and replacing text with conditions and formatting

- Accessing the dictionary, thesaurus, and autocorrect options
  - Correcting misspelled words
  - Looking up words in the dictionary and thesaurus
  - Enabling and editing autocorrect options for words
- Unit 3, Formatting Text
  - Changing fonts and styles
    - Previewing fonts that you can use
    - Changing the font of selected text
    - Applying predefined styles
  - Formatting pages, columns, and borders
    - Changing the format for the content of the entire document
    - Applying templates for document types
    - Changing the layout of the document with columns
    - Creating borders for the document and paragraphs
  - Applying predefined paragraph styles
    - Accessing and moving the styles toolbar
    - Experimenting with predefined styles
    - Using keyboard shortcuts for styles
  - Creating and saving paragraph styles
    - Creating a new paragraph style
    - Making rules for paragraph styles
    - Saving styles to use in other documents
- Unit 4, Designing Documents
  - Working with headers and footers
    - Accessing headers
    - Adding footers to pages
    - Making a different first page
    - Editing headers and footers
  - Inserting tables and graphics
    - Adding a table to a document
    - Removing tables, rows, and columns
    - Inserting photos and clip art
  - Adding sections and page breaks
    - Creating section breaks within the document

- Editing section breaks
- Manually adding page breaks
- Creating a table of contents
  - Exploring a table of contents
  - Using styles and sections for generating a table of contents
  - Editing a table of contents

The learning outcomes describe the actions that will help the learner achieve the instructional goal of each topical unit. Verbal nouns continue to support the parent objective by demonstrating the activity the learner will do to achieve the needed behavior within each topical unit and again within the overall instructional goal for the technical training. It is important to define the learning outcomes for the course because these set the expectations for the participant, for you, the technical trainer, and also for the client or manager that may be enrolling their employees into the technical training class.

 NOTE Some approaches to defining the topical units and the learning outcomes also include a prediction of the duration of the task. For the example in this discussion, I'm not adding time constraints because the point is to see how you, a technical trainer, will assess learners' needs and define the topical unit, the learning outcomes, and ultimately the learning objectives for your seminars.

Writing the Learning Objectives

Now that the instructional goal has been broken down into topical units and the topical units have been broken down into learning outcomes, you are ready to fully define the learning objectives. The *learning objective* is the end product of breaking down the instructional goal, the topical units, and the learning outcomes. It clearly defines the behavior that participants will be able to do as a result of your training. It's important to define the learning objectives through this breakdown of goals because you're starting with a broad definition of learning outcomes and moving to the very specific, measurable outcome of the learning.

Learning objectives must focus on the end result of the learning: how the participants will ultimately use what you've taught them. This focus and objective of the learning helps organizations predict the value of your technical instruction, the expectations that their staff will be able to accomplish, what will and will not happen as a result of the seminar, and how participants will perform their roles in the organization more completely. Note that learning objectives do not address how the instruction will take place, but only what the end result of the instruction will be.

In most circumstances learning objectives are written based on each learning outcome you've defined. This means, of course, that you'll have many learning objectives for the entire technical training course. To some trainers this comes as a surprise because they've created just one broad learning objective for the entire course. Because learning objectives focus on the specific actions that learners will gain as a result of the course, you must define the complete learning objectives that you will provide to the learners and to the organization.

By completely defining the learning objectives, you're also setting expectations for several of the learning stakeholders:

- **Participants**   There's no confusion as to what the participants will learn in the course and be able to perform once the training is completed.

- **Organization and management**   The organization and management will have a clear understanding of what the technical training will provide for their employees.

- **Human resources department**   If the organization has a skills set database, that is, a central location for tracking training and competency, then it becomes easier to define resource capabilities for tasks and assignments within the organization based on the completion of technical training and the learning objectives of the training.

- **Technical trainer**   By creating or reviewing the learning objectives, the technical trainer understands the expectations of the organization and the participants that the trainer must be able to meet and to help the learner accomplish.

In the following example I've created the learning objectives for just the first topical unit in the Microsoft Word training scenario:

- **Microsoft Word fundamental seminar**—Participants will be able to create new word processing documents, define page layouts, format text, configure tabs and indents, insert artwork, manipulate text, and configure print options.

- Unit 1, Getting Started with Microsoft Word
  - Defining the Microsoft Word interface
    - Defining what Microsoft Word is and is not
      - Identify the purpose of Microsoft Word, what Word can help them accomplish, and identify the boundaries of Microsoft Word.
    - Interacting with Microsoft Word as a word processor, not as a typewriter
      - Explain how Microsoft Word is a word processor, what a word processor allows users to accomplish, and the advantages of Microsoft Word versus a typewriter.
  - Entering text
    - Typing text
      - Interact with Microsoft Word to enter text into the program, experience automatic text wrapping, follow the cursor, and use the keyboard to interact with the program.
    - Using the keyboard to navigate through the text, and using the mouse to move to new positions in your document
      - Participants will use the keyboard and mouse to fully operate the Microsoft Word software, move throughout their documents, and navigate to specific places in Microsoft documents.

- Accessing menus and buttons
  - Touring the menus
    - Participants will use the mouse and keyboard to access menus and commands, become familiar with common features of Microsoft Word, and learn how to select and deselect commands through the menu bar.
  - Experimenting with common buttons
    - By the end of this training, users will know how to save, print, format, indent, and use several other common Microsoft Word commands by using the button bar.
  - Hiding and showing toolbars
    - Participants will be able to use the View commands to customize the Microsoft Word interface to reveal and hide toolbars and ribbons in the Microsoft Word software.
- Saving, printing, and accessing documents
  - Saving a document to different computer locations
    - Using the Save and Save As commands, participants will learn the mechanics and features of saving a document in multiple versions to more than one locale.
  - Accessing saved documents
    - Once a document has been saved, the learners will access the computer location and open the document through their computer's operating system and by using the Microsoft Open command.
  - Printing a document to various printers
    - Learners will be able to preview and print their document to their printer by use the Microsoft Word Print command and the printer buttons.

Yes, it does take some time and thought to develop the learning objectives, but it's part of the requirements-gathering process for effective technical training. The learning objectives may pass through several rounds of revisions before they are ultimately approved by the learners, the organization, or by the client that is paying for the seminar. The process of creating the learning objective helps distinguish what will be covered in the class and communicates what participants will be able to do with the technical training you've provided.

Measuring Learner Competencies

Often, to teach an effective class and to deliver the learning objectives, you'll need to determine the learner competencies. Understanding the learner competencies means that you'll assess what the learner already knows about the material you're about to teach. In a technical training environment this is important because assumptions about the background, education, and experience of the learners can directly influence your ability to teach an effective class. In other words, if you think your participants know more than they do, they'll be lost, confused, and frustrated in your training session.

Trying to train participants that aren't adequately prepped for your training and that don't comprehend the material because of poor assumptions equates not only to a loss of time and training dollars, but also could have a long-term impact when the learner returns to production to implement the technologies your class was to deliver. You can imagine the costly losses a person could easily cause an organization, for example, by misunderstanding how to defragment a hard disk versus how to format a hard disk. In technology training it's essential to create measurements to understand what your learners already know before you teach them new information.

Measuring learner competencies also helps you, the instructor, determine what you should be teaching. You can tailor your presentation to match the needs of the learners based on their current knowledge, experience with the technology, and the outcome of your knowledge assessments. Whenever you go about measuring learning competencies, whether it's in the first few moments of a course or at course registration, it's important to follow the rules and policies of your organization. How you measure and record learner competencies should always mesh with the human resource guidelines that your company has in place. You don't want to cause fears or concerns on the learners' behalf when you're attempting to determine what they do or don't know about the technology you're about to teach.

Creating Course Prerequisites

It's important for participants in a technical seminar to be technically competent enough to grasp the learning objectives without delaying the progress of the class. Prerequisites create knowledge boundaries that ensure all participants have at least the same base amount of knowledge to ensure the course progresses in the timeline allotted to deliver the learning objectives. From a participant's perspective, it's frustrating when the technical trainer must stop the flow of the course to explain remedial concepts to a few learners who aren't prepared to take the class. Prerequisites should be identified prior to the start of the course, but more importantly, prerequisites should be enforced before learners enroll in the seminar.

Prerequisites define the needed knowledge the participants are expected to have in order to grasp the concepts you'll be teaching. They also set expectations for the participants about how the information you'll be sharing builds on the skills they already have. When there's a gap between what the learner knows and needs to know, there's a need for remedial training, completion of qualifying seminars, and direction for what the learner must complete in order to register for the technical training. Prerequisites can have a negative connotation in some training environments, but they're actually helpful to the learner. If learners don't have the needed knowledge to grasp what you're going to teach, it's a waste of training dollars, but also a waste of their time to take the course.

To create prerequisites, you'll examine the learning objectives of the course and determine what prior knowledge and experience is needed to grasp these tasks. For example, to install and configure a network router, the participant should have a working knowledge of Ethernet networking principles, experience configuring TCP/IP, and have completed a basic networking course. For the entire course you would examine each learning objective and determine what the participant should already know to fully grasp the topic you'll be teaching. Once you've determined all of the course prerequisites, it's ideal to summarize the prerequisites into three or four qualifications for the participants.

 NOTE Prerequisites are only an effective method to qualify learners for the material if they are enforced. In my opinion, too many technical training centers and corporate educators don't enforce the prerequisites so they can ensure sales and volume of learners in the classroom. This can directly affect the trainer's ability to effectively teach and the qualified learners' ability to learn.

While prerequisites are a great method to screen for qualified learners, you may also need to perform pre-class assessments. A pre-class assessment can be a test, an exercise, or an interview with the learners to determine their level of competencies in the technology. For example, a class on software development may have prerequisite courses that the learners have to complete, but an assessment would measure their depth of understanding on key concepts. By measuring the learners' understanding prior to the course, the instructor can tailor the course to address specific topics, coach varying levels of learners, and prepare examples that more precisely meet the learners' needs.

Administering Assessment Exams

Pre-course assessment exams are an excellent tool to quickly measure the learners' knowledge about the technology, assess their depth of understanding, and determine how prepared they are for the material you're about to teach. Assessment exams can be administered at the launch of your class or prior to your class start date as part of the screening process for learners to register. Whatever approach you take to conducting an assessment exam, clearly communicate the purpose of the exam and the outcome of the assessment exam.

There are some general rules you should follow when creating and administering assessment exams:

- **Include questions based on the course prerequisites.** You'll want to confirm that learners understand the prerequisites for the course. Aim for common, mainstream questions that participants will be able to quickly answer if they understand the prerequisites. Don't focus these questions on the tricky, obscure facts that don't prove comprehension through experience.

- **Write effective multiple-choice questions.** Effective multiple-choice questions should have a clearly stated objective that the learner can relate to and then choose the best answer for. There are many different psychological approaches to writing effective questions, but the most widely accepted approach is to include one answer that's tempting but obviously wrong, one plausible answer that's actually a distracter, and two answers that are similar but one of which is the best answer.

- **Test the participants' comprehension, not their memory.** The goal of the pre-course assessment is to test the learners' comprehension of the subject matter based on their experience with the technology. Frame your questions in scenarios and direct statements, and avoid ambiguous statements. Avoid trick questions so that the focus is on the course material, not on test taking.

- **Create answers that are of the same length for each question.** A trick I learned long ago is that the longest answer is often the correct answer. If you don't want test takers to use this approach, try to write all of the answer choices with the same approximate number of words. Along these same lines you should have the same number of answer choices for each question.

- **Use independent answers for your questions.** Independent answers means that only one choice is correct of the number of choices presented. This means you won't be using "all of the above" or "none of the above" type answers. Craft your answers to be independent of one another so that learners must choose only one correct answer.

- **Communicate the purpose of the assessment.** Some people get nervous about taking any type of exam, so it's best to explain the purpose of the pre-course assessment to your audience. Explain to the class that the assessment helps you understand the background of the learners, what areas they are strong in, where you should focus your attention, and that the assessment is not graded in any way.

Learners enroll in technical training with different goals and objectives: desire to learn new skills, improve their work performance, pass a certification exam, and learn the technology you're teaching. The participants' prior knowledge can directly affect their ability to achieve their goals and grasp the concepts you're teaching. When instructors think of assessments and prerequisites, it's easy to think of what correct information the learner has, but there can also be incorrect experiences that affect the learning needs. For example, consider a student who has incorrectly learned how to subnet IP addresses and how this skewed knowledge could affect a networking technology course. Or consider a student who has had a bad experience with a Microsoft technology and how they may now be biased toward any Microsoft product.

One of the best methods to assess learner needs and to measure competencies is to talk with your learners before the class begins. Ask them questions about how they expect to use the course materials, what they're expecting from the course, and what they like about the technology you're going to teach. Their responses, stories, anecdotes, and remarks about the technology can give you insight into their perceptions, concerns, interests, and aversions to the technology you're going to teach. It's good to understand what prior knowledge, good or bad, the learner is bringing into the classroom so that you can adjust your presentation accordingly.

VIDEO   See the video *Exploring the ADDIE Model.*

Introducing the ADDIE Model

As a technical instructor you should be at least aware of the ADDIE model from a high-level perspective. The ADDIE model is an approach to developing the instruction that you'll teach to your participants. ADDIE is an acronym for Analysis, Design, Development, Implementation, and Evaluation. ADDIE is more embraced by instructional designers than by instructors, but there's a symbiotic relationship between the people who design the training and the people who deliver the training. When the instructors and the instructional designers are in synch with how the performance needs are assessed, how the learning needs are developed, and then how the content of the course satisfies those objectives, training becomes much more effective. Good instructional design, especially in technical content, makes the training and learning more enjoyable.

The ADDIE model is often twisted, adapted, and shoehorned to an organization's instructional systems development (ISD) model. Your organization may have a cyclic approach to designing their classroom and web-based training deliverables, or they may have a rapid development approach to get training started as quickly as possible. These approaches to instructional design are probably still based on the widely accepted ADDIE model. ADDIE isn't the panacea for all instructional design, just as training isn't the cure-all for performance gaps in an organization, but it's a good place to start. Figure 2-1 is the typical ADDIE model instructional design.

For your CompTIA CTT+ examination you should be familiar with the five components of the ADDIE model. While you may not be developing instructional content, it will help you become a better instructor because you'll understand the process and the five stages of instructional design. The ADDIE model will also be referenced throughout the remainder of our time together in this book, as the five stages of instructional design map to several areas of technical training. Finally, before we hop into these stages, realize that your role as the technical trainer is greatly affected by how well the instructional designers have followed the recommendations of the ADDIE model and designed a well-thought-out course for you to teach.

Figure 2-1
The ADDIE model describes the activities of each phase of instructional design.

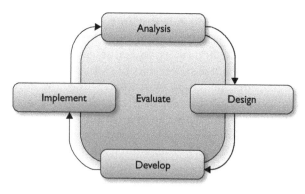

Analyzing the Learning Need

Understanding how instructional assets are developed can help you understand how learners' needs were assessed prior to the start of the technical seminar. The most common assessment type of learners' needs, and really what has been discussed thus far in this book, is *instructional analysis*, which is the process of determining training needs. *Task analysis* is the process of a learning professional, trainer, instructional designer, or learning consultant, serving as a business analyst to evaluate the expected behavior changes and expected knowledge the participant will have as a result of the training. Task analysis also reviews the audience, the depth of content for the course, and the type of training that will best satisfy the learning need.

Task analysis reviews the type of work the learner is doing now in relation to how the work is being performed and how the workflow and associated processes may change as a result of the new technology. In other words, task analysis examines how the technology you'll be teaching will change how the learner completes their role in the organization. Task analysis considers how the learners' work will be performed differently as a result of the technology you'll be teaching and addresses the best approach to teaching the technology. Sometimes task analysis may also consider the available time for learning, the depth of what must be taught, and the learning style of the audience.

While task analysis focuses on why training is needed and the expected outcomes of training, performance analysis focuses on broader organization goals. *Performance analysis*, a key component of human performance technology, creates an assessment of current performance and then creates a map to future optimal performance. Performance analysis is often founded on the idea that performance suffers not because of educational deficiencies, but because of organizational constraints. Organizational constraints, such as unclear goals, faulty workflows, lack of clear instruction for organizational processes, and unbalanced rewards and recognition systems, all contribute to performance gaps—not educational gaps. Performance analysis aims to better the organization through process improvement, not through education about tasks.

Performance assessment documents what optimal performance means to an organization, defines the gap between the current state and the desired future state of performance, and creates a method to achieve optimal performance. As part of this assessment there's often a cost-benefits analysis to determine if the cost, energy, and organizational change is actually worth reaching optimal performance. The plan for optimal performance may include training as a byproduct, but not necessarily as a key element to reaching organizational goals. Performance analysis is usually done prior to the launch of the ADDIE model. Performance analysis, in some organizations, is folded into their ADDIE model to help see the difference between tasks that should be done and tasks that will affect the performance objectives for the organization as a whole.

Designing the Technical Training

The second phase of the ADDIE model is the design of the technical training. It is in this phase that the direction and content of the technical training is determined. The design phase is based on the outcome of the analysis phase. Instructional designers will determine what the best approach is for knowledge transfer, what must be included in the training, and what the expected learning outcomes of the training are based on the learning needs. Instructional designers will often say that designing the technical training must be efficient, effective, and appealing.

Efficient training means that there is enough training to transfer the knowledge to the learners so they can complete the associated tasks and have recall of what the instructor taught. Efficient training is likely weighted so that prioritized topics receive more time and the trainer doesn't linger on lower-prioritized topics. Training efficiency also addresses the cost of the seat and the value of the knowledge the trainer has for the recipients of the training. When you consider, for example, a classroom with a dozen learners, the salary of the learners, the time away from production, the cost of the facilities, the cost of the instructor, and the cost of the design of the materials, efficiency in learning must address the total cost of learning.

Effective learning means that the experience in the classroom will help the learners better complete their role in the organization. Effective learning thinks of the end result of the training—how the learner will apply what they've learned in the organization. Effective learning is about teaching the correct information in the correct approach so that the learners will retain what they've learned and be able to apply the information in their roles in the organization. Effective learning is dependent not only on good, clear design, but on the ability of the instructor to teach the content clearly, with authority, and in a manner that will help the participants learn and retain the course content.

Appealing training is best represented when the participants understand how the training will help them better achieve their roles in the organization. The learners can clearly see what the training is going to include, what the outcomes of the training will be, and how the training is important to their lives and roles in the organization. Appealing training is also training that is exciting because of the way the training is conducted, the teaching style of the instructor, and the experiences that the class will provide for the audience.

The design phase also addresses how the training will be conducted: web-based training (WBT), classroom instruction, demonstrations, one-on-one training, peer mentoring, or a host of other approaches can be used to accomplish the learning goals. How the training will be conducted is usually influenced first by the learning goals of the organization, the time allotted to complete the training, and the strategies that best align with the culture and learning style of the audience. The combination of learning needs, organizational goals, and learning styles should always be considered when designing the content and direction of a technical course.

As you might expect, the design phase directly addresses the specific topics that the course will include to meet the learning objectives of the organization. It's during this process that the specifics of the course content are determined, priority is assigned to the content, and the depth of explanation that is needed based on the completed instructional and performance analysis is determined. The identification of the course content is just the first step—the logical sequencing of the materials, consideration of the flow of the course, and the audience all affect what goes into your technical training and how it'll be best presented.

Instructional designers will (or should) create a *design strategy document*, sometimes called the detailed design document, that identifies the strategy of the course, the content of the seminar, the order of learning topics, and the overall direction of the learning for the organization. In most organizations a learning officer, project champion, or director will review and approve the design strategy document to confirm that the direction of the course is mapping to the learning goals of the organization. This document should include all of the following components:

- **Technical training scope**   Defines what the technical trainer will accomplish, the topics the course will and won't cover, timing for the course, approved and recommended techniques for teaching the learning objectives, and the expected outcomes from the training.

- **Constraints and assumptions**   Constraints are anything that limits options, such as versions, types of hardware, specific dates for training, budgets, duration of the class, or qualifications for the trainer. Assumptions are anything that's believed to be true, but hasn't yet been proven to be true. Assumptions may include resource availability, longevity of the technology, changes in the technology, learning goals, and interest in the technical course.

- **Course structure**   The prioritization of the course objectives, how the objectives were weighted and scored, workflow of the course, and how the structure supports the identified learning objectives.

- **Course context**   The context describes where the learning will take place, such as in a classroom, on the job, by web-based training, or with a combination of elements. The context should also address the learning activities, to a degree, that will be utilized to support the learning objectives. For example, in a classroom the learning activities may be lecture, labs, and conversations, but on-the-job training may be more mentoring, examples, and coaching.

The design phase of the ADDIE model is really about how the designers will manipulate the interactions within the learning environment. The design phase addresses the learner, expected outcomes for the learner, the learning environment, how the learners may interact with one another, and how the instructor will interact with the learners. These instructional elements are the design components that influence the degree of course efficiency, effectiveness, and appeal for the organization and the learners.

Developing the Course Material

The development phase of the ADDIE model is the actual creation of the course materials. This phase is based on the outcomes of the analysis and design phase, and it's the heart of what instructional designers do in an organization. Instructional designers will take the outcome of the design phase; examine the weighting, direction, and prioritization of the course content; and begin creating the materials that the instructor will utilize to deliver the class.

Depending on the structure of the class, the type of training being conducted, and the duration of the education experience, the designers will create the course assets. For example, a simple task may need only a job aid and five-minute web-based training video, whereas an overview of a complex new operating system may require an entire day of instructor-led training, a course workbook, and exercises and labs to engage the learner. The scope of the learning needs directly affects what the instructional designers will include in the course content.

The development phase involves more than just instructional designers; technical writers, subject matter experts, multimedia experts, copy editors, and more will be involved in this phase of the course development. Development of the course can involve the instructor, usually when they're needed to comment on or to review the material during development. More likely the technical trainer is involved in the earlier phases of the ADDIE model and then not needed during the development stage.

One important aspect of the development phase is quality control. *Quality control* is the inspection of what has been created to prevent mistakes from the learners. As a technical trainer, you may find it embarrassing when you're teaching a class and students take joy in calling your attention to a mistake in the user guide. It's not just the embarrassment for the instructor, but mistakes in the manuals, job aids, and other training deliverables can have a negative effect on the appeal of the class. If you've ever taught a technical course where it's obvious the writer, designer, and quality controllers didn't have experience with the subject matter, you've experienced this pain. This is why the technical trainer should be closely involved during the development portion of the ADDIE model. Technical trainers are often the last to see the course content though they have the most exposure to the learners and stakeholders.

Quality control and quality assurance are not the same thing. While quality *control* focuses on inspecting the project work to discover errors before the learners do, quality *assurance* is a prevention-driven process of doing the work properly the first time. Quality assurance defines the ground rules for quality expectations, best practices for estimating creation timelines and resource capabilities, and procedures to proof, prove, and verify the project work before the deliverables move into an intense inspection in quality control. While quality assurance and quality control seem similar, quality assurance is about doing the work properly the first time; quality control inspects the project work to prove the existence of quality.

Implementing the Technical Course

The implementation phase of the ADDIE model focuses on the actual delivery of what's been designed and developed for the learners. This is the bulk of the model, where the instructor will be conducting the training in either a classroom environment or through web-based training. The transition between the development phase and the implementation phase may overlap, depending on the organization's preferences, for pilot groups of training, train-the-trainer programs, and for "super user" groups. This overlap between development and implementation also serves as a type of quality control for the training, as the early sessions of training can expose errors, flaws, and inaccurate instructions.

The implementation phase is also considered part of the effective management of the learning logistics; all of these elements that are needed for the training to be a successful event are:

- Participant enrollment and tracking
- Classroom reservation, temperature, and configuration
- Adequate classroom materials, such as table tents for name placards, markers, whiteboards, flipcharts, courseware, and job aids
- Technical configuration of computers, networks, hardware, software, overhead projectors, and any other technical resource needed to satisfy the course objectives
- Instructor confirmation and communication for training locale and times
- Information for instructor and participants for immediate help, information, and maps and directions when appropriate
- Refreshments when appropriate for the class participants

The goal of the implementation phase, of course, is to implement the training that has been analyzed, designed, and developed so that the learners of the course can achieve the learning objectives. The implementation of the technical training keeps in alignment with the designed course and aims to reach the learning objectives, while remaining in alignment with the learning goals of the organization. This does not mean that the technical instructor cannot, or should not, adapt the course materials to teach a more effective class. Adapting the course for the learning styles in the learning environment is always a good idea to help the participants reach their learning objectives and to support the goals of the organization.

When you consider new technical training that your organization may be deploying, there will likely be train-the-trainer programs. These courses can be developed internally or through third-party vendors. Train-the-trainer programs are considered part of the implementation phase because you have to ramp up on the technology you'll be teaching. Train-the-trainer programs should give the instructor all of the information they're expected to deliver as part of the course—and sometimes more. It's always a good idea for the technical trainer to know more than what's promised to be delivered in the course, rather than just the course requirements. This is part of the mastery of the topic and can present opportunities for additional conversations and examples in the class.

In technology training the instructor should confirm that the technical requirements, such as server disk space, hardware requirements, access to appropriate networks, and available software, are supplied. It's embarrassing and frustrating to start a class, only to learn in front of a dozen participants that the hardware isn't configured properly, the network access is blocked, and the software you're about to teach is an older version than what's expected. Part of implementation, as you might expect, is to prepare the learning environment for the best possible delivery of the information. This rule is no different for the virtual classroom environment; the technical trainer must review the connection requirements, communicate with the remote learners before class starts, and confirm that the virtual classroom is ready to present the needed material.

During the technical training, keep a log of any technical or content issues that happen in class. Issues are any disruption in the course that must be rectified before the course continues and should be corrected before the course is offered again. Common issues could be technical settings that don't allow labs and demonstrations to work properly, course exercises that are vague or confusing, and errors in the learners' classroom workbooks. There's often, in my experience, a disconnection between the instructional designers and the technical trainer. Treating each role as a solo rather than a group effort doesn't support the learning objectives. Finally, during the actual teaching of the course, the technical trainer should never criticize the material, the course designers, or the technology that's being taught in front of the participants. If the material is faulty it should be reported to your supervisor so that the materials can be corrected for future classes.

Evaluating the Technical Course

The last component of the ADDIE model is the evaluation of the technical course. Evaluation actually happens throughout the ADDIE model, but it's the last phase I've not discussed. The evaluation measures the effectiveness of the training, the quality of the course, and the instructor's performance, along with the overall analysis, design, and development of the course. Figure 2-2 captures all levels of the Kirkpatrick evaluation approach, discussed next.

Evaluations are often seen as a judgment on the instructor's performance, which to some extent is true, but the primary use for an evaluation should be focused on how the performance, content, and learner experience can improve. Evaluation of the technical course can first be done in-house to measure the ability of the course and the instructor to meet the goals of the training program; this evaluation approach is called *formative*. The more common evaluation approach is the *summative* evaluation, and it continues through the life of the training program.

When most instructors think of evaluations, they are envisioning the end-of-class one-page review. These evaluations are useful, but only at a topical level for the organization. The end-of-class evaluations aren't always a true reflection of the instructor or the course quality. Participants often rush through the evaluation jotting perfect scores

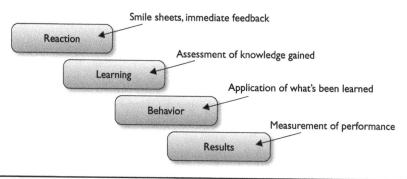

Figure 2-2   Evaluations move through reaction, learning, behavior, and results.

and no comments, and then rush out the door like sophomores on the last day of school. These end-of-class evaluations are also often lacking in content because the participants may fear that the instructor will read their comments and scores.

Over the last few years, since 1998, the popularity and effectiveness of Donald Kirkpatrick's Four Levels Evaluation Model has soared for many organizations. This four-tier approach to reviewing the effectiveness and benefits of training measures the whole breadth of learning for adult participants. You should not only be familiar with these four levels of evaluation for your CompTIA CTT+ certification, but you should also consider implementing these evaluations in your organization.

Conducting the Reaction Evaluation

The first level of Kirkpatrick's evaluation is the reaction evaluation. This evaluation is most commonly distributed at the end of class to gauge the participants' reaction to their training experience. Your organization might call these evaluations "feedback forms" or "course evaluations." The purpose of this initial step is to gain immediate feedback to the training to determine how the participants feel about the course. This evaluation lets participants share their experiences and captures if they're upset or disappointed by the class.

The reaction evaluation aims to determine if the training was successful and enjoyable and met the learners' needs. Organizations structure this evaluation not only to determine the instructor's ability to train on the topic, but also to determine if the training was worthy of the participants' time. This level of evaluation can also capture comments on the training environment, any technical issues in the course, and how effective the course material was. When an organization uses just this level of evaluation, as many do, it's of paramount importance to follow up with the responders and the trainer on any issues that happened in the course. Many companies are now using the first level of evaluation as part of the learning management system (LMS) to document learners' participation and transcript of course completion.

Administering the Learning Evaluation

The learning evaluation focuses on the increase in participant knowledge as a result of the training. For this learning evaluation to be effective, you'll first need a "before" assessment of the knowledge, and then you'll have to conduct a post-training assessment. Assessment exams before and after the class are the most common approach for this evaluation, but they aren't always the most effective. Interviews with the participants can be a good method to administer the learning evaluation, but this approach can be time-consuming.

In the technical training environment, assessment exams do make a quick and somewhat reliable approach for testing knowledge. The design of the pre- and post-class exams should reflect the same skill sets and topics that are tested, so that the same learning objectives are measured in both exams. In other words, you don't want to make either exam tougher or easier than the other. While assessment exams may be easy to create and administer, they are not cost-effective if the exams aren't well designed and paired on the same objectives and scoring.

Reviewing the Behavior Evaluation

The behavior evaluation attempts to determine if the course participants applied the learning and changed their behavior as a result of the training. This analysis, depending on the topic, can be done right away or even several months after the course. For example, you might teach a technical class on installing a certain technology. Participants in the seminar should be able to leave your training and go install the technology just as you taught them. The immediate behavior evaluation would determine if the technology was installed properly, while the long-term behavior evaluation would determine if the technology continued to be installed properly.

Other technical courses, such as new processes, workflows, and software usage, aren't as easy to measure because the behavior may not be immediately evident in the participants' jobs. The organization will have to review, interview, and assess the ongoing behavior of the participants to confirm that their behavior and utilization of the training is effective. A quick snapshot of before and an interview afterwards, such as with installing the technology, doesn't apply to every condition. People's behavior changes over time—and this assumes that people also have an opportunity to actually use the training and change their behavior based on what they've learned.

Measuring the Results Evaluation

The fourth level of Kirkpatrick's model is the results evaluation. This evaluation determines the effect of the training on the organization as a whole. This evaluation reviews how the training has affected how the organization operates, the betterment of the processes, the decline of technical issues, and even the improved morale of the employees. More likely, however, this evaluation level uses current management systems to measure key performance indicators to compare before-and-after statistics that may be linked to the trainer's contribution in the organization.

Key performance indicators will vary by organization, but common factors are volume of business; reliability of hardware, software, or technical solution; return on investment; and quality scoring. The difficulty with this evaluation is to prove that there is a direct correlation between what the instructor has taught, the behavior that changed in the participants' responsibilities, and the positive and negative circumstances within the organization. The size and scope of the technical training and the number of participants in the course also directly affect the organization's ability to measure the results.

Chapter Summary

Technical training is always based on the learners' needs. The organization should work with the technical trainer, the technical subject matter experts, and the learners to determine what information is needed to complete their assignments and do their work with more accuracy, efficiency, and productivity. This assessment of learners' needs is the first step in successful training because it helps to ensure that the training will include the content that's needed. Determining the learners' needs is a fundamental activity to determine what the training should include to be meaningful to the learners and the organization.

The instructional goal is part of assessing learners' needs because it defines the learning objectives and expected outcomes of the course in a clear, high-level statement. Some organizations may call the instructional goal the "course overview" or the "course description," but the purpose is always to communicate what the course will accomplish. The instructional goal helps the organization, the participants in the course, and the instructor to be in agreement as to what the course will achieve. Instructional goals help all the parties involved set expectations, but they also help the instructor set boundaries as to what will and will not be included in the course content.

The instructional goals help define the learning objectives for the technical training. Learning objectives describe the increased knowledge that participants will have once they complete the course. Learning objectives are created by first defining the topical units that will be included in the course. The topical units are a type of course outline that will then be broken down into learning outcomes. For each topical unit a learning outcome will elaborate on how the topical unit will be applied in the organization as a result of the technical training. The actual learning objective is based on the learning outcome. The learning objective is a statement that clearly defines how the behavior of the participants should change by applying the technical knowledge in the training.

As a technical trainer you'll need to measure the learner competencies to help you prepare to teach. This can mean creating course prerequisites, administering pre-course assessment exams, or even just conversing with participants to gauge their experience with the course subject matter. When you can assess how well versed the participants are in the course technology, you can then adapt your lecture, edit course labs, and offer more precise information to help learners achieve their goals for the course. Of course, you're not changing the content of the course or altering the learning objectives, but tailoring the course to address the learners' needs.

The ADDIE model is an instructional design model that can help you prepare to teach a great technical course. The ADDIE model is an acronym to describe the five common stages for instructional design and development. *Analysis* focuses on determining the learning needs, documenting why the training is needed, and considering what the learning objectives and goals for the training may be. *Design* defines the direction and content of the technical training. *Development* is the actual creation of the course content and material. *Implementation* is the trainer's delivery of what's been developed for the course content. *Evaluation* is the review of the course's ability to satisfy the learning objectives and instructional goals.

All courses should pass through an evaluation, and a recently embraced model is Kirkpatrick's Four Levels Evaluation Model. The first level is the *reaction* evaluation, which is the end-of-course evaluations the class completes to rank their overall satisfaction with the instructor and training. The second level is the *learning* evaluation, which aims to measure the increase in learner knowledge as a result of the course. The *behavior* evaluation, the third level in Kirkpatrick's model, determines if the actions of the participants have changed as a result of what they've learned in the training. The final level in the model is the evaluation of *results* the training had on the organization's performance indicators, such as profits, efficiency, or reliability of technical solutions.

Key Terms

aDDIE model An instructional design model that uses the phases of Analysis, Design, Development, Implementation, and Evaluation to describe the five cyclic stages of instructional design and development.

analysis The first phase of the ADDIE model. This phase determines the learning needs, why the training is needed, and the learning objectives and goals for the training.

assessment exams Often given as a course prerequisite to determine the depth of knowledge and experience a participant has on a given technology.

behavior evaluation The third level of Kirkpatrick's evaluation model measures the change in learners' behavior as a result of the course. The behavior measurement is the determination of actual usage and implementation of what's been taught in the technical training.

course prerequisites A determination of the existing knowledge that the learner must have, either through prior training or experience, to enroll in a technical training course.

design The second phase of the ADDIE model defines the direction and content of the technical training.

development The third phase of the ADDIE model is the actual creation of the course content and material.

education In the adult domain, education is defined as the broad goals of transferring knowledge from one individual to another with the intent to direct and influence the course of an individual's life.

dvaluation The fifth and final phase of the ADDIE model is the review of the course's ability to satisfy the learning objectives and instructional goals.

implementation The fourth phase of the ADDIE model is the trainer's delivery of what's been developed for the course content.

instructional goal An instructional goal is a statement that defines the high-level objectives for the course. It's a statement that communicates the broad learning objectives and expected outcomes of the course.

Kirkpatrick's Four Levels Evaluation Model Don Kirkpatrick developed four levels of training evaluation: reaction, learning, behavior, and results. Each level of evaluation becomes more involved and generally takes longer to implement, do well, and see actual measurements.

knowledge application   The evidence that knowledge transfer has actually occurred. Knowledge application is evident in the application of the skills, the fulfillment of the course expectations, and the return on the training investment.

knowledge transfer   In a technical training environment, knowledge transfer happens when accurate information is transferred from the instructor to the learner.

learning evaluation   The second level of Kirkpatrick's evaluation model attempts to assess the knowledge gained as a result of the training session. This level may use a pre- and post-course assessment to measure competence.

learning need   Describes what the learner needs to know to operate within the organization, complete a specific task or role, or manage a given technology.

learning objectives   Define the increased knowledge that learners will have as a result of the specifics of the training. Learning objectives are the specific goals of the specific content of the training course. Learning objectives define the exact application of the knowledge, not how the knowledge will be transferred from the instructor to the participants. Learning objectives are the end product of the breakdown of the instructional goal, the topical units, and the learning outcomes. Learning objectives clearly define the behavior that participants will possess as a result of the technical training.

learning outcome   A statement that describes what a topical unit will accomplish. Learning outcomes communicate the purpose of each component in a topical unit.

reaction evaluation   The first of the four levels of Kirkpatrick's evaluation model. The reaction evaluation is the immediate, end-of-course evaluation, sometimes called "smile sheets," to measure the participant's overall satisfaction with the course. These are called smile sheets to quickly measure how "smiley" participants are. Some evaluations may even use a scale from sad face to neutral face to happy face to measure learner reactions.

results evaluation   The fourth and final level of Kirkpatrick's evaluation model measures the overall results of the training on the organization as a whole. This evaluation can measure key performance indicators, such as profitability, efficiency, or the reliability of technology, as direct outcomes from the training session.

topical units   An outline topology of what the technical training will include. Topical units are based on the course learning objectives.

training   Focuses on the skills, tools, and competencies to help people complete their roles in an organization.

Questions

1. You are a technical trainer for your company and you're prepping to deliver a new course. Your manager has asked you to define the learning needs for the course. Which one of the following statements best describes the learning needs?

   A. It's what the participants need to know to complete their tasks within the organization.

   B. It's what management needs to know that your technical content will and won't include.

   C. It's what the learners need to know so they can prepare for your technical course.

   D. It's the assessment of what will and won't be included in the technical training.

2. What term best describes the phenomenon of knowledge moving from one individual to another?

   A. Knowledge gained

   B. Knowledge transfer

   C. Knowledge transmission

   D. Education

3. You are coaching a new employee on her role as a technical trainer in your company. The employee is slightly confused on the difference between education and training. What is the difference between education and training?

   A. There is no difference between education and training, as both aim to edify the learners.

   B. Education aims to direct and influence a person's life, while training focuses on the skills and tasks.

   C. Education focuses on the pedagogical approach, while training focuses on the andragogical approach.

   D. Training is for adults in a corporate environment, while education is for adults in a learning institution.

4. What term describes the high-level objectives for a course?

   A. Topical units

   B. Course description

   C. Course objectives

   D. Instructional goal

5. A manager has asked you, a technical trainer in your organization, to define the learning objectives for a new technical training course you have proposed. What are learning objectives?

   A. Learning objectives define the skills gap learners have in their roles and responsibilities.

   B. Learning objectives define the increased knowledge that learners will have as a result of the specifics of the training.

   C. Learning objectives define the design phase of the ADDIE model.

   D. Learning objectives define how the instructor will create the course content to satisfy the needs of the organization and to target the key performance indicators.

6. You are developing the learning outcomes for a technical course. What must exist so that you can clearly and completely define the learning outcomes?

   A. Course outline

   B. Course objectives

   C. Topical units

   D. Training objectives

7. What component is best described as the end product of the breakdown of the instructional goal?

   A. ADDIE model

   B. Course objective

   C. Learning objective

   D. Learners' needs

8. Which phase of the ADDIE model is concerned with the direction and content of the technical training?

   A. Analysis

   B. Design

   C. Development

   D. Implementation

9. You are coaching a new trainer on the ADDIE model. Which one of the following components is not one of the five phases of the ADDIE model?

   A. Design

   B. Document

   C. Implementation

   D. Evaluation

10. Which one of the following answers best describes what happens in the analysis phase of the ADDIE model?

    A. The instructor analyzes the information that will be taught to the learners.

    B. The participants reflect on what information, skills, and behaviors they need to complete their roles in the organization.

    C. The organization completes task analysis to determine what information, skills, and behaviors employees need to complete their roles in the organization.

    D. The instructor analyzes the learners to determine their prerequisites and qualifications for the course instruction.

11. Which one of the following best describes the ADDIE model?

    A. The ADDIE model is an approach to developing the instruction that you'll teach to your participants.

    B. The ADDIE model is the learning life cycle.

    C. The ADDIE model describes the adult learning process.

    D. The ADDIE model describes the instructor's role to Analyze, Define, Discuss, Implement, and then Explore the training topics.

12. During the design phase of the ADDIE model the constraints and assumptions must be analyzed. Which one of the following statements is the best example of a design constraint?

    A. The instructor should be certified in the given technology.

    B. The course will use commercial off-the-shelf training materials.

    C. The course must be completed in seven hours of training.

    D. The instructor will help design the course content.

13. What is the course context?

    A. The objectives that will be covered in the course

    B. The type of instructor that will teach the course

    C. The locale of the instruction

    D. The follow-up instruction for the participants

14. During the development phase of the ADDIE model it is essential that the organization, designers, and instructors carefully review the course to keep mistakes out of the course materials. What term best describes the inspection of what's been created to keep mistakes from the learners?

    A. Quality assurance

    B. Quality control

    C. Scope verification

    D. Education verification

15. The implementation phase of the ADDIE model describes the effective management of learning logistics. All of the following are examples of learning logistics except for which one?

    A. Selection of the material to use in the training

    B. Participant enrollment and tracking

    C. Classroom reservation, temperature, and configuration

    D. Adequate classroom materials

16. Which level of Kirkpatrick's evaluation model focuses on the increase in participant knowledge as a result of the training?

    A. Learning

    B. Behavior

    C. Reaction

    D. Results

17. An organization is measuring the connection between an increase in productivity and the training you've recently conducted. What type of evaluation is the company implementing?

    A. Reaction

    B. Results

    C. Performance

    D. Return on investment

18. Which one of the following statements best describes the behavior evaluation?

    A. Smile sheets

    B. Increased efficiency

    C. Application of learning

    D. Decrease in the number of errors

19. All of the following are outcomes of creating the learning objectives except for which one?

    A. Participants will know what they can expect to learn in the course and be able to perform once the training is completed.

    B. Management will have a clear understanding of what the technical training will provide for their employees.

    C. The human resources department can assess skills for pay increases, promotions, and downsizing.

    D. The technical trainer will create and review the expectations of the organization and the participants that the trainer must be able to provide and help the learner accomplish.

20. You're working with the instructional designers to define the learning objectives for a new course you're creating. When defining the learning objectives, what should you always keep in mind?

    A. The experience of the participants

    B. How the participants apply the information to their organizational roles

    C. What management expects from the course and the key performance results

    D. What tasks the course should include

Questions and Answers

1. You are a technical trainer for your company and you're prepping to deliver a new course. Your manager has asked you to define the learning needs for the course. Which one of the following statements best describes the learning needs?

    A. It's what the participants need to know to complete their tasks within the organization.

    B. It's what management needs to know that your technical content will and won't include.

    C. It's what the learners need to know so they can prepare for your technical course.

    D. It's the assessment of what will and won't be included in the technical training.

    A. Learning needs describe what the technical training will enable the participants to do as a result of the training. The learning needs should address the specific tasks and responsibilities the learners will achieve through the technical course. B is incorrect, as learning needs don't address management's concern for what's included in the course. C is incorrect because this answer describes course prerequisites and course prep for a technical course. D is incorrect, as this statement describes the boundaries of the course, not the learning objectives.

2. What term best describes the phenomenon of knowledge moving from one individual to another?

    A. Knowledge gained

    B. Knowledge transfer

    C. Knowledge transmission

    D. Education

    B. Knowledge transfer is the goal of technical training, as information is transferred from one individual, usually the technical trainer, to the learners.

Choices A and C are not valid choices, as these don't describe the knowledge transfer process. D is incorrect, as education is described as the broad goal of transferring knowledge from one individual to another with the intent to direct and influence the course of an individual's life. Education, from primary school to college, helps the person identify strengths and weaknesses and exposes interests that will influence the direction of the person's career and motivations.

3. You are coaching a new employee on her role as a technical trainer in your company. The employee is slightly confused on the difference between education and training. What is the difference between education and training?

   A. There is no difference between education and training, as both aim to edify the learners.

   B. Education aims to direct and influence a person's life, while training focuses on the skills and tasks.

   C. Education focuses on the pedagogical approach, while training focuses on the andragogical approach.

   D. Training is for adults in a corporate environment, while education is for adults in a learning institution.

   B. Of all the choices this is the best answer because education has loftier goals of motivating, directing, and influencing the choices in a person's life. Training focuses on the completion of tasks and actions individuals need to operate in their roles within an organization. A is incorrect; there is a distinct difference between training and education. C is incorrect, as the pedagogical model does focus on children, while the andragogical approach focuses on adults; both approaches can be applied for education or training. D is incorrect, as this statement doesn't clearly define the difference between education and training.

4. What term describes the high-level objectives for a course?

   A. Topical units

   B. Course description

   C. Course objectives

   D. Instructional goal

   D. The instructional goal defines the high-level objectives for the course. It's a statement that communicates the broad learning objectives and expected outcomes of the course. A, topical units, actually describes the breakdown of the instructional goal into an outline format. The course description and course objectives may be part of the instructional goal, but choices B and C don't accurately answer the question.

5. A manager has asked you, a technical trainer in your organization, to define the learning objectives for a new technical training course you have proposed. What are learning objectives?

   A. Learning objectives define the skills gap learners have in their roles and responsibilities.

   B. Learning objectives define the increased knowledge that learners will have as a result of the specifics of the training.

   C. Learning objectives define the design phase of the ADDIE model.

   D. Learning objectives define how the instructor will create the course content to satisfy the needs of the organization and to target the key performance indicators.

   B. Learning objectives define the increased knowledge that learners will have as a result of the specifics of the training. Learning objectives are the specific goals of the specific content of the training course. Learning objectives define the exact application of the knowledge, not how the knowledge will be transferred from the instructor to the participants. Answer A actually describes the identification of skills gaps and the assessment of learners' needs. Learning objectives are part of the assessment phase of the ADDIE model, not the design phase (choice C). Learning objectives don't address the specific organizational goals (choice D), but rather the specific learning needs.

6. You are developing the learning outcomes for a technical course. What must exist so that you can clearly and completely define the learning outcomes?

   A. Course outline

   B. Course objectives

   C. Topical units

   D. Training objectives

   C. The learning outcomes are based on the topical units for the technical training session. Topical units are like a course outline, but choice A does not clearly and completely answer the question. B is incorrect, as the course objectives are not a prerequisite to creating the learning outcomes. Training objectives, choice D, is not a valid answer for this question.

7. What component is best described as the end product of the breakdown of the instructional goal?

   A. ADDIE model

   B. Course objective

   C. Learning objective

   D. Learners' needs

   C. The learning objective is the final product of breaking down the instructional goal. Learning objectives clearly define the behavior that participants will be able to do as a result of your training. A, the ADDIE model, describes the phases of instructional design, not the instructional goal. The course objective, choice B, is not a valid answer for this question. D is incorrect, as learners' needs are the assessment of what the learners' need to know to complete their role in the organization.

8. Which phase of the ADDIE model is concerned with the direction and content of the technical training?

   A. Analysis

   B. Design

   C. Development

   D. Implementation

B. The design phase of the ADDIE model defines the direction and content of the technical training. A is incorrect, as the analysis phase determines the learners' needs for the technical training. C is incorrect, as development is the actual creation of the course content based on the assessment and course design. D, implementation, is incorrect, as this is the phase where the instructor actually teaches the course to the participants.

9. You are coaching a new trainer on the ADDIE model. Which one of the following components is not one of the five phases of the ADDIE model?

   A. Design

   B. Document

   C. Implementation

   D. Evaluation

B. Document is not one of the five phases of the ADDIE model. The correct phases of the ADDIE model are Analysis, Design, Development, Implementation, and Evaluation. Choices A, C, and D are incorrect because these answers are part of the ADDIE model.

10. Which one of the following answers best describes what happens in the analysis phase of the ADDIE model?

   A. The instructor analyzes the information that will be taught to the learners.

   B. The participants reflect on what information, skills, and behaviors they need to complete their roles in the organization.

   C. The organization completes task analysis to determine what information, skills, and behaviors employees need to complete their roles in the organization.

   D. The instructor analyzes the learners to determine their prerequisites and qualifications for the course instruction.

C. The analysis phase of the ADDIE model is the process of determining training needs and task analysis—it's the expected learning outcomes of what your training class will accomplish for your participants. Task analysis is the process of a learning professional, trainer, instructional designer, or learning consultant, serving as a business analyst to evaluate the expected behavior changes and expected knowledge the participant will have as a result of the training. Task analysis also reviews the audience, the depth of content for the course, and the type of training that will best satisfy the learning need. Choices A, B, and D are incorrect as these statements do not reflect the actual activities of the analysis phase.

11. Which one of the following best describes the ADDIE model?

    A. The ADDIE model is an approach to developing the instruction that you'll teach to your participants.

    B. The ADDIE model is the learning life cycle.

    C. The ADDIE model describes the adult learning process.

    D. The ADDIE model describes the instructor's role to Analyze, Define, Discuss, Implement, and then Explore the training topics.

A. The ADDIE model is an approach to developing the instruction that you'll teach to your participants. ADDIE is an acronym for Analysis, Design, Development, Implementation, and Evaluation. Choices B, C, and D are incorrect, as these statements do not define the ADDIE model.

12. During the design phase of the ADDIE model the constraints and assumptions must be analyzed. Which one of the following statements is the best example of a design constraint?

    A. The instructor should be certified in the given technology.

    B. The course will use commercial off-the-shelf training materials.

    C. The course must be completed in seven hours of training.

    D. The instructor will help design the course content.

C. Of all the choices the constraint of completing the training in seven hours is the best example. A constraint is anything that limits your design options. A is incorrect, as this is a recommendation, not a requirement. B is incorrect, as this answer still allows the designer to choose from many different training materials. Answer D is incorrect; while this answer may be considered a constraint to an extent, it's not the best answer because it doesn't define the degree of contribution the instructor will make in the training content.

13. What is the course context?

    A. The objectives that will covered in the course

    B. The type of instructor that will teach the course

    C. The locale of the instruction

    D. The follow-up instruction for the participants

    C. The context describes where the learning will take place, such as in a classroom, on the job, by web-based training, or a combination of elements. The context should also address the learning activities, to a degree, that will be utilized to support the learning objectives. Choices A, B, and D are incorrect, as these choices don't describe the context, but rather the content, instructor requirements, and the post-class support.

14. During the development phase of the ADDIE model it is essential that the organization, designers, and instructors carefully review the course to keep mistakes out of the course materials. What term best describes the inspection of what's been created to keep mistakes from the learners?

    A. Quality assurance

    B. Quality control

    C. Scope verification

    D. Education verification

    B. Quality control is the inspection of what has been created to prevent mistakes from the learners. A, quality assurance, is the quality plan and requirements to create the materials properly the first time. C, scope verification, is a project management term to describe the acceptance of the course materials by the key stakeholders. D, education verification, is not an applicable term for this question.

15. The implementation phase of the ADDIE model describes the effective management of learning logistics. All of the following are examples of learning logistics except for which one?

    A. Selection of the material to use in the training

    B. Participant enrollment and tracking

    C. Classroom reservation, temperature, and configuration

    D. Adequate classroom materials

    A. The selection of the material to use in the training is part of the ADDIE model's design phase. Choices B, C, and D are incorrect, as these choices are learning logistics.

16. Which level of Kirkpatrick's evaluation model focuses on the increase in participant knowledge as a result of the training?

    A. Learning

    B. Behavior

    C. Reaction

    D. Results

    A. The learning evaluation focuses on the increase in participant knowledge as a result of the training. This learning evaluation often requires a "before" assessment of the knowledge and then a post-training assessment. B is incorrect, as the behavior evaluation measures the application of what's been taught. C, the reaction evaluation, is the immediate, end-of-training evaluation to measure participant satisfaction. D, results evaluations, are the final level of the Kirkpatrick model and measure the overall effect the training had on the organization.

17. An organization is measuring the connection between an increase in productivity and the training you've recently conducted. What type of evaluation is the company implementing?

    A. Reaction

    B. Results

    C. Performance

    D. Return on investment

    B. This is an example of the results evaluation, as this is a review of the actual effect the training had on key performance results, such as productivity. Answer A is incorrect, as reaction evaluations are the immediate feedback from the course participants on the effectiveness of the course. C and D are incorrect choices because neither performance nor return on investment is one of the four levels of the Kirkpatrick evaluation model.

18. Which one of the following statements best describes the behavior evaluation?

    A. Smile sheets

    B. Increased efficiency

    C. Application of learning

    D. Decrease in the number of errors

    C. Of all the choices the application of learning is the best answer because the application of learning describes the behavior evaluation. The behavior evaluation attempts to determine if the course participants applied the learning and changed their behavior as a result of the training. A, smile sheets, is incorrect, as this is a component of the reaction evaluation. Choices B and D are incorrect, as these are representative of the results evaluation.

19. All of the following are outcomes of creating the learning objectives except for which one?

    A. Participants will know what they can expect to learn in the course and be able to perform once the training is completed.

    B. Management will have a clear understanding of what the technical training will provide for their employees.

    C. The human resources department can assess skills for pay increases, promotions, and downsizing.

    D. The technical trainer will create and review the expectations of the organization and the participants that the trainer must be able to provide and help the learner accomplish.

    C. An outcome of the learning objectives is not necessarily for human resources to assess skills for pay increases, promotions, and downsizing. This may be an end result of the training, but it's not a direct product of creating the learning objectives. Choices A, B, and D are incorrect, as these choices accurately reflect the outcomes of the learning objectives.

20. You're working with the instructional designers to define the learning objectives for a new course you're creating. When defining the learning objectives, what should you always keep in mind?

    A. The experience of the participants

    B. How the participants apply the information to their organizational roles

    C. What management expects from the course and the key performance results

    D. What tasks the course should include

    B. The learning objectives should always consider the end result and goal of the training: how participants will apply the information to their organizational roles. In other words, how will the learners use what you've taught them? Answer A is incorrect; the experience of the participants isn't a consideration for the learning objective creation. C is incorrect, as key performance will be an outcome based on the ability of the participants to accurately use what's been taught them, assuming that the correct instructional needs have been identified. The tasks of the course should be considered, but choice D isn't the best answer, as the tasks will be defined based on the correct identification of the learning objectives.

Managing the Technical Classroom

In this chapter you will:
- Prepare the classroom for learning
- Manage the course logistics for materials and technology
- Address classroom issues and distractions for learners
- Design course materials and handouts
- Create a comfortable learning environment

The technical classroom can present challenges that aren't found in other training environments. Teach a class on project management, for example, and all you'll need is a whiteboard, the class desks and chairs, and the course workbook. Teach a class on Microsoft Office, databases, or computer repair, and things suddenly get more complex. Now you'll need to prepare the classroom for technical training, make certain the computer exercises work as planned, check network connectivity, confirm software and hardware compatibility, and handle a host of other technical concerns. More prep time goes into technical training than into other types of training.

Learners come into a technical training session with all sorts of expectations. Not only do they expect to learn new information from you, the technical expert on the topic you're teaching, but they also expect the classroom configuration to be perfect. When there are glitches, technology errors, or the classroom is not prepped properly, it not only reflects poorly on you, the front line for the training organization, but it also deters from meeting the learning objectives of the course. Participants will get very frustrated when they can't complete exercises or practice the material, or if they watch your demonstrations fail.

It's easy to understand their frustrations—you're teaching busy people, people that need the technical information you're teaching for their career and businesses. When they're in class, they're away from their jobs, and their responsibilities are piling up on top of the technical training you're giving them. No one, especially IT people, wants to waste time in a class that's falling apart due to technical problems. From the trainer's perspective it's embarrassing when the room isn't configured properly. Learners don't know that you, the technical trainer, weren't necessarily the person that was supposed to configure the room for their class.

NOTE Some would say that the technical instructor is ultimately responsible for configuring the classroom. While this might be true under ideal circumstances, it's not always the case. I've worked as a contract-based technical trainer flying from organization to organization to teach different technical topics. Often I couldn't have access to the training room until Monday morning just moments before class began. Occasionally I was surprised to learn that the room wasn't configured as promised and that there wasn't much time to try to fix the problem before the learners arrived. Maybe you've found yourself in that situation too; the key is to remain calm, not blame anyone, assess the problem, and then make a plan of attack to fix the problem.

Classroom management is more than fixing a poor classroom setup. Classroom management is ensuring that the room is prepared to support the learning objectives. In fact, everything you do in the classroom should be to support the learning objectives. Classroom management is guiding and directing participants' conversations, actions, and total learning experience toward the achievement of the instructional goals. Everything that you have control over in the classroom, from the lighting to the technology to the logistics of the classroom configuration, falls into the broad category of classroom management.

While your role is that of technical trainer, your responsibility is to boost and support the learning experience for the users. As you enter a classroom as the trainer, think of your preparations, your lecture, your demonstrations, and all your actions from the perspective of the learner. When you shift your vision from instructor to a participant, your effectiveness as a technical trainer will soar. Always consider how what you say and do as the instructor may affect the participants' ability to learn.

Configuring the Learning Environment

Some trainers just call it a "classroom"; that's fine, but try to think of that big room where you teach as a learning environment. The learning environment is the space where learning happens—and in today's world it doesn't have to be just the traditional classroom space. Sure, you have the obvious alternatives of web-based training and remote meetings, but you also have the ability to leave the classroom, see the actual technology installed, learn on the job, and to learn by doing. Of course, the bulk of the learning, especially for your CompTIA CTT+ examination, focuses on the traditional classroom environment or the virtual classroom environment.

The learning environment needs to be configured to support the educational goals of the organization. This means that you'll need the classroom prepped for the technology you're teaching, but you'll also want to clean, organize, and make the classroom comfortable for learning. Too many organizations allow their classrooms to be used as a spare room for storage, not as a pristine and revered room for expanding knowledge.

Configuring the learning environment is all about preparing the space to support the instructional goals. This means that while the instructor is prepared to teach the technical topic, the space where the learning will happen also needs to be prepared.

View your classrooms through the learners' eyes, not the trainer's, and it'll be clearer what needs to be done to prepare your training rooms for learning, not just teaching. It's always more important that learners learn than that trainers train.

NOTE The learning environment can also be the web environment that CompTIA calls the *virtual classroom space*. Most of the objectives in this chapter deal with the physical classroom. Throughout this book I will specifically address the virtual classroom space. If you're prepping for the CompTIA written exam, you should be familiar with the management of both virtual classrooms and traditional, instructor-led classrooms.

Preparing the Physical Space

Years ago when I lived in Chicago, a client assigned me to teach a technical class on-site. I took the "L" and two buses to arrive at the facility where I was to teach, only to discover that this location was not an office park, but an oil refinery. It was loud, stinky, and dirty—and that was before I even made it to the training room. The room they'd created for the training was their break room—right next to the shop floor where thousands of gallons of fuel were being processed every second.

The computers were arranged on folding tables under buzzing, flickering fluorescent lights. There was hardly any room for keyboards, mice, and certainly not for the class workbooks. I had to speak over the consistent churn of the factory—and just stop talking during the frequent roar of equipment. Other workers, unaware of the training, would ramble in for a candy bar and soda. A few people actually ate their snack and watched me teach. It was not, as you might imagine, an environment conducive to learning.

A good learning environment starts with the training room. The training room should be large enough to support the maximum number of people recommended for the class. If the class will allow 12 people to attend, organizations should not pack 19 people into the space. When too many people are in the classroom, the number of participants can detract from the learning of the whole group. The shape of the classroom should be rectangular, with clear lines of sight to the front of the classroom; forget classrooms that are shaped like an *L* or that have columns throughout. The ideal classroom has ceilings in the 10-foot range and allows the trainer to walk freely through the room, accessing each participant without bumping into other learners, and has a door to keep out hallway noise. The rows of desks should be amply spaced so that you (and the class participants) can move through the aisles freely—think first-class spacing rather than coach.

First impressions matter for learning. Your classroom space should be neat, clean, have a pleasant smell, and be organized. Boxes of old materials, supplies, and random computer parts should be stored somewhere else—not in the classroom. When learners come into a disorganized, messy classroom, they're immediately distracted by the junk and may begin to dread having to spend much time in the classroom. A messy classroom that's littered with stored supplies sends a message that storage in this space is more important than learning in this space.

As part of your classroom preparation you or a staff member should clean the whiteboards, wipe down the desks and chairs, clean the dust off the computers, and vacuum the floor. If you're using flipcharts in your classroom, make certain the first page of the flipchart is blank or has a welcome message—not the notes from the last group that used the classroom. It's also a nice touch to organize your markers, erasers, and desk items. You want the room to look and feel neat, welcoming, and organized. Any visual aid, such as a prop or poster, should be neat, organized, and support the learning objectives.

Temperature in classrooms is always an important consideration—especially if you're running several computers in the space. The heat from the monitors, printers, and other devices can begin to cook as the day wears. Be aware of your participants' body language: are they pulling on sweaters and jackets or do they appear comfortable? As the trainer, you're moving, talking, and may have on a suit jacket—you'll probably feel warmer than your learners. A good temperature for training is 70 to 72 degrees Fahrenheit (that's 20.5 to 21.6 degrees Celsius), but that's a recommendation. Crank up the air or heat as needed.

One of the most important elements of a training room is effective lighting. I dread fluorescent overhead lights in a classroom because they can flicker, buzz, and provide bright, harsh light. My preference is for track lighting or recessed lighting, but I don't always have a choice. My point: make do with what you have. When possible use natural lighting—as long as it doesn't cause a glare, make the room too warm, or serve as a distraction from the learning. If you're using an overhead projector, test the lights and your demonstration before class begins. It's frustrating for the learners in the back of the room to be unable to see your demonstration because the lights are too bright. Asking participants if they can see is fine, but it's smarter to find out before class actually begins.

How you configure the classroom can affect how the class operates, what the training feels like for the learners, and the energy level in the room. Many classrooms are arranged in the typical classroom style, as in Figure 3-1, where the desks face the front of the room in rows. There's nothing wrong with the approach, as it keeps all eyes toward the instructor and the presentation screen, and suggests the seriousness of the classroom. From a technical point of view this configuration is good too because computers can be quickly accessed and cables can be configured and neatly positioned.

Another approach, as in Figure 3-2, arranges the computers, workbenches, and hardware along the perimeter of the room. This configuration is ideal for technical classes that are lab-driven, such as a CompTIA A+ hardware class. This classroom setting allows the instructor to be at the top of the U for demonstrations, but allows the participants to swivel back to their workstations to practice what they've learned. This approach allows the instructor to move about the room and to shadow, coach, or interact with learners as needed. The one drawback of this approach, however, is that there

Figure 3-1
The typical classroom configuration aims the learners' view toward the front of the classroom.

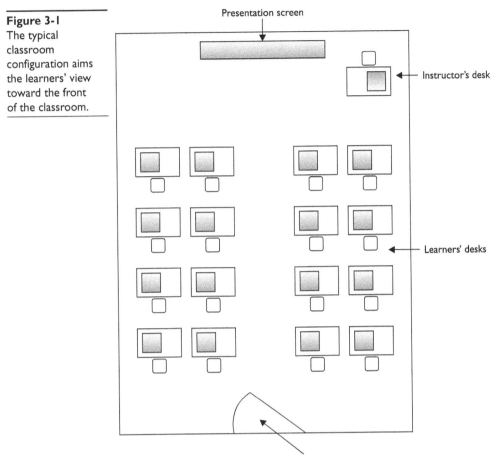

Presentation screen

Instructor's desk

Learners' desks

Exit at back of room—minimal interruptions

can be a constant distraction to see what's on the workbench rather than what the instructor is presenting.

Whatever approach you take in configuring your classroom, you should avoid one of the most common pitfalls for many instructors: hiding. It's easy to hide behind your computer monitor, a podium, or even at the back of the room. The people in the classroom are on your side—they want you to teach a good, solid class and to do well in your presentation. Participants want you to be visible and to make eye contact, and they want to see you and your body language. Fifty-five percent of communication is nonverbal; if your participants can't see you, they are losing a significant portion of your message.

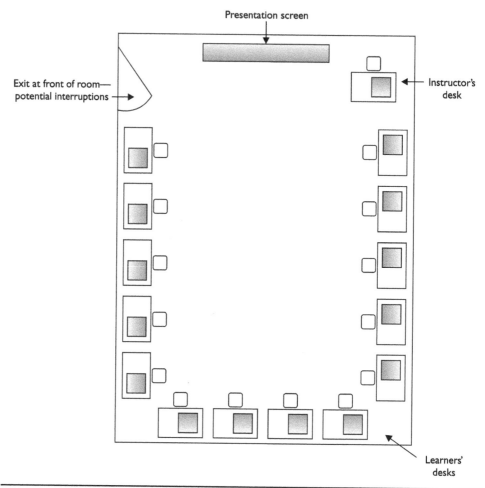

Figure 3-2 U-shaped classroom configurations are ideal for lab-intensive classes.

Planning the Course Logistics

If you've ever arrived to teach a technical class only to realize the training materials weren't shipped, the computers weren't configured, or worse still, no one was expecting you, then you know how frustrating poor handling of logistics can be. Course logistics involve all of the moving parts that need to come together before you actually arrive to teach the class. Course logistics may be outside of your role, but an effective trainer makes certain that everything is in place to teach an effective class.

One of the biggest elements of course logistics is the where-and-when portion of scheduling the course. You, the training coordinator, the facilities coordinator, and the participants all need to know the exact location of the class and when the class will commence and end. If you're teaching for a client at their location, contact the client personally, and find out the training location and time. In some instances you'll have to be escorted from the front door to the training room, so it's smart to bring at least two contact names and numbers. When you have only one contact for a training site, invariably that contact will be running late the day of your training.

Books, software, and any other course materials should also be delivered to the training center or training room well before class starts. It's unprofessional and disruptive when materials arrive late—or not at all. Again, communicating with the vendor, the client, and the facilities coordinators can help make certain the materials are delivered to the correct room by the correct time. Having the books ahead of the class start also allows you to peruse the manuals and to confirm that they are the correct version for the course you'll be teaching. Some instructors also like to place the manuals in specific locations in the classroom to guide participants to where they should be seated. This approach can keep the back row of the classroom configuration from having the most learners.

When you arrive early to the classroom, connect your computer to the overhead projector as soon as possible. Sometimes overhead projectors can be stubborn to synchronize and may require a reboot or two of your computer. By taking care of this pesky business first, you're assured that your computer is ready for you before any learners arrive and well before the class start time. Once your computer is connected to the overhead projector, then you can go about your business of prepping the room and organizing your materials.

Depending on the type of class you'll be teaching, technical logistics may need to be coordinated. You may need to know computer and network passwords, network storage path locations, and where electrical and network outlets are. You may want to randomly select a few computers and confirm that the software is loaded, that there is network connectivity, and that the keyboard, mouse, and operating system are functional for your class.

Another big part of logistics is the coordination of refreshments. If your training center provides breakfast, drinks, and snacks throughout the day, you'll want to coordinate when these items will be available. Armed with this information you can time your breaks so that participants can refill their coffees, grab some cookies, and return to class in unison rather than in a disruptive trickle. As the trainer you should not be first in line for the breakfast items, snacks, and drinks. Keep the focus on the learners in all parts of the training. In fact, I always recommend that trainers not have any of the snacks—drinks are fine, but it's not professional to start the training day by greeting your learners while you're munching on a big donut.

Write down the name and numbers of any on-site technical support. Keep with you throughout the training event the contact information for anyone who will support the overhead projector, network, access to the classrooms, or other interaction with the training location. When there's a problem, you can quickly contact the support, get the problem resolved, and keep the class moving.

NOTE Be certain to publicly thank the person who solves the technical issue—never embarrass them or put them down for a problem in the classroom.

There are also logistics for the end of the course. If learners are completing evaluations as part of the course time, you'll need to know the web address for the evaluation or to determine who will provide and collect the paper-based evaluation forms. When class is done, ask learners to collect all their belongings and throw away their trash, and thank them for doing so. You'll want to wipe down the whiteboards, discard any used pages from flipcharts, and tidy up the room. Just because you may not have found the room in perfect condition doesn't mean that you should leave it in less than perfect condition.

Teaching the Perfect Class

Some would argue there's no such thing as a perfect class, but I'd say they were wrong. There can be a perfect class, as I know I've taught many and I'm sure you have too. Some participants will always find something to criticize in a class: the instructor's jokes weren't funny, the coffee was cold, the computer gave an error message, or the materials had a typo. As an instructor realize now that some people won't ever rate your class with perfect scores, but that doesn't mean that you won't do all that you can to give a perfect presentation.

Assuming that you have clear learning objectives, understand the material to be taught, and that you've created a link between what you are about to teach and the learners' responsibilities, you can teach a perfect class. You can take many steps to prepare the room, manage the class, and to create a wonderful learning environment beyond just lecturing and demoing the technology. Training perfection is often the result of subtle things that learners may perceive but be unaware of, for example, not pacing when you're teaching, or speaking clearly during lectures, or ensuring the room is comfortable, tidy, and lit appropriately for learning.

While participants may not always recognize a perfect class, a less-than-perfect class is always evident. If the room isn't prepped properly, the instructor isn't prepared for the delivery, or the hardware and software aren't configured, it's obvious to the participant. In fact, problems at the start of the course can affect the way the remainder of the course is seen. A small problem that could have been prevented can magnify other problems in the delivery of the course. There's something about "the smell of blood in the water" that brings out the sharks in participants. They have expectations about the time they're investing in your class, and when these expectations aren't met, you can expect a docile group of people to turn hostile.

 NOTE In Chapter 6 I'll explore the attributes of teaching, how to teach well, and the mechanics of public speaking. This chapter focuses more on the preparation and classroom configuration to set the stage for effective instruction.

Managing the Learning Environment

When you're the instructor, you're in charge of the learning environment. This doesn't mean you need to be a dictator, but rather a good, effective manager. You need to take charge of the physical space, lead the conversations, and have an authoritative, yet approachable, attitude in the classroom. Always consider this from the learners' perspective; when they come to class, they may have anxiety about the class topic, their time away from responsibilities, and who they'll be spending the next several hours or days with. Participants want to go to an organized, meaningful class led by an expert.

They assume that you, the technical trainer, must be the expert since you're teaching the technology. They assume that you know everything there is to know about the technical topic you're about to teach because you're the instructor. You should, of course, satisfy that assumption through your pre-class preparations, and know your topic to a few notches higher than what's expected of you in the classroom. In other words, you should prepare for the entire scope of the class, but extend your comfort level beyond the expectations of the learners. When you are fully prepared, it is easier to speak with confidence, be in control, and anticipate learners' needs.

But there's more to managing the learning environment than just teaching. It's in all of your communication. There's the obvious oral communications, which I'll discuss later in this book, but there's the written communications too. If you use whiteboards or flipcharts, you must be aware of what you write and how you write it. When you write as part of your presentation, you must use legible handwriting that everyone in the classroom can see. Always write your messages in the top two-thirds of the flipchart or whiteboard; when you write in the lowest third, it's hard for everyone to see your messages.

In technical classes it's useful to draw quick illustrations for participants. While sometimes you may need quick, ad hoc drawings, it's a good idea to plan out the drawings you're illustrating for your class. If you know what you're about to draw based on your prep time or from previous classes, you can draw the figure faster and with more confidence. When an instructor is illustrating a concept, it's usually because the esoteric nature of the topic is better explained in a figure than in a conversation. If the figure confuses the learner even more, then the drawing is a detriment, not a help.

If you're going to speak with your audience as you draw or write on the whiteboard, pay attention to when you speak and when you draw. In other words, don't speak with your back to your audience. Sometimes, when illustrating a point, it makes more sense to align the drawing and your conversation. If you must draw or write while you speak, at least turn your body so that you can project your voice out toward your audience rather than speaking directly to the whiteboard.

A good practice is to examine the markers you'll be using in your class to confirm that the markers are appropriate for the drawing surface. You don't want any permanent ink markers getting mixed into your batch of dry erase markers because you'll certainly grab the permanent marker during your class and leave your training mark forever. If you're a contract-based instructor, it's a good idea to bring a set of markers with you to the classroom. This ensures that you have different colors of dry erase markers, and you can add variety to whiteboard drawings by using different size marker tips for your classroom topics.

Lighting is important in your classroom, as you want to confirm the participants can read what you're presenting on the overhead. Fluorescent tube lighting doesn't give you many choices on how to dim, position, or manage streams of light—usually just "on" or "off." If you must teach in a classroom with fluorescent light, experiment with turning only half the lights on, adding lamps, or using natural lighting. If your training room has track lighting or recessed lighting, you might be able to dim the lights, change the spotlight effects, and utilize preset lighting functions. In any case, make certain that what you're writing is adequately lit, glare free, and viewable by all of the course participants. Watch for shadows, colors that fade away under certain lighting, and where you stand, so that you're not backlit or casting your shadow onto what students are trying to read.

VIDEO   See the video *Preparing the Classroom*

Adding Presentation Software

Another aspect of classroom management that deals with communications is the presentation software you'll use as a teaching tool in your class. PowerPoint is the de facto standard for training presentations in a classroom. Unfortunately, it's also one of the worst tools to support effective training. This isn't because PowerPoint is bad software; it's because PowerPoint is not used very well.

If you've ever sat through a "death by PowerPoint" meeting or training session, you know the pain of poorly designed and utilized presentations. Few things are more painful in training than to sit through a slide deck that's loaded with long paragraphs of text and then to have the instructor read the text off the slide. When that happens, I'd prefer that someone just drop a projector on my head.

When you're creating your PowerPoint slideshow, the basic rule to follow is the KISS rule: Keep It Simply Simple. For starters, all of your content should directly support the learning objectives of the presentation; if it's in your slideshow, it must be related to what you want learners to learn. The design of the slides should be neat, organized, and easy to view. Use a dark font on a light background; I prefer black letters on a faded yellow background. The contrast between text and color should be easy on the eyes. I prefer Arial 28 pt for headlines, and Arial 24 pt for body text, though any sans serif font is a good choice.

NOTE   Avoid uppercase letters, underlining, italics, or reverse fonts where the letter is white and the background is a darker color. When your message is stylized, it's a distraction from the learning.

In PowerPoint you can choose from all sorts of fancy templates loaded with graphics, flashy animations, and color schemes. It's fun to play with these templates, but the best approach is the simple slideshow where your message speaks more loudly than the medium that delivers it. I highly recommend that trainers not use animations, slide transitions, and sounds in the presentation. The instructor, not the slideshow, should be the focal point for delivering the message. When you add effects and animations, these can distract from the message of the class rather than boost the message you want to convey.

Your slideshows should also follow the storytelling model: have a beginning, the middle content, and a definite ending to the presentation. The beginning slides should introduce you, the course objectives, and what learners can expect from the class. Any timing information, such as break schedules and lunches, should be communicated as well. The introductory slides are a good place to discuss not only the agenda for the class, but also your experience and ice breakers for the class, and to get the participants excited about what you'll be teaching.

The middle content is the meat of your presentation. Organize the materials in a logical, progressive order to move through the course content. Keep the slide content short—no more than 15 words maximum per slide is ideal. Each line of text, as shown in Figure 3-3, should just be the key thoughts; your lecture is where you expound on the thoughts. Keep in mind, people can read faster than you can speak, so synch the slide content to the message without putting too much or too little information into the slides. If you'll have frequent demonstrations or exercises throughout your lecture, use a common icon to represent these activities. For example, a beaker might be used to represent a lab exercise, while a pair of sunglasses might represent a demonstration. If you use these same simple elements throughout the course, learners will anticipate what they'll need to do in the class, and you can direct their behavior with little instruction. These visual clues also help you to pause for labs, demonstration, conversation, and other activities.

Figure 3-3
Slides should have just key thoughts and no more than 15 words total.

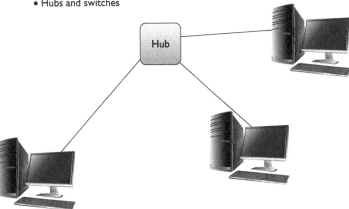

Ethernet Networking

• Frame-based networking
• Twisted-pair wiring
• Network card interface
• Hubs and switches

Hub

A slideshow that's just full of text can be a bit dry and boring. Grab some screen captures and add some clip art or photos to engage your learners. Of course, make certain that the content you add is actually related to the course material. It's not recommended to grab clip art of a guy wearing 12 hats just because he's cute, but if the clip is related to one person serving multiple roles in an organization, that may be appropriate. The type of clip art and photos you add to your slideshows should always mesh with the topic of the training and the audience you'll be speaking with.

Long, uninterrupted slideshows are an invitation to nap—especially if you dim the room lights for that movie theater effect all trainers seem to enjoy. While you may be a profound speaker, your participants may not be profound listeners. Break up presentations with lots of interactions, questions, quick surveys, and exercises. By incorporating these quick, impromptu activities into your lecture, you'll keep your learners involved, motivate them to pay attention, and you'll confirm the reception of what you're teaching.

A cordless presentation tool that lets you move around the room and still navigate your slideshow is one of the best aids for a technical instructor. If you're forced to use a mouse to advance your slides, you're anchored to your desk and separated from where your audience will be looking. Use caution: just because you can roam to all corners of the room and change the slides doesn't mean that you should. Ideally you should stand to the left of the presentation screen, as people generally read left to right. Your audience will look at you first and then onto the information on the slide being displayed. A cordless presentation tool also allows you to use body language and hand gestures, and adds professionalism to your presentation.

Adding Classroom Features

Your organization might have preset best practices for all of its trainers to follow. The organization might dictate the dress code, templates for the presentation software, and even the type of markers you're allowed to use in the classroom. Perhaps you have more freedom in how you teach and interact with your participants, and in the extras you decide to add to your classroom. All instructors should be professional, well-groomed, friendly yet authoritative, and use the tools available to best support the learning objectives.

You might consider adding some practices and features to your classroom to support the learning objectives. The extras that I'll discuss in this section might seem controversial to you. Some instructors have embraced these additions, while others despise bringing these elements into the classroom. In either case, what's most important in your decision to add, experiment with, or ignore these additions is how well they support the learning objectives for your class. If you can reason that adding one or two of these elements does enhance learning, make the training event memorable, and generate energy among your participants, then it's a good idea to add these features to your classroom. At the least, however, I hope you'll consider these additions and how they may help you become a better technical instructor and support the learning goals of your organization.

Creating Learning Handouts for Participants

Learning handouts go by many names: job aids, learner assistants, cheat sheets, reference cards. Whatever you call your handouts, they are given to your participants to help them learn and retain the course information. Your handouts may be created by instructional designers rather than you, but if the design and creation of the handouts is left up to you, there are several rules and guidelines you should follow. Chief among these guidelines is that the handouts should always support the course objectives. In other words, don't distribute a handout for Microsoft Excel during a Microsoft Word course, or even distribute handouts for advanced technical topics in a fundamentals course. Just use common sense.

All people learn, to some extent, through visual clues, but handouts support the visual learners' need to see facts, figures, and information to best receive that information. Handouts also give the learners a "take-away" deliverable for the class that they can keep at their desk for quick reference. A good handout organizes information in a logical, easy-to-access, and easy-to-read manner. Clean, good design isn't easy, but you can do some logical things to make handouts that people will keep and utilize:

1. **Sketch your handout on paper first.** There are lots of choices for desktop publishing software, but it's best to sketch out your design on paper before firing up your favorite software. When you sketch out the design on paper, you plot out the flow of information, headlines, and graphics, and imagine how the final product will look. Your layout process will also flow much more smoothly because you'll know what information goes where in the handout.

2. **Choose the right font.** Fonts affect the message; consider the Cartoon font versus Times New Roman. You wouldn't expect to use the Cartoon font for a seminar on TCP/IP subnetting. Generally you'll want to use the same font for the entire handout, though some designers swear a headline font should be serif, while the body font is best in sans serif. Whatever approach you take, follow the same style and limit the number of fonts in the document. Use too many different fonts, and your handout will appear jumbled and messy.

3. **Clearly communicate.** Handouts should provide quick, accurate information, not long passages of text. Use quick, exact sentences, bulleted points, and simple directions. Imagine the learner back at her desk following the quick steps in the handout to create a macro in Microsoft Word. If she's reading an essay to do the steps, the handout isn't as useful as fast step-by-step instructions. Also keep the amount of information to a minimum so as not to overwhelm the learner. As the old adage goes, don't try to put eight pounds of directions in a five-pound bag.

4. **Aim for neat.** Handouts that are neat have lots of whitespace for notes, margins, and space between ideas. Sloppy handouts are jammed with information and don't provide an easy, clean method to move through the information. Your headlines should visually break up the text, segment ideas,

and help learners quickly find the information they need. Figures are fine on your handout, but make certain they're legible—don't make screen captures too small to be useful or so large that you can't add much information. Avoid all capitalized text, dingbats, and icons that don't support the message of the handout.

5. **Incorporate color and shading.** A little splash of color is more powerful than a handout full of rainbows. Headlines, warnings, and key facts in blue, red, or green on white paper can really pop and get the readers' attention. If you add too much color, your handout will appear sloppy, and the color won't add any value to the deliverable. If color printing isn't an option for your handout, experiment with adding shading to key areas of the handout. You can create grayscale boxes and artwork to break up the stark black-and-white printing and still call attention to key details.

6. **Emulate a design.** If someone has created a handout that's neat, thought-out, and balanced with information and whitespace, base your design on theirs. It's not stealing or copyright infringement, you're just modeling your information on their design to create something for your learners that works. Of course, the content of your handout must be different from the model, but the look and feel of the original design can serve as a good base for what you create.

Handouts are good memory joggers for post-class utilization, but they can also be used in class to help learners learn. For example, you might create a handout with the usual facts and information, but insert fill-in-the-blank information for learners. Then in a group exercise you can walk the learners through the handout, and they can interact with the information by adding the correct answers. You can also create *memory maps* to help learners interact with the handout in class and learn the information you've shared. A memory map is an illustration of a process or activity with key points to help the participant remember the information.

Some organizations have moved away from the concept of learners having an actual class workbook, but instead use a collection of handouts throughout the class. While this model is less costly than creating a workbook for each participant, it can be overwhelming for the learners to have many single sheets of paper if they aren't organized, logical, and neatly designed. Whatever approach you take to creating your handouts, proofread the handout, document learner feedback regarding the handout, and update your handout as needed for future classes.

Considering the Room Color

Guess which room color promotes longer wavelengths and promotes brain activity: a room that's painted with red, orange, or yellow, or a room that's painted with green, blue, or violet. The colors red, orange, and yellow have been proven to stimulate brain activity, while green, blue, and violet actually promote relaxation. I'm not saying that I'd like to teach an intense technical topic in a room that's painted red, but color does affect how learners are able to learn, concentrate, and focus.

Selecting the interior design for your training room may be well beyond your responsibilities as a trainer, but understanding how current room color can affect your learners is important. If you're in a subdued, peaceful room with dim lights and a full belly from lunch, chances are you'll be feeling relaxed, comfy, and ready for a snooze. As a trainer, your recognizing the power of color and how your participants react to the room gives you an opportunity to take action to promote learning, keep participants involved, and to put all that you can into your arsenal of learning tricks.

First, add colorful images to your slideshow. While you don't want loads of unrelated, cluttered artwork in your presentation, adding artwork to presentations doesn't cost anything, and it's a powerful way to add color. I've experimented with using just a bright orange square background in my presentations during exercises and classroom quizzes to visually wake up the students. It's not an amazing difference between a blue background or the orange background, but people notice the orange square more than the dark blue square. It's anecdotal, but you might consider experimenting with color elements in your slideshow, as long as it's not distracting, to see how learners' energy and involvement may change.

Another way to inject color into a classroom space is to add posters that are related to your technical topic. If you were teaching a networking class, for example, you might use color to represent the servers, workstations, routers, and other network components. The chart directly supports the learning objective, but the color can support the brainwaves and interest. Some training rooms may already have posters that actually can distract from the learning—yes, even the motivational posters that are popular—I sometimes take them down or cover them with my colorful banners and posters that are related to the course topic.

Get creative to add color and to support the learning objectives of your class. Instructors have long used party decorations to create a festive mood, create interest and excitement in the room, and to link the décor to the training objectives. You might also consider adding little toys and trinkets such as modeling clay to your exercises and lecture to keep learners involved and to use the toys as part of the learning experience. You can use colorful markers, wear a bright tie or scarf, and have participants complete exercises with different colored fonts, markers, or highlighters. These approaches add color, help the learners interact, and are good visual aids for your seminars.

Adding Music to Your Classroom

There's a constant debate among instructors on adding music to the classroom during labs and exercises. Some instructors believe music is intrusive, distracting, and can prevent learners from concentrating. Other instructors, and I happen to be in this camp, believe music can support learning objectives, be soothing and relaxing, and make the classroom space more enjoyable. Whatever approach you take, however, always be aware that if the music is bothering someone in the class—that is, the music is keeping them from learning—then the music should be turned off.

The type of music you select to play should be appropriate to the classroom setting. Calm, soothing music without words (like the New Age and Smooth Jazz genres) is ideal for most classes. Rock 'n' roll, country, and even classical can be too noisy and distract from learning, though there may be exercises and opportunities where this music is appropriate. It's the beats per minute that basically determines how soothing and relaxing the environment may be. Listen to a Tom Waits tune versus a piano melody by Jim Brickman, and you'll get the idea of which type of music is most appropriate for your class.

Even if you don't like music to be played during labs and exercises, you should experiment with playing some music before class starts. The music can be welcoming when students walk into the classroom, rather than entering a deathly silent space. On breaks and after class, music can also liven up the atmosphere—and when the music stops, there's an audible clue that it's time for the class to continue. Music can affect the mood of your participants, get them excited to be in the training, and hint that your class is going to be exciting and fun.

Some organizations have a rolling slideshow prior to the class starting or during breaks. The rolling slideshow is an auto-advanced presentation that has news, announcements, information about the training facility, and other information. If your organization uses such a slideshow, consider adding some music to the presentation to offer a richer multimedia experience. The music you select should be positive, uplifting, and must not detract from the learning experience.

Chapter Summary

Managing the technical classroom is a large portion of delivering an effective class for learners. When the classroom is configured properly, clean, well-lit, and organized, learners immediately sense the professionalism and seriousness of the class they're about to start. When the classroom is messy, the computers don't operate as expected, and the instructor must stop the presentation to troubleshoot issues and errors on the computers, students will be less than enamored, frustrated, and deterred from learning. As with most things in training, preparation is the key to effective classroom management.

The physical space of the classroom must be conducive to learning. This means noise from the surrounding environment should not interfere with the learning, the classroom desks and computers should be positioned in a logical manner to support the style of the class, and things such as storage boxes should be removed from the classroom if they aren't part of the class. Not only should the classroom space be quiet and arranged for the presentation, but also the room itself should be both rectangular and a suitable room to host a training function. When choosing a classroom, consider that ceiling height affects the acoustics, natural light may help or hinder the classroom space, and the temperature should be comfortable.

Instructors and the training organization should communicate the logistics of the classroom space. Access to the room, how the equipment will be secured, and information for the delivery of the books should be determined well in advance of the class start time. The instructor should also confirm how the technology in the classroom will be configured. This can mean that the instructor is the person configuring the technology or that a technician at the client's site is doing the configuration. When the instructor isn't the person prepping the room, the instructor should arrive early and confirm the configuration, gather usernames and passwords, and get network information the class may need to operate.

To teach a perfect class requires prep time to clean, organize, and arrange the class-room. Participants might not recognize the preparation that went into the classroom space, but it'll be obvious if the room isn't ready for training. Classroom management is a big portion of teaching an excellent class; this means leading conversations and us-ing whiteboards and even flipcharts. The instructor's penmanship, lighting, and inter-actions with what's been written or drawn all contribute to the education of the participants. The instructor must be aware of the learners' perception of all that she says and doesn't say, and how she leads the class through the information.

Slideshows such as PowerPoint should be a support tool for the instructor—not something that replaces the instructor. PowerPoint slideshows should follow a clean, simple approach to help guide the instructor and the class through ideas and conversa-tions. Slideshows should not be packed with text and then read to the class. The same idea is true with classroom handouts—they should be neat, organized, and concise. Too much information in the slide deck or in the handouts can be a distraction to the learning process, as students may be looking for information more than learning the key information.

Room color and music are two other elements to consider in classroom manage-ment. While the color of the room may be beyond the instructor's control, the instruc-tor may be able to add color through posters, markers, toys that support the classroom objectives, and even through the clothes the instructor wears. Music, often a controver-sial topic, should be appropriate to the classroom environment, soothing, and not disruptive to any of the learners. Music can also serve as an audio clue that class is ready to resume at the end of the breaks.

Key Terms

classroom lighting   The consideration of the type of lighting in the classroom, such as track lighting, recessed lighting, fluorescent lighting, or natural light and how the lighting can be manipulated to best support the learning objectives.

classroom seating configuration   The typical classroom configuration where the tables, chairs, and computers are all aligned the same and facing the front of the room, where the instructor will present.

cordless presentation tool   A device like a cordless mouse that will allow the instruc-tor to roam around the room and still click through the presentation. Some devices have features to navigate forwards and backwards and may include a laser pointer.

course logistics   All of the coordination of materials, software, hardware, classroom equipment, security information, access to data, refreshments, travel, communications, and any related aspects of preparing and managing the classroom environment.

KISS rule   A heuristic for designing slides, handouts, or instructional tools that means you'll Keep It Simply Simple.

learning environment   The classroom space where learning through technical train-ing is expected to happen.

learning handouts   Additional information for the learners that is distributed to help support the learning objectives. Handouts may be called job aids, learner assistants, cheat sheets, or reference cards.

nonverbal communication   The posture, facial expressions, and body language that affect the message of the instructor. Fifty-five percent of all communication is nonverbal.

room color   Color does have an effect on the learners' brain activity. Red, orange, and yellow stimulate brain activity, while green, blue, and violet promote relaxation.

stage presence   The presence the instructor has when presenting to learners; it's the ability to appear comfortable while commanding the audience's attention and being in charge in the classroom.

U-seating configuration   The classroom chairs and tables create a U-shape, often along the perimeter of the room, where the attendees will pivot from looking at the instructor to the materials and equipment on their desks.

visual aids   Anything that you use, such as a prop, the whiteboards, or a flipchart, to visually demonstrate the concepts of the class to the learners.

Questions

1. Which one of the following statements best describes the concept of a learning environment for technical training?

   A. It's the space where learning happens.

   B. It's the technical equipment and software that contribute to the education of the learners.

   C. It's the management of the classroom space for the participants.

   D. It's anywhere that allows students to learn something new.

2. Jan is teaching an ongoing technical class in a room that can comfortably accommodate 12 people. Management would like to increase the number of participants to 18 to reduce the number of training days for the organization. What is the detriment of adding more people to the training room?

   A. More than 12 people in the training room will likely diminish the effectiveness of the training.

   B. More than 12 people in the training room will cause the room to be stuffy.

   C. More than 12 people in the training room will cause Jan to have better classroom management skills.

   D. More than 12 people in the training room is a good idea, as the total number of needed classes will be reduced over time.

3. All of the following characteristics of a classroom should be removed and managed except for which one?

   A. Storage boxes of computer parts

    B. Stacks of manuals from related classes

    C. Fluorescent lighting

    D. Natural lighting

4. You are cleaning a classroom space for your next assignment. The classroom has a flipchart that you likely won't use. What should you do with the flipchart?

    A. Move the flipchart to the back of the classroom.

    B. Make certain the first page of the flipchart has a "welcome" message.

    C. Turn the flipchart around so it's not a distraction to the users.

    D. Move the flipchart to the right side of the presentation area.

5. What's the best range of temperature for a technical training class?

    A. 68–70 degrees Fahrenheit

    B. 70–72 degrees Fahrenheit

    C. 72–74 degrees Fahrenheit

    D. 71–73 degrees Fahrenheit

6. You are coaching Frank, a new instructor in your company, on the best approach to teaching a technical class. In your evaluation you notice that Frank is staying behind the instructor's desk rather than coming out from behind the desk to interact with the participants and to present the material of the classroom. What term is assigned to the interaction and ownership of the classroom space?

    A. Classroom management

    B. Classroom ownership

    C. Trainership

    D. Stage presence

7. Fred is a technical trainer and he's teaching a printer repair class. He's arranged his classroom in a U-shaped configuration so that learners can swivel and face him during the presentation and then swivel back to their workbenches for access to the hardware the class will use. What's the one disadvantage to this approach?

    A. Learners at the sides of the classroom won't be able to see Fred.

    B. Learners at the back of the classroom won't see Fred as well as users along the sides.

    C. Learners may be distracted by what's on the workbench rather than listening to what Fred has to say.

    D. Fred won't be able to make eye contact with learners as they're working on their labs.

8. What percent of communication is nonverbal?

   A. 50 percent

   B. 55 percent

   C. 65 percent

   D. 80 percent

9. A trainer has arrived to teach a technical class and discovers that the room has not been configured properly, the materials that were shipped to the training center can't be found, and the overhead projector isn't functioning with her laptop. What term best describes the failures in this scenario?

   A. Course objections

   B. Course constraints

   C. Course logistics

   D. Course expectations

10. What's the first thing a trainer should do when arriving at the training room?

   A. Connect the laptop to the overhead projector.

   B. Confirm the hardware and software are present.

   C. Enable music for the welcome time.

   D. Locate the course materials.

11. For an instructor to teach a perfect class, several elements must exist. Which one of the following is not one of the elements that directly contribute to a perfect class?

   A. Learner recognition of the instructor's subject matter knowledge

   B. Clear learning objectives for the course

   C. Instructor expertise on the subject matter

   D. Linkage between the course content and the learners' role in the organization

12. You're coaching Mary, a new trainer in your organization, about how best to use the whiteboard in the classroom. You advise her to not use the lowest third of the whiteboard when writing in class. Why is this good advice?

   A. People don't remember things in the lowest portion of the whiteboard.

   B. The lowest portion of the whiteboard is hard to see.

   C. The lowest portion of the whiteboard should be used for the question parking lot.

   D. The lowest portion of the whiteboard usually has more glare than the upper two portions.

13. What's the maximum number of words you should have on a PowerPoint slide?

    A. 15

    B. 20

    C. 24

    D. 32

14. Which one of the following presentation tools can help the instructor be most effective in the classroom during presentations?

    A. Cordless presentation tool

    B. Cordless mouse

    C. Laser pointer

    D. Teacher's manual

15. Wendy, a technical trainer in your company, recommends that John present at the left of the presentation screen in the classroom. Why is this a good idea?

    A. Most people read from left to right, so participants will see John first and then the content of the screen.

    B. Most people read from left to right, so with John at the left he won't be interfering with what they're reading on the presentation screen.

    C. John should actually stand to the right of the screen; as most people read from left to right they'll see John last.

    D. It doesn't matter where John stands as long as he doesn't stand in front of the presentation screen to interfere with what's on the overhead projector.

16. All of the following are valid reasons for creating and distributing handouts in a technical class except for which one?

    A. Appeal to visual learners

    B. Appeal to kinesthetic learners

    C. Provide future reference

    D. Support the course objectives

17. What term best describes a handout that is an illustration of processes, key activities, or information designed to help the learner remember the information through the illustration rather than through rote statements of facts and ideas?

    A. Memory map

    B. Knowledge art

    C. Memory matrix

    D. Acrostic

18. Which one of the following colors stimulates brain activity the least?

    A. Red

    B. Orange

    C. Green

    D. Yellow

19. Mary is teaching a class on database security, and she wants to get the learners involved and hold their attention in the classroom. She's decided to add some party favors, modeling clay and little toys, to the desks to bring color and some fun to the class. What must Mary do to ensure that this addition is worthwhile for the learners?

    A. Make sure all of the learners have the same trinkets.

    B. Make sure the trinkets support the learning objectives.

    C. Link the trinkets to key facts about the roles of the participants.

    D. Demonstrate how the trinkets are to be used.

20. Thomas is interested in adding music to his class during the labs and exercises. What is the primary concern for adding music to the classroom?

    A. The music must support the learning objectives.

    B. The music must not be a detriment to the learning.

    C. The music must not be offensive.

    D. The music should be approved by the students.

Questions and Answers

1. Which one of the following statements best describes the concept of a learning environment for technical training?

    A. It's the space where learning happens.

    B. It's the technical equipment and software that contribute to the education of the learners.

    C. It's the management of the classroom space for the participants.

    D. It's anywhere that allows students to learn something new.

    A. The best answer is that technical training happens most often in a classroom space, called the learning environment. The equipment and software describe the technical props and supporting details for the class, not the actual learning environment, so choice B is incorrect. C describes the management of the learning environment, not the actual learning environment. D is tempting, but it's not the best answer, as the learning environment is a space designated specifically for learning. The learning environment does not describe on-the-job training or learning in production, but describes a designated space for learning in most scenarios.

PART I

2. Jan is teaching an ongoing technical class in a room that can comfortably accommodate 12 people. Management would like to increase the number of participants to 18 to reduce the number of training days for the organization. What is the detriment of adding more people to the training room?

   A. More than 12 people in the training room will likely diminish the effectiveness of the training.

   B. More than 12 people in the training room will cause the room to be stuffy.

   C. More than 12 people in the training room will cause Jan to have better classroom management skills.

   D. More than 12 people in the training room is a good idea, as the total number of needed classes will be reduced over time.

   A. When an organization adds more than the recommended number of people to a learning environment, the increase in the number of people is usually a detriment to the effectiveness of the training. This is because the room can't easily accommodate that number of people, the instructor's attention to each student is decreased, and the chatter and distractions among the students may increase. B is incorrect because there's no evidence that the room's heating and cooling won't be able to manage the additional participants. C is incorrect because more people in the classroom won't necessarily equate to Jan having better classroom management skills; in fact, Jan may discover a need to have better classroom management skills. D is incorrect, as adding more people to the classroom may reduce the overall duration of the classroom, but the best answer is that the room can't easily accommodate the additional learners and keep the class effective.

3. All of the following characteristics of a classroom should be removed and managed except for which one?

   A. Storage boxes of computer parts

   B. Stacks of manuals from related classes

   C. Fluorescent lighting

   D. Natural lighting

   D. Of all the choices only natural lighting is what should remain. If possible, use natural lighting in the classroom space. Choice C, fluorescent lighting, is tempting to choose, as many classrooms may already be lit with fluorescent lights, but these can be managed not to disrupt learning. Choices A and B should obviously be removed from the classroom to promote a neat and organized learning environment.

4. You are cleaning a classroom space for your next assignment. The classroom has a flipchart that you likely won't use. What should you do with the flipchart?

   A. Move the flipchart to the back of the classroom.

   B. Make certain the first page of the flipchart has a "welcome" message.

   C. Turn the flipchart around so it's not a distraction to the users.

   D. Move the flipchart to the right side of the presentation area.

> **B.** If there's a flipchart in the classroom, even if it's not going to be used, either make certain the first page of the flipchart is blank so it's not a distraction, or add a welcome message to the first page. Choices A and D don't address what may be on the flipchart and may make the room appear cluttered. C, turning the flipchart around, could hide the notes from a previous class, but doesn't best answer the question as with a welcome message to greet the participants.

5. What's the best range of temperature for a technical training class?

   A. 68–70 degrees Fahrenheit

   B. 70–72 degrees Fahrenheit

   C. 72–74 degrees Fahrenheit

   D. 71–73 degrees Fahrenheit

> **B.** The recommended range for a comfortable training room is 70–72 degrees Fahrenheit. Choices A, C, and D are not the best choices for the answer. Bear in mind, however, that the comfort of the learners is what's most important—if people feel warm or cold, regardless of the recommended temperature, it will distract them from the course content.

6. You are coaching Frank, a new instructor in your company, on the best approach to teaching a technical class. In your evaluation you notice that Frank is staying behind the instructor's desk rather than coming out from behind the desk to interact with the participants and to present the material of the classroom. What term is assigned to the interaction and ownership of the classroom space?

   A. Classroom management

   B. Classroom ownership

   C. Trainership

   D. Stage presence

> **D.** Stage presence describes the showmanship, ownership, and control of being in front of participants and leading an effective presentation. Answer A, classroom management, includes the concept of stage presence, but is more about managing the entire learning space to promote learning. Answers B and C are not the best choices because classroom ownership and trainership aren't valid technical training terms.

7. Fred is a technical trainer and he's teaching a printer repair class. He's arranged his classroom in a U-shaped configuration so that learners can swivel and face him during the presentation and then swivel back to their workbenches for access to the hardware the class will use. What's the one disadvantage to this approach?

   A. Learners at the sides of the classroom won't be able to see Fred.

   B. Learners at the back of the classroom won't see Fred as well as users along the sides.

   C. Learners may be distracted with what's on the workbench rather than listening to what Fred has to say.

   D. Fred won't be able to make eye contact with learners as they're working on their labs.

   C. Classrooms that utilize the U-shaped configuration must combat the distraction of the hardware from the lecture. A and B are not the best choices because learners throughout the room will be able to easily see Fred, as the space will be unobstructed between their seats and the center of the classroom. Fred must, however, lecture from the top of the U. When Fred walks into the middle of the U-shape, learners on the sides of the room may not be able to see Fred easily. D is incorrect because Fred doesn't need to make eye contact with the learners during the exercises.

8. What percent of communication is nonverbal?

   A. 50 percent

   B. 55 percent

   C. 65 percent

   D. 80 percent

   B. Fifty-five percent of communication is nonverbal. Body language, facial expressions, and posture all are part of the nonverbal communication. Choices A, C, and D are incorrect, as these answers don't accurately reflect the percentage of communication that is nonverbal.

9. A trainer has arrived to teach a technical class and discovers that the room has not been configured properly, the materials that were shipped to the training center can't be found, and the overhead projector isn't functioning with her laptop. What term best describes the failures in this scenario?

   A. Course objections

   B. Course constraints

   C. Course logistics

   D. Course expectations

> C. Course logistics describes all of the moving parts that need to come together before the instructor arrives to teach. Course logistics may be outside of the trainer's role, but an effective trainer makes certain that everything is in place in order to teach an effective class. Answers A, B, and D are all incorrect, as the only correct answer is course logistics. Choices A, B, and D are not valid technical training terms.

10. What's the first thing a trainer should do when arriving at the training room?

    A. Connect the laptop to the overhead projector.

    B. Confirm the hardware and software are present.

    C. Enable music for the welcome time.

    D. Locate the course materials.

> A. The first action the technical trainer should always do is to connect the laptop to the overhead projector to confirm that the laptop is working properly with the overhead projector. While the other choices are all important, it's best to first establish the communication with the overhead projector, as this process can sometimes take the longest to complete. D, locating the course materials, is likely the second instructor activity, followed by confirming the hardware and software configuration (answer B), and then lastly enabling the welcome music for the classroom (answer C).

11. For an instructor to teach a perfect class, several elements must exist. Which one of the following is not one of the elements that directly contribute to a perfect class?

    A. Learner recognition of the instructor's subject matter knowledge

    B. Clear learning objectives for the course

    C. Instructor expertise on the subject matter

    D. Linkage between the course content and the learners' role in the organization

> A. To teach a perfect class, the learner doesn't need to recognize the level of expertise the instructor has in the subject matter, so this choice is the best answer. B, C, and D are all incorrect choices because clear learning objectives, instructor's expertise, and the link between the course content and the learner role must exist in a perfect class.

12. You're coaching Mary, a new trainer in your organization, about how best to use the whiteboard in the classroom. You advise her to not use the lowest third of the whiteboard when writing in class. Why is this good advice?

    A. People don't remember things in the lowest portion of the whiteboard.

B. The lowest portion of the whiteboard is hard to see.

C. The lowest portion of the whiteboard should be used for the question parking lot.

D. The lowest portion of the whiteboard usually has more glare than the upper two portions.

B. Mary should not use the lowest third of the whiteboard because it's hard to see. Answer A is incorrect, as there's no evidence people won't remember what's in the lowest third of the whiteboard. Answer option C is incorrect, as the "question parking lot" doesn't have to be in the lowest third of the whiteboard. A question parking lot is an area of the whiteboard that's reserved for questions that aren't necessarily relative to the current topic that you'll answer later in the class or after class. Answer D is incorrect, as there's no evidence there's more glare at the bottom of the whiteboard than at the top.

13. What's the maximum number of words you should have on a PowerPoint slide?

   A. 15

   B. 20

   C. 24

   D. 32

A. The ideal maximum number of words per slide is 15. Choices B, C, and D are incorrect, as more than 15 words make the slide look messy and jumbled and provide more information than the participant can easily absorb.

14. Which one of the following presentation tools can help the instructor be most effective in the classroom during presentations?

   A. Cordless presentation tool

   B. Cordless mouse

   C. Laser pointer

   D. Teacher's manual

A. The cordless presentation tool allows the instructor to move away from the computer and interact with the class while still advancing the slide deck. B, the cordless mouse, may work similarly to the cordless presentation tool, but this isn't the best answer. Answer C is incorrect. The laser pointer may be a good tool, and many cordless presentation tools have laser pointers included, but this isn't the best answer. The teacher's manual, choice D, doesn't help the instructor during a presentation.

15. Wendy, a technical trainer in your company, recommends that John present at the left of the presentation screen in the classroom. Why is this a good idea?

   A. Most people read from left to right, so participants will see John first and then the content of the screen.

   B. Most people read from left to right, so with John at the left he won't be interfering with what they're reading on the presentation screen.

   C. John should actually stand to the right of the screen; as most people read from left to right they'll see John last.

   D. It doesn't matter where John stands as long as he doesn't stand in front of the presentation screen to interfere with what's on the overhead projector.

   A. Because most people do read from left to right, they'll see John first and then the text on the screen. B is incorrect, as people will see John first and he can quickly point to key facts to his left on the overhead screen. Answer C is incorrect, as the point isn't to see John last, but for John to introduce the information on the screen. D isn't the best choice, as John should stand to the left of the screen to introduce the information, not just anywhere in the classroom.

16. All of the following are valid reasons for creating and distributing handouts in a technical class except for which one?

   A. Appeal to visual learners

   B. Appeal to kinesthetic learners

   C. Provide future reference

   D. Support the course objectives

   B. Kinesthetic learners learn by doing, such as by completing a lab or exercise. Visual learners, answer A, can learn by seeing the visual clues the handouts provide. Choices C and D are also incorrect, as handouts do provide future reference and can support the course objectives.

17. What term best describes a handout that is an illustration of processes, key activities, or information designed to help the learner remember the information through the illustration rather than through rote statements of facts and ideas?

   A. Memory map

   B. Knowledge art

   C. Memory matrix

   D. Acrostic

A. A memory map is an illustration that helps the learner remember key facts and information through an illustration. It's ideal to show a process from start to end, but can be designed for many learning applications. B, knowledge art, and C, memory matrix, aren't actual learning tools, so these choices are incorrect. D, an acrostic, is a word device, such as ADDIE, where each letter in the word represents a word that describes the process, facts, or information.

18. Which one of the following colors stimulates brain activity the least?

A. Red

B. Orange

C. Green

D. Yellow

C. Green, blue, and violet do not stimulate brain activity to the extent that choices A, B, and D do. When considering colors to inject into your presentation, you should choose colors that do stimulate brain activity, such as red, orange, or yellow.

19. Mary is teaching a class on database security, and she wants to get the learners involved and hold their attention in the classroom. She's decided to add some party favors, modeling clay and little toys, to the desks to bring color and some fun to the class. What must Mary do to ensure that this addition is worthwhile for the learners?

A. Make sure all of the learners have the same trinkets.

B. Make sure the trinkets support the learning objectives.

C. Link the trinkets to key facts about the roles of the participants.

D. Demonstrate how the trinkets are to be used.

B. Of all the choices the best answer is that Mary should make certain that the trinkets support the learning objectives. While there's enjoyment from the modeling clay and toys, if they don't support the learning objectives, they can be a detriment to the class. Choice A is incorrect, as it's not necessary for all of the learners to have the same trinkets. C is incorrect, as Mary needs to link the trinkets to the learning objectives, not to the roles of the participants. D is incorrect, as Mary doesn't need to demonstrate how the trinkets are to be used, but should instead demonstrate how the trinkets support the learning objectives.

20. Thomas is interested in adding music to his class during the labs and exercises. What is the primary concern for adding music to the classroom?

   A. The music must support the learning objectives.

   B. The music must not be a detriment to the learning.

   C. The music must not be offensive.

   D. The music should be approved by the learners.

B. While all of the choices have merit, the best answer is that the music should not be a detriment to the learning. A is incorrect, as music doesn't directly support the learning objectives, but can make the class more enjoyable for the learners. C is incorrect, as it's true that the music should not be offensive, but this is better supported through the fact that the music should not be a detriment to the learning. Offensive music would be a detriment, but so too could loud rock 'n' roll during an intense lab. D is a good choice, but it's not the best because if the music is bothering a learner, it would be a detriment to the learning and should be stopped.

PART II

Methods for Effective Instruction

■ **Chapter 4** Engaging Learners Through Instructional Methods
■ **Chapter 5** Managing Instructional Materials

Engaging Learners Through Instructional Methods

In this chapter you will:
- Explore the concept of training versus facilitating technical courses
- Adapt your training approach to the different adult learning styles
- Learn about Kolb's Learning Cycle for adult education
- Understand Gagné's Theory of Instruction
- Apply the Cognitive Learning Theory to technical courses
- Utilize the Constructivist Learning Theory
- Facilitate technical courses, group exercises, and demonstrations

Some people might argue that a person with years of technical expertise can teach a technical topic. While years of experience can contribute some merit and value to a successful trainer, it really takes more than just knowing the topic to teach the topic. If you've ever taken a speech class, you know that the fundamental rule is to first know your topic. The second rule is to know your audience. After those two rules, however, things can get real soupy as to what makes a good trainer a great trainer. In this chapter you'll learn about some fundamental rules of great training, and also some advanced ideas to make training engaging for learners.

Pedagogy is often used to describe the process of teaching; it's the vocation and strategies for teaching. Pedagogy is more closely related to teaching children than adults. "Pedagogy" is Greek and it means to lead the child. *Andragogy*, however, describes the science and applications used to teach adults. "Andragogy," also Greek, means "manleading," which is most commonly associated with leading adults. Adult education has many theories, some of which I'll discuss in this chapter, which describe how adults learn. Andragogy was developed into the Theory of Adult Education by Malcolm Knowles. The Theory of Adult Education, and really the subject matter for this chapter, defines the methods by which adults learn and how an instructor can facilitate the learning.

113

Theories aside, technical trainers need to know and recognize the most common adult learning styles. Adults learn differently and have preferences for how they absorb information. These preferences of learning may not be clearly stated by the learner, but a good trainer can recognize when a class participant is engaged, absorbing and thinking about the information. These learning clues help the instructor teach more effectively by tailoring the course to the recognized learning styles. Basically, you'll pay attention to how learners learn and then change your teaching style to accommodate the learning style. It's always more important for participants to learn than it is for the trainer to teach. In other words, as always, focus on the participants, not the instructor.

Trainers that teach in a virtual classroom can also apply the theories of adult education to their teaching styles. By interacting with participants through the virtual classroom, the instructor can recognize learning preferences and use the technical tools the virtual classroom provides to help learners learn better. While technical trainers often have no access to the nonverbal clues of communication, the virtual classroom does provide opportunities for more collaboration, experimenting with the technology to discover learning, and utilizing hands-on training in lieu of lecture-driven training.

Training the Technical Participant

When most adults think of training, they probably think of what they've experienced from grade school into college: the teacher stands at the front of the room and drones on about a topic. This style of training is technically called the *didactic approach*, and it is the traditional, instructor-led training where the focus is strictly on a specific topic. For example, a trainer using this approach to teach Microsoft Word would use a systematic, formal approach to introduce a Microsoft Word topic, lecture on the topic, demonstrate the topic, allow the participants to experiment on the topic, review the topic, and then move forward. This instructive style is fairly common and well-received by participants because it's logical, proven, and is what most learners are used to.

The problem with using the didactic approach for adult learners in a technical environment is that adults learn differently than children. The didactic approach may be well-suited for an elementary school or even college lecture hall, but when the class focus is on a technical topic and you have only a few hours to facilitate real, in-depth learning, the approach can be lacking. Technical participants often want to get the meat of the course, try out the technology in the safe classroom environment, and to tinker with the options, features, and choices the technology may provide. Technical participants often learn best by doing, discovering, and experimenting.

The idea of learners discovering their learning may seem odd to some experienced trainers. This andragogical approach is best described as trainer-facilitation: the learners learn the technology by working with the technology. It's what Aristotle likely had in mind when he said, "We learn by doing." Technical trainers have an advantage that many other types of trainers do not: they can guide learners to experiment, to discover what does and doesn't work, and to practice in a safe, nonwork environment.

Facilitating a Technical Class

Technical training is becoming more and more about facilitating rather than teaching. Facilitating a class means that the trainer guides the participants through the designed course materials to each objective. Facilitating takes the complex, that is, the technical subject matter, and makes it easier for the participants to understand. Facilitation of a technical class means that you are leading the learners to the key objectives and helping them mentally absorb what they need to know. The subtle difference between teaching and facilitating is that *teaching* is usually aimed more toward children and rudimentary skills; *facilitation* is the delivery and demonstration of a predefined course of objectives.

The most common approach to adult education is still the instructor-led course through lecture. Lecture is a fast way to disperse lots of information to a group of people. The problem with lecture, however, is that most adults retain only about 25 percent of what they hear but nearly 75 percent of what they do. Lecturing may be fast and easy to prepare for, but it's not always the best use of the participants' classroom time and dollars. To be a good lecturer, you'll need to be interesting, use some humor to keep participants' interests, and pause often to engage your audience with questions and input. Lecturing in a technical class requires that you use lots of samples, analogies, and even demonstrations to keep your audience involved.

Questions are your best friend as a technical trainer. It might be easy for the participant to ignore the instructor during a long, windy lecture, but it's difficult to ignore a direct question during the lecture. This isn't intended to embarrass a person who may be losing interest in your fascinating talk, but it keeps participants focused on the discussion, as they realize they may be called on to answer a question. Some guidelines you should follow when asking questions to get learners involved are

- **Know your questions and answers.** When you're preparing for a technical course that requires some lecture, plan ahead on what you're going to ask. By planning ahead you're armed with good questions instead of trying to deliver material, manage the class, and think on-the-fly of good questions to involve learners.

- **Silence is golden and uncomfortable.** When you offer a question for the class to answer, don't rush to answer the question if no one does. Wait through the awkward silence for the class to answer a question. If no one proffers an answer after a relatively long pause, rephrase the question to prompt the participants. If there's still no answer, suggest the participants look up the answer in their manual, the Internet, or other source. Get them involved and let them discover the answer.

- **Create open-ended questions.** Open-ended questions allow students to expound on what they've learned. For example, why is TCP/IP version 6 better than version 4? Close-ended questions have a direct answer without any explanation. For example, what's the first layer of the OSI Model?

- **Questions beget questions.** When a learner answers an open-ended question, you can come back to their answer in the form of another question. This does require you to think on your feet a little bit, but it can help all of the learners see the technology you're teaching from different angles.

Questions in a lecture can generate a group discussion for the participants. As the technical trainer you'll listen to what the group's saying and add comments and questions to direct the conversation. In a classroom where some learners aren't familiar with one another a group discussion can be intimidating, so introduce learners to one another. For example, Susan may be shy in the group, so you might in the midst of the conversation say, "Susan, you're experienced in that arena, what's your take?" This introduces Susan as someone with experience, gives her a little boost in the class, and gets her talking with the other participants.

Facilitating a technical class also means that you're demonstrating the technology for the learners. Imagine that you're teaching an A+ hardware class for a group. From the learners' perspective it may be boring if during the entire class you're lecturing from a book about hard drives, network cards, and power supplies without ever actually holding up a physical computer component. In a technical class you want to link what you're lecturing about to the physical application of your topic. So in that A+ class you can be more effective by gathering the group around a computer and removing the power supply, the network card, and the hard drive. Then, ideally, you'll send the participants back to their workbenches to try the same activity.

 NOTE The CompTIA CTT+ examination is for all types of technical trainers. When you consider that technical trainers could teach anything from Microsoft Office to networking, databases, and even custom applications, it's a broad audience. The examples I'm using throughout this book are mainstream, but don't let that affect your exam prep. The exam focuses on the practice and theories of training, not the technical content you and other professionals teach.

When you follow this model, you're addressing the needs and understanding of the learners through a logical approach rather than through a sequential lecture. In your lecture you first answer for the learners why this topic is important by explaining how the topic is linked to their work role. Next, you're explaining the technical concept by training them on how the technology functions. Through the demonstration you're showing the learners how to interact with the technology. Finally, by assigning an exercise you're allowing the learners to experience the technology and explore the if-then relationship of interacting with what they've already learned. This is the discovery of the information, the discovery of knowledge. You're facilitating the learners by coaching them toward the discovery.

Teaching Technology for Different Learning Styles

It's no secret that we all have preferences for how we learn. Even as you're preparing to pass the CompTIA CTT+ examination you have a preference for how you learn the theories, objectives, and skills needed to pass the examination. Adults need a direct connection between the seminar they are attending and how it will apply to their lives. Children, in the pedagogical approach, don't necessarily need that same connection, as they're going to school because they're required to do so, mom and dad are making them, and that's where all their friends are.

Adults are busy and have responsibilities, and being forced to attend a class doesn't necessarily inspire them to learn the course content. While they are in a class, the work is piling up back at their job, their daily routine has been interrupted, and their responsibilities don't necessarily pause for the training you're going to deliver. Adults need to know why the training is important to their lives. Once they understand and accept the purpose of the training, they'll be more interested in the training as they see the value of what they are about to learn.

Assuming that the participants in your class are willing to learn, you can adjust your teaching style to accommodate the learning style of your participants. Adults learn information in two main approaches:

- **Active learning** The learner is actively involved in the technology and topic. Exercises, practice, hands-on activities, and interactions with the instructor and other participants are used. Active learning comes from hands-on involvement with the technology you're teaching.

- **Passive learning** The learner absorbs information through listening, reading, and reason. The participant accepts what the instructor says and then uses that information on exams, in feedback, and in the workplace.

Passive learning is the traditional classroom environment where the instructor assumes the participant is a "blank slate" and void of any preconceived opinions or notions about the technology. The instructor, primarily through lecture, imparts the wisdom to the participant. The learner takes notes, memorizes facts, and regurgitates information. The instructor in the learning relationship is considered to be a master of the technology and is steeped in experience in the technology, but is not necessarily an expert at training. Passive learning in technical classes is evident when the class structure requires a rote lecture, and then the learners follow a cookbook lab manual to complete a hands-on exercise.

Active learning, as you might have already guessed, requires the participants to be involved and emotionally attached to the technology being taught. The instructor assumes that the participants do have relative knowledge about the technology and challenges the participants to expand their understanding. This challenge isn't a negative activity, but is presented through questions, scenarios, and case studies that require in-depth thought and exploration. Through demonstrations, hands-on labs, and experiments the participants confirm and discover knowledge about the technology. In active learning the instructor isn't just a talking textbook, but serves in a consultative and facilitative role to lead learners to new information.

I'm sure you can see the difference between the active and passive learning methods, but I want to make clear that one method isn't necessarily better than the other. In some classes it may be appropriate for the instructor and participants to use the passive learning style. You may prefer to use the active learning approach—but that's the idea of the learning and teaching preferences. Participants are going to have their preferences too. The practicality of the two styles is that adults learn by using both approaches. Some concepts are better learned passively, while other technical topics require hands-on, active learning.

If the goal of training is to increase workers' performance through the acquisition of new skills and understanding, then the evidence of reaching the goal is gathered by observing the behavior of the participants post-class. The expected outcomes of participants' behavior, such as the ability to operate a new piece of equipment, use a specific software, or to configure hardware, are actually tied to the profitability, stability, and reduction of operational costs to maintain the technology. The information you teach must be directly linked to the organization's increased performance in order to meet management expectations. For this outcome to actually happen based on your training, you need to help the learners answer four questions in their learning:

- **Why is this important to me?** You need to show how the training topic is related to the learner's role and responsibility within the organization. Participants may come to class already armed with this information, but it's a topic to address in your opening statements and throughout your lecture in the class.

- **What am I expected to do with this information?** Learners need to know what is expected of them as a result of the training. This should be fairly obvious in most classes, but sometimes it's not. Consider a class on Microsoft Word that covers how to create a table of contents. If the learners don't understand what they'll be using the table of contents for, the information is dismissed because they don't see the value of what you're teaching them. This could be because the course objectives don't all apply to the learner.

- **How will this work in production?** In the classroom environment, situations and lab exercises are structured to give learners a good foundation. In operational and production environments, however, circumstances, other software and hardware, and policies may affect the actual implementation and utilization of the technology. The classroom environment is usually a pristine, orderly environment and not always reflective of what the user may face in the workplace.

- **What if this and this happen?** This last type of question shows that the learner is understanding the concepts and creating "if-then" scenarios to apply their knowledge. For example, a learner may ponder "if this software works accordingly, then what will happen if I add this parameter?" The learner is thinking beyond the classroom and trying to apply what's been delivered to their roles and responsibilities, to understand at a deeper level, and to anticipate how the technology will affect their current processes.

As a technical trainer you can anticipate these types of questions and actions by observing the feedback, verbal and nonverbal clues, and interactions of each participant. This observation helps you gauge the depth of understanding of the participants, and then you can adjust your teaching style accordingly. The technical skills are the easiest to learn and observe; you'll see the individual do the correct steps to get to the desired results. The behavioral skills, however, are evident only when the learner understands the steps needed, but also wants to apply the skills to get the expected results. The behavior and attitude are in alignment with the needed skills to operate within the domain of the technology correctly.

The most common learning style model, and one you should be familiar with for your CTT+ examination, is the VAK Model. The VAK Model describes the learning styles of visual, auditory, and kinesthetic. Some learners learn better by watching and observing, such as through your demonstrations. Auditory learners prefer you to lecture and explain concepts to them, as they learn best through auditory signals. Finally, and some would argue most importantly, is the kinesthetic learner. The kinesthetic learner must touch, experience, and interact with the subject matter in order to learn the technology.

 NOTE An addition to this learning style model is called VARK, which adds reading to the list of visual, auditory, and kinesthetic styles.

The reality is that most people can learn through all of these learning styles, but they prefer a particular approach. I like to experience technology to understand it, so I know I'm a kinesthetic learner, but I also like to hear good lectures from experts. This duality of learner style isn't unusual—you probably can learn things in multiple combinations too. Four common blended learning styles are variants on the VAK Model to describe how people learn:

- **Tactile/kinesthetic learners** These learners remember by doing. In technology classes you'll probably find that most of your exercises and guided instruction are geared toward this type of learning style—because you have to interact with the technology to understand it. Any class that you teach that has a lab component is appealing to the tactile/kinesthetic learner.

- **Auditory/verbal learners** These learners like to listen to you explain technical concepts. If you've ever had a person in your class record your lecture because they feel they can learn by listening, then you've identified an auditory learner. These types of learners may like a good lecture, but they also like to interact with the instructor and other people in the classroom. Group conversations and opportunities to discuss questions appeal to these learners.

- **Visual/verbal learners** People who like to listen to you talk, but also like it when you write down key notes on a whiteboard or through a PowerPoint presentation, are considered visual/verbal learners. They like to watch and hear. A good technical lecture that includes a slide deck, demonstrations, and notes jotted on a whiteboard will appeal to these learners.

- **Visual/nonverbal learners** These learners like to see demonstrations, videos, illustrations, and charts. They learn best by watching you interact with the technology or demonstrate esoteric concepts by walking them through a figure or workflow. Lectures don't appeal to this type of learner, so you'll need to spice up your talk with more interactions and demonstrations.

VIDEO See the video *Exploring the ADDIE Model.*

David Kolb, a learning theorist, specialized in the concept of experiential learning—that is, that people best learn through their experiences and how the experiences are applied to their roles and responsibilities within an organization. Kolb's learning theory is based first on how learners receive information in a training session and then on how the learners internalize the information you've taught them. Kolb's Learning Cycle has four elements that create a cycle of learning and understanding, as seen in Figure 4-1. Technically the learning can start at any of the elements, as the cycle is like an ongoing spiral based on experience and current understanding. The four elements, concrete experience, observation and reflection, forming abstract concepts, and testing knowledge in new situations, all contribute to comprehensive learning.

According to Kolb's model there are four distinct types of learners:

- **Divergers** These people utilize concrete experience and reflection to best learn. The learners wants to experience the technology you're teaching, but they must understand how the information will be applied in their jobs and lives. These learners are sometimes referred to as "concrete-reflective."

- **Assimilators** These learners want to know the very specific directions to reach a desired result. They want to understand the step-by-step instructions to apply the technology in their work and lives. These learners are sometimes called "abstract-reflective" learners.

Figure 4-1
Learning can start at any of the learning elements in Kolb's Learning Cycle.

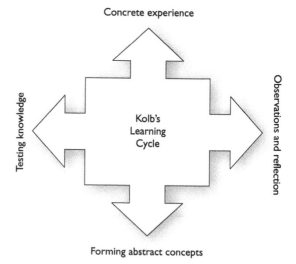

- **Convergers** These people thrive with detailed, hands-on activities with the technology in order to learn how the technology works. They prefer to be active in labs and testing rather than in lecture-driven training. These learners are sometimes called "abstract-active" learners.

- **Accommodators** These learners are similar to the convergers, but they're more inclined to experiment with the technology, create "what-if" scenarios, and to combine knowledge to see the outcome. These learners like a loosely structured training event that allows them time to test their theories and understanding of a technology. These people are sometimes referred to as "concrete-active."

As with all of the learning theories, people tend to gravitate toward one of the defined learning styles, but can appreciate and learn from the other learning styles. Rarely is one person unable to learn from more than one approach to the training and understanding. One of the drawbacks of Kolb's Learning Cycle, however, is that it doesn't allow for individuals to jump over or bypass one of the learning stages. In technology training, people may move from learning style to learning style based on the topic, their comfort level with the topic, and how the training course is designed.

Exploring Learning Theories

There are lots of different opinions and research on how people learn. As a technical trainer your job is to help people understand the technology you're teaching so that they can apply the information in their lives and in their jobs. All of this begins, of course, with the depth of your understanding of the technology. With that in mind, consider how you learn new topics, how you retain information, and how you process technical concepts. When I first started teaching technical classes way back in 1993, my supervisor told me a great nugget that's stuck with me: If you want to know something, really know something, teach it.

When you prepare to teach, there's a new type of pressure that's introduced into the learning process. What you learn, what you understand about teaching, will affect how your participants learn and understand. There's a new level of responsibility attached to your approach to learning, as what you teach others, right or wrong, can have huge ramifications on their businesses, careers, and lives. Participants enter the classroom with the assumption that you're the expert in the technology, and they'll look to you for guidance on how they'll receive, process, and apply the information.

By understanding the learning theories, you'll have more insight into your classroom preparations, but also insight into your learners. You'll be able to recognize the type of learners in your classrooms, adjust your teaching style to accommodate the participants, and grow into a more facilitative approach to training. The learning theories in this section may not actually affect how you and others learn, but they can affect how you teach. It's dangerous for an instructor to force their learning style preferences onto their audience, because the participants in the class may not have the same learning style as the instructor. My point being, recognize your learning style to help you learn better; then recognize the learning styles of your participants to help you teach better.

Understanding Gagné's Theory of Instruction

No discussion on learning is complete without a brief look at Robert Gagné's Conditions of Learning. Gagné was a psychologist who trained pilots in the U.S. Air Force. He went on to develop theories about how humans learn and what the domains of learning are. Gagné believed that the expected outcomes of education require specific training in consideration of the type of learners in the education process. In other words, the trainer accommodates the learning style. The fundamental beliefs of Gagné are

- When people learn, the learning cumulates, allowing people to understand more and more complex topics and to change their behavior accordingly.

- Learning is the avenue by which people become good members of a society.

- Learning and the environment both affect the behavior of the individual.

Learning, in Gagné's theory, is dependent on the learner having a complete understanding of the prerequisite tasks. The organization fails the learner when the organization assumes the learner understands the subtasks and sets expectations for the learner accordingly. For example, imagine a trainer teaching a database management course with the false assumption that the learners understand how data is entered into the database, how a server operates, or even how the data can be accessed.

Gagné defined five categories of learning that affect instructional design, instructor-led training, and even virtual classroom training today:

- **Verbal information** The learners need the instructor to teach the information in logical segments, provide enough information so that the learners can comprehend and process the concepts, and to link the topic to the learners' roles and lives.

- **Intellectual skills** Learners will use prerequisite skills and knowledge to process new, relative knowledge, to experiment with the technology to solve a problem for deeper understanding, and to apply new information to current problems.

- **Cognitive strategies** The learners will internally process what the instructor is teaching by using their learning strategies.

- **Attitude** The learners' attitudes toward the training, the instructor, the technology, and themselves affect their abilities to learn. The instructor can reward and recognize proper behavior to promote good learning.

- **Motor skills** The learners will complete a physical movement by first learning the correct movement from the instructor, practicing the correct movement over and over, and then will refine the movement based on feedback and the outcomes of the movement.

In addition to these five categories of learning, Gagné also posits that there are nine instructional events that promote the learner's cognitive processes, as seen in Figure 4-2. These nine instructional events don't necessarily result in learning. In these nine instructional events the instructor can help the participant prepare for learning, guide the learner through the subject matter, and transfer information to the learner. The nine instructional events are

- **Gain attention**   The instructor must get the participants' attention by linking the subject matter to the participants' lives and making the topic interesting.

- **Inform objectives**   Learners need to know what the instructor is going to teach, and the objectives help the learners anticipate and set expectations for the class.

- **Stimulate recall of prior knowledge**   Based on past experiences or previous training, the instructor builds new information on working memories of the participants.

- **Present stimulus material**   The instructor teaches the objectives in an interesting, engaging way.

- **Provide learning guidance**   The instructor helps the learners understand the new material through demonstration, repetition, and applied examples such as case studies.

- **Elicit performance**   The instructor offers time for the learners to practice the new information through exercises, additional demonstrations, and confirmation of understanding.

- **Provide feedback**   Learners need feedback on their performance and understanding; this can mean corrections and reinforcement or confirmation of understanding.

- **Assess performance**   The instructor may test the learners' knowledge through an assessment exam, an exercise without coaching, or through other methods for the learners to show understanding of the material.

- **Enhance retention and transfer**   The instructor makes a determination of skills learned by the participants; the participants apply the skills and are able to retain and retrieve the information at will.

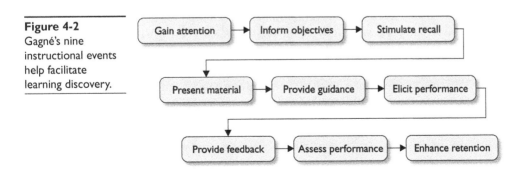

Figure 4-2
Gagné's nine instructional events help facilitate learning discovery.

These nine instructional events can map to the ADDIE Model and to portions of the Kirkpatrick Four Levels Evaluation Model. It's important to note that these instructional events don't actually make learning happen, but they massage the conditions for learning and then confirm if the information transfer has actually taken place. It's certainly possible for a person to attend a training and learn nothing, either through their own determination or the instructor's faulty guidance and preparation.

Exploring the Cognitive Learning Theory

The Cognitive Learning Theory focuses on how people process and retain information. This theory is less concerned with the behavior the learning brings about than with how the learning happens internally within each participant. The Cognitive Learning Theory begins with the instructional design and its effect on learning. Good instructional design, according to the Cognitive Learning Theory, creates materials, web-based training, and presentations that ultimately create the right conditions for learning to happen.

If a trainer subscribes to the Cognitive Learning Theory, she'll work to adjust her lectures, course demonstrations, exercises, and even the class structure to five learner activities:

- **Determine what needs to be learned.** The participant internally determines what information they need to pay attention to because the information is new, it interests them, or they've predetermined the link of the information to their lives. The instructor must get the learners' attention with each topic, help the learners see the importance of the information, and encourage the learners that they can master the skills the information requires.

- **Build upon existing knowledge.** Learners need to process the information by linking what the instructor is teaching to existing knowledge. The trainer can help this process by relating the new knowledge to information the learner has already experienced.

- **Structure the knowledge.** Learners will mentally structure the new information the trainer is teaching in a manner that best suits them for processing time, recall, and mental organization. Trainers can facilitate this process by stressing the learning objective, keeping topics in small segments that make it easier for learners to process, and by using illustrations and organized presentations to promote learner recall.

- **Integrate the new knowledge.** Learners won't have layers of knowledge, but will integrate the new information with existing information where they know both older and new information as one comprehensive component of knowledge. Trainers should clearly and accurately present the new information in a logical manner to help the learners accept and understand what's being taught.

- **Reinforce the new knowledge.** Learners can reinforce the new information by practicing what they've learned until they've perfected the skills the new knowledge requires. The instructor can help with the process by offering practice time, exercises, feedback, and by testing the learners' comprehension. Learners will also need an opportunity to consistently use the information so they don't lose what they've learned.

While the primary focus of the Cognitive Learning Theory is that the individual learners will accept, process, store, and retrieve the learned information, there's also responsibility for the instructor to teach the information in a manner that helps the learner learn. In that same vein, the instructional designers must create course content that's logical and that creates an environment where the learners can accept, process, and have opportunities to practice the newly received information. Practice doesn't always mean exercises in the Cognitive Learning Theory; practice could also mean quizzes, tests, and group conversation for recall.

Using the Constructivist Learning Theory

The Constructivist Learning Theory has been influenced by many learning psychologists and leaders, but none more so than Jean Piaget. In his view, and the most widely accepted belief of the Constructivist Learning Theory, is that the learners' cognitive development is based on their experiences. The outcome of a learning opportunity, whether in the class or through self-led discovery, is that the learners make sense of the experience based on the outcomes of the current and previous learning experiences. While there is practical application of the Constructivist Learning Theory in adult education, much of the focus of this theory is in the pedagogical domain.

In the Constructivist Learning Theory the learner is considered a unique individual with his own approach to learning by making sense of the experience. The instructor is a facilitator or guide to help the learner make sense of the information by teaching, offering analogies, and providing opportunities to explore the information through labs, exercises, and demonstrations. The primary characteristic of the Constructivist Learning Theory is that the instructor facilitates the information, and it's the learner who makes the discovery of the information, processes the information, and stores the information as new knowledge until it is assimilated into existing knowledge.

The Constructivist Learning Theory has the following characteristics:

- The learning experience must be linked to the learners' roles, responsibilities, or personal lives.

- Learners examine the tasks in the learning experience and define what the outcome of the tasks will create.

- Learners examine the tasks, break down the tasks into subtasks, and create the expected outcome.

- Learners will work with other participants and be guided by the instructor to the discovery of information.

- Learners will discover alternative approaches to reach the same expected outcomes.

Because Constructivist Learning Theory has evolved over the years (primarily since 1980), it goes by many different names and has influences into other learning theories. Constructivist Learning Theory may also be known as "Performance-Based Training," "Goal-Based Learning," "Problem-Based Learning," and my favorite, "Cognitive Apprenticeship."

Facilitating Technical Content

While learning theories are interesting to consider, they're a bit tougher to actually apply. The goal of learning theories and their application, I believe, is to make the instructor pause and consider how the learners receive, process, and store information for recall. When you consider the different studies on how participants learn, receive, process, store, and recall information, it can help you, the instructor, be better at framing your technical class to create a more learner-centered approach. If the goal of technical training is to impart knowledge that can be applied in the individual's role and life, then it's more important for the participant to learn than it is for the instructor to teach.

Teaching technical content creates opportunities for demonstrations, hands-on activities, and experimenting with the technology. Most technical courses fall into a rhythm of four parts, as in Figure 4-3. First, the instructor tells the class what the objectives of the module or lesson are. Second, the instructor lectures and demonstrates the technical concept. Third, the instructor gives an assignment or exercise that the class completes with or without the instructor's input. Finally, the instructor offers a review of the information and might offer a quiz to test understanding.

While there's nothing wrong with the four-step approach to teaching technical content, there may be opportunities for more in-depth learning that the instructor is overlooking. The four-step approach to teaching technology can also make the technical trainer apathetic to the portions of the class where the instructor isn't readily involved. An instructor who's teaching the same material over and over might go on "autopilot" and let the class run itself. The class and presentation may not be a bad experience, but

Figure 4-3
Technical training often follows a four-step approach to learning.

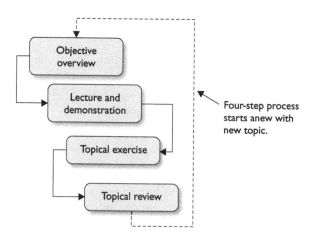

the fulfillment of the course goals may be missed because the instructor isn't truly teaching, just talking.

Creating Group Exercises

Group exercises allow participants to interact with one another, complete complex exercises, and play different roles in a simulated environment. For example, a group of participants in a server operating-system class could each play a role in configuring their servers, communicating with other servers in their group, and setting and testing security for user accounts. This hands-on experimentation can resemble real-world scenarios and allow the learners to see how configuration might actually happen in the real world.

Group exercises can also serve as a time management technique if the class is lagging on completing their labs and assignments on time. You can, if the course allows you to, shift the individual-led exercises to group exercises by pairing some of the more experienced learners with the learners who are new to the technology. You'll need to use caution with this approach, however, as you don't want to offend any learners or remove opportunities for individuals to experience the technology and practice the knowledge.

If you decide to create group exercises in your technical classes, you'll need to identify who'll be in what group. It's easy to make that decision based on where people are sitting in the classroom, but this isn't always the best approach. Based on observation you might choose who'll be with whom to help the class and learning proceed. This can also be a helpful classroom management approach if you have some people who are visiting with each other more than focusing on the learning. Ideally you'll also define the roles that the members of the group will play. Some instructors let the adults determine who'll do what in the group exercise, but sometimes this can backfire because people aren't always willing to lead or be led.

When you start the group exercise, you'll need to clearly communicate the expectations of the exercise. Define the purpose of the exercise, what the expectations of the group are, and what the outcome of the exercise should be. Your group exercise should have an interdependent element to the exercise so that all the people in the group can (and are required to) contribute to the learning outcomes. You don't want one person to charge through the exercise and complete all of the tasks, leaving the other learners out of the process. You also don't want the group to be frozen with indecision about who'll do what in the exercise.

As the group is working the technical trainer should visit each group to observe the process. Ask the group how the exercise is going, if they have questions, and ask who is doing what in the activity. This prompting can keep the group moving forward so the exercise doesn't stall or lose its appeal. Group exercise can invite chitchat among the participants, so it's important to visit each group and keep them moving toward the objectives. You can also include a countdown of how much time is remaining for the group to complete their exercise and to stay on task.

Teaching with Games and Simulations

No one wants to go to a boring class—especially the technical trainer. Games and simulations are exercises that you can use to spice up the class, get people involved, and help participants learn the information with better retention. Games must, however, be relevant to the course objectives; it's not a good idea to host a checkers tournament just because you have the time in class. Games in a technical class can be a great way to review the material and keep people involved in the class. I'm fond of using a game right after lunch to get participants thinking about our topic again. After lunch is also a good time for a quick game, as people can be a bit drowsy and need some interaction.

Simulations, especially in the virtual classroom, can emulate a real-world problem or interaction with a complex software, or can create a mock environment for learners to experiment in without interrupting production, live data, or servers. You can imagine how a simulation could allow learners to experiment with different router settings in a WAN technology class without changing the actual values on a router. The simulation allows the learner to experiment, test, and troubleshoot scenarios in a safe environment before applying their practice in a production environment.

Simulations require planning for effective design and anticipation of how the activity will proceed. Some computer simulations are really just a guided series of "hot spots" that require the user to click a specific area to advance to the next screen. This approach can help the user interact and complete a specific series of steps, but doesn't allow the user to see the outcome of choosing an incorrect option. A robust simulation would include branching and different methods of reaching the same outcome. For example, a simulation in Microsoft Word could allow the user to navigate through the menu bars to a specific command, right-click the mouse and choose from the pop-up menu, or even to use a keyboard shortcut.

Games are a good method to create some friendly competition in the classroom. It's easy to break the team into different groups and quiz each team on the topics. You can also get creative with the game and have the groups complete a specific task. For example, in a computer troubleshooting class you could create a game out of who can diagnose and repair a computer problem the fastest. While games can providing some fun and interaction, it's important that the game underscores the learning objectives, not just the fun competition among the participants. Limit the time allotted for the game, and always end the game with a review of how the activity will help the learners retain the information and apply it in their roles and lives.

Demonstrating the Technology

One of the best ways to teach technical topics is to offer demonstrations. Demonstrations give you, the instructor, an opportunity to show, not tell, what the capabilities and limitations of the technology are. Imagine trying to tell a person who's never created a formula in Microsoft Excel all the steps to making the formula happen. Or imagine describing how to configure DHCP (Dynamic Host Configuration Protocol) services for a new technician. These complex topics actually become pretty simple when you can demonstrate the activity.

Demonstrations do require some framework:

- **Know exactly what you're going to accomplish in the demonstration.** If you don't know the exact steps the participants are to follow, you'll just end up confusing the people in your class. Practice the demonstration before class to a level of mastery that you can easily show others the steps to complete the activity. If the topic is complex and has many steps, you might create a "cheat sheet" or put the steps on the overhead projector or in the virtual classroom to prompt you and your participants.

- **Demonstrate with a slow, steady pace.** For some demonstrations you'd no doubt be able to breeze through the steps quickly and easily just based on your experience with the technology. Unfortunately, when you move quickly through the actions, it doesn't give learners an opportunity to follow along and absorb the steps you're taking. You might also adjust your mouse pointer to help learners follow your actions on the screen.

- **Match what the learners will see.** If your computer screen isn't configured the same as the screens of learners in your classroom, you'll just add confusion. When learners compare their environment, such as hardware or software, and they see a difference, such as added buttons or features, they'll immediately wonder why your demonstration is different than their configuration. They'll likely have doubts about whether their environment is configured properly for the class, and then they'll be lost as you go deeper into the demonstration.

- **Let other people drive.** In a virtual environment and in the classroom you can get more people involved by letting them lead the demonstration. You can have someone take control of the demonstration while you walk them through the steps. This gives the individual a chance to practice the technology, keeps the group engaged, and puts the focus back on the learners rather than on you, the expert trainer.

While demonstrations are a good method to show people how the technology works, you'll want to balance the number of demonstrations you offer. Too many demonstrations and the participants can feel like they're only watching and not learning. Not enough demonstrations and the technical class can feel like one long lecture. Examine your content, find the most complex topics, and aim to demonstrate these activities for your learners. You might also elect to use some of the exercises as a pseudo-demonstration where you'll walk the learners through the exercise rather than let them work at their own pace.

Chapter Summary

Teaching technical topics requires a mastery of the technical content, the ability to deliver the needed information in a logical, acceptable format, and the insight to lead learners to discovery of the information. Technical training is based on the identified objectives that will help the learners perform better in their roles and responsibilities.

The activities, facilitation, and exercises in the class must all be in alignment with the learning objectives for the class to be successful. The technical trainer must position the class lecture, demonstrations, and exercises to be learner-centric rather than trainer-centric.

Technical trainers need to be aware of the learning styles in the room. Active learning happens when the learner is involved with the technology and learns through hands-on activities and exercises. Passive learning happens when the learner absorbs the lecture, group discussions, and readings about the technology. Either learning style requires that the learners understand why the information is important and how it will contribute to their role in the organization; they'll be more receptive to learning the technology than if they were uncertain why they needed to know what you're teaching.

The most common model of learning styles is called the VAK Model, which stands for visual, auditory, and kinesthetic. Visual learners prefer to learn through demonstrations, multimedia, charts, figures, and slideshows. Auditory learners prefer to learn through lecture and even multimedia. Kinesthetic learners prefer to learn through hands-on activities; they want to learn by doing, interacting with the technology, and experimenting with the subject matter. There's a variation on the VAK Model called the VARK Model. The "R" in this model represents the learners who prefer to learn by reading and writing.

Learning theories are beliefs that describe how people learn. Gagné's Conditions of Learning essentially states that all learning is cumulative on past learning experiences. Through learning people become good members of society and control personal behavior. An alternative theory, the Cognitive Learning Theory, focuses on how people process and retain information.

Trainers who subscribe to the Cognitive Learning Theory believe that learners determine what needs to be learned, how to structure the information based on existing knowledge, integrate the new knowledge, and through practice reinforce the knowledge. Finally, the Constructivist Learning Theory is that learning capabilities, capacity, and willingness to learn are based on the learner's cumulative experiences.

Regardless of the learning theories the instructor believes, she must make a concerted effort to shift the class from simply teaching to involved facilitating. Facilitation gets the people in the class involved with the technology and shifts the focus of the class from the instructor to the learners' interactions with the technology. Group exercises and group discussions can get the people in the classroom involved with one another to see interpretations of knowledge, create interdependent, simulated, real-world activities, and to offer some cross training of experience. Demonstrations can also provide a good facilitation technique, as the instructor can show how the technology works rather than simply telling how the technology works.

Key Terms

accommodators These learners are similar to the convergers, but they're more inclined to experiment with the technology, create "what-if" scenarios, and combine knowledge to see the outcome of their combinations. These learners like a loosely structured training event that allows them time to test their theories and understanding of a technology. These people are sometimes referred to as concrete-active.

active learning The learner is actively involved in the technology and topic through exercises, practice, hands-on activities, and interactions with the instructor and other participants. Active learning comes from hands-on involvement with the technology you're teaching.

andragogy Used to describe the science and applications used to teach adults. Andragogy, Greek, means man-leading, which is most commonly associated with leading adults. It was developed into the Theory of Adult Education by Malcolm Knowles.

assessing performance One of nine categories of learning as defined by Gagné. The instructor may test the learners' knowledge through an assessment exam, exercise without coaching, or other methods for the learner to show understanding of the material.

assimilators These learners want to know the very specific directions to reach a desired result. They want to understand the exact step-by-step instructions to apply the technology in their work and lives. These learners are sometimes called abstract-reflective learners.

attitude Part of Gagné's Conditions of Learning. The learners' attitude toward the training, the instructor, the technology, and themselves affects their abilities to learn. The instructor can reward and recognize proper behavior to promote good learning.

auditory/verbal learners These learners like to listen to an instructor explain technical concepts. These types of learners may like a good lecture, but they also like to interact with the instructor and other people in the classroom. Group conversations and opportunities to discuss questions appeal to these people.

Cognitive Learning Theory A theory that focuses on how people process and retain information. This theory is less concerned with the behavior the learning brings about than with how the learning happens internally within each participant. The Cognitive Learning Theory begins with the instructional design and its effect on learning.

cognitive strategies Part of Gagné's Conditions of Learning. The learners will internally process what the instructor is teaching by using their learning strategies.

Constructivist Learning Theory A theory that believes the learners' cognitive development is based on their experiences. The outcome of a learning opportunity, whether in the class or through self-led discovery, is that the learners make sense of the experience based on the outcomes of current and previous learning experiences.

convergers These people thrive with detailed, hands-on activities with the technology in order to learn how the technology works. They prefer to be active in labs and testing rather than in lecture-driven training. These learners are sometimes called abstract-active learners.

divergers These people utilize the concrete experience and reflection to best learn. The learners want to experience the technology you're teaching, but they must understand how the information will be applied in their jobs and lives. These learners are sometimes referred to as concrete-reflective.

eliciting performance   One of nine categories of learning as defined by Gagné. The instructor offers time for the learner to practice the new information through exercises, additional demonstrations, and confirmation of understanding.

enhance retention and transfer   One of nine categories of learning as defined by Gagné. The instructor makes a determination of skills learned by the participants; the participants apply the skills and are able to retain and retrieve the information at will.

gain attention   One of nine categories of learning as defined by Gagné. The instructor must get the participant attention by linking the subject matter to the participant lives and making the topic interesting.

inform objectives   One of nine categories of learning as defined by Gagné. Learners need to know what the instructor is going to teach, and the objectives help the learner anticipate and set expectations for the class.

intellectual skills   Part of Gagné's Conditions of Learning. Learners will use prerequisite skills and knowledge to process new, relative knowledge, to experiment with the technology to solve a problem for deeper understanding, and to apply new information to current problems.

Kolb's Learning Cycle   David Kolb defined four elements that create a cycle of learning and understanding. Adult learning can begin at any of the elements, as the cycle is like an ongoing spiral based on experience and current understanding. The four elements are concrete experience, observation and reflection, forming abstract concepts, and testing knowledge in new situations.

motor skills   Part of Gagné's Conditions of Learning. The learner will complete a physical movement by first learning the correct movement from the instructor, practicing the correct movement over and over, and then refining the movement based on feedback and the outcomes of the movement.

passive learning   The learner absorbs information through listening, reading, and reason. The participant accepts what the instructor says and then applies the information on exams, feedback, and in the workplace.

pedagogy   Used to describe the process of teaching; it's the vocation and strategies for teaching. Pedagogy is more closely related to teaching children than adults. Pedagogy is Greek and it means to lead the child.

present stimulus material   One of nine categories of learning as defined by Gagné. The instructor teaches the objectives in an interesting, engaging way.

providing feedback   One of nine categories of learning as defined by Gagné. The learners need feedback on their performance and understanding; this can mean corrections and reinforcement or confirmation of understanding.

providing learning guidance   The instructor helps the learner understand the new material through demonstration, repetition, and applied examples such as case studies.

Robert Gagné's Conditions of Learning   This theory states that the expected outcomes of education require specific training in consideration of the type of learners in the education process. The trainer must recognize and accommodate the learning style of the participant.

stimulate recall of prior knowledge   One of nine categories of learning as defined by Gagné. Based on past experiences or previous training the instructor builds new information on working memories of the participant.

tactile/kinesthetic learners   These learners remember by doing. Any hands-on exercises or lab components are usually appealing to the tactile/kinesthetic learner.

VAK Model   This model describes the learning styles of visual, auditory, and kinesthetic. Some learners learn better by watching and observing, such as through your demonstrations. Auditory learners prefer you to lecture and explain concepts to them, as they learn best through auditory signals. The kinesthetic learner must touch, experience, and interact with the subject matter in order to learn the technology.

verbal information   Part of Gagné's Conditions of Learning. The learner needs the instructor to teach the information in logical segments, provide enough information so that the learner can comprehend and process the concepts, and to link the topic to the learners' roles and lives.

visual/nonverbal learners   These learners like to see demonstrations, videos, illustrations, and charts. They learn best by watching an instructor interact with the technology or demonstrate esoteric concepts by walking them through a figure or workflow.

visual/verbal learners   These learners like to listen to you talk but who also like it when you write down key notes on a whiteboard or through a PowerPoint presentation are considered visual/verbal. A good technical lecture that includes a slide deck, demonstrations, and notes jotted on a whiteboard will appeal to these learners.

Questions

1. What term is most commonly used to describe the teaching of adults?

   A. Pedagogy

   B. Andragogy

   C. ADDIE

   D. VAK Model

2. You are coaching a new technical trainer on the importance of lecture versus hands-on activities. What percentage of lecture do most adults actually remember?

   A. 25 percent

   B. 50 percent

   C. 75 percent

   D. 10 percent

3. You are preparing your questions for a new technical class, and you want to add plenty of open-ended questions in the class. Which one of the following is not an example of an open-ended question?

   A. Why is TCP/IP the most popular network protocol?

   B. How do network cards communicate with the router?

   C. Can TCP/IP provide secure communications?

   D. What are the steps to configure a server with TCP/IP?

4. There are two primary large categories of adult learning styles. Which learning style is best described as the participant having a "blank slate" of knowledge?

   A. Passive learning

   B. Active learning

   C. Pedagogical learning

   D. VAK Model

5. What is the VARK Model?

   A. Video, Audio, Reading, Knowledge

   B. Visual, Audio, Reading, Knowledge

   C. Visual, Action, Reading, Kinesthetic

   D. Visual, Audio, Reading, Kinesthetic

6. Blended learning styles describe learners who prefer a combination of learning attributes. Which blended learning style would include learners who like a lecture, but also like to interact with group and instructor conversations in order to learn?

   A. Tactile/kinesthetic learners

   B. Auditory/verbal learners

   C. Visual/verbal learners

   D. Visual/nonverbal learners

7. Kolb's Learning Cycle describes the four elements of learning. Which one of the following elements is not part of the four elements of the Learning Cycle?

   A. Concrete experience

   B. Observation and reflection

   C. Forming abstract concepts

   D. Challenging information

8. In Kolb's Learning Cycle he describes four distinct types of learners. Which type of learner utilizes the concrete experience and reflection to best learn?

A. Accommodators

B. Divergers

C. Convergers

D. Assimilators

9. In Kolb's Learning Cycle he describes four distinct types of learners. Which type of learner prefers detailed, hands-on activities like labs and exercises with the technology?

A. Accommodators

B. Divergers

C. Convergers

D. Assimilators

10. Gagné defined five categories of learning that directly affect how instructors teach and instructional design. Which one of these five categories is most likely associated with the concept of the learner internally processing what the instructor is teaching?

A. Attitude

B. Cognitive strategies

C. Intellectual skills

D. Motor skills

11. In Gagné's Theory of Learning he posits that there are nine instructional events that facilitate learning. What is the first instructional event that the technical trainer must do?

A. Gain attention

B. Inform objectives

C. Present stimulus material

D. Enhance retention and transfer

12. In Gagné's Theory of Learning he posits that there are nine instructional events that facilitate learning. Which instructional event is best characterized as the instructor providing classroom time for the learner to experiment with and test the new information?

A. Providing learning guidance

B. Eliciting performance

C. Enhancing retention and transfer

D. Providing feedback

13. One of the learning theories all instructors should be familiar with is the Cognitive Learning Theory. Which one of the following statements best describes the Cognitive Learning Theory?

   A. The Cognitive Learning Theory describes how people learn based on prior experience.

   B. The Cognitive Learning Theory states that the trainer must accommodate the learning styles.

   C. The Cognitive Learning Theory posits that there are four levels of training evaluation.

   D. The Cognitive Learning Theory describes how people process and retain information.

14. The Cognitive Learning Theory has five training requirements that instructors must adopt in their classes to be successful. Which one of the following is not one of the five training requirements of the Cognitive Learning Theory?

   A. Determine what needs to be learned.

   B. Control the learning environment.

   C. Structure the knowledge.

   D. Build upon existing knowledge.

15. You are a technical trainer in your company, and you're teaching a group of trainers about the different learning theories. One of the trainers asks about the Constructivist Learning Theory. Which one of the following statements is part of the Constructivist Learning Theory?

   A. Work will expand to fill the time allotted to it.

   B. Adults only remember 25 percent of what they hear, but 75 percent of what they do.

   C. The instructor facilitates the information, and the learner discovers the learning.

   D. The instructor must get the learners' attention.

16. In the Cognitive Learning Theory which learner activity is met through exams and quizzes?

   A. Reinforce the new knowledge.

   B. Integrate the new knowledge.

   C. Structure the knowledge.

   D. Build upon existing knowledge.

17. Andi is a trainer who subscribes to the Constructivist Learning Theory. As a lead trainer in her organization she's teaching other trainers about the theory. Which one of the following statements would Andi not include as part of the Constructivist Learning Theory in her peer coaching?

A. The learning experience must be linked to the learners' roles, responsibilities, or personal lives.

B. Learners must learn the material even if they do not want to accept the new information.

C. Learners examine the tasks, break down the tasks into subtasks, and create the expected outcome.

D. Learners will work with other participants and be guided by the instructor to the discovery of information.

18. Most technical training courses fall into a cycle of four parts to the training delivery. Which one of the following answers describes the correct ordering of the four parts of technical training?

A. Tell the overview, lecture the content, assign an exercise, review the information

B. Tell the overview, lecture the content, assign an exercise, demonstrate the information

C. Tell the overview, gain an assessment, assign an exercise, review the information

D. Tell the overview, demonstrate the technology, gain an assessment, assign an exercise

19. An instructor is teaching a technical class, but some of the course participants are lagging behind and taking too long to complete the hands-on exercises. Which one of the following techniques can the trainer use to keep the participants on track and finish the course within the given time constraints?

A. Elect to not complete some of the exercises.

B. Partner the slower-paced participants with the advanced participants for the exercises.

C. Partner the slower participants with other slower-paced participants.

D. Simply demonstrate the exercises rather than have the class complete the exercises.

20. You are a technical trainer for your organization, and you want to include a demonstration for a technical concept in the course. In your preparation for the demonstration there are several rules you should follow. Of the following, which guideline doesn't apply to demonstrations?

A. Know exactly what you're going to do in the demonstration.

B. Demonstrate at the same pace as if you were in a production environment.

C. Your screen should match what the learners will see on their screen (assuming it's a software demonstration).

D. Choose a participant and allow them to drive through the demonstration.

Questions and Answers

1. What term is most commonly used to describe the teaching of adults?

   A. Pedagogy

   B. Andragogy

   C. ADDIE

   D. VAK Model

   B. Andragogy is the term used to describe the teaching of adults. A, pedagogy, is the term used to describe the teaching of children. C, ADDIE, describes the analysis, design, development, implementation, and evaluation of instructional design. D is incorrect, as the VAK model describes the three primary learning styles of visual, audio, and kinesthetic.

2. You are coaching a new technical trainer on the importance of lecture versus hands-on activities. What percentage of lecture do most adults actually remember?

   A. 25 percent

   B. 50 percent

   C. 75 percent

   D. 10 percent

   A. Most adults retain only about 25 percent of what they hear. B, C, and D are all incorrect values. Incidentally, most adults retain nearly 75 percent of what they do, which is why hands-on exercises are important in technical classes.

3. You are preparing your questions for a new technical class, and you want to add plenty of open-ended questions in the class. Which one of the following is not an example of an open-ended question?

   A. Why is TCP/IP the most popular network protocol?

   B. How do network cards communicate with the router?

   C. Can TCP/IP provide secure communications?

   D. What are the steps to configure a server with TCP/IP?

   C. Of all the examples choice C is not an open-ended question. Choice C is asking for a specific yes or no answer. Choices A, B, and D are all considered open-ended questions and require the respondent to answer with a detailed explanation, not a yes or no.

4. There are two primary large categories of adult learning styles. Which learning style is best described as the participant having a "blank slate" of knowledge?

A. Passive learning

B. Active learning

C. Pedagogical learning

D. VAK Model

A. Passive learning is the traditional classroom learning style where the instructor assumes the participant is a "blank slate" and void of any preconceived opinions or notions about the technology. B is incorrect because active learning describes the participant's role in the learning as actively involved. C is incorrect because pedagogy is directed toward the learning of children, not adults. The VAK Model, choice D, is incorrect, as this model describes the visual, audio, and kinesthetic approach to learning.

5. What is the VARK Model?

A. Video, Audio, Reading, Knowledge

B. Visual, Audio, Reading, Knowledge

C. Visual, Action, Reading, Kinesthetic

D. Visual, Audio, Reading, Kinesthetic

D. The VARK Model adds reading to the typical VAK Model. It describes the four learning styles and preferences of the adult learner as Visual, Audio, Reading, Kinesthetic. The other choices are incorrect, as they do not answer the question correctly.

6. Blended learning styles describe learners who prefer a combination of learning attributes. Which blended learning style would include learners who like a lecture, but also like to interact with group and instructor conversations in order to learn?

A. Tactile/kinesthetic learners

B. Auditory/verbal learners

C. Visual/verbal learners

D. Visual/nonverbal learners

B. These types of learners may like a good lecture, but they also like to interact with the instructor and other people in the classroom. Group conversations and opportunities to discuss questions appeal to these people. Answer A is incorrect, as tactile/kinesthetic learners remember by doing and prefer to follow exercises and labs. C is incorrect, as visual/verbal learners like to listen to you talk, but also like it when you write down key notes on a whiteboard or through a PowerPoint presentation. D, visual/nonverbal learners, like to learn from demonstrations, videos, illustrations, and charts.

7. Kolb's Learning Cycle describes the four elements of learning. Which one of the following elements is not part of the four elements of the Learning Cycle?

   A. Concrete experience

   B. Observation and reflection

   C. Forming abstract concepts

   D. Challenging information

   D. Challenging information is not one of the four elements of Kolb's Learning Cycle. The four elements are actually concrete experience, observation and reflection, forming abstract concepts, and testing knowledge. Choices A, B, and C are incorrect, as these answers are actually part of Kolb's Learning Cycle.

8. In Kolb's Learning Cycle he describes four distinct types of learners. Which type of learner utilizes the concrete experience and reflection to best learn?

   A. Accommodators

   B. Divergers

   C. Convergers

   D. Assimilators

   B. Divergers are people who utilize the concrete experience and reflection to best learn. The learners want to experience the technology you're teaching, but they must understand how the information will be applied in their jobs and lives. A is incorrect, as accommodators experiment with the technology and consider "what-if" scenarios with the information. C is incorrect, as convergers are people who thrive with detailed, hands-on activities with the technology to learn how the technology works. They prefer to be active in labs and testing rather than in lecture-driven training. D is incorrect, as assimilators want to know the very specific directions to reach a desired result. They want to understand the exact step-by-step instructions to apply the technology in their work and lives.

9. In Kolb's Learning Cycle he describes four distinct types of learners. Which type of learner prefer detailed, hands-on activities like labs and exercises with the technology?

   A. Accommodators

   B. Divergers

   C. Convergers

   D. Assimilators

   C. Convergers are people who thrive with detailed, hands-on activities with the technology to learn how the technology works. They prefer to be active in labs and testing rather than in lecture-driven training. A is incorrect, as accommodators experiment with the technology and consider "what-if" scenarios with the information. B is incorrect, as divergers are people who utilize the concrete experience and reflection to best learn. The learners want to experience the technology you're teaching, but they must understand how the information will be applied in their jobs and lives. D is incorrect, as assimilators want to know the very specific directions to reach a desired result. They want to understand the exact step-by-step instructions to apply the technology in their work and lives.

10. Gagné defined five categories of learning that directly affect how instructors teach and instructional design. Which one of these five categories is most likely associated with the concept of the learner internally processing what the instructor is teaching?

    A. Attitude

    B. Cognitive strategies

    C. Intellectual skills

    D. Motor skills

    B. Cognitive strategies describes how the individual will internally process the information the technical instructor is teaching. A is incorrect, as attitude describes the participant's attitude toward the training, the technology, and even the trainer. C is incorrect, as intellectual skills describes the ability of learners to use prerequisite skills and knowledge to process new, relative knowledge; experiment with the technology to solve a problem for deeper understanding; and to apply new information to current problems. D, motor skills, describes the physical action the learner perfects as a result of the training and practice with the movement.

11. In Gagné's Theory of Learning he posits that there are nine instructional events that facilitate learning. What is the first instructional event that the technical trainer must do?

    A. Gain attention

    B. Inform objectives

    C. Present stimulus material

    D. Enhance retention and transfer

    A. The first instructional event that the technical trainer must do is to gain attention. Gaining attention at the launch of each section of learning helps the learners feel engaged with the material and helps them link the message to their role in the organization. B is incorrect, as inform objectives is the second instructional event. C, present stimulus material, happens when the instructor is teaching the technical topic. D, enhance retention and transfer, is the last instructional event.

12. In Gagné's Theory of Learning he posits that there are nine instructional events that facilitate learning. Which instructional event is best characterized as the instructor providing classroom time for the learner to experiment with and test the new information?

   A. Providing learning guidance

   B. Eliciting performance

   C. Enhancing retention and transfer

   D. Providing feedback

   B. Eliciting performance is the opportunity in class for the learners to experiment and test the information and knowledge of the technical topic. A, providing learning guidance, happens when the instructor teaches, demonstrates, and coaches the learners through the technical topics. C, enhancing retention and transfer, is incorrect, as this choice is actually referring to the instructor making a determination of skills learned by the participants. D, providing feedback, happens throughout the course, as the learners need feedback from the instructor on their performance in the class.

13. One of the learning theories all instructors should be familiar with is the Cognitive Learning Theory. Which one of the following statements best describes the Cognitive Learning Theory?

   A. The Cognitive Learning Theory describes how people learn based on prior experience.

   B. The Cognitive Learning Theory states that the trainer must accommodate the learning styles.

   C. The Cognitive Learning Theory posits that there are four levels of training evaluation.

   D. The Cognitive Learning Theory describes how people process and retain information.

   D. The Cognitive Learning Theory describes how people process and retain information. All learners have a unique approach to processing, storing, and retrieving information. The Cognitive Learning Theory begins with the instructional design and carries through the technical content. A is incorrect, as this statement describes the Constructivist Learning Theory. B is incorrect, as this statement best describes the Gagné Theory of Instruction. C is incorrect, as this answer describes the Kirkpatrick Four Levels Evaluation Model.

14. The Cognitive Learning Theory has five training requirements that instructors must adopt in their classes to be successful. Which one of the following is not one of the five training requirements of the Cognitive Learning Theory?

    A. Determine what needs to be learned.

    B. Control the learning environment.

    C. Structure the knowledge.

    D. Build upon existing knowledge.

> **B.** Control the learning environment is not one of the five training requirements of the Cognitive Learning Theory. The five requirements are determine what needs to be learned, build upon existing knowledge, structure the knowledge, integrate the new knowledge, and reinforce the new knowledge. Choices A, C, and D are incorrect answers, as these are part of the five requirements of the training in the Cognitive Learning Theory.

15. You are a technical trainer in your company, and you're teaching a group of trainers about the different learning theories. One of the trainers asks about the Constructivist Learning Theory. Which one of the following statements is part of the Constructivist Learning Theory?

    A. Work will expand to fill the time allotted to it.

    B. Adults only remember 25 percent of what they hear, but 75 percent of what they do.

    C. The instructor facilitates the information, and the learner discovers the learning.

    D. The instructor must get the learners' attention.

> **C.** In the Constructivist Learning Theory the instructor is a facilitator that guides the learners to the discovery of information. A is incorrect, as this statement describes Parkinson's Law. B is incorrect, as this is a general statement about adult retention in the classroom environment. D is incorrect, as this statement is the first instruction event in Gagné's Theory of Instruction.

16. In the Cognitive Learning Theory which learner activity is met through exams and quizzes?

    A. Reinforce the new knowledge.

    B. Integrate the new knowledge.

    C. Structure the knowledge.

    D. Build upon existing knowledge.

> **A.** Reinforcement of the new knowledge happens through quizzes, exercises, and exams in the class to test the learners' retention of what's been taught. B is incorrect, as integrating the new knowledge can be facilitated by the instructor teaching the course in a logical approach. C is incorrect, as structuring the knowledge happens in the participant's internal cognitive processes. D is incorrect, as the instructor and the participants can use relative knowledge to accept new knowledge.

,

17. Andi is a trainer who subscribes to the Constructivist Learning Theory. As a lead trainer in her organization she's teaching other trainers about the theory. Which one of the following statements would Andi not include as part of the Constructivist Learning Theory in her peer coaching?

   A. The learning experience must be linked to the learners' roles, responsibilities, or personal lives.

   B. Learners must learn the material even if they do not want to accept the new information.

   C. Learners examine the tasks, break down the tasks into subtasks, and create the expected outcome.

   D. Learners will work with other participants and be guided by the instructor to the discovery of information.

   B. In the Constructivist Learning Theory learners won't accept or learn the material if they do not see the advantage of the material—the knowledge—in their roles and responsibilities within the organization or in their lives. Choices A, C, and D are incorrect, as these answers are all factual statements regarding the Constructivist Learning Theory.

18. Most technical training courses fall into a cycle of four parts to the training delivery. Which one of the following answers describes the correct ordering of the four parts of technical training?

   A. Tell the overview, lecture the content, assign an exercise, review the information

   B. Tell the overview, lecture the content, assign an exercise, demonstrate the information

   C. Tell the overview, gain an assessment, assign an exercise, review the information

   D. Tell the overview, demonstrate the technology, gain an assessment, assign an exercise

   A. The correct order of the typical four-step model to teaching is simply for the instructor to give an overview of the course, model, or topic; then the instructor will lecture the content and assign an exercise. Finally, the instructor will review the information for clarity and to confirm participants' understanding. Choices B, C, and D are incorrect choices, as these answers do not reflect the correct ordering of the four-step learning cycle.

19. An instructor is teaching a technical class but some of the course participants are lagging behind and taking too long to complete the hands-on exercises. Which one of the following techniques can the trainer use to keep the participants on track and to finish the course within the given time constraints?

A. Elect to not complete some of the exercises.

B. Partner the slower-paced participants with the advanced participants for the exercises.

C. Partner the slower participants with other slower-paced participants.

D. Simply demonstrate the exercises rather than have the class complete the exercises.

> **B.** Of all the choices, the best option is to partner the slower-paced participants with the faster-paced advanced participants. This option still allows the participants to complete the exercises, but creates a group exercise solution. A and D aren't good choices, as the exercises should be completed by the class to reinforce the learning. Choice C isn't a good solution, as partnering the slower-paced participants with one another won't necessarily increase the speed of the course.

20. You are a technical trainer for your organization, and you want to include a demonstration for a technical concept in the course. In your preparation for the demonstration there are several rules you should follow. Of the following, which guideline doesn't apply to demonstrations?

A. Know exactly what you're going to do in the demonstration.

B. Demonstrate at the same pace as if you were in a production environment.

C. Your screen should match what the learners will see on their screen (assuming it's a software demonstration).

D. Choose a participant and allow them to drive through the demonstration.

> **B.** Of all the choices this is the best answer because you should actually demonstrate at a slower, steady pace so all of the participants can follow along with your demonstration. Choices A, C, and D are incorrect because these are good practices for an effective demonstration.

Managing Instructional Materials

In this chapter you will:
- Learn the details of developing course materials
- Design effective materials for learner objectives
- Select vendor-provided materials
- Determine make-or-buy decisions for classroom resources
- Manage materials in the virtual classroom
- Customize classroom materials for learner needs

While most of the CompTIA CTT+ examination focuses on the trainer's ability to teach a technical topic, you'll also need to be familiar with training materials. Most technical trainers don't actually design and develop the course materials, though they should be involved in the process. The course materials—whether they be course workbooks, job aids, or even your PowerPoint slides—in the eyes of the learners are linked to you, the instructor, even if you didn't create the materials. You need for the course materials to be professional, organized, and focused on the learning objectives for the participants.

The design and development of the course materials may be completed by a professional instructional designer. Ideally, the instructors and the designers will work together on some level to discuss the flow of the course, exercises, and the amount of information that should go into a course and into the course materials. Commercial off-the-shelf course materials, if considered, should be evaluated for how accurately the materials satisfy the learning objectives. It's fairly easy to find course materials for mainstream technologies, but custom software, niche hardware, and internal technical processes usually require the course materials to be designed specifically for the training events.

The course materials serve as a tool in the trainer facilitation, not as a replacement for it. Not just anyone can grab a workbook and start teaching a class. In fact, if that were to happen, it'd probably be a painful class to sit through. The course materials help guide the instructor to guide the participants; they don't act as the primary lead through the course. This means the instructor should not read from the materials or constantly reference the workbook to the learners. The course materials should be used only when necessary in the course, not as a primary component of the course.

Determining the Make-or-Buy Decision

When an organization makes the determination to host technical training, one of the first conversations is always about the materials that the course will provide. People have a tendency to think of course materials first because they're one of the few tangible take-aways from the course, though this logic is actually flawed. Before the conversation dives into the course materials, the conversation should actually focus on the outcome of the course. The course stakeholders, including the instructor and key users of the technology product, should be involved in what the goals of the course are to be. It doesn't profit an organization to focus on course materials that may not cover the learning objectives.

Once the learning objectives have been clearly defined and documented, the organization should find the best materials for the course. They may even discuss the need for course materials—many organizations have bypassed using them. Workbooks were once considered a necessity for adult education, but now are often seen as a waste—especially if the learners aren't using the materials post-class. The cost of creating the workbooks can be significant, involving writers, designers, printing, and shipping. Many organizations have embraced the concept of workbook development, but are using a web-based format to deliver the content. This model saves on costs for printing, keeps the resources readily available beyond the classroom, and makes corrections and updates easy to manage.

Still, organizations must often consider the purchase of vendor-based solutions versus solutions that can be made in-house. The make-or-buy decision isn't always a financial one when time, skills, resources, and experience are factored into the decision. There are pros and cons to both decisions, and the value for the organization must be clear: which solution best supports the learning objectives of the course and is also sensitive to costs and schedule. In this section I'll help you compare and contrast buying versus building a solution for your technical classes.

Considering Financial Impact of Course Materials

If you've never tried to make course materials, you might be surprised at the amount of time it takes to develop quality course materials. The truth is, it's time-consuming and often painful to develop course materials that are going to support the course objectives and fit within the time constraints of the technical class. To develop course materials internally, you'll need several different resources:

- **Project manager**   Organizes the stakeholders and keeps the project in scope, on schedule, and within cost constraints
- **Subject matter expert in the technology**   Guides and identifies the concepts, tasks, and actual steps needed to complete the learning objectives
- **Trainer of the technology**   Determines the length of the course topics, the exercises, and the learner-centric preferences

- **Writer**   Works with the subject matter expert, trainer, and instructional designer to write the flow of the activities and concepts in the course material

- **Instructional designer**   Formats the writer's content, creates screen captures, and designs the course into manageable sections of learning for the learners and instructors

- **Editor**   Edits the writer's text, oversees the instructional designer formatting, and aims for consistency throughout the materials

- **Proofreader**   Reads the drafts of the course material with an eye toward accuracy, typos, and any grammatical errors

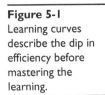

While it's possible that one person could serve in multiple roles in the course development, it's more likely that you'll need a separate person for each role in the development and publishing of the materials. Each of these individuals will, of course, have a cost associated with their contributions to the materials. If your organization has never created course materials, you'll succumb to the first-time, first-use penalty: the first time you try a new endeavor you'll be penalized in time and monies as part of the learning curve. When you attempt something for the first time, you'll have to pass through the learning curve, as in Figure 5-1.

Learning curves can be costly because you usually don't know how long it'll take you to reach a level of efficiency where using the learned processes becomes cost-effective. If your organization is going to continue to develop course materials internally on a regular basis, then the initial costs of learning to develop them may be worthwhile. If the organization is going to be developing the materials just once or for just a few instances, then there needs to be a detailed examination of the worth of developing the materials internally at all. It may not be worth the financial costs of attempting to develop the materials when you consider the time invested for a short-term commitment.

When considering whether to make the materials or to buy the materials, also consider the number of workbooks you'll be creating. The ratio of the cost per workbook to the number of participants may affect the make-or-buy decision. For example, the largest cost in creating the course materials is not the printing, but the labor and skills needed to create the first copy. The time of the project manager, writer, trainer, subject matter expert, instructional designer, editor, and proofreader will cost the same if you're printing 10 manuals or 500 manuals. Once the course manual has been created, the cost of printing the manual is relatively low—and most printers will offer a price break based on the quantity of printing.

Figure 5-1
Learning curves describe the dip in efficiency before mastering the learning.

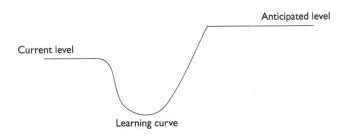

Generally, the more people that pass through training, the lower your cost per course manual will be. When an organization has a relatively small number of people to pass through a training event, it's probably not cost-effective to develop the materials in-house because the cost of each manual for the small event isn't cost-effective. But when the organization has a mass of people to pass through the training, the overall cost of each manual is reduced. The size of the training audience directly affects the feasibility of buying or building.

 NOTE The real advantage of making in-house materials isn't the cost factor, but the control factor. When you develop the materials in-house, you'll have more control over the content, screen captures, and the direct linkage from the classroom to production.

Considering Internal Development Solutions

If your organization elects to develop the course materials in-house, take several precautions. Planning is paramount to any successful project—and developing course materials will be a project. All projects, as the project management expressions goes, fail at the beginning, not the end. If you do nothing else in your project planning time, always define clear project requirements. Your development of the course will go much more smoothly if you know exactly what must be delivered.

Creating training materials can be a time-consuming activity. All of the people involved in the decision to bring the course material development in-house must take a hard look at the expected delivery date for the materials and determine if that's feasible or not. This examination of the scope of the material development and the amount of time to develop the material is based on the assumption that there are resources within the organization that can actually develop the materials. It takes special skills, from editing to designing, to create good, solid course materials. If these skill sets do exist internally, there's also a need to determine if the resources have operational duties to attend to in addition to developing the materials, or whether the development will be their full-time role for the duration of the course development process.

It's also common for stakeholders to have a negative perception of materials that are developed internally versus materials that are purchased from a vendor. The internal skill sets may be credible, but there's often some mystique attached to purchased materials over homegrown materials. It's often harder to accept the validity of materials that John down the hall created versus the slick, packaged materials purchased from a company in New York City. The organization may need to stress quality control and to sell the internal product to the internal stakeholders.

Another concern when developing materials in-house is the expected outcome. While most instructional designers and trainers think of course materials as used in the classroom environment, there's an increasing demand for web-based training, videos, and resources. These deliverables require additional skills and specialized software. The cost and learning requirements of the software may be enough to consider outsourcing the project to a vendor or looking for commercial, off-the-shelf solutions.

Of course it's important to make the correct decision at the launch of the in-house development initiative. When there are production issues, laws and regulations, and even government funding tied to training initiatives, the organization can't be late on launching and completing the training. If your organization doesn't have a skilled resource to develop the materials, it's a great idea to hire a subject matter expert to at least determine the time estimate for the project and to coach the development team along. As a general rule, the longer it takes to develop course materials, the more costly the materials will be.

Designing Effective Technical Classes

While the goal of this book is to help you become a better technical trainer—and to pass the CompTIA CTT+ certification exams—it's important to understand what goes into the design of technical classes. In your role as a technical trainer you may never have the opportunity to actually design a technical class, but understanding the process can give you insight into the learning objectives. As mentioned in an earlier discussion of the ADDIE model of instructional design, the first *D* in ADDIE represents the design phase. Design in ADDIE isn't the hands-on writing and publishing of the work; that's the development phase. Design in ADDIE is the determination of what the course is supposed to accomplish.

When an organization looks to design a class, they're determining what's important for the learners to learn. The organization wants to define what the expected outcomes of the training will be and how the knowledge transfer will happen. In a perfect world this process would bring together the key stakeholders: subject matter experts, instructional designers, technical trainers, management, and users of the technology. The goal would be to determine what the users need to know, what the organization expects the users to accomplish with the technology, and what methods are best suited to accomplish these goals.

Unfortunately, for many organizations the process starts with some big, dreamy goals of what the class will accomplish, and then the vision is reduced to hours and dollars. Training is expensive when you factor in the "seat time" for the attendees to be learning rather than producing and supporting the organization's bottom line. No training, however, can be more expensive than training when you factor in the cost of mistakes, wasted time, and frustration of users. Organizations must balance how much training is needed in relation to the return on investment for the time in the classroom.

Designing a technical course is tough work. The designers need to establish the primary goals of the training, determine the realistic amount of time to teach the technical topics, and map out the plan for the implementation of the course. Designers have to calculate how much time is needed to effectively transfer the knowledge and to complete the exercises, and also determine some breathing room for classroom issues, breaks, and group conversation. There's a wealth of planning that goes into the initial design of technical training.

Preparing for Effective Technical Training

Designing a technical training course begins with understanding why the technology is being implemented. You need to understand the root cause for the technology to understand how to design the course around the root cause. Technology is rarely implemented, at least in businesses, because it's fancy; technology must solve a problem or seize an opportunity, and that's where root cause analysis begins.

For our conversation, assume that you'll be involved in the design of your next technical course. In your organization that may or may not be the norm, but for your CTT+ examination and as an excellent technical trainer, it's good to peek into the design process. Designing effective training is really about creating a learner-centric environment. This doesn't mean that everything's about the learner enjoying the class; it's more about creating a symbiotic relationship between the organization and the learner.

Examine Figure 5-2. The organization needs the employee to accomplish a new task using some new technology. The effective usage of the new technology supports the goals, missions, strategy, and objective of the organization. The users, however, are primarily concerned with doing the task to complete their roles and responsibilities. Sure, the users may have some interest in supporting the organization, but the immediate focus is to do their work well as part of their employment. Of course the users doing the work satisfy their personal objectives, but they also support the organization as a whole.

There are some flaws in this assumption of the win-win relationship. First, the organization must understand why the technology is needed and how it supports the broader vision of the organization. The organization first needs to know how the technology will help the company be more profitable or how it cuts costs. Efficiency and productivity are sometimes tough to track due to Parkinson's Law—that work expands to fill the time allotted to it. A new technology making the process faster doesn't necessarily equate to the organization being more productive. Just because I can complete a task that used to take an hour in 15 minutes doesn't mean I necessarily will. Regula-

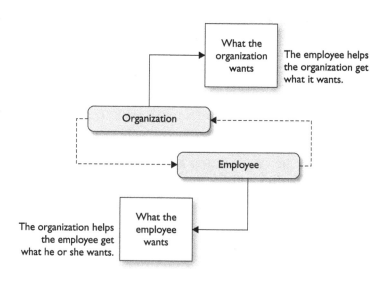

Figure 5-2
Ideally, employees and organizations work together in a symbiotic relationship.

What the organization wants

The employee helps the organization get what it wants.

Organization

Employee

The organization helps the employee get what he or she wants.

What the employee wants

tions and laws are really cost avoidance because you must adhere to regulations and laws or there will be penalties and lawsuits that your organization may have to pay. Technology has helped organizations adhere to new regulations: consider accounting, health care, and manufacturing laws and how technology has helped ease the necessity of new regulations. My point is that organizations must see the value in the implementation of the technology, or they won't see the value in training their employees.

Employees, the other side of the equation, must also see the value in the technology. It's fairly common for employees to resist any technical change. Employees may have mastered their processes, the technology, and have learned through experience the bells, bugs, and whistles of a given technology. Unless they really despise the current technology or can see the big benefits of the new technology, they probably won't buy into the change. Change is difficult but can be eased with motivation. The motivation in changing technology is really generated through education—and not just in the classroom. There must be pre-training communication as part of designing the technical course. Adults need to know what's changing, how it affects them, how it affects their roles and responsibilities, and what the organization's expectations are. It's no secret that adults are more willing to learn if they understand why the change is happening and how it affects their job.

Designing the technical training course is the examination of what the organization needs to satisfy its mission and objectives, but also what the employee is required to do to support that higher goal. The employee, the person who will become the learner in the classroom, has the greatest influence on using the technology correctly in order to support the organization's goals. Therefore, the designers of the technical course have a lofty responsibility to determine the exact needs of the training to support the organization as a whole.

Ensuring Quality Course Design

Quality is a term that people talk about but don't often define. When most people talk about quality, especially in technical course design, they mean a reliable, enjoyable experience that achieves the instructional goals. Quality is really about meeting objectives and key performance indicators, and the experience of the class. Quality can only be met, however, by first defining what quality is for the course. To have quality technical training, you must first define what quality is.

The first step in designing a quality technical class is to define what the boundaries, or scope, of the training will be. Based on the needs analysis of the training, the subject matter experts and other key stakeholders will contribute to what they believe the course should include. This can be a mishmash of ideas and input, but there needs to be some ordering of what the learners will need to come out of the class knowing. The most logical way to break down the course topics is to relate the performance outcomes of the organization to the tasks in the technology. If an organization is migrating to a new contact management system, the training should be based on what the goal of the contact management system will be: sales, customer tracking, marketing efforts, or active order fulfillment. Based on the root cause, again, the tasks can be identified for the audience; it's a different skill set to use a contact management system for sales than it is to use it for order fulfillment.

PART II

Storyboards are one approach to define the flow of activities in the process of identifying the actual tasks the employees will complete in the software. Figure 5-3 is a storyboard for order fulfillment. Storyboards are quick sketches and drawings of how the individual will interact with the technology to get to the desired result. The interactions are really the interactions with the technology to utilize the technology to achieve the desired result of the workflow. Storyboards show the process, not the technology—remember, the technology is just a tool to help get the job done.

Adults like to learn things in chunks. You don't go to a class on Microsoft Word and start the class by printing and making the table of contents. There's a logical workflow to creating a document, saving a document, editing a document, and so on. The flow of the work, the design of the course, and the course activities all follow a logical approach. These logical steps often build on one another and help keep the class activities orderly. The idea of design, teaching, and learning in chunks of information also keeps the class in an anticipated rhythm of what's next in the workflow for productivity.

NOTE   One of the worst classes I've ever sat through was really poorly designed. The class started with the first menu in the software and went through each command. Then we moved onto the next menu, and so on. By the end of the day I was exhausted and hadn't learned much. Poorly designed courses don't help the trainer teach a good course. When you're teaching a poorly designed course it's best to chuck the materials and just take charge and teach.

Organizations should develop a style manual and standard operating procedures for the development and design of courses. A style manual defines the language, gram-

Figure 5-3
Storyboards tell a story of a process in a technical environment.

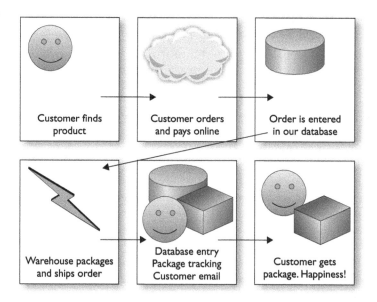

mar practices, and generally accepted approach for writing the course content. Standard operating procedures for instructional designers define the rules and procedures for the content of the course. For example, a standard operating procedure could define the order of elements within a module: overview, demonstration, exercise, review, and quiz. The standard operating procedure could also define the type of artwork to be used in the manual, the screen captures, and the maximum number of steps in an exercise.

The style guide and standard operating procedure create a uniform, consistent approach for the course participants. This helps participants feel at ease with the repetition in the approach and anticipate the next portion of the course, and keeps the design consistent. The style guide is especially important when there are multiple designers contributing to one course. All of the designers should follow the same methodology and flow for the course to prevent a mismatched hodgepodge of exercises. Having a clear vision of all exercises, modules, and instructor materials for all types of training for an organization is ideal. This approach allows participants to understand how the course flow will happen regardless of the topic they're learning.

Beyond designing the course is the development of the course. There's sometimes a blurry line between development and design. Purists of the ADDIE model say that design sets the vision and expectations for the course. Other educational gurus might disagree with this belief and say that the developers should follow the high-level design of the course, but treat the high-level design more as a recommendation than a mandate. This conflict, or appearance of conflict, can be unique to each organization, but it's best to understand at the launch of the instructional design process what the expectations are for the final product.

Controlling Materials in the Virtual Classroom

While virtual classroom trainers can still utilize course workbooks and job aids much as standard classroom trainers do, virtual classroom trainers have some constraints. The largest drawback of materials in a virtual classroom environment is that the instructor can't actually see if the participant is on the correct page and location in the work. Audio clues and repetition are needed to direct the virtual learner to where exercises and labs are located and to confirm that the participant is following along. You can imagine the frustration a learner will have in a virtual classroom environment if the printed course materials are misnumbered, formatted incorrectly, or don't provide detailed instructions because they're more likely to rely on the printer materials than in a traditional classroom structure.

It's because of this desire of the virtual learner to rely heavily on materials that the virtual classroom instructor must take extra efforts to bring the learner away from the printed materials and into the web-based software for the virtual learner. In the virtual classroom the instructor needs to make extra efforts to involve the learner, do more demonstrations, and to perform walkthroughs with the learners than to just set them loose to complete course book activities. Some technical topics will require learners to complete the course activities in a cookbook approach; it's best to get the learners involved rather than to leave them on their own to follow the course materials.

Many technical courses are designed first for the classroom environment, with face-to-face instruction, and then are ported to the virtual classroom environment. While there's nothing terribly wrong with this approach, drawbacks and issues can creep into the adaptation. When classroom-based training and instruction aren't accurately mapped to the virtual environment and the issues and challenges of remote learning aren't accurately considered, then the virtual trainer will have problems to manage. Ideally, virtual classroom materials are designed specifically for the virtual classroom, rather than adopting a one-size-fits-all mentality of utilizing the same materials for the traditional classroom and the virtual classroom environments.

Managing Virtual Classroom Material Challenges

"Materials" in a virtual classroom means more than just the course workbook and job aids. Materials in the virtual classroom can mean anything the instructor can show to the learner. Note the word "show." Because you'll be teaching in a virtual environment, you can show your learners a slide deck, demonstrations, drawings, multimedia events, and other trainer-learner interactions to promote learning. Showing your learners is better than telling your learners—because you're using the technology of your web-based classroom to pull the learner into the learning process.

If you've ever sat through a web-based class where it's simply a voice over a Power-Point presentation, you know how mind-numbingly boring it can be. Learners don't want hours of lectures and slides in a virtual environment—and they probably aren't going to learn much with this approach either. Learners want you to show them the technology, show them how the components of the technology actually work, and let them experiment, as much as possible, with the technology. Learners learn differently in a virtual classroom than in a traditional classroom because they can't make eye contact, read your body language, and pick up other nonverbal clues to contribute to their understand and learning. In light of this, you have to make extra efforts to get them involved and learning by using technical tools.

 VIDEO See the video *Configuring the Virtual Classroom*.

In whatever web-based training platform you use to teach your classes you usually have some standard elements and characteristics:

- **Whiteboard** Where your slides appear, where you can share multimedia files, and where you can draw figures and illustrations on-the-fly.

- **Chat** Some area of the web-based software where you and the users can type messages directly to one another, either with everyone in the group, or just among a few participants.

- **Student monitoring** Some area of the interface where users can "raise their hand"; change a status indicator like green, yellow, or red; or participate in polling for group questions.

- **Demonstration area** Some virtual classroom software allows the instructor to share their desktop so that the users can see the instructor interact with the technology.

- **Role configuration** Roles are usually moderator, instructor, host, student, or something similar. The instructor may be able to change the roles so that a participant can do the demonstration for the class.

Your web-based training software may have similar and additional features. For your CompTIA exam you won't be tested on the specifics of any particular remote conferencing software interface, just on the high-level components like those I've shared here. On the more practical side of things, however, it's essential for you to be very familiar with how to operate and manage the technical aspect of the virtual classroom. It's distracting and confusing for learners when the instructor is fumbling with the interface to teach the class, rather than focusing on the course content. Your expertise in a virtual classroom environment begins with the management of the classroom as an extension of your abilities as a technical trainer.

The virtual classroom environment is an extension of your learner materials. Adults learn through visuals, so use this to your advantage to help your participants learn and to engage them in the materials. Create figures as you lecture to illustrate complex topics, rather than just lecturing on the topic. If you're teaching software, show the software as you lecture so the participant can see, literally, what you're talking about. If you have multimedia clips, such as recorded demonstrations or videos that explore the topic you're teaching, share them with your learners. One of the primary goals of a virtual classroom trainer is to involve the participant in the class by engaging the participant, not just lecturing to the participant.

Virtual classrooms often allow the instructor's mouse pointer to be changed to a highlighter, a larger arrow, or to some other cueing device to help learners see the interaction. Don't move the mouse too quickly, for learners need to be able to follow where you're pointing and what you're doing on the screen. In the virtual classroom you'll also need to pay attention to how you arrange the learning content. You don't want to clutter the screen with a slide deck, illustrations, multimedia, chat, and other windows. Screen real estate for the learner becomes more and more scarce when there are more and more sections to pay attention to. As with all learning, simple is best—less is more.

Selecting Media Visuals for Learners' Needs

While you cannot actually make eye contact with learners in a virtual classroom environment, you can engage the learners through the visuals on their computer screen. Using the correct visual is essential to correct engagement; adding some clip art to a slide because it's cute can actually be a deterrent to learning, as the participants may wonder what the clip art has to do with the materials. They may wonder if they're missing a connection between the random artwork and the message and content of what they're seeing on their screen. Such clip art and figures are called *decorative visuals*—they're pretty, but don't add value, only decoration to your lecture.

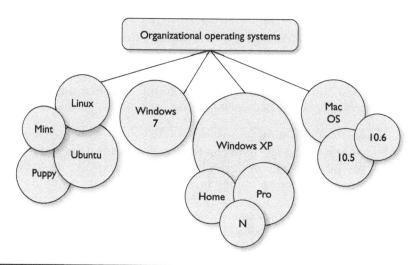

Figure 5-4 Organizational artwork arranges topics by classification.

Most visuals in a virtual classroom environment (and in course materials) are *representational art*. Representational artwork represents the actual technology, line drawings of concepts, and screen captures or photographs from the technology. This type of artwork shows the learners how the concept is applied. Throughout this book I've used representational art to show the concepts of technical training without adding any decorative artwork. All of the icons and the line drawings in this book are representational artwork of concepts. Representational artwork is the most common type of artwork for most virtual classrooms.

Some artwork, however, is more organizational in nature, as in Figure 5-4. As its name implies, organizational artwork organizes concepts, ideas, and related material. In Figure 5-4 I've created some organizational artwork to visualize the topography of several different computer operating systems. While you may argue that this is also a representational artwork, and you'd be correct, it's also considered organizational because the artwork organizes concepts into different categories by different operating systems.

In Figure 5-5 I've taken the information on the different categories of operating systems and created a pie chart to represent the distribution of operating systems within the company. Bar charts, pie charts, and other graphics that show quantitative relationships are called *relational graphics*. For example, your web-based training classroom may allow you to take a survey of your participants and then show the results in a bar chart.

Figure 5-5
Relational graphics
show distribution
of data.

Some technical classes might use a mnemonic visual to help people remember facts. One mnemonic from my networking days was for the layers of the Open Systems Interconnect (OSI) Model—"*All People Seem To Need Data Processing*"—which stands for:

- Application
- Presentation
- Session
- Transport
- Network
- Data link
- Physical

Transformational artwork shows changes over time. In technology, you could use a timeline to show how operating systems have progressed since DOS, then Windows, then Windows NT 3.51, Window 95, NT4, and on and on. The transformational artwork shows the transformation or evolution of a technology or concept from starting point to the most recent status of the concept. Of course whatever type of visuals the instructor uses, the visuals should contribute to the learners' understanding of the concept, not detract from the learning. The instructor should explain how the visual supports the concept, and when possible, interact with the visuals by using the pen or highlighter tool, assuming one exists, within the virtual classroom software to help express the purpose of the visual.

Chapter Summary

Training materials are a support to the instructor and the classroom learning process, not a replacement for the instructor. Training materials are, however, one of the largest expenses in the training proposition considering the time to create the materials and the cost of producing the materials. Organizations must examine the scope of the training needs, the size of the audience, the expertise within the organization, and the longevity of the training to determine the make-or-buy decision for the training materials. Often it may be more cost-effective to buy the materials, but the commercial off-the-shelf solution doesn't provide the exact details that an in-house developed set of materials can offer. It won't take a lengthy discussion to see the pros and cons of making the materials versus purchasing readymade materials from a reputable vendor.

If the organization decides to make the materials in-house, then there must be a clear, documented decision as to what will and won't be included in the training materials. Roles and responsibilities will need to be defined, and a project manager will need to own the planning, monitoring and controlling, and execution of the project to ensure that all of the requirements are captured and included in the final deliverable. One of the largest components of the internal creation of the training materials is the design of the technical class.

The design of the technical class determines what will and won't be included in the training class due to cost, feasibility, and timing of the course. A needs analysis and task analysis will need to be conducted for the organization to determine what must be included and should be included based on the priorities of management, the users, and the learning objectives for the course. Designers also have to consider how much can be allotted to each training topic and still fit within the confines of the course schedule. Too much or too little time on a given topic can be a costly mistake if the user isn't going to use a particular feature or if a concept is not explained to the depth needed for production.

All training, traditional classroom-based or in the virtual classroom environment, must present a value proposition for the design of the course materials and content. The value proposition is the study of the return on investment for the training and how the training will save the organization money, increase revenue, or both. Some training may be required as part of continuing education or for regulations—but this too is likely a savings of fees that the organization would have to pay if it did not meet the training obligations of the regulations.

Virtual classrooms have challenges when it comes to using the materials as part of the course. In a traditional classroom environment the instructor can hold up the materials and point to a specific portion of a page to corral participants. In a virtual class environment the learners may not be able to see the instructor—and may see only the content of the virtual classroom screen space. The instructor needs to take extra steps to ensure participants are following along and engaged in the lecture and conversation, and to use the technology to teach a learner-centric approach, rather than just hosting a long telephone call.

Virtual classroom trainers should be familiar with how to interact with the whiteboard to load slides, add illustrations, and create drawings during the lecture. While a person in a traditional classroom environment can raise their hand to ask a question, there may be electronic versions of this concept in the virtual environment—either through chat or through a student monitoring panel in the software. Instructors should also use demonstrations to support the dialogue and interactions with the students in the software. The goal of the virtual classroom is to involve and engage the learner to overcome the limitations of not being able to see the instructor and her nonverbal clues and body language. Visuals, demonstrations, and exercises can all help the remote learner feel engaged and involved in the virtual classroom.

Key Terms

chat   Some area of the web-based software where the instructor and the users can type messages directly to one another, to everyone in the group, or just among a few participants.

decorative visuals   Clip art and pictures that are used more for decorations than as teaching elements; decorative visuals can be a learning distraction if they don't support the learning environment.

demonstration area   Some virtual classroom software allows the instructor to share their desktop so that the users can see the instructor interact with the technology.

first-time, first-use penalty   The first time an endeavor is attempted by a person or organization there are likely to be additional cost and time requirements for the implementation of the technology or training.

learning curve   The negative curve of productivity tracking that happens when learning a new technology, process, or approach. The learning curve is often described as a short-term backward trend in productivity to move to long-term trends in efficiency.

make-or-buy decision   The process an organization completes to determine the value proposition of making the course materials internally or purchasing standardized materials from a vendor.

mnemonic visual   A visual and a mnemonic device to help people remember key facts and information.

organizational visuals   Artwork that is used to organize concepts, group similar topics, and demonstrate logical grouping of things.

Parkinson's Law   Work expands to fill the time allotted to it.

relational visuals   Graphics that show relationships among data; for example, bar charts and pie charts are relational graphics.

representational visuals   Artwork that represents the actual technology, line drawings of concepts, and screen captures or photographs from the technology. This type of artwork shows the learners how the concept is applied.

role configuration   In the virtual classroom environment roles are usually moderator, instructor, host, student, or something similar. The instructor may be able to change the roles so that a participant can do the demonstration for the class.

standard operating procedures   The rules for instructional designers to define the expectations and procedures for the content of the course development.

storyboard   A series of drawings to visualize a process, event, or workflow; storyboards help course designers see how a task should be completed to better teach a technical concept.

student monitoring   An area of the web-based training interface where users can "raise their hand"; change a status indicator like green, yellow, or red; or participate in polling for group questions.

style manual   Defines the language, grammar practices, and generally accepted approach for writing the course content.

transformational artwork   A visual aid that shows how change has happened over time.

whiteboard   The area in a virtual classroom software environment where slides appear, where the instructor can share multimedia files, and where the instructor can draw figures and illustrations.

Questions

1. You work for an organization that is making a determination to make or buy the classroom materials. You're helping the organization identify the positive aspects of creating the materials in-house. Which one of the following is not a viable positive reason to make the materials rather than buy the materials?

   A. Competent resources

   B. Time available to create the materials

   C. Importance of subject matter

   D. Control of topic inclusion

2. There are several roles needed to create course materials. Which role is best described as the person who will guide and identify the concepts, tasks, and steps needed to complete the learning objectives?

   A. Project manager

   B. Subject matter expert

   C. Writer

   D. Trainer

3. What term is given to the condition that a new endeavor will likely take longer and cost more because it's never been attempted?

   A. First-time, first-use penalty

   B. Parkinson's Law

   C. Law of Diminishing Returns

   D. Learning curve

4. Which one of the following is a perceived concern stakeholders may have about internally developed materials?

   A. Control over the resources is better with a vendor.

   B. The content is better with a vendor.

   C. Control over the content is better with a vendor.

   D. The quality is better with a vendor.

5. Your organization has decided to make their course materials internally rather than purchase the materials through a vendor. Your organization has not, however, created materials internally before. Based on this information complete this statement: The longer it takes to develop course materials, the materials will be _____.

   A. Better in quality

   B. Higher in costs

   C. Lower in quality

   D. Likely to fail

6. What does the first *D* in ADDIE represent?

   A. Design

   B. Development

   C. Doing

   D. Duration

7. An organization has determined to create its course materials internally rather than hire a vendor to create the materials. The designer believes the course development and design will take six weeks to create, but reports that the design will most likely take nine weeks to complete in case there are delays or issues in the development. If you subscribe to Parkinson's Law, how long will it take to complete the design and development of this course?

   A. Six weeks

   B. Nine weeks

   C. Ten weeks

   D. Unknown

8. Ben is an instructional designer for his company. Management has demanded that quality be met in all course designs. To achieve quality what must first be defined?

   A. What quality is

   B. What the responsibilities of the designer are

   C. What the expectations for the end user will be

   D. What the requirements of the course are

9. Annie and Samantha are drawing the flow of a task for their technical class. Each step of the task is defined and drawn to represent one section of the workflow. What term is given to the drawing of the steps to complete the task?

   A. Action items

   B. Work authorization system

   C. Process configuration mapping

   D. Storyboarding

10. Martin wants to create a guide for all language, grammar preferences, and generally accepted practices for the language and tone used for all course documentation. What type of document does Martin want to create?

    A. Guidebook

    B. Writers' manual

    C. Style manual

    D. Standard operating procedure

11. You're teaching a course in a virtual classroom. What area is generally described as the primary portion of the learning interface where slides, illustrations, and demonstrations take place?

    A. Focal point

    B. Platform

    C. Whiteboard

    D. Learning space

12. John is an instructor for his organization, and he's been asked to design and develop a new technical course for his company. When John is preparing to design and develop the course, what's the first step in creating a quality technical class?

    A. Define the schedule for the course.

    B. Define the scope of the course.

    C. Define the delivery channels for the course.

    D. Define the project ground rules.

13. Which one of the following statements best describes how adults learn technical topics?

    A. Adults learn topics from simple to complex.

    B. Adults learn by watching demonstrations.

    C. Adults learn in chunks.

    D. Adults learn through mistakes.

14. Holly is a technical instructor for her organization. She usually teaches technology in the traditional classroom environment, but her manager has asked her to teach a class through a virtual classroom software. The class she is to teach is usually done in the traditional classroom environment, as there are many labs where the participants will install hardware into computers. All of the following are challenges this scenario will present for Holly except for which one?

    A. Logistics of shipping hardware to participants

    B. Timing of the course duration

    C. Communication and direction

    D. Oversight of the technical labs

15. Knowing that adults learn through visuals, what can you do as a virtual instructor to ensure that adults are following along with you as you demonstrate the technology through a virtual classroom environment?

    A. Change your mouse pointer to a larger icon to help learners follow along.

    B. Send the learners screen captures of the demonstration.

    C. Share the software with the learners through the virtual classroom.

    D. Add lots of pictures and clip art to liven up the presentation.

16. What type of artwork can an instructor use to show how a technical concept is applied?

    A. Representational artwork

    B. Organizational artwork

    C. Topographical artwork

    D. Relational graphics

17. Henry is creating a slide deck for a technical class on databases. In his slides he's created a graphic that shows all the different categories of databases and their characteristics. What type of artwork has Henry created?

    A. Representational artwork

    B. Organizational artwork

    C. Topographical artwork

    D. Relational graphics

18. Gina is teaching a technical class for her organization. In her slide deck she has created a graphic to help people remember the ordering of twisted-pair wires in a network cable. What type of graphic has Gina created?

    A. Mnemonic graphic

    B. Representational graphic

    C. Acronym graphic

    D. Relational graphic

19. Which one of the following is a relational graphic?

    A. Drawing of a network

    B. Picture of a network card

    C. Pie chart

    D. Classification of data types

20. Beth has created a slide deck that you are reviewing for her technical class. You notice that on each slide Beth has added some clip art that's not really relevant to the material. What type of art has Beth actually added?

    A. There's not enough information to know.

    B. Extraneous

    C. Decorative

    D. Relative

Questions and Answers

1. You work for an organization that is making a determination to make or buy the classroom materials. You're helping the organization identify the positive aspects of creating the materials in-house. Which one of the following is not a viable positive reason to make the materials rather than buy the materials?

   A. Competent resources

   B. Time available to create the materials

   C. Importance of subject matter

   D. Control of topic inclusion

   C. The importance of the subject matter is the best answer of all presented; if the subject matter is important enough to determine that training should be conducted, then there should be a corresponding importance for the supporting course materials. A, B, and D are incorrect choices, as the presence of competent resources, time, and control of the topic are all valid reasons to create the content in-house.

2. There are several roles needed to create course materials. Which role is best described as the person who will guide and identify the concepts, tasks, and steps needed to complete the learning objectives?

   A. Project manager

   B. Subject matter expert

   C. Writer

   D. Trainer

   B. The subject matter expert is the person who knows the technology to the degree of being able to identify all of the needed steps to complete the learning objectives. Choice A, the project manager, organizes and manages the work for creating the materials. C, the writer, interviews the subject matter expert and then writes the documentation. D, the trainer, actually teaches the course as it's been designed to the best interests of the learners.

3. What term is given to the condition that a new endeavor will likely take longer and cost more because it's never been attempted?

   A. First-time, first-use penalty

   B. Parkinson's Law

   C. Law of Diminishing Returns

   D. Learning curve

A. The best answer is the first-time, first-use penalty. When an endeavor has never been attempted, the first-time, first-use penalty is often enacted, as the endeavor will likely take longer and cost more than has been predicted. B is incorrect, as Parkinson's Law describes the phenomenon that work expands to fill the time allotted to it. C, the Law of Diminishing Returns, is not applicable in this question, as it describes the economical condition that the yield of work remains constant, so additional labor won't exponentially reduce the amount of time needed to complete the work. Because the yield is the same, each unit of resource, that is, labor, will actually produce less than the previously added resource. D, the learning curve, describes the condition that an organization may take a dip in efficiency during the learning of a new technology to later realize an increase in efficiency and productivity.

4. Which one of the following is a perceived concern stakeholders may have about internally developed materials?

   A. Control over the resources is better with a vendor.

   B. The content is better with a vendor.

   C. Control over the content is better with a vendor.

   D. The quality is better with a vendor.

   D. Of all the choices presented stakeholders will most likely associate the quality of the resources to be better with a vendor than with an internally developed course workbook. Choices A and C are incorrect because control over the resources and over the course content is better with internal resources. B is incorrect; better content isn't necessarily true with a vendor, as the content can be identified internally based on needs of the technology users.

5. Your organization has decided to make their course materials internally rather than purchase the materials through a vendor. Your organization has not, however, created materials internally before. Based on this information complete this statement: The longer it takes to develop course materials, the materials will be _____.

   A. Better in quality

   B. Higher in costs

   C. Lower in quality

   D. Likely to fail

   B. Of all the choices this is the best answer because the longer it takes to develop materials, the more resources will be utilized in the production of the materials. A and C are both incorrect because there's no evidence that taking longer to create materials will increase or decrease the quality of the materials. D is incorrect, as the materials aren't likely to fail just based on the production time of the materials.

6. What does the first *D* in ADDIE represent?

   A. Design

   B. Development

   C. Doing

   D. Duration

   A. ADDIE means Analysis, Design, Development, Implementation, and Evaluation and describes the general process of instructional design, delivery, and evaluation of the course, instructor, and behavior of the participants after the course. Choices B, C, and D are incorrect.

7. An organization has determined to create its course materials internally rather than hire a vendor to create the materials. The designer believes the course development and design will take six weeks to create, but reports that the design will most likely take nine weeks to complete in case there are delays or issues in the development. If you subscribe to Parkinson's Law, how long will it take to complete the design and development of this course?

   A. Six weeks

   B. Nine weeks

   C. Ten weeks

   D. Unknown

   B. Parkinson's Law states that work expands to fill the time allotted to it. When the designer allows additional time for errors or mistakes by adding three weeks of "padded time," then development will naturally expand to fill that time. A, C, and D are incorrect because these do not support the details of Parkinson's Law.

8. Ben is an instructional designer for his company. Management has demanded that quality be met in all course designs. To achieve quality what must first be defined?

   A. What quality is

   B. What the responsibilities of the designer are

   C. What the expectations for the end user will be

   D. What the requirements of the course are

   D. To achieve quality, Ben must know exactly what the course is to deliver. If Ben doesn't understand the scope of the work, or the scope of the work has not been completely defined, then the quality of the work is likely to suffer because expectations have not been set. Answer A is needed to some extent, as the definition of quality should be defined within the standard operating procedures for the organization, but this answer doesn't satisfy the question as completely as knowing what the requirements for the course are. B is incorrect; Ben's responsibilities don't necessarily affect quality, as he needs to satisfy the scope of the course development requirements. C is incorrect, as the expectations of the end user will be set and delivered by the needs analysis for the course design, not by the content and quality of the course workbook and materials.

9. Annie and Samantha are drawing the flow of a task for their technical class. Each step of the task is defined and drawn to represent one section of the workflow. What term is given to the drawing of the steps to complete the task?

   A. Action items

   B. Work authorization system

   C. Process configuration mapping

   D. Storyboarding

   D. This is an example of storyboarding, as Annie and Samantha are drawing the flow of the tasks as if they were drawing a story. Action items, choice A, is not a valid answer for this question. B, a work authorization system, is not applicable to this scenario, as a work authorization system determines how work is authorized to continue. C is not the best choice, as process configuration mapping describes the illustration of a process or procedure within a system, not the flow of activities to complete a task.

10. Martin wants to create a guide for all language, grammar preferences, and generally accepted practices for the language and tone used for all course documentation. What type of document does Martin want to create?

    A. Guidebook

    B. Writers' manual

    C. Style manual

    D. Standard operating procedure

    C. Martin wants to create a style manual for his organization. A style manual defines the style, that is, the tone and voice, of the course materials. Choice A, a guidebook, doesn't answer the question, as "guidebook" is common terminology for course design and development. B, a writers' manual, is tempting, but not the preferred language. D, a standard operating procedure, isn't the best choice, as this answer describes the practices for completing a procedure, such as printing or binding the documents.

11. You're teaching a course in a virtual classroom. What area is generally described as the primary portion of the learning interface where slides, illustrations, and demonstrations take place?

    A. Focal point

    B. Platform

    C. Whiteboard

    D. Learning space

    C. A whiteboard is the portion of the learning environment where your slides appear, where you can share multimedia files, and where you can draw figures and illustrations on-the-fly. Choices A, B, and D do not describe the teaching interface for the virtual classroom environment.

12. John is an instructor for his organization, and he's been asked to design and develop a new technical course for his company. When John is preparing to design and develop the course, what's the first step in creating a quality technical class?

    A. Define the schedule for the course.

    B. Define the scope of the course.

    C. Define the delivery channels for the course.

    D. Define the project ground rules.

    B. John first needs to define the scope of the course. The scope defines what will and will not be in the course. Knowing the scope helps define the delivery date, costs, expectations, and boundaries for the course deliverables. A is incorrect, as the project scope can help determine the schedule for the course. C is incorrect, as the delivery channels, such as instructor-led or virtual classroom, are actually part of the project scope. D is incorrect, as the project ground rules are important, but they are the most essential element of the quality concerns for the class.

13. Which one of the following statements best describes how adults learn technical topics?

    A. Adults learn topics from simple to complex.

    B. Adults learn by watching demonstrations.

    C. Adults learn in chunks.

    D. Adults learn through mistakes.

    C. Of all the choices C is the best answer, as adults learn in chunks. Answer A is incorrect because not all topics that adults learn could be considered simple. B isn't the best choice because adults learn through many different avenues, not just through demonstrations. Even in demonstrations, however, adults still learn in chunks; an instructor would not demonstrate the entire software, but would create segments of learning for the adults. D is incorrect, as trial and error is a good way to learn, but not all adults learn through their mistakes.

14. Holly is a technical instructor for her organization. She usually teaches technology in the traditional classroom environment, but her manager has asked her to teach a class through a virtual classroom software. The class she is to teach is usually done in the traditional classroom environment, as there are many labs where the participants will install hardware into computers. All of the following are challenges this scenario will present for Holly except for which one?

   A. Logistics of shipping hardware to participants

   B. Timing of the course duration

   C. Communication and direction

   D. Oversight of the technical labs

   B. Of all the choices the timing of the course duration should not be affected by the virtual training environment. Choices A, C, and D are incorrect answers, as Holly may experience challenges with the hardware, communication and direction, and oversight of the technical labs.

15. Knowing that adults learn through visuals, what can you do as a virtual instructor to ensure that adults are following along with you as you demonstrate the technology through a virtual classroom environment?

   A. Change your mouse pointer to a larger icon to help learners follow along.

   B. Send the learners screen captures of the demonstration.

   C. Share the software with the learners through the virtual classroom.

   D. Add lots of pictures and clip art to liven up the presentation.

   A. In a software demonstration the instructor should change the mouse pointer to a larger icon to help learners follow along. B is incorrect; screen captures might be helpful in step-by-step directions, but it's probably too confusing to follow the screen captures and the demonstration in the classroom. C is incorrect; sharing the software is a good idea so learners can interact and learn by doing, but it doesn't support the demonstration and visual method of learning. D is incorrect; adding lots of clip art and pictures can actually be a detriment to learning if the artwork doesn't support the lecture. In addition, the question asked about how the instructor could support the visual approach to learning during classroom demonstrations.

16. What type of artwork can an instructor use to show how a technical concept is applied?

   A. Representational artwork

   B. Organizational artwork

   C. Topographical artwork

   D. Relational graphics

   A. Representational artwork shows how a technical concept is applied, such as how networks function, how databases store data, or how computer hard disks work. B is incorrect, as organizational artwork organizes components, such as categories of hardware, software, networking, and data. C is incorrect, as there's not a classification of instructional artwork called topographical artwork. D is incorrect, as relational artwork is illustrated in pie charts, bar charts, and other data graphics.

17. Henry is creating a slide deck for a technical class on databases. In his slides he's created a graphic that shows all the different categories of databases and their characteristics. What type of artwork has Henry created?

   A. Representational artwork

   B. Organizational artwork

   C. Topographical artwork

   D. Relational graphics

   B. This is an example of organizational artwork, as Henry has organized the types of databases and characteristics. A is incorrect, as representational artwork shows how technical concepts work. C is incorrect, as there's not a classification of artwork called topographical. D is incorrect, as relational graphics are elements like pie charts and bar charts.

18. Gina is teaching a technical class for her organization. In her slide deck she has created a graphic to help people remember the ordering of twisted-pair wires in a network cable. What type of graphic has Gina created?

   A. Mnemonic graphic

   B. Representational graphic

   C. Acronym graphic

   D. Relational graphic

   A. This is an example of a mnemonic graphic, as it helps people remember the ordering of networking wiring. Mnemonic graphics use a phrase or form a word to represent a concept. B is incorrect; representational graphics show how a concept is actually applied. C is incorrect; there's not a visual called "acronym graphics" in technology training. D is incorrect, as relational graphics are pie charts, bar charts, and categorization of data.

19. Which one of the following is a relational graphic?

    A. Drawing of a network

    B. Picture of a network card

    C. Pie chart

    D. Classification of data types

    C. A relational graphic is best described as a visual that shows distribution of data, such as a pie chart. A and B are incorrect, as these are examples of a representational graphic. D is incorrect, as classification of data types is actually an organizational graphic.

20. Beth has created a slide deck that you are reviewing for her technical class. You notice that on each slide Beth has added some clip art that's not really relevant to the material. What type of art has Beth actually added?

    A. There's not enough information to know.

    B. Extraneous

    C. Decorative

    D. Relative

    C. This is an example of decorative art. Decorative art, as in this example, is placed in the presentation as decoration, not to support the message of the slide. Decorative art doesn't contribute to the message of the presentation and can be a distraction. A is incorrect; there is enough information to know based on the scenario presented. B is incorrect; while the art may be described as "extraneous," this isn't a valid term for artwork in the learning domain. Answer D is incorrect, as "relative" isn't a term used to describe artwork in the learning domain.

PART III

Establishing Instructor Credibility and Maintaining Communications

■ **Chapter 6**   Instructing with Confidence
■ **Chapter 7**   Leading a Successful Class

Instructing with Confidence

In this chapter you will:
- Understand training fundamentals
- Learn how to act as a professional trainer
- Manage classroom participants
- Prepare for an excellent training session
- Maintain the learning environment
- Link the learning to the participants' lives

You may be a great technical trainer, you may be launching your training career, or you might be somewhere between the two—but all trainers can learn how to be better presenters. Excellent trainers have a certain essence that sets them apart from other speakers and educators—they have what actors call a *stage presence*. Something magical happens when the trainer steps in front of an audience: participants feel welcome, engaged, interested. The speaker's body language, energy, and voice all subtly communicate confidence, knowledge, and comfort in the training topic.

The level of confidence a trainer feels, or at least projects, can be based on years of experience, trial and error through teaching, self-study, education, and emulation of other successful trainers. What isn't always so apparent, however, is that the trainer may have a stomach of butterflies, be sweating bullets, and be focusing intently on each word, phrase, and topic. Excellent speakers aren't always what they appear—excellent speakers are sometimes actors looking to grow into genuine comfort in front of an audience. In either case, the participants' perception is that the instructor is a professional, and the instructor's image helps the learners have more confidence in what's about to be taught.

In your career as a trainer you'll need to find and develop your teaching style—the rhythm, language, and diction you use in your vocal delivery, how you stand before your audience, and how you present the course material. Think back on some of your favorite speakers; each probably had their own approach to teaching. Some speakers walk through the room and engage learners individually, while others may be stationary and engage learners through eye contact, depth of knowledge, and no-nonsense lecture. Other trainers may be funny, have real-world anecdotes to share, and ask questions to get people involved in the classroom. While all of these teaching styles are different, probably all of your favorite presenters have a common trait in their approach to teaching: confidence.

When an instructor has confidence in their topic, in their ability to teach, and in themselves as a trainer, the participants can feel this energy. When the trainer lacks confidence, or at least the ability to act confidently, participants can sense this unease, and their attitude toward the trainer can diminish. To appear confident, you can do several things beyond just being familiar with the course content. In this chapter you'll learn some characteristics that separate the good trainers from the great trainers. You'll explore the fundamentals of training that will immediately affect the success rate of your training endeavors.

Establishing Instructor Fundamentals

Here's a secret: no one wants to go to a technical training session if it's going to be boring, painful to sit through, and led by an instructor who's stammering. In other words, the people in the classroom want you to be exciting, energetic, and full of wisdom to impart. The people in the classroom want you, the expert trainer, to teach a great class. The participants want you to be successful. When people enroll in a class, they're hopeful that the class will help them achieve some specific goal: do their job better, learn a skill, or advance their career. They're counting on you to help them reach that goal.

Your first step to becoming a great trainer is to know and accept that the people in the class are on your side. So many trainers I've met and coached have a false belief that the people in the room are against the trainer—not true! The people in the room are your allies, cheering for you to do well, because if you don't, it's an awful time for them. Use this energy to advantage by embracing the positive energy the audience gives you before the class begins. That's right, you don't project confidence and excitement only when the class starts, but in all the prep work leading up to the first words in your presentation.

The basic element of great technical training is, of course, preparation. You must be versed in the subject matter, or you won't have the mental assurance to speak on the topic with confidence. I know; I've made the mistake of believing I could fake my way through a class with my good looks and quick smile. Wrong. Excellent training is about the technical topic, not the technical trainer. So you've heard that speech often enough— know your topic in order to teach your topic. Nothing new there. What may be new to you, however, is that how you know your topic affects how you teach it. You need to examine the topic from your participants' point of view. Understanding how the participants will apply the information can direct how you teach.

The fundamentals of training, and really it's the mechanics of public speaking, all begin with knowing your topic—and then knowing your audience. You'd probably present your topic differently if you were speaking at a funeral versus a comedy club. The same is true in the classroom. How you speak should be appropriate for the audience and their goals. Public speaking has some basic rules you should adopt not only for your CTT+ examination, but for your success in the classroom.

Preparing to Train

You're probably an expert in the topics you teach; that's why you're the go-to trainer (or soon will be). Still, technology changes so rapidly that you constantly have to be preparing, learning, and researching the subtle changes that hot fixes, upgrades, and service packs bring to your technical prowess. As part of preparing to teach a technical class, you'll need to confirm any changes to the technology that may affect what you're used to seeing. You don't want to get before your audience and be surprised when buttons, commands, and features have been moved or updated. In technical classes you must always confirm that the software and hardware the participants have will match what you'll be teaching from.

While you may be an expert in the technology you're teaching, you can bet that the person configuring the classroom environment for you may not be. Technical classes that require the classroom to be configured a particular way for labs and demonstrations must also be checked before class begins. You can imagine the horrors of teaching a networking class, for example, where routers, switches, and servers are to emulate a WAN environment and discovering the room hasn't been configured properly. I've had the pain of assuming the room was properly configured—even with a script and step-by-step instructions—only to learn early in the class that my assumption was false. It's embarrassing and classroom configuration problems cause big delays in your teaching time. It's imperative if your class depends on a proper configuration, that you confirm the preparation.

Create a checklist that will prove the room is configured correctly so you can quickly confirm preparations before class begins. Ideally the classroom is configured well in advance of your training start time, but when classroom space is a scarce commodity and you may be travelling to the training site, that's not often a reality. Communication is your mitigation approach if you can't have physical access to the training room before your event begins. Stress the importance of having a properly configured room—and find out the soonest you'll have access to the classroom. You must confirm the technology is configured properly, and arrive early enough to rectify any problems before participants start arriving. You don't want to be frantically running from PC to PC correcting problems as students arrive and want to chat with you over coffee and donuts.

 NOTE When you do find a messy scenario in the classroom and you need to fix the problem, use the classroom projector to help. Create a message explaining what's happening and what you're doing. This way you can concentrate on fixing the problem and not be interrupted (as frequently) by students who are curious why you're ignoring them.

Knowing your audience is important for a technical trainer. You need to know who'll be attending the class, what their goals are from the class, and, if possible, what their experience level with the technology is. If your class uses an assessment exam as part of the course prerequisites, this information can offer some insight about the course participants. You might need to speak with your supervisor or, if working as a vendor, your client, to gain some insight into the people in the classroom. This can help you tailor your presentation, anticipate concerns, and identify participants who are more advanced or need some remedial work. By understanding who your audience is, you can teach with more confidence that you're meeting the learners' needs.

Another part of preparing to train is your personal grooming and dress. Always dress appropriately for the learning environment. In some organizations this means men wear suits and ties and women wear business suits. In other organizations you may wear a standard training shirt with your company's logo emblazoned on it. Clothes should fit well, look pressed, and have a clean, attractive look. In other words, don't dig your old bowling shirt out of the bottom of the closet for your class. Wrinkles, missing buttons, and stains all communicate that you aren't professional. Shoes should always be neat, polished, and free of mud and dust; seriously, polish your shoes and replace the shoelaces when they break rather than tie them back together.

Commonsense grooming is needed for men and women. Invest a few dollars in a fingernail scrub and a manicure set. If you wear fingernail polish, fill in any chips and choose a professional color. People will look at your hands when you teach and point to objects on the overhead and in the software. When your fingernails are jagged, dirty, and unkempt, you're giving the wrong message to your participants. I believe having clean, trimmed fingernails communicates, even subconsciously, that you pay attention to the details. Before you go to speak, always check your breath and teeth to make certain remnants of the breakfast or lunch aren't evident. If you're wearing pants, do a zipper check in the restroom and have a quick glance at your nostrils in the mirror. I know, it sounds silly, but it's best to create a ritual of the basic hygiene to avoid an embarrassing situation in front of your class.

The final act of preparation is the mental mindset. You need to ease your anxieties and relax before you present. You don't want to be gasping for breath and sweating like you've just finished a marathon. Knowing that you're prepared to teach and reminding yourself that you're an expert in the technology will help alleviate many fears, but here are some tried approaches to managing stage fright:

- **Know your space.** Once your room is configured, walk through all of the pathways in the room. Walk around the perimeter of the classroom, walk down the central aisle, or wander through each row of desks. As you move about the room get comfortable with the idea that you own this space and you're free to move through it. Gain familiarity with your work environment.

- **Visualize a great class.** Just as golfers do before they take their shot, visualize a successful outcome of what you're about to do. By imagining yourself teaching a great class you're mentally preparing yourself for a successful time with your participants. I like to visualize lots of energy, happy people in the classroom, and class flowing without a problem or delay. While this doesn't always work for me, I find that I'm usually able to teach with a calmer, happier disposition than when I don't visualize a great class.

- **You're the expert.** All of these people came to hear you speak, and they know you're the expert in the technology you're about to teach them. Embrace their confidence and remind yourself how the participants want you to lead a fantastic class. You're steeped in experience, know how the class is going to progress, and can teach others what you already know.

- **Take some deep breaths.** If you're really anxious about teaching, get away from the classroom, and find a place where you take 10 to 20 deep-belly breaths. Breathe in deeply and slowly exhale all the air. As you do these repetitions of breathing go ahead and visualize the successful class you're about to teach.

- **Stretch your body.** Another relaxation technique I rely on is to stretch before I present. I put my hands on my hips and roll my torso by dipping forward, to my right, backwards, and then to my left. I'm a runner, so often I will go ahead and do some simple stretches for my back and legs—this helps me relax and takes my mind off of the classroom.

If after all of your preparations and relaxation techniques you're still full of fright, you're not alone. Mark Twain said, "There are two types of speakers: those that are nervous and those that are liars." It's common to have some nervous feelings before you present. To be a successful technical trainer, you don't have to be the world's greatest orator, but understanding the basics of public speaking can differentiate you from other trainers. Experience, maturity in the profession, and confidence in knowing what you're about to deliver all contribute to great classes.

NOTE   One avenue to get more time presenting is through Toastmasters International—a great organization to help people become better public speakers. You can find them online at www.toastmasters.org.

Maintaining a Positive Learning Environment

Preparing for a successful technical class is essential, but it's also important to maintain the positive energy and dynamics of a class as you teach. It won't help the learners if your preparations and pre-class exercises go well, only to have the class fall apart. Maintaining a positive learning environment is really about managing the classroom and the participants. Your goal for classroom management should always be to maintain a positive, learner-centric training environment. To this end, technical trainers must guard against remarks that may be interpreted as bias and inappropriate for the classroom. This means you don't comment or joke about sexual topics, race, religion, culture, and age.

You are the leader of the class, so you'll have to lead. Most participants in the class will assume that you're in charge of the class flow, so you should take that assumption to heart. Participants will look to you to define the lecture, timings, and dictate when events like breaks, exercises, and conversations may happen. If things in the classroom get rowdy, errors happen, or people are having too much social time, you must step in and take charge of the situation. Of course this means in a friendly, yet authoritative tone.

Because the participants will look to you for guidance, communicate any news that affects the learners. People want to know when class will start (if you're teaching multiple days to the same group of people), when you'll break for lunch, what time they'll be dismissed, and any other timing for the course. Adult learners want to know what's going to happen—they can then focus on the course content and not wonder when they'll be done for the day. I always like to write the schedule of events on the whiteboard, including the modules and topics I'll be teaching for the day, and then wipe off each topic or break as it's been completed.

PART III

People feel tethered to their phones, laptops, and other gadgets. These gadgets, like toy races in second grade, detract from learning. Participants might not like this, but I always ask them to turn their phones off when I teach. Invariably someone won't and their phone will ring in the middle of an intense lab with some obnoxious ringtone. Texting and e-mails are detriments to learning in tough, technical classes where hands-on activities and in-depth lectures demand focused attention. You'll need to take charge and make the request for phones to be turned off, put away, and referenced only on breaks.

Another detractor from learning are questions that just aren't related to what you're discussing. While I generally believe questions are a sign that participants are thinking about what you're saying, you'll need to manage questions that aren't related to the learning objectives for the course. Queries that aren't relevant take away time from topics that are essential for the course objectives. Some questions you might be able to answer quickly and move on, but as a general rule you'll need to take questions that aren't part of the current course and move them to a question parking lot. A *question parking lot* is where you'll document questions that don't fit in the confines of the current course, but you'll answer them after class. It's also appropriate to put questions you don't know the answer to in your parking lot. Tell the learner that you don't know the answer, but that you'll find it out. Then you can move on with your class and find an answer later. Putting the question in public view ensures that you'll find out for the participant—and it helps you to remember your obligation of finding the answer.

 VIDEO See the video *Managing Questions in a Time-Constrained Class.*

Maintaining a positive learner environment means that you take charge of the room and control any element that is a distraction from the learning experience. This can mean an ongoing management of the technology that's being utilized in the classroom, asking people in the hallway outside your class to be quiet, or keeping learners on task rather than chitchatting with one another. As the leader in the classroom you'll need to be involved and ready to assist learners. Some trainers like to assign learners an exercise and then leave the classroom—not usually a good idea. You should be available throughout the labs, walk around the room and check in with learners, and watch the learners in case they're stumped or have a question. Being available even though you may not be needed can help learners' confidence in the labs because they realize they can experiment with the technology, and you'll be there to help them in case there's a problem.

Managing Learners in the Classroom

It's easy to manage things like computers, overhead projectors, and classroom configurations—managing learners, however, can be a tough task. Most people when they come to a technical class are there to learn and want to have an enjoyable time doing it. Some people, however, come to class with ulterior motives, disruptive personalities or emotional drama, or they see class time as paid time off. Not only can these learners make the instructor's day miserable, but they also can interrupt and hinder other people in the class from learning. These troublesome participants have to be managed, corralled, or, in some horrible instances, dismissed from the class to keep the learning moving forward.

Other learners who have to be managed may have a fine personality, but they're not keeping pace with the instructor. Often these learners don't have the technical background to grasp what the instructor is teaching. When an individual enrolls in a class and they don't meet the prerequisites for the course, they're likely to have difficulty achieving the learning objectives—and they can slow other people's learning. The other end of the pace spectrum must be examined too—when learners are zooming far ahead of the instructor. These learners may already have the technical competence, but their quick completion of exercises, fast answers, and desire to show their smarts can also affect other learners.

Managing the learners in the classroom isn't just about dealing with difficult people. It's also the process of the instructor getting people involved in the class. When people are shy, have inhibitions about asking questions, or want to hide in the back and surf the Web, the instructor must step in to get these people involved without causing embarrassment. Managing the learners means that you're consistently checking in with the learners, observing their behavior during lecture and labs, and looking for clues as to what excites and motivates the learner.

Involving Learners in the Training

Training a technical class is more effective, and frankly more enjoyable for the instructor, when learners are engaged in the learning. You want people to ask questions, add comments, and to hear their oohs and ahhs when they learn something they can apply in their lives. What's really boring, and really scary, is when your audience looks at you without any feedback. Imagine a room full of learners staring at you like an oil painting. It's a tough day when no joke, no technical war story, no software Easter egg excites your learners.

You can begin to engage your learners before class even starts by sending them e-mails defining the course overview and expectations or by welcoming the learners to the class as they enter your training room. I like to work the room by introducing myself, asking a few questions of each person I meet, and introducing learners to one another. This approach, I believe, takes down an imaginary wall between the learner and the instructor. I've been to many classes, and I bet you have too, where the instructor doesn't mingle with the learners, but treats them almost with disdain. The reality is probably the instructor is more focused on teaching the topic than thinking about engaging the audience, but the perception can make a bad impression on the participants.

Nonverbal communications from the instructor to the learners can help get people involved. Nodding your head, not speaking when other people are talking, posture, and even body movement can encourage people to say more or stop their conversation. Eye contact is one of your best tools to create rapport and show that you're paying attention to the learner. Even if you've heard the question a hundred times, don't cut off the learner, but make eye contact, nod your head in agreement, and let the learner speak. Letting the learner speak shows respect, but it also keeps the learner engaged and contributing to the class.

If you had to pick one nonverbal quality to use for the rest of your training days, it would be to simply smile. When you smile as an instructor, no matter the circumstance, it shows your confident control of the problem, and how you're competent and can deal with the issue. Smiling with your face—not just your mouth—shows the group you're involved, relaxed, and happy to be there. Learners often emulate what the

PART III

instructor does—if you panic, are bored, or are longingly looking outside, so too will the learners.

You can also manage your learners through verbal communications that build encouragement and get them involved in the class. When learners make statements and ask questions, these are opportunities for you to get other learners involved and to make the learners feel that their participation is welcome. Try phrases like these to encourage participation in classroom conversations:

- Good thought. Let's explore that in more detail.
- Tell me more about...
- I'm glad you brought that up because...
- Who else would like to add a comment on this...
- Excellent question. Let's see what happens if...

As a general rule you want to avoid "why" questions when you're trying to encourage participation. Why questions can be good when you've built rapport and you're testing your audience, but often why questions can seem argumentative and put people on the defense. Open-ended questions are good methods to encourage participation, but when you just want quick answers, close-ended questions help people participate without feeling obligated to discuss things in detail in front of peers and strangers. For example, rather than asking why is one database server better than the other, you might ask what are some characteristics of one specific database server and then compare and contrast them with the other technology. This phrasing is an open-ended question and lets the class discover the learning rather than defend an opinion.

While you, the technical trainer, ask questions to get people involved and to test comprehension, people in your classes ask questions for lots of different reasons:

- **I want to know more.** This is what I think of first when people ask me a question in a technical class—and you probably do too. Questions are a great sign that people are interested in the topic and listening to what I have to say. The context of the question, however, may be a clue that I didn't explain a topic very well or that people misunderstood what I was trying to convey. It's important to not only answer the question, but also to mentally examine why the question was asked. If it's apparent there's a misunderstanding, you'll need to pause, ask some follow-up questions to understand why the question is asked, and then explain the answer. Never be embarrassed to correct yourself in class—that's a sign of a professional. Your job is to send these learners out with the best information possible, so if you've misspoken, correct the problem and move forward.

- **Look at me, I'm smart.** Some folks like to ask questions so they can show you, their peers, and perhaps managers in the classroom how brilliant they are. These folks see questions as an opportunity to show others how insightful they are, how they're ready to move up in the organization, and how they've mastered the technology beyond anyone else in the room. This can be irritating for the instructor, especially when it happens over and over from the same person, but the best response is to answer questions with tact. If the question isn't relevant, swiftly move the question to the question parking lot and promise to get to that topic if there's time or after class. And then move right along with your teaching.

- **I gotcha.** A tiny fraction of learners will enjoy trying to embarrass the trainer with gotcha questions. They aren't interested in knowing the technology, but would rather make the instructor look bad by announcing an error or misperception, or they just want to make the instructor squirm for their satisfaction. While every scenario is different, as soon as I recognize the person is being smarmy and sardonic I'll give them a genuine smile, laugh a little, and either answer their question or put the question in the question parking lot. Sometimes it's best to just be direct and tell the person that you're not going to debate the merits of a decision or technology, but focus only on how to properly use the technology that's been selected.

NOTE I must admit this is my least favorite type of question asker. When these people pipe up, over and over, they distract from the learning. You can often see the exasperation on the other participants when the gotcha questions start. If the ill-mannered questions persist, I'll catch the person one-on-one and ask them if everything's okay in the class. If they respond positively, I'll gently acknowledge the nature of their questions and ask if we can discuss these types of questions directly rather than distract and confuse the other learners. That often ends the misery.

- **Delay, delay, delay.** Some people don't want to get back to work or on with the class, or like to play "stump the trainer" with weird questions. These folks ask long-winded, rambling questions or test your patience by asking you to repeat things or to show them a different approach, or by asking some other goofy question. It may take some time to see if their questions are genuine or are genuine attempts to eat up time and delay the end of the class. To manage these folks, you can quickly summarize answers, move questions to the question parking lot, and simply let them know their question isn't relevant to the course material.

In most cases you want people to ask questions when they're sincere. Depending on the class time constraints and your teaching style, how you handle questions may vary. Some instructors like the class to move forward like a conversation where people can interject thoughts and questions on every topic. Other instructors prefer questions to happen at the end of a section of slides or when prompted. There's really not a right or wrong approach, as each class, schedule, participant, and instructor preference differs. What must happen in each class, however, is that the instructor should explain to participants how questions will be managed in the classroom so everyone knows what to expect.

When a question is proffered, the instructor should first repeat and often rephrase the question to ensure she understands what's been asked. This saves time by not answering a misunderstood question, and it gives the individual who asked the question an opportunity to correct any misunderstandings. This process also makes certain that everyone in the group has heard the question, as they may have a similar question to ask. When you rephrase a question for clarity, don't be in a hurry to blurt out the answer; pause and ponder for a couple of seconds to make certain you understand the context and meaning of the question.

Of course you'll treat the participants with respect. Don't belittle people based on the questions they've asked, as this only makes you look foolish, demeans the individual, and will hamper the group participation. One of the worst questions you can ask a participant is, "Did that answer your question?" It seems like a good follow-up, and you may be sincere in your query, but think how it can make the learner feel. What if your answer didn't answer their question? Now the learner has to say no, maybe make you look bad, or appear foolish in front of others because they didn't understand what you were explaining to them. Instead instructors should ask, "Would you like me to go into more detail on this?" Or "Do you have other questions we can explore on this topic?" These types of questions allow the learner to tell you if they want clarifications or if they're okay with what you've offered.

When you ask for questions or feedback, make certain you're involving the whole room. I like to visually scan the room clockwise to make certain I've not missed anyone with questions or comments—and this ensures that I'm not favoring one side of the room over the other. It can also help to move to different parts of the room so people don't feel self-conscious about speaking up in front of the group.

Finally, be honest. Some questions that are likely to come up in class you won't know the answer to. You can't lie or fudge your way through these questions. Tell the participant that you don't know, but you'll find out. When you make a promise to find out, do your research and find out for the participant. If you fail to find an answer for the participant during class hours, follow up with the answer via a phone call or e-mail. Not only is this part of the instructor's job, but it's a good characteristic to keep your word. This builds your reputation as a trainer, and now you're armed with new information should the same question be asked again.

Dealing with Learner Behavior

If you believe in Pareto's Law, the 80/20 Rule, you'll see that about 80 percent of the class participants are easy to manage and work with. Technically, Pareto's Law states that 80 percent of the effects come from just 20 percent of the causes. The 20 percent of the learners are the causes you'll have to manage. These are the people with intermittent issues, disruptions, or a failure to participate in the learning. In my experience as a technical trainer, I'd say more than 80 percent of the people that come to class are adults, are capable of working well with others, and are polite to me and their peers. I can report a sliver of folks that are rude, mean-spirited, and don't want to be in the class. Some participants are friendly, but friendly to the point of being chatty, silly, and disruptive in the class.

The goal of the technical trainer is to help the participants learn the course objectives so they can apply the knowledge in their employment and lives. The technical trainer is not, by definition, a counselor, a life coach, or a mediator—though these are often characteristics that a trainer needs in order to manage, control, and facilitate a class with people that are causing problems. When people are rude and disruptive in class, I've always considered that it's not personal to me, but rather they have some issues and stress in their lives beyond the classroom. While I can't solve problems, I can address their behavior and keep their disruption of the other participants to a minimum.

 NOTE An anecdotal observation that I've shared with other trainers for years is there's always at least one learner in the class who just can't get with the program. The degree of the problems this one person presents varies from class to class, but invariably you'll find at least one person who doesn't fall into the same groove of the class like the rest of the participants. As soon as I recognize this participant I start taking actions to mitigate their behavior.

Some of the biggest disruptions in today's technical classes are learners who lecture in their comments and questions. You've probably experienced this scenario: open the floor for discussion, and the participant takes the opportunity, every opportunity, to drone on about the technology, the company that makes the technology, and why the technology won't work in their environment. And then when others enter the conversation, this same person adds their counterpoints. It's exhausting for the trainer and for other people in the room. What often ends up happening is that the other participants don't contribute anything because they don't want to hear the inevitable lecture.

To combat these verbose learners, the instructor needs to make certain other participants are given a chance to contribute. You may need to wait for a pause in the person's lecture and to step in and ask if other people have anything to add. Another approach is to establish a ground rule for the class that everyone should contribute before any one person contributes twice. If the individual doesn't take the hint, it's not inappropriate to speak with the individual on a break. In your conversation you'll acknowledge that you appreciate their input, but they aren't giving other learners a chance to participate. You cannot allow one person to railroad conversations and manipulate the class time.

Some learners consider class time a social time. These people visit and chitchat with their friends and colleagues in the room. Their idle chatter can be disruptive to other learners and to the instructor as she tries to teach. As always, the instructor must not aim to embarrass these learners, but needs to put a stop to the disruption. First, the instructor can tell the group as a whole to please keep side conversation to breaks, as the extra noise can be distracting to others in the room. If this doesn't squelch the problem, then the instructor can address this issue directly when the chatter continues by saying something to the effect of "I'm sorry, John. What was your comment?" This will catch John's attention, and he'll usually get the hint.

PART III

Another approach is to just stop talking and watch the people who are chatting. Wait until they're done talking, and then they'll realize you've paused for them. Chatters will usually catch on to your acknowledgment, apologize, and then you can continue with the class. In the worst-case scenario you may need to speak directly to the person about their disruptions. Catch the person on a break and ask if everything is okay. It's possible there's a technical issue they need your help with, but more than likely it's just social time with a friend. Then politely ask the person to keep their ad hoc conversations for breaks, as they're disrupting other learners.

Some learners see the classroom as their personal group therapy, and they'll bring up work and personal issues that aren't relevant to the learning objectives. This is especially true when you're teaching a group of people from the same company. In this environment the learner feels that the class time is an opportunity to commiserate about issues within the organization rather than to focus on the learning materials. When this situation happens, the instructor must not acknowledge the issue, but rather bring the conversation back to the learning objectives. This can usually be done by politely saying, "I'm sorry, but I'm not following how that concern is relevant to our class topic?"

Some participants don't want to be in the class for any number of reasons. The participant may feel that they're above and beyond the technology you're teaching, don't see the value in the training, or they don't like learning in the classroom environment. You might also encounter learners who are in class simply because their manager told them to go. While these participants may not be a strong disruption to the class, they have the potential to distract the other learners. You should try to assess why they're withdrawn from the class participation, and then address the issue by linking the content to their roles and lives. You might do this by asking the person questions about the material, having them do a demonstration for the class, or by setting up lab partners to get everyone involved.

Finally, the worst type of participant is the brute. This person is rude, obnoxious, and can attack you and the learners in the classroom. This person, I've gathered, is this way all the time—not just in your class. You cannot take it personally; just assume that this person has issues and problems that are beyond classroom management. Always be calm, polite, but firm and direct. Don't respond to their attacks; answer their questions or address their concerns, but don't return the hostility. When responding, first recognize the behavior, pause for a moment, and then address the concern. Sometimes the pause may be enough for the person to recognize their behavior and they'll apologize.

If the boorish behavior continues, you must tell the individual in clear terms that they are welcome to contribute to the class discussion and ask questions, but they cannot attack you or other people in the room. If the attacks continue, speak to the person one-on-one, again without returning the hostility, and ask if you've offended the person or if they're upset with something you've said in the class. Likely you've not, but you're giving the person an opportunity to rectify their behavior. In the worst-case scenario you may need to ask the individual to leave the class due to their disruptions. Depending on the organization, you may need to immediately bring in a supervisor or your learning manager to address the problem with the individual.

NOTE I've been teaching technical topics in the corporate world and in universities since 1993. In all this time I have encountered only three memorable incidents of completely abrasive behavior. Of the three, I've only asked one person to leave the classroom. My point isn't to share my track record, but to acknowledge that most people come to class with a desire to learn, not to be mean.

Managing student behavior can be a challenging part of the trainer's job. The instructor wants to teach a group of happy, willing, and interested people, not babysit. Unfortunately, you will have to manage how people behave in the classroom, as what one person does affects the other people's ability to learn. Always be polite, never embarrass the individual, and quickly deal with problems and issues to keep the class moving forward. Your job is to achieve the learning objectives, and disruptive behavior is a hindrance to that goal.

Chapter Summary

Training with confidence means that the instructor already possesses confidence. Good trainers can lead a class through the objectives, present the material, and answer questions about the technology. A great technical trainer, however, can get people excited to be in the class, create synergy among the participants, and transfer the knowledge needed for people to accurately apply the technology in their jobs and lives. Successful technical training begins with the trainer fully preparing for the class and understanding the subject matter. Great technical trainers prepare themselves, the participants, and the classroom for a successful training event.

Technical trainers should look professional in their dress and appearance. The first impression an instructor makes on a learner is often based on how the instructor appears for the class. Sloppy, wrinkled clothes; dirty shoes; and ties with gravy stains all send the wrong messages to the participants. The instructor should always dress for the audience and project professionalism in the classroom. You do not want your wardrobe or appearance to be a distraction from the learning processes, so always give yourself a once-over look in the mirror.

No matter how much the instructor knows the material and is prepared to teach the technical class, he must consider the technical configuration of the classroom. Arrive early to ensure that the classroom is configured properly so that your class operates smoothly and as planned. Arriving early at the training center can also give you a chance to physically and mentally prepare for the training. You'll do some stretches, some breathing exercises, and find a moment to gather your thoughts and steel your nerves before the training begins.

Once the class begins, you'll deliver the technical training, but you'll also be managing the learners in the class. While most people come to a technical class with the intent of learning and participating, some learners have other objectives. You'll need to recognize learner behaviors and address how the learners may be affecting other people in the room. Unrelated questions, side conversations, and mobile phones can all distract people from your teaching. You'll have to address these issues in a polite, but firm, conversation to remind participants why they're in the class. While you want people to enjoy the class, you may need to remind them that the focus of the class is on learning.

Key Terms

classroom checklist A checklist of the required technical configurations of a classroom to confirm that a technical class has been properly prepared so that the technical training may begin.

nonverbal communication The body language, eye contact, posture, and gestures that affect the verbal communication and messages sent between people. Fifty-five percent of all communication is nonverbal.

Pareto's Law Eighty percent of the effects come from just 20 percent of the causes. In technical training this is relevant to participant management, as you'll discover 80 percent of the classroom disruptions come from just 20 percent of the participants.

public speaking The act of an individual standing before a group of peers, colleagues, and strangers, and speaking on a concept.

question parking lot A section of the classroom whiteboard or flipchart that's dedicated for questions that aren't necessarily relevant to the class topic, but the instructor will answer later in the course or after the class.

stage fright The dread and anxiety a person feels before and during public speaking; stage fright can hinder the technical trainer from delivering a successful training session.

stage presence The confidence, speaking abilities, and ownership of the technology, training space, and leadership of the classroom by the technical trainer.

Toastmasters International A nonprofit organization established to help people be better public speakers

trainer confidence The self-assurance and belief that a trainer has to teach, control, and manage the technical classroom.

visualization The mental process of imagining a successful activity, such as a sporting event, but for the technical trainer it's the vision of teaching a technical topic.

Questions

1. Beth is about to teach a technical class at a client's site. The technical class requires the classroom be configured with multiple networks, servers, and databases. Beth would like to have access to the training room a day before the class begins, but due to travel restrictions she can't. Beth's supervisor assures Beth that the room will be configured properly by the technician at the client's site. Which one of the following is the best choice of action for Beth in this instance?

   A. Beth should send detailed instructions to the client on how to configure the classroom.

   B. Beth should call the client to make certain the room is configured properly by walking the client's technician through each step of the configuration process.

   C. Beth should cancel the class and move it to a date when she can configure the classroom.

   D. Beth should create a configuration checklist to ensure the classroom is configured properly.

2. Beth is about to teach a technical class at a client's site. The technical class requires the classroom be configured with multiple networks, servers, and databases. Beth would like to have access to the training room a day before the class begins, but due to travel restrictions she cannot. Beth's supervisor assures Beth that the room will be configured properly by the technician at the client's site. Which choice is the best example of mitigation with the client and of the risk that the classroom may not be configured properly?

   A. Create a script to configure the classroom.

   B. Schedule a backup date for a replacement class.

   C. Communicate with the technician who's configuring the classroom.

   D. E-mail the supervisor and demand access to the training room.

3. You are teaching a technical class for a client, and you'd like to know some information about the people who'll be attending your class. Why is it important for you to know who'll be attending the class and their technical background before your class begins?

   A. So you can identify any learners from a past class

   B. So you can prepare to teach the learners

   C. So you can identify learners who may be disruptive

   D. So you can identify who the most important learners in the class are

4. Jane is coaching Mike on how to prepare to teach a live class. She's giving Mike some ideas on how to deal with stage fright. All of the following are examples of stage fright except for which one?

   A. Fear of looking foolish in front of an audience

   B. Nervous feeling before starting the class

   C. Excessive sweating and stammering when beginning the class

   D. Feeling out of breath when speaking to an audience

5. Most participants in a technical training have what type of assumption about the technical trainer before class begins?

   A. The trainer won't know the technology.

   B. The trainer will be boring.

   C. The trainer will be an expert.

   D. The trainer won't be able to help me.

6. What term is assigned to an area of a whiteboard where questions that are not relevant are documented for future reference or consideration?

   A. Question parking lot

   B. Question warehouse

   C. Question corner

   D. Questions and issues

7. You are teaching a class to a large group of people on how best to implement a technology. You've noticed four or five people outside of your classroom door having a loud conversation that is disrupting the class. Which one of the following is the best method to handle this situation?

   A. Open the door and ask the people to be quiet, as you're having a class.

   B. Tell the class to take a break, and let the people in the hallway know they are disrupting your class.

   C. Talk louder in the classroom.

   D. Move next to the door, but continue to lecture so the people in the hallway will realize there is a class in session.

8. Henry is about to teach a technical class, and he wants to engage the learners as soon as possible for the training event. Which one of the following activities can Henry do to make the learners feel welcome and engaged?

   A. Greet the learners as they arrive for the training event.

   B. Put a welcome slide on the overhead screen.

   C. Make certain all of the course workbooks have been distributed.

   D. Ensure that the classroom is configured properly.

9. Which one of the following activities can show that you're interested in what the person is saying and help build rapport in the technical classroom?

   A. Introducing yourself as people enter the classroom

   B. Making eye contact when people speak to you

   C. Moving about the room as you lecture

   D. Distributing books, pens, and classroom supplies before learners arrive for class

10. Rick is teaching a technical class, and he'd like to get all of the learners involved in the classroom conversation. All of the following are good to say to get other learners involved in the conversation except for which one?

    A. Tell me more about…

    B. I'm glad you brought that up because…

    C. Who else would like to add a comment on this…

    D. That's not a good solution because…

11. Janet is teaching a class for her organization. In the class she asks a question about how the technology works. Janet then follows up with another question: "Why do you think that is?" for the student that answered. What problem can happen when Janet asks a question using the word "why"?

   A. There's no problem—this is a good practice, as people need to know why.

   B. The learner may not know why their answer was correct.

   C. Janet may appear foolish because she may not know why and is actually seeking help.

   D. The learner may feel defensive about their answer.

12. Jon has asked a question in the class that's long, elaborate, and full of technical jargon. You suspect the question is actually to show off his technical prowess. There are many responses you can offer to Jon in this situation. Which one is the least effective as used by a technical trainer?

   A. Show Jon all the reasons why his question is flawed.

   B. Answer Jon's question quickly and precisely, and then move on with class.

   C. Tell Jon you appreciate his thoughtful question, but you don't have the time to answer the question now, but maybe later.

   D. Ask Jon to keep his questions to a more concise format for time's sake.

13. A person in your class is asking you long, detailed questions that aren't really related to the course material. You suspect the reason is they are using the question time as a tactic to delay returning to work. Which one of the following approaches is the best course of action in this scenario?

   A. Answer their questions fully and completely, as you don't really know why someone is asking the question.

   B. Ask the person to keep their questions relevant to the course content.

   C. Show the person how their question is flawed.

   D. Remind the class that questions are a tool, not an excuse to waste time.

14. A learner asks a question in your technical class. What's the first thing you should do?

   A. Answer the question as quickly and efficiently as possible.

   B. Write the question down for reference later.

   C. Repeat the question for everyone to hear.

   D. Ask why the learner wants to know the information.

15. Which one of the following questions should a technical trainer never ask?

   A. Did I answer your question?

   B. Do you understand the demonstration?

   C. Can you hear me there in the back?

   D. What's your favorite thing about this technology?

16. Jennifer is teaching a new technical class for her organization. One of the participants in the class has asked Jennifer a detailed question that Jennifer doesn't know the answer to. What's the best response Jennifer can give?

    A. That question isn't relevant to this course.

    B. That question is good and we'll be covering it later today.

    C. I don't know the answer to your question, but I can find out.

    D. I don't know.

17. You are teaching a technical class, and Martin adds a comment after every statement people in the room make. This is causing many people in the room to be weary of contributing, as they don't want to hear what Martin has to add to their comments or questions. How should you manage this situation?

    A. Ask Martin to be quiet.

    B. Tell the class that everyone should contribute before Martin contributes again.

    C. Privately ask Martin to let other people contribute without adding comments.

    D. Ask Martin to leave the class.

18. Mary is teaching a technical class for her organization. Two participants in the class, Steve and Sam, are having a side conversation that is distracting the other learners in the classroom. Which one of the following is the first response that Mary should use to stop the distracting chatter?

    A. Mary should ask the class as a whole to keep side conversations to breaks, as they are distracting to other participants.

    B. Mary should ask Sam and Steve what they are discussing.

    C. Mary should tell Sam and Steve that their conversation is interrupting the class.

    D. Mary should privately tell Sam and Steve to stop their chatter.

19. Ned is teaching a class for his organization. During a group conversation Amanda begins talking about her personal life and the issues she's experiencing. Which one of the following could Ned say to bring the conversation back on track?

    A. Ned shouldn't acknowledge the personal issues, as this is out of the scope of the class.

    B. How is this relevant to the subject matter in this course?

    C. Who cares about your issues and drama?

    D. Why are you introducing this topic during the class?

20. Donald is teaching a technical class for his organization. Donald has years of experience in the technology and is regarded as one of the top trainers on the subject matter. One of the students, Jim, is becoming rude and irate with Donald about the technology, Donald's competence, and how stupid he thinks the training is. Which is the best response for Donald in this scenario?

   A. Tell Jim to calm down.

   B. Explain to Jim how he's wrong.

   C. Ignore Jim and continue with the class.

   D. Ask Jim to leave the class.

Questions and Answers

1. Beth is about to teach a technical class at a client's site. The technical class requires the classroom be configured with multiple networks, servers, and databases. Beth would like to have access to the training room a day before the class begins, but due to travel restrictions she can't. Beth's supervisor assures Beth that the room will be configured properly by the technician at the client's site. Which one of the following is the best choice of action for Beth in this instance?

   A. Beth should send detailed instructions to the client on how to configure the classroom.

   B. Beth should call the client to make certain the room is configured properly by walking the client's technician through each step of the configuration process.

   C. Beth should cancel the class and move it to a date when she can configure the classroom.

   D. Beth should create a configuration checklist to ensure the classroom is configured properly.

   D. Beth should create a checklist to test the room's configuration. A is not the best choice, as her supervisor has already made arrangements with the client to configure the training room. B isn't the best choice; communicating with the client is a good idea, but the checklist is proof that the room is configured properly. In addition, it's not feasible for Beth to walk the client through the configuration over the phone and may be demeaning to the client. C isn't likely to happen, as Beth probably doesn't have the authority to cancel and reschedule the class.

2. Beth is about to teach a technical class at a client's site. The technical class requires the classroom be configured with multiple networks, servers, and databases. Beth would like to have access to the training room a day before the class begins, but due to travel restrictions she cannot. Beth's supervisor assures Beth that the room will be configured properly by the technician at the client's site. Which choice is the best example of mitigation with the client and of the risk that the classroom may not be configured properly?

A. Create a script to configure the classroom.

B. Schedule a backup date for a replacement class.

C. Communicate with the technician who's configuring the classroom.

D. E-mail the supervisor and demand access to the training room.

C. Communication is always the best mitigation plan, as this lets Beth and the technician discuss any issues or concerns with the classroom configuration. Beth could also share the checklist with the technician to ensure that the room has been configured properly. Choice A, creating a script, is feasible with some classes, but there's no evidence in the question that a setup script will work with the classroom configuration. B isn't a good choice, as Beth should first take actions to ensure the current classroom is configured properly. D isn't likely either, as travel constraints are the reason why Beth can't access the room early, not the supervisor's restrictions.

3. You are teaching a technical class for a client, and you'd like to know some information about the people who'll be attending your class. Why is it important for you to know who'll be attending the class and their technical background before your class begins?

A. So you can identify any learners from a past class

B. So you can prepare to teach the learners

C. So you can identify learners who may be disruptive

D. So you can identify who the most important learners in the class are

B. It's always a good idea to know your audience before a class begins so you can prepare to teach the class. Knowing your audience means that you understand the learners' goals and motivations for the class, not what their status or title in the organization may be. Choice A is incorrect; while it's nice to see learners from previous classes, this isn't the best answer for the question. C is incorrect; it would be difficult to determine whether a learner would be disruptive based on their background with the technology. D is incorrect, as all of the learners in the class are important—not just some of the learners.

4. Jane is coaching Mike on how to prepare to teach a live class. She's giving Mike some ideas on how to deal with stage fright. All of the following are examples of stage fright except for which one?

   A. Fear of looking foolish in front of an audience

   B. Nervous feeling before starting the class

   C. Excessive sweating and stammering when beginning the class

   D. Feeling out of breath when speaking to an audience

   B. It's natural to feel nervous before starting a technical class—and some would say that's a common and good experience for the instructor. Choices A, C, and D are incorrect, as these are characteristics of stage fright.

5. Most participants in a technical training have what type of assumption about the technical trainer before class begins?

   A. The trainer won't know the technology.

   B. The trainer will be boring.

   C. The trainer will be an expert.

   D. The trainer won't be able to help me.

   C. Most people who come to class have an opinion that the technical trainer will be an expert in the technology. They assume that because the trainer is teaching a topic, they are already an expert in the technology. Choices A, B, and D are incorrect choices, as most people don't believe that the trainer won't know the technology, will be boring, or will be unable to help.

6. What term is assigned to an area of a whiteboard where questions that are not relevant are documented for future reference or consideration?

   A. Question parking lot

   B. Question warehouse

   C. Question corner

   D. Questions and issues

   A. The question parking lot is a tool instructors can use to record questions that aren't relevant to the subject matter. The question parking lot is an area of the whiteboard where questions can be documented for future reference in the class, at the end of the class, or after the official class time has ended.

7. You are teaching a class to a large group of people on how best to implement a technology. You've noticed four or five people outside of your classroom door having a loud conversation that is disrupting the class. Which one of the following is the best method to handle this situation?

   A. Open the door and ask the people to be quiet, as you're having a class.

   B. Tell the class to take a break, and let the people in the hallway know they are disrupting your class.

   C. Talk louder in the classroom.

   D. Move next to the door, but continue to lecture so the people in the hallway will realize there is a class in session.

   A. The best response is to immediately deal with the problem. You should open the door and politely ask the people in the hall to move away from the door, as you have a class in session. B is incorrect, as the timing of a break may not be appropriate for the class. C is incorrect, as talking louder doesn't ensure that the people will move away from the door or be quiet. D is also incorrect, as moving next to the door and continuing your lecture doesn't ensure that the people will move away from the door or be quiet.

8. Henry is about to teach a technical class, and he wants to engage the learners as soon as possible for the training event. Which one of the following activities can Henry do to make the learners feel welcome and engaged?

   A. Greet the learners as they arrive for the training event.

   B. Put a welcome slide on the overhead screen.

   C. Make certain all of the course workbooks have been distributed.

   D. Ensure that the classroom is configured properly.

   A. One of the best methods of engaging learners is to welcome them as they enter the classroom. Henry can introduce himself, introduce learners, and converse with the learners to make them feel at ease in the classroom before the training event begins. B is incorrect; putting a welcome slide on the overhead screen isn't a bad idea, but it's not the most welcoming activity Henry can do. C and D are not the best choices, as the learners should receive their workbooks as part of the class, and Henry should confirm the classroom configuration before the learners arrive.

9. Which one of the following activities can show that you're interested in what the person is saying and help build rapport in the technical classroom?

   A. Introducing yourself as people enter the classroom

   B. Making eye contact when people speak to you

   C. Moving about the room as you lecture

   D. Distributing books, pens, and classroom supplies before learners arrive for class

B. Making eye contact is one of the best methods to show your interest in what a person is saying. Eye contact is part of nonverbal communications. A is incorrect; while it's good to introduce yourself to people as they enter the classroom, you still must build rapport and pay attention to their introductions. C is incorrect, as moving about the room as you lecture can be a good teaching technique, but it's not the best method to build rapport with learners. D is incorrect, as classroom supplies and workbooks should be distributed before the learners arrive.

10. Rick is teaching a technical class, and he'd like to get all of the learners involved in the classroom conversation. All of the following are good to say to get other learners involved in the conversation except for which one?

   A. Tell me more about…

   B. I'm glad you brought that up because…

   C. Who else would like to add a comment on this…

   D. That's not a good solution because…

   D. Rick shouldn't tell someone their answer isn't a good solution and then lecture the participant. This can cause the learner to feel embarrassed and even to withdraw from participation in the class. A better response would be something to the effect of "Let's examine this in more detail. Who else has a solution?" Choices A, B, and C are all effective ways to get people involved in the conversation.

11. Janet is teaching a class for her organization. In the class she asks a question about how the technology works. Janet then follows up with another question: "Why do you think that is?" for the student that answered. What problem can happen when Janet asks a question using the word "why"?

   A. There's no problem—this is a good practice, as people need to know why.

   B. The learner may not know why their answer was correct.

   C. Janet may appear foolish because she may not know why and is actually seeking help.

   D. The learner may feel defensive about their answer.

   D. When instructors ask learners why something is right or wrong, it actually can make the learners feel defensive about the answer they gave. The instructor may have the right attitude of trying to lead people to learning discovery, but "why" questions can make people feel like they are being challenged. A is incorrect because asking why is not a good practice for adult education. Choice B is tempting, but it's not the best answer to this question. C is incorrect, as Janet likely knows the answer, but is trying to get people involved in the conversation.

12. Jon has asked a question in the class that's long, elaborate, and full of technical jargon. You suspect the question is actually to show off his technical prowess. There are many responses you can offer to Jon in this situation. Which one is the least effective as used by a technical trainer?

    A. Show Jon all the reasons why his question is flawed.

    B. Answer Jon's question quickly and precisely, and then move on with class.

    C. Tell Jon you appreciate his thoughtful question, but you don't have the time to answer the question now, but maybe later.

    D. Ask Jon to keep his questions to a more concise format for time's sake.

    A. Of all the choices this is the best answer because you don't want to embarrass Jon or open an opportunity for a technical debate on the technology. Choices B, C, and D are all good responses, as these keep the trainer in charge of the situation and keep the class moving along at a good pace.

13. A person in your class is asking you long, detailed questions that aren't really related to the course material. You suspect the reason is they are using the question time as a tactic to delay returning to work. Which one of the following approaches is the best course of action in this scenario?

    A. Answer their questions fully and completely, as you don't really know why someone is asking the question.

    B. Ask the person to keep their questions relevant to the course content.

    C. Show the person how their question is flawed.

    D. Remind the class that questions are a tool, not an excuse to waste time.

    B. It's acceptable to remind the class to keep their questions relevant to the course content. An occasional question that's outside of the course content may be understandable, but a series of questions that aren't relevant are usually an indicator that something is amiss and needs to be addressed. Answer A isn't the best choice because in-depth answers for unrelated questions don't help achieve the learning objectives of the class. C is incorrect, as the instructor should never embarrass a person in the class. D is also incorrect, as this statement could potentially embarrass the person in the class.

14. A learner asks a question in your technical class. What's the first thing you should do?

    A. Answer the question as quickly and efficiently as possible.

    B. Write the question down for reference later.

    C. Repeat the question for everyone to hear.

    D. Ask why the learner wants to know the information.

C. When someone asks a question in class, it's best to repeat the question so that everyone can hear the original question. This also ensures that you understand the question the learner is asking. While choice A is tempting, it's better to confirm the understanding of the question and to make certain others hear and understand the question before giving an answer. B is incorrect because you don't always need to write down every question asked in class. D is not a good choice, as why the learner wants to know something isn't as important as understanding the question and repeating the question for the class.

15. Which one of the following questions should a technical trainer never ask?

   A. Did I answer your question?

   B. Do you understand the demonstration?

   C. Can you hear me there in the back?

   D. What's your favorite thing about this technology?

A. When an instructor asks if they've answered a person's question, they're putting the person in an awkward position. It's possible that the instructor didn't answer the question and that the person may feel foolish for saying no. It's also possible that the person doesn't want to say no and contradict the instructor. It's better for the instructor to ask if the person has other questions about the topic or wants the instructor to provide more information. Choices B, C, and D are not good choices because these are all good questions that an instructor should ask as part of classroom management.

16. Jennifer is teaching a new technical class for her organization. One of the participants in the class has asked Jennifer a detailed question that Jennifer doesn't know the answer to. What's the best response Jennifer can give?

   A. That question isn't relevant to this course.

   B. That question is good and we'll be covering it later today.

   C. I don't know the answer to your question, but I can find out.

   D. I don't know.

C. The best answer is to tell the participant that she doesn't know, but will find out the answer for the learner. Choice A is incorrect, as the question may be relevant to the course. B isn't the best answer, as Jennifer shouldn't bluff or lie about the answer that she doesn't know. D is incorrect, as Jennifer shouldn't just leave the answer as "I don't know"; there should be some follow-up for the question.

17. You are teaching a technical class, and Martin adds a comment after every statement people in the room make. This is causing many people in the room to be weary of contributing, as they don't want to hear what Martin has to add to their comments or questions. How should you manage this situation?

A. Ask Martin to be quiet.

B. Tell the class that everyone should contribute before Martin contributes again.

C. Privately ask Martin to let other people contribute without adding comments.

D. Ask Martin to leave the class.

C. The best choice presented, and the most difficult option for the instructor, is to privately ask Martin to allow other learners to contribute without Martin adding comments. This keeps learners involved and keeps disruptions to a minimum. A and B are incorrect choices, as these options may embarrass Martin. It is possible Martin is wanting to be helpful, but his comments are having an opposite effect. Choice D isn't the best choice, as the instructor should first address the situation with Martin privately.

18. Mary is teaching a technical class for her organization. Two participants in the class, Steve and Sam, are having a side conversation that is distracting the other learners in the classroom. Which one of the following is the first response that Mary should use to stop the distracting chatter?

A. Mary should ask the class as a whole to keep side conversations to breaks, as they are distracting to other participants.

B. Mary should ask Sam and Steve what they are discussing.

C. Mary should tell Sam and Steve that their conversation is interrupting the class.

D. Mary should privately tell Sam and Steve to stop their chatter.

A. The best choice is that Mary should make a general announcement that side conversations should be kept to breaks. This lets everyone know that the chatter isn't appreciated, and Mary has addressed the problem without necessarily embarrassing Steve or Sam. B isn't a good answer, as it doesn't matter what Sam and Steve are discussing, their side conversation should be squelched. C isn't a good choice, as this direct statement would likely embarrass Sam and Steve. D is a good option, but only if Sam and Steve don't first respond to Mary's request for the whole group to limit conversations.

19. Ned is teaching a class for his organization. During a group conversation Amanda begins talking about her personal life and the issues she's experiencing. Which one of the following could Ned say to bring the conversation back on track?

    A. Ned shouldn't acknowledge the personal issues, as this is out of the scope of the class.

    B. How is this relevant to the subject matter in this course?

    C. Who cares about your issues and drama?

    D. Why are you introducing this topic during the class?

    B. Of course the best choice is to bring the topic back to the subject matter. Ned should use tact and diplomacy, but the focus of the conversations should be on the course material, not personal issues. A isn't the best choice because Ned does need to keep the group conversation on the materials in the class. C and D are rude and don't bring the conversation back to the course materials. Ned, and all technical trainers, should not attempt to embarrass learners.

20. Donald is teaching a technical class for his organization. Donald has years of experience in the technology and is regarded as one of the top trainers on the subject matter. One of the students, Jim, is becoming rude and irate with Donald about the technology, Donald's competence, and how stupid he thinks the training is. Which is the best response for Donald in this scenario?

    A. Tell Jim to calm down.

    B. Explain to Jim how he's wrong.

    C. Ignore Jim and continue with the class.

    D. Ask Jim to leave the class.

    D. Of all the choices presented this is the best choice. While it's rare than an instructor will need to ask someone to leave a class, it's sometimes necessary when a participant is being belligerent. Choices A, B, and C aren't the best answer because these do not confront the problem and keep the class moving forward. Asking someone to leave is usually the last option for an instructor, but it is a viable choice in some scenarios.

Leading a Successful Class

In this chapter you will:
- Embrace public speaking fundamentals
- Present with confidence and charm
- Use your voice to motivate and engage learners
- Manage the classroom environment
- Consider speech and the virtual classroom

Think back on some of your favorite instructors and speakers from technical classes, college, and conferences you've attended. When you imagine listening to these great teachers and speakers present, I bet some things they did, things they said, and how they behaved have stuck with you over the years. Some of your memories may have been the humor the speaker put into the topic or the good stories they shared to relate to your world. Some of the speakers may not have been terribly inspiring, but they were so experienced in their field that they spoke with ease and confidence.

All great speakers share a common trait: they can connect with their audience. Great speakers can make a connection that the audience can feel; the connection is electric, charming, and inspiring. A good connection between the speaker and the audience starts by first bridging the difference between the audience members—by using a common experience, an interest in the subject matter, or some humor that all of the participants can relate to. This initial bridge tells the audience that the speaker is just like them. Then the speaker, usually, gives a tiny insight into why the audience should pay attention—why the speaker deserves the audience's attention. First, you build the connection to the audience and second, you demand attention.

But making connections to your participants isn't a quick formula; it's all based on genuine interest in the subject matter and in the outcomes of the technical training. The connection between speaker and participants is initiated and then built upon as the training continues. Just like your favorite speakers, they make a connection, but then through their knowledge, speech, and control of the topic they keep the audience involved, interested, and thinking. Great speakers have subtle verbal and nonverbal powers that command attention, interest, and respect from their audience. Great speakers are in control of how they communicate verbally and nonverbally and choose their words, gestures, and posture carefully to convey the right message to the audience. In this chapter you'll explore the elements that can turn your good presentations into great, memorable training events.

Training like a Professional

You've already learned about creating the perfect learning environment for your classroom. In the instructor-led training you'll configure the room, ensure the software and hardware are working, and keep the room tidy and professional. In the virtual classroom environment you'll ensure connectivity, coordinate time zones, and complete the logistics of materials, access, and participants. These things are the mechanics of training—the elements that should be completed and perfected before every class you offer.

While the mechanics of training are essential contributions to the effectiveness of your training session, the heart of training is the instructor delivery. The instructor's ability to connect with the audience, control the presentation, and speak with confidence and good diction is paramount to successful training. If the audience can't understand the instructor, finds the nervous tics and habits distracting, or the instructor rambles on in a monotone voice, the participants will be bored, angry, and ready to bolt from the class. Trainers need to be strong in the voice and confident in their abilities to utilize effective public speaking to connect with their audience, and to maintain the training relationship.

You've probably heard that more people are afraid of public speaking than death—not a good thing to consider if you're speaking at a funeral. Public speaking is often dreaded because the speaker is the center of attention. The speaker is expected to lead, motivate, inspire, and convey information to the silent group of peers, professionals, colleagues, and strangers. Stage fright can rattle the most intelligent speakers, but the professional speakers don't lose the nerves, they just learn to control them. Through experience you'll become more savvy and equipped to manage and channel your nervous energy into your delivery and into positive energy in the classroom. First, you must embrace the basics of public speaking. Sure, you may have already completed a train-the-trainer type course or a speech class, but there's always room to improve for all public speakers (even me!).

Speaking with Clarity

If you're sipping a frosty beverage on the beach with your best friend, you'll probably talk differently than if you were in a meeting with the CEO of your company. That's one of the cornerstones of public speaking—know your audience and adapt your speech to them. This doesn't mean you talk down to people or try to impress them; it means you adapt your speaking style to what's appropriate. Technical training demands that you speak the way your audience expects: with clear, distinct ideas that can be easily understood. Great trainers speak conversationally and aren't haughty, robotic, or breathy. They're natural, but they're also professional.

To be professional in how you speak begins with your articulation. To articulate your message means that you speak clearly and distinctly. Articulation describes how you speak each word that comes out of your mouth; poor articulators slur their words together and are sometimes called lazy talkers. Pronounce each word distinctly, properly, and with enunciation. The easiest way to articulate is to slow down your talk and to be more conversational in your facilitation. You must articulate for your learners so they'll understand the messages you're conveying, but also so that you maintain the participants' interest in the class. If you don't articulate your words, people will get bored with your lecture and will quickly tune you out.

 NOTE If you play a brass instrument, such as a trumpet, you're likely familiar with the concept of embouchure. *Embouchure* describes how you shape your lips and tongue to play the instrument most effectively. In speech there's also an "embouchure" to consider: a smile. When you smile as you talk, you'll naturally slow down, and it's easier to articulate and speak with authority. And you'll look nicer too.

When you articulate your message, it also becomes easier to project your voice. Projection is speaking loud enough so that people in your audience can hear you without sounding like you're yelling to the back row. Projection is mastered through proper breathing as you speak. If you've ever felt out of breath during a talk, and every trainer likely has, you've mistimed your breathing. To speak well, first adjust your posture. As a trainer you're on your feet most of the time, and it's easy to let your posture slip. Of course, like Mom said, stand up straight. When you stand straight, pay attention that your shoulders don't creep up to your ears; keep your shoulders down and natural, otherwise you'll ache and you'll lose your projection. When you stand up straight, your chest rises and your gut is relaxed.

You don't need to gulp air like you're about to go underwater, but you do need effective breathing to project your voice. The diaphragm is your secret weapon to projecting your voice without wearing yourself out. The diaphragm is what sucks air in and out of your lungs, as it's located right below your lungs. Take a deep breath right now and your chest expands. Exhale and your chest flattens—that's your secret weapon at work. When you speak, breathe in and use the diaphragm to help throw your voice. Learn to control how quickly your diaphragm pushes air out, and you can talk louder and softer without gasping for your next breath.

 NOTE I believe that breathing in through the nose gives you deeper breaths and more control of your projection. I also think you won't look as silly as being a mouth breather.

How you say something is often more important than what you say. Your inflection affects the meaning of the message. For example, you could say, "This software is fantastic." How you emphasize the words affects how people interpret the meaning of the words. You can add sarcasm, interest, puzzlement, excitement, and other meanings into one little sentence and change the meaning every time you say it. Inflection can help you create some humor in the class, but also create some interest in your speech. People that have monotone speech patterns have little or no inflection in their voice—boring! Inflection is the pepper in your technical talks.

Speaking with Your Voice

You don't have to possess a deep, booming voice to be an effective speaker (especially if you're female). Clear pronunciation, crisp dialogue, projection, and inflection all contribute to an effective speaking voice. All of these elements together help you connect with your audience, but you also need a natural, relaxed approach in your speech. If you're mechanical and robotic, these elements will seem forced and distract from the importance of your message. The best advice I can offer is to use all of these elements, but also to be conversational. You can still project and articulate and be a good conversationalist. While you're focusing on controlling your voice, it's really the message that's the most important element of the training. You should aim for a conversational tone that's professional and authoritative, but friendly and interested in the audience's reception of what you're saying.

How you use your voice is what will contribute to your success as a trainer. Use variety in your pitch, pace, emphasis, and even the volume of your voice to affect the meaning and effectiveness of your message. If you're excited about what you're teaching, and I'll assume that you are, you'll probably already have a good deal of variety in your voice—because it's natural. You do have to monitor your pace and tension when you're excited, because there's a tendency to talk faster when you're emotionally tied to a topic. It's good to be excited and interested in what you're teaching, but for variety try the opposite tactic to talking faster: slow down and actually lower your volume to build tension and interest from your audience.

NOTE If you're like me, you hate to hear the sound of your voice. A couple times a year I'll record one of my presentations and force myself to listen to how I'm speaking. It's painful, but it also helps me to be a better speaker. I listen to my articulation, diction, and my projection. I try to find areas where I can improve and how I can speak more clearly to my audiences.

It's easy to think about your voice and how it affects your message, but there's another component to public speaking, and that's the lack of your voice. Silence. Use silence and pauses to give people an opportunity to ponder what you've said, to invite people into the conversation, and to build tension for what you're about to say. Imagine how a nice pause would work when you say, "The most important thing you should take from this module is…" The silence makes people want to hear what's coming next; it's the anticipation of new knowledge. Sometimes silence can feel painful—three seconds might feel like an hour, but it's effective and it gives people time to think and formulate their response.

Vocalizations are the "ums" and "uhs" that creep into your talk when you're thinking. These filler noises are pauses that allow you to think about how your sentence is going to end, where your train of thought is going, or what's a wise answer to a question. Unfortunately, ums and uhs make the instructor look less than intelligent and can be a distraction to your audience. Here's the key to removing ums and ahs from your public speaking: remove them from all of your speaking. Start listening to your speech when you're hanging out with friends, chatting on the phone, or in meetings with colleagues—listen for your fillers and then delete them from your talk. It's not easy, but the ongoing exercise makes you persistently aware of what comes out of your mouth. In lieu of the filler sounds you'll offer something wonderful—silence. I can attest that when you're just silent for a second rather than dropping in the fillers, you will seem wiser, your thoughts and speech will be more coherent, and your effectiveness as a professional trainer will skyrocket.

NOTE While the most common vocalizations are ums and uhs, other fillers that trainers rely on are *literally, super, basically, well, like, okay,* and phrases like *I know it, let's see, if you will,* and *could you repeat that for me.* Fillers are just Styrofoam words and remove value from your talk.

As an instructor you want to be enthusiastic to keep variation and interest in your message. Enthusiasm helps other people get excited about what you're teaching and keeps their interest in the topic. Fake enthusiasm, however, comes off like a sales pitch, or worse, like a kindergarten teacher. If you're not interested in the topic, get interested in how the topic will help the people in your classroom—that usually helps trainers to pep things up in their talk.

Connecting with Your Audience

The first minute of your talk is the most important minute of the entire class. It's your opportunity to capture the audience's attention, build rapport, and connect with your learners' needs. The first minute of your class is considered so important because everyone will give you their attention and interest. The audience is curious what you're going to be like as a speaker and how you'll make the class interesting and helpful for them. They want to know if you'll be intelligent, funny, motivating, or just boring. It's in the first minute that your audience will begin to judge you and what they think of your teaching style.

Use this first minute of their attention to your advantage—keep them interested, curious, and motivated about your technology. Here are some clever ways to get people interested and motivated in your class:

- *Be funny.* Quick, humorous lines can put people at ease and make them like you. I sometimes like to say, "For this class your organization has selected one of the greatest minds and leaders in this technology. Unfortunately, that person couldn't make it, so I'm here to share what I know." I like this line because, well, I am one of the greatest minds and leaders, but the line keeps me humble and lets people in the audience know I'm just a regular guy. I don't want to intimidate, but would rather be accessible and down-to-earth. It's also a quick line that usually gets a laugh. Usually.

- *Have something interesting to say.* Interesting facts about the software or technology you're teaching can really draw people into the class. If you've done your homework and know why the people are taking the class, it'll be easier to find a good opener. For example, if your class is interested in passing an associated certification exam, you might share some facts about the test, the salary of the people who've passed the exam, or how the current class will help them pass the test.

- *Present a question.* Questions are good openers because they make people ponder a topic and get them involved in the class. For example, you might ask what personal goals the people in the class expect to achieve from the course. This broad question asks people to think about the course objectives and how they want to apply them to their lives. The question must be phrased, however, so that people don't feel silly for not knowing an answer. You don't want to ask specifics about the technology if people haven't been involved with the technology yet—they may not know how to answer.

- *Share a story.* I often like to start my presentation with a story that's related to what I'm teaching. One class I teach often is IT Project Management; in this class I'll begin with, "In the most complicated IT project I ever managed a rat nearly bit my nose off." It's a true story and it gets people curious about how a rat and IT project management could be related—and how my nose was nearly chomped off. The story approach must be compelling and relevant to the topic at hand; this wouldn't be a very good story for a class on Microsoft Word.

All of these suggestions are linked to the beginning of the class, but you must also consider what you'll do past the first minute. Once you've made the initial connection with your audience, keep the energy going. Discuss the class you're teaching by summing up what's ahead for the participants. I don't like to linger on every detail of the class agenda. Before class begins I create a slide with the module topics, the anticipated breaks, and the time when the class will be dismissed. A fast review of the topics is ideal; a detailed breakdown of topics, exercises, and quizzes along with breaks, lunch menus, and the course evaluation is painful. Remember, you've already captured the audience's attention—keep it going.

Throughout the technical course, build on the relationship you have with your participants. When new modules or topics are introduced to the course, you can treat the topic like a new chance to renew or expand your audience's attention. Use humor, facts, or stories about the topic to get the participants interested in what you're going to detail in your lecture and labs. Connecting with your audience continues through the class—and if you're teaching several classes to the same participants, you can carry your connection forward. People want to feel connected to you, the instructor, because you're the expert and you're helping them move their careers, lives, and responsibilities forward. Make that connection and you'll instantly be a better trainer.

Managing Learning Momentum

If you've ever taught a class, you've found there's a rhythm and momentum to a good class. You introduce a topic, people are interested, and you lecture, demonstrate, and answer questions. People practice their concept in the lab, take a break, and are ready to move forward. Classes that are full of disruptions, led by an unorganized instructor, and that have participants who don't see the value of the training will creep by, and learning objectives likely won't be met. The instructor must manage the classroom environment, but also manage and encourage the focus of the learners on the learning objectives and accustom people into a rhythm of learning.

Your behavior often influences the behavior of the people in the classroom. If you're nonchalant, disorganized, joking with people too much, and telling unrelated stories, then people in the class will get the message that what you're teaching isn't really that important. If you're professional, focused, and speak in an authoritative and friendly conversational tone, then people will (usually) pay attention, follow your directions, and find the rhythm of learning. Participants in technical training will mirror what the instructor does—because the instructor is instructing not just in the learning objectives, but in the behavior and attitude toward the learning objectives.

Instructors must be cognizant of the participants' behavior, body language, and feedback as a reflection of the instructor's performance. In other words if people look bored, you're boring; if people look interested, you're interesting. Your audience is giving you a constant ongoing evaluation that should guide your voice, enthusiasm, and involvement with your participants. Don't ignore what people are telling you just because they aren't speaking.

Maintaining Learner Interest

Sometimes class participants will lose all interest in the class, become vocal about the course content, nod off to sleep, or even leave the classroom in disgust. When it comes to classes that have fallen apart, there are two types of instructors: those who have experienced it and those who haven't experienced it yet. Of course the best way to avoid total failure in the classroom is to be adequately prepared for what you're about to teach, to know your audience, and to confirm the learning objectives with the class participants. There are, however, some tactics that you can use to keep people interested in what you're teaching.

First, pay attention to your audience. Body language, questions, and the paralingual attributes of their questions and comments can offer insight into their level of energy and interest in the class. Often one of the first signs that you're losing your audience is that people begin talking to one another—not only is this rude, but it's a signal that you're not interesting them, so they'll chitchat about office romance, cupcakes, and the World Series of Poker. This chatter gets other people whispering, and pretty soon you have a room full of adults all having their own conversations that have nothing to do with the learning objectives you're offering. Your class has fallen apart.

It's not always so drastic; there are signs that your audience is losing interest:

- People are sending text messages.
- There are giggles and snorts when you've not said anything funny.
- You can see people working on their computers when you've not assigned an exercise.
- Arms are crossed, people are fidgeting, mouths are tight.
- People are subtly looking at their watches for a clue as to when you're going to end their misery.
- You can hear someone snoring.

If you're paying attention to your audience, then you'll know when you're losing them. When you've lost your audience, you must concentrate your efforts on winning them back. Sometimes this is as easy as taking a ten-minute break to get people moving, stretching, and away from the topic. Often, however, it's your presentation and lack of enthusiasm that are probably the culprit. Assuming you've prepared for the class and understand the material, you need to check your excitement and your involvement with the materials and the people in your class. Get excited, insert some passion into your talk, and speak with clarity, interest, and animation. You might need to ask questions, show a demonstration, or use a quick pop quiz to get participants and yourself re-interested in the learning objectives.

Sometimes people are just rude and will keep right on talking while you're presenting. You might try to talk louder or walk over to where the participants are chatting while you continue your animated lecture, but that doesn't always work. You might just stop talking and look at the participants who are talking; talkers have likely tuned you out, but the absence of your voice can get their attention and make them realize how rude they're being. The worst-case scenario, but sometimes it's necessary when talkers are distracting other learners, is to simply ask the talkers to quit talking. I usually like to make a general statement rather than calling out people by name, for example, "I understand some of you are more interested than others in this technology, but chatter disrupts the class and keeps your colleagues from learning. Please don't talk while others are trying to listen."

I once was presenting to roughly 200 people in a large auditorium in a hospital. The auditorium was a bowl-shaped room, and I was in the back of the auditorium, at the top of the bowl, when I was being introduced. As I made my way down the center aisle to polite applause, I managed to slip and fall in front of these 200 people. Of course if you're going to fall and risk injury, it's always best to do it in a hospital, but thankfully the only thing that was injured was my pride. So I fell—I'm human. I jumped up, took a bow, laughed it off, and went on with my talk. My point being that mistakes will happen, and if you try to cover up mistakes, misstatements, or outright fabrications, people will notice, and your reputation and effectiveness will be diminished.

When you make a mistake or misspeak, it's better to acknowledge the mistake and set the record straight. You don't want people to think you're lying, an idiot, or a lying idiot. Mistakes distract from the class and keep people from learning. Mistakes take the attention off of the topic and can confuse learners, be amplified in the classroom, and make the instructor look foolish. When you recognize you've made a mistake, correct yourself, don't belabor the mistake, and move right along. You're human—and your audience will appreciate the direct candor and correction.

Presenting with Charm

After you've been teaching for years you'll develop your style of teaching and a certain level of comfort being in front of an audience. You can do some things now to greatly improve your training skills—even if you're an expert trainer and a confident public speaker. First, eavesdrop on your audience. I don't mean this in a negative, creepy way—

but listen to the side conversations your participants are having on breaks and before and after class. Sometimes you'll hear things that can help you adjust your presentation or change your behavior to be a better trainer.

Listening to your audience also helps you become a better performer. While the bulk of a trainer's time is spent teaching and facilitating, you also need a certain level of performance in class. Smiling, being witty without being obnoxious, and having direct, prepared answers and demonstrations can elevate your reputation as a professional trainer. Performance also means there's a level of entertainment in the classroom. Entertainment doesn't mean just humor—though that's often a big part of it. What I mean by being entertaining is to captivate your audience, to speak with purpose, and to convey with your voice and actions that you understand the importance of what you're teaching. You make the connection between the content of the class and the day-to-day application of the technology.

Often technical trainers start off with excitement regarding the technology, but over time the excitement fades. Teaching the same class over and over can wear out your excitement and passion for the course. Ideally you'll have some variety in the class you teach, but this isn't always feasible. I know from my experience how insane training can be. One of my first training assignments was to teach a four-hour class on calendaring software twice a day, five days a week, for a year. I am not kidding—the pay was incredible for a young trainer like me, and everyone else knew better than to take on the assignment. By the end of the second month I could give the presentation in my sleep. I had the same jokes, same approach, same examples for all of the classes—and it started to show. I had to mix things up, keep the class fresh, while adhering to the learning objectives, and find ways to have fun in the classroom.

Being present in each class and not following a script as if I were performing at some small-town dinner theater, I made it through the experience and became a better trainer because of it. And that's what you'll need to do to—be present and mindful of each class you teach. Just because you've heard the same comments and questions 30 times before this class doesn't mean you shouldn't use the same passion and intensity in responding. You must focus on each learner's objectives in each class you teach. If your mind begins to wander, that's when someone will ask an amazing question that'll confound you.

Another way of presenting with charm is to find a way to connect with your audience. You can do this through your introductions and ice breakers. An ice breaker is some type of exercise that allows the people in the room to meet one another, learn about each other, and have a little fun in the process. Some instructors use elaborate games to get people comfortable with the classroom and the people they may be working with in the seminar. Other classes, especially smaller classes with time constraints, keep ice breakers to a quick exercise. If everyone in the room already knows one another or the class is short on time, you'll need to "break the ice" when you start the class. Ice breakers are usually funny and insightful, so you don't need to tell a long-winded story about your pet dog that died when you were a child. Keep it light and relevant to the class.

NOTE An ice breaker that I despise is when an instructor asks the participants to go around the room and introduce themselves to the group. I used to do this until I realized what a waste of time it is—and how many people dread the activity. Remember, most people don't like to speak in public, and here trainers are requiring people to do that first thing in a class. Instead of this approach I ask everyone to stand, and then I tell the class they have X number of minutes to meet three new people in the class. If it's a multiple-day class with lots of people, we'll do this ice breaker a couple of times. It's easier, faster, and more fun than the traditional spotlight introductions.

While most train-the-trainer courses tell you to be anchored and not to move around, you can actually be a better performer by adding some movement to your training. Sure, you don't want to be doing laps and pacing in the classroom, but movement keeps people watching you. It's ideal to stand to the left of your slideshow, but I also like to move to different places in the room so it doesn't feel like I'm just talking to one side of the audience. With remote pointers you can teach from around the room, and you can see what your participants are doing. When you're anchored, people know where you're going to be, but when you move in the classroom, you can connect more easily with more people.

And that's what good training is really all about—connecting with the people in your class. Eye contact is part of the connection, but it's emotional involvement you bring to your presentation that tells people you care about their learning. You can't learn that from a class, a book, or even another trainer—it's something that you have to invent and give to your learners. When you truly understand how the information you're giving others will affect their lives and how this information may affect the lives of others, then the emotional attachment is genuine and felt by your learners. Connecting with your audience is one the biggest goals of a performer—and that's what you're doing when you're helping people improve their lives and their careers.

VIDEO See the video *Ice Breakers for Technical Training*.

Reviewing and Summarizing Content

In virtual classrooms and with traditional classrooms, you'll need to summarize and review the content you've shared with your participants. Reviewing the content keeps what you've taught fresh in people's minds and helps them retain what they've learned. Reviews can be conversations, pop quizzes, recaps, and games. Most people learn new information based on what they already know—and in a technical class you'll need to connect new concepts to older concepts you've already covered. Transitioning from a topic you've covered to a new topic helps people make that link—you'll show them how what they already know can be related to a new concept.

Reviewing what you've done means you'll use simple statements that reference what the learners have experienced to introduce new concepts. Reviewing concepts in quick statements is one of the best transitioning methods you can use. Transitioning from topic to topic should be subtle and seamless. For example, in a word processing class you might show how to format just a sentence, then a paragraph, and then the entire document. With this logical transition from one simple concept to the next it's logical to the learners, and the transition is almost invisible. But think how new learners may struggle with the concept of formatting if you were to jump straightaway to creating formatting styles and rules in the word processing software. Now you've gone from formatting a sentence to creating complex styles without any transition or related concept for the learners.

It's been said, many times, that repetition is the mother of all learning. By doing a task or explaining a concept over and over, individuals grasp the concept and begin to master the technology. This idea is most evident in motor skills: riding a bike, juggling, or installing a hard drive. The first time you try an activity it may seem impossible to do, but after repetition your brain, eye-hand coordination, and body all synch up, and you master the task. Eventually, with enough practice, you can do the activity almost without looking or thinking about what you're doing. When you're teaching a technology, be patient and give your learners time to practice what you've taught and what they're to accomplish in their exercises.

Sometimes you'll want to pause in the class and look back on what's been accomplished—especially in longer seminars. A technical class that'll last for five days is packed with information and concepts the learners are to retain. At the end of each day of the class you can review what you've covered for the day, and at the start of each morning you can give a quick review of what's been covered so far in the class. This review time, especially at the launch of each day, helps learners recall what's already been taught to prepare for the new information you'll be sharing that day. If you just launch right into technical topics without helping learners recall what's already been shared, there's no definite mental linkage to the older concepts, and learning can become more challenging.

In shorter classes you still may want to offer intermediate reviews to give learners opportunities to pause and reflect on what's been taught. These intermediate reviews don't have to be lengthy, but they're helpful whenever you take breaks to adjust their minds back to learning and to prepare for new material in the class. You can make reviews fun and interesting by creating pop quizzes, playing a game with the material, or by creating a lab that challenges people to complete a series of tasks based on what you've already covered. If you've noticed that people in the class are struggling with certain concepts, this is a clear sign that reviews are needed to make certain that people understand the information you're teaching.

Summaries, like a closing argument in a court case, are the final review for the entire course. Summaries don't re-teach the entire course, but rather focus on the most important elements or headlines from the material. Summaries show learners the logical progression of where they started in the course to where they've ended—it's the trail of breadcrumbs from the first concept to final topic you've taught. Summaries don't need to be a lengthy, step-by-step outline of the course, but rather a conversation about what you've taught and what the learners have learned. Summaries help learners see all that they have been exposed to over the course and how they'll apply the information to their lives.

Summaries are also a good time to ask learners if they have questions or concerns about any of the material. Because summaries come at the end of the course, learners often have a tendency to stay quiet on what's been taught—they're ready to leave the class. This isn't necessarily a bad thing, but you still need to give learners the opportunity to ask questions and comment on the material. Sometimes it's appropriate to ask the learners questions; you want to keep them involved and excited about the material before you send them off to apply what they've learned.

Chapter Summary

Great speakers first know their topic, and then they use verbal and nonverbal techniques to persuade, inform, and teach their audience on the topic. Great speakers have charm and stage presence that comes from years of practice, but also from following the fundamentals of public speaking. As a technical instructor your goal may not be to persuade your audience, but to educate them on how to use the technology in their lives and jobs. Like a public speaker, however, you must first know your topic and then connect the information you have to share with the value the information has for the learners in your class.

When you speak, you must speak with clarity. Diction and enunciation directly affect the message you're giving your learners; if participants are struggling to understand what you've teaching, they won't be able to grasp the information. Technical trainers must articulate their thoughts in an easy-to-follow, friendly, but authoritative voice. Articulation also helps the instructor to project their voice so that everyone in the room can hear what's being shared. Projection doesn't mean yelling, but it means speaking so that learners can easily hear the words you're saying. Posture and breathing directly affect your projection and articulation.

Your voice is your primary instrument to teach. No one wants to hear a monotone speaker drone on for hours regardless of how fascinating a new piece of technology may be. Use inflection to vary your voice and to affect the meaning of what you're saying. Technical trainers often get excited about the technology, or nervous about teaching, and both attributes can affect the pace of the message. It's essential to slow down the pace of your talk so that learners can follow the information that you're sharing with them. When you speak too quickly, the presentation will be rushed, and the information may be lost on your participants.

Vocalizations, such as ums and uhs, are filler sounds that devalue your message and can make you look stumped or nervous. Vocalizations should be removed from your talk. Instead, trainers should either continue to teach in a conversational tone or insert silence when thinking. Silence during training isn't a bad thing at all; just because there's a void in the noise doesn't mean the trainer needs to fill it. Silence can build tension, offer opportunities for people to ask questions, and allow the trainer to think of how best to answer questions.

Often technical trainers think so much about what they're doing and what they're saying that they forget to think about their audience. Communication in a classroom isn't one-way; the trainer should also consider the feedback the audience is sharing. Feedback from the audience can be verbal with comments and questions, or nonverbal through body language. Being perceptive about the participants' nonverbal communications helps the instructor to determine their level of interest, confusion, or participation in what's being taught. Body language is immediate feedback to the instructor's level of performance and an opportunity to adjust, when necessary, the message, interaction, or pacing of the course.

Classroom management includes more than presenting the learning objectives. Classroom management means you're keeping participants involved and synchronized with your message. Interactions with participants keep the conversation from being one-sided and add variety and interest to the message you're teaching. Sometimes participants will become bored or lose interest in the topic regardless of how knowledgeable and charming you are as the presenter. These participants aren't achieving the learning objectives and need to be managed and brought back into the course so they're not a distraction to the other learners.

Throughout the course you'll offer intermittent reviews to keep information fresh for learners. Reviews can serve as transitions from one technical concept to the next and can be summations of what you've taught, opportunities for questions, and even pop quizzes. Reviews might also be disguised as classroom games, quizzes, or conversations. Finally, as with every chapter in this book, you'll want to offer a summary of what you've taught. Summaries discuss all of the key information the course has covered and should be linked to the learning objectives. Summaries are opportunities to clarify points and objectives and allow learners to ask any final questions about the course content.

Key Terms

articulation   Speaking with clarity and distinction to increase the likelihood of the message being understood by the class participants.

diaphragm   A respiratory muscle that helps to bring air into and out of the lungs. The diaphragm helps with voice projection in public speaking.

ice breakers   Activities, stories, or introductions to "break the ice" in a classroom environment to make people feel comfortable with one another and the instructor.

inflection   The variation and pitch in voice that affects the meaning of the message.

pace   The speed and tempo of spoken communication that may affect the ability of learners to comprehend what's being shared.

paralingual   The meaning beyond the spoken word—characterized by tone, inflection, and body language—that affects the meaning of the message.

projection   The ability to speak with enough clarity and volume so that the participants can hear the message.

review   Periodic refreshers of what has been taught in the course to help learners remember and recall key information.

summaries   End-of-course summations of what's been taught; the focus is on the learning objectives and most important elements of the technical training.

transitions   The process of moving from one technical concept to another in a smooth, seamless manner so that participants will learn new information based on what they've already learned.

vocalizations   The filler words and phrases, such as "uhs," "ums," and "like," that distract from the value of the spoken message.

Questions

1. Beth is observing a class that Lenny is teaching. In Lenny's presentation he's talking fast and slurring his words. Beth understands the technology, but feels that Lenny can be a better presenter. What advice should Beth offer to Lenny to help him become a better instructor?

   A. Articulate your words for the learners.

   B. Use tone to affect the excitement and enthusiasm in your message.

   C. Breathe deeply so it's easier to articulate.

   D. Stand up straight so it's easier to breathe and articulate.

2. What term best describes the volume and strength of a person's voice?

   A. Articulation

   B. Projection

   C. Embouchure

   D. Depth

3. You are helping a new trainer become a better public speaker. Which one of the following items is the best advice to give a new trainer regarding speaking well?

   A. Have good posture.

   B. Wear comfortable shoes.

   C. Breathe deeply.

   D. Over-articulate the message.

4. What part of the human body helps with breathing and projecting your voice? Choose the best answer:

   A. Lungs

   B. Mouth

   C. Diaphragm

   D. Brain

5. Nancy is teaching a class that she's taught several times before. In her presentation, however, she's ending many sentences with a higher tone that makes it sound like she's asking a question when she's not. What term is assigned to this scenario?

   A. Dialect

   B. Sarcasm

   C. Rhetorical pitch

   D. Inflection

6. You are teaching a technical class for your organization, and you want to use your voice to build tension and interest in a specific point about the

technology. Which one of the following statements is the best method to build tension in your message?

A. Speak quickly with smooth gestures.

B. Slow your pace, but increase your gestures.

C. Slow your pace and lower your voice.

D. Increase your pace and lower your voice.

7. One of the tools an instructor can use in their class is silence. Silence has many effects on the message and participants. Silence has the following effects in a technical class except for which one?

A. Builds tension in the classroom

B. Creates interest and drama in the classroom

C. Gives participants an opportunity to ponder

D. Allows the instructor to rest her mind

8. Beth is teaching her first class, and you're watching her performance to help her become a better technical trainer. In the class Beth is saying "uh" several times in each sentence. You make a note of this, as you want Beth to be a better trainer. What term best describes the "uhs" Beth is adding to her talk?

A. Nervous energy

B. Vocalization

C. Stress voice

D. Stage fright

9. Beth is teaching her first class, and you're watching her performance to help her become a better technical trainer. In the class Beth is saying "uh" several times in each sentence. You make a note of this, as you want Beth to be a better trainer. What recommendation would you make to Beth to remove the distracting words from her speech?

A. Use silence instead.

B. Speak faster.

C. Memorize her lecture.

D. Rely more on notes for her thoughts.

10. Complete this statement: The _____ is the most important part of a technical training class.

A. Summation

B. First minute

C. Instructor

D. Course material

11. Henry is teaching a technical class that he's taught at least 20 times before. In the class, however, participants are nodding off, surfing the Internet, texting, and chatting with one another. Which one of the following is the likely cause of the lack of learner interest in the class?

    A. The topic is boring.

    B. The participants already know the topic.

    C. Henry has failed to link the topic to the learners' responsibilities.

    D. Henry has taught the class too many times and is experiencing instructor burnout.

12. Regina is teaching a technical class, and she notices that the participants in the room look bored with her lecture. What should the participants' body language tell Regina?

    A. The participants have had too much information.

    B. The participants need a pop quiz.

    C. Regina needs to speak with enthusiasm and not be boring.

    D. Regina needs to move around the room to create interest.

13. What's the best approach to avoid having a technical class fall apart?

    A. Take control of the classroom, and let people know you're in charge.

    B. Demand respect and attention from the participants.

    C. Be funny.

    D. Be prepared.

14. Fran is teaching a technical class to 20 network engineers. In her class she notices that a few of the participants are chatting with one another. The chatter is disturbing other people in the classroom, and Fran needs to control the situation. What advice would you offer to Fran in this scenario?

    A. Tell the people who are chatting to be quiet.

    B. Move to where the people are chatting in the room.

    C. Talk louder so that the chatter isn't distracting from the message.

    D. Ask the people who are chatting to leave.

15. Eric is teaching a technical class for his company. Eric realizes that he has misstated a key piece of information, and several people wrote down the information. Eric knows that people probably haven't realized the misstatement. What should Eric do in this instance?

    A. Keep talking and ignore the misstatement, as people in the class don't realize the mistake.

    B. Keep talking, ignore the misstatement, and address it only if people realize the error.

C. Address the error at the summation.

D. Immediately correct the error.

16. What is an ice breaker?

 A. Transition

 B. Method to break bad news

 C. Method for participants to learn about each other and the instructor

 D. A story that introduces a technical topic

17. Thomas is a technical trainer for his organization, and he wants to introduce some new methods for reviewing course materials with participants. All of the following are examples of reviews except for which one?

 A. Conversations

 B. Pop quizzes

 C. Transitions

 D. End-of-class summations

18. An instructor is teaching a class how to install a rack-mounted server. The participants in this class will be installing hundreds of these servers over the next six months, so the instructor must make certain the users are doing the procedure properly. Which one of the following solutions could the instructor provide in class to ensure that people will follow the installation process correctly? Choose the best answer:

 A. Have the participants in the class repeat the installation process several times.

 B. Demonstrate how the install process needs to happen.

 C. Provide a step-by-step checklist for the installation process.

 D. Create a video of the installation process that will be available for the participants to review should they need to during an installation.

19. What term best describes the final summation of course content at the conclusion of the class?

 A. Summary

 B. Conclusion

 C. Review

 D. Abstract

20. These two elements directly affect the instructor's projection and articulation:

 A. Posture and breathing

 B. Knowledge and posture

 C. Pitch and breathing

 D. Breathing and knowledge

Questions and Answers

1. Beth is observing a class that Lenny is teaching. In Lenny's presentation he's talking fast and slurring his words. Beth understands the technology, but feels that Lenny can be a better presenter. What advice should Beth offer to Lenny to help him become a better instructor?

   A. Articulate your words for the learners.

   B. Use tone to affect the excitement and enthusiasm in your message.

   C. Breathe deeply so it's easier to articulate.

   D. Stand up straight so it's easier to breathe and articulate.

   A. The best answer is that Lenny needs to articulate his words for his participants. When Lenny is slurring his words, he has what some people call "lazy lips." Lenny needs to slow his pace and distinctly pronounce each word without over-articulating, but remain conversational. Tone can affect the message, but this isn't the best answer, so choice B is incorrect. C isn't a valid statement; breathing deeply doesn't help articulation, but it does help projection. D is also incorrect, as the best answer is to articulate—breathing doesn't directly affect the articulation, nor does good posture.

2. What term best describes the volume and strength of a person's voice?

   A. Articulation

   B. Projection

   C. Embouchure

   D. Depth

   B. Projection is the volume of a speaker's voice and its ability to carry throughout the classroom. A is incorrect, as articulation describes the distinction and clarity of the message. C is incorrect, as embouchure describes the placement of the lips and tongue that affect the message, though this term is mainly applied to people who play a brass or woodwind instrument. D is incorrect, as depth isn't a valid term for public speaking.

3. You are helping a new trainer become a better public speaker. Which one of the following items is the best advice to give a new trainer regarding speaking well?

   A. Have good posture.

   B. Wear comfortable shoes.

   C. Breathe deeply.

   D. Over-articulate the message.

A. The first step in speaking well is to adjust your posture. This act helps you breathe more easily, speak from the diaphragm, and project your voice. B, wearing comfortable shoes, is good advice for instructors, but it's not the first advice for becoming a great speaker. C is incorrect; breathing deeply will help with projection, but having good posture will not only help you breathe deeply, but will also help you to look professional. D isn't correct, as over-articulation can be annoying and distracting in the classroom.

4. What part of the human body helps with breathing and projecting your voice? Choose the best answer:

   A. Lungs

   B. Mouth

   C. Diaphragm

   D. Brain

C. The diaphragm is the best answer, as it's the muscle that helps the lungs to breathe in and to exhale. Voice coaches and consultants often advise people to "speak from their diaphragm" to have enough breathe to project their voice and speak without being breathy. Choices A, B, and D are all incorrect; while the lungs, mouth, and brain all help the instructor project the voice, the best answer is the diaphragm muscle, as its primary job is to help inhale and exhale.

5. Nancy is teaching a class that she's taught several times before. In her presentation, however, she's ending many sentences with a higher tone that makes it sound like she's asking a question when she's not. What term is assigned to this scenario?

   A. Dialect

   B. Sarcasm

   C. Rhetorical pitch

   D. Inflection

D. This is an example of an inflection. Inflections are the desired shift in tone that add or remove emphasis from the meaning of the message. In this instance the inflection could cause confusion or irritation in the classroom. A is incorrect, as dialect describes the regional accent of how a person speaks, such as the southeastern United States versus the northeastern United States. B is incorrect; sarcasm is achieved by inflection, but its intent is usually to provide humor. C is incorrect, as this isn't a valid term.

6. You are teaching a technical class for your organization, and you want to use your voice to build tension and interest in a specific point about the technology. Which one of the following statements is the best method to build tension in your message?

A. Speak quickly with smooth gestures.

B. Slow your pace, but increase your gestures.

C. Slow your pace and lower your voice.

D. Increase your pace and lower your voice.

C. The best solution is to slow your pace and lower your voice. This action creates interest and can build tension and drama into your message. A is incorrect, as speaking faster can be exciting, but it doesn't build tension. B is a tempting choice, as you are slowing your pace, but an increase in gestures can be distracting. D is also incorrect, as increasing your pace and lowering your voice doesn't build tension and may distort the message you're trying to convey.

7. One of the tools an instructor can use in their class is silence. Silence has many effects on the message and participants. Silence has the following effects in a technical class except for which one?

A. Builds tension in the classroom

B. Creates interest and drama in the classroom

C. Gives participants an opportunity to ponder

D. Allows the instructor to rest her mind

D. Of all the choices this is the best answer, as silence is meant to be used as a tool to build tension, give pause, and allow the participants to consider the message. Choices A, B, and C are incorrect, as these are attributes and achievements of using silence in the classroom.

8. Beth is teaching her first class, and you're watching her performance to help her become a better technical trainer. In the class Beth is saying "uh" several times in each sentence. You make a note of this, as you want Beth to be a better trainer. What term best describes the "uhs" Beth is adding to her talk?

A. Nervous energy

B. Vocalization

C. Stress voice

D. Stage fright

B. Vocalizations are the filler words like *uh, ah, like,* and other phrases that don't add value to the message. Choices A, C, and D are incorrect choices. Nervous energy and *stage fright* are basically the same concept, though stage fright is a better term, as it describes the fear of public speaking. Stress voice isn't a valid public speaking term.

9. Beth is teaching her first class, and you're watching her performance to help her become a better technical trainer. In the class Beth is saying "uh" several times in each sentence. You make a note of this, as you want Beth to be a better trainer. What recommendation would you make to Beth to remove the distracting words from her speech?

    A. Use silence instead.

    B. Speak faster.

    C. Memorize her lecture.

    D. Rely more on notes for her thoughts.

A. One of the best solutions to remove vocalizations from speech is to use silence instead. The best recommendation, though not one of the choices, is to remove the vocalization from all areas of speech—even when not teaching a technical class. B is incorrect, as speaking faster won't necessarily remove the vocalizations from the speech. C is incorrect, as memorizing her lecture isn't a likely solution, as Beth will need to interact with the participants, not just deliver a speech. D is also incorrect—as relying heavily on notes doesn't necessarily remove the vocalizations from her speech.

10. Complete this statement: The _____ is the most important part of a technical training class.

    A. Summation

    B. First minute

    C. Instructor

    D. Course material

B. The first minute is the most important part of a technical training class. It allows the instructor to get the attention and interest of the participants. A is incorrect; while the summation is important, it's not as important as the first minute of the class. If the technical trainer has not captured the interest of the participants, then the summation isn't going to be valuable. C is incorrect; the instructor is an essential element to the technical training class, but the class can't happen without the instructor. In addition, it's the instructor's presence in the first minute that's vital to capturing the participants' attention and interest. D is incorrect; course material is important in many technical classes, but it's not the most important element of the class.

11. Henry is teaching a technical class that he's taught at least 20 times before. In the class, however, participants are nodding off, surfing the Internet, texting, and chatting with one another. Which one of the following is the likely cause of the lack of learner interest in the class?

    A. The topic is boring.

    B. The participants already know the topic.

    C. Henry has failed to link the topic to the learners' responsibilities.

    D. Henry has taught the class too many times and is experiencing instructor burnout.

C. Of all the choices this is the most likely answer. When Henry fails to link the topic to the learners' responsibilities, the participants won't see the value in the training. A is incorrect; the topic may be dry, but it's the instructor's role to generate interest in the topic by linking the information and objectives to the learners' lives and responsibilities. The instructor must show why the information is important and present the information with enthusiasm. B is incorrect; if the participants already knew the topic, they most likely would not be taking the technical class. D is incorrect; Henry may have taught the class many times and may be bored with the course content, but it's Henry responsibility to link the learning objectives to the lives of the participants in the learner-centered classroom.

12. Regina is teaching a technical class, and she notices that the participants in the room look bored with her lecture. What should the participants' body language tell Regina?

    A. The participants have had too much information.

    B. The participants need a pop quiz.

    C. Regina needs to speak with enthusiasm and not be boring.

    D. Regina needs to move around the room to create interest.

C. The best answer is that Regina needs to speak with enthusiasm and not be boring. The nonverbal clue from the participants is that they are bored with the content and need Regina to not be boring. A is incorrect; the information in the classroom is to be relevant to what the learners need to accomplish and meet the learning objectives. B is incorrect, as boredom doesn't necessarily equate to needing a pop quiz in the class. D is incorrect; movement can help create some interest, but this isn't always the best choice. If Regina is speaking in a monotone voice, movement won't necessarily generate interest in what she's saying.

13. What's the best approach to avoid having a technical class fall apart?

    A. Take control of the classroom, and let people know you're in charge.

    B. Demand respect and attention from the participants.

C. Be funny.

D. Be prepared.

> D. Being prepared is the best method to keep a technical class from falling apart. If the technical trainer isn't prepared and well-versed on the subject matter, then he's likely to not hold the attention of the participants. A and B are incorrect choices, as instructors can't demand attention and respect from people in the class—demands for respect often fail and just saying you're in charge of the classroom doesn't necessarily make it so. C is incorrect, as being funny is a good way to maintain interest, but being prepared is a higher priority in technical training.

14. Fran is teaching a technical class to 20 network engineers. In her class she notices that a few of the participants are chatting with one another. The chatter is disturbing other people in the classroom, and Fran needs to control the situation. What advice would you offer to Fran in this scenario?

    A. Tell the people that are chatting to be quiet.

    B. Move to where the people are chatting in the room.

    C. Talk louder so that the chatter isn't distracting from the message.

    D. Ask the people who are chatting to leave.

    > A. Simply telling the people who are chatting to be quiet is the best answer presented. Choices B and C aren't good answers because these choices don't address the problem directly. D isn't the best choice, as the people may just need to be refocused on the content, not necessarily asked to leave the class.

15. Eric is teaching a technical class for his company. Eric realizes that he has misstated a key piece of information, and several people wrote down the information. Eric knows that people probably haven't realized the misstatement. What should Eric do in this instance?

    A. Keep talking and ignore the misstatement, as people in the class don't realize the mistake.

    B. Keep talking, ignore the misstatement, and address it only if people realize the error.

    C. Address the error at the summation.

    D. Immediately correct the error.

    > D. The best answer is to immediately correct the error. If Eric ignores the mistake, his reputation could be tarnished. Choices A and B are not the best answer, as these choices allow Eric to keep talking as if the mistake hadn't happened. These choices could allow people to leave the class with faulty information. Choice C is not correct, as correcting the mistake at the class summation allows the mistake to exist until later in the class. By immediately correcting the error, the topic is fresh in the participant's minds and easier to understand and mentally correct.

16. What is an ice breaker?

    A. Transition

    B. Method to break bad news

    C. Method for participants to learn about each other and the instructor

    D. A story that introduces a technical topic

    C. An ice breaker is usually a fun exercise that allows people in the classroom to learn about each other and the instructor. A, transition, is not a correct choice because transitions are the subtle shifts from one topic to another. Choices B and D are incorrect because these answers do not describe what an ice breaker is.

17. Thomas is a technical trainer for his organization, and he wants to introduce some new methods for reviewing course materials with participants. All of the following are examples of reviews except for which one?

    A. Conversations

    B. Pop quizzes

    C. Transitions

    D. End-of-class summations

    D. The end-of-class summation is different than a review, as it covers everything that the course has included. Reviews are quick statements and recaps of what's just been taught and can serve as transitions to new topics. Choices A, B, and C are incorrect choices, as conversations, pop quizzes, and transitions are all examples of reviews.

18. An instructor is teaching a class how to install a rack-mounted server. The participants in this class will be installing hundreds of these servers over the next six months, so the instructor must make certain the users are doing the procedure properly. Which one of the following solutions could the instructor provide in class to ensure that people will follow the installation process correctly? Choose the best answer:

    A. Have the participants in the class repeat the installation process several times.

    B. Demonstrate how the install process needs to happen.

    C. Provide a step-by-step checklist for the installation process.

    D. Create a video of the installation process that will be available for the participants to review should they need to during an installation.

    A. Repetition is the mother of learning. By repeating the process many times, the participants will learn by doing and will be more comfortable installing the server as part of their job responsibilities. Choices B, C, and D are all good practices, but these solutions don't require that the participants actually practice installing the server and learn by doing.

19. What term best describes the final summation of course content at the conclusion of the class?

   A. Summary

   B. Conclusion

   C. Review

   D. Abstract

   A. The end-of-course summation is simply called a summary. Summaries provide learners a final digest of everything that's been covered in the course. Choices B, C, and D are not valid choices, as conclusions, reviews, and abstracts are not used at the end of a technical training course. Note that reviews are intermittent summations of the material throughout the course, not just at the end.

20. These two elements directly affect the instructor's projection and articulation:

   A. Posture and breathing

   B. Knowledge and posture

   C. Pitch and breathing

   D. Breathing and knowledge

   A. Posture and breathing directly affect the instructor's ability to project her voice and the articulation of each word. Choices B, C, and D are incorrect, as knowledge and pitch don't affect projection and articulation.

PART IV

Leading Group Facilitation

- **Chapter 8**   Managing Learner-Centered Instruction
- **Chapter 9**   Promoting Learner Engagement
- **Chapter 10** Motivating and Involving Learners

Managing Learner-Centered Instruction

In this chapter you will:
- Implement performance-based training
- Analyze learner tasks
- Explore Bloom's Taxonomy
- Train to the psychomotor domain
- Manage learner emotions
- Recognize learner values in adult education
- Review the cognitive domain
- Encourage learners to comprehend and apply knowledge
- Implement cognitive domain verbs in technical training

In the perfect world of training you'll show up to teach your technical class and participants will show up to learn. You'll have a clear communication on what the course objectives are, and learners will have the same expectations for the course. While this is the ideal training scenario and probably the norm for most technical trainers, there are days and classes when this doesn't jive. Imagine a technical class where learners have different expectations than what you do; you're prepared to teach the course objectives and the participants are prepared to learn something else slightly different.

This slight difference in what you're prepared to teach and learner expectations is usually due to pre-class communications. If you're teaching in a public training center and sales reps are making promises about the course content without telling you about those promises, you're sunk. Or if managers are adding more and more objectives to a course without allotting more time for the training, you're sunk. Or if people have just a few items they want to learn and want to browse the Web the remainder of the class, you're sunk. There must be a consistent message on what the course objectives are, and it's one of the fundamentals you'll consider when you launch a training session.

This is just part of creating the learner-centered environment: Making the learner the most important person in the classroom is the foundation of effective adult education. Managing the learner-centered environment takes some finesse. Adult learners want to know why the training is happening, why they need to learn the material, and why the information is important. If you can establish the answers to these questions right away, you'll have an easier time teaching and keep the material focused on the learners. Throughout the course you'll likely need to revisit why the information is important for each topic and course objective. When learners lose interest or don't see the value in the training, you'll need to implement classroom management to engage learners and keep them focused on what they need to know as part of the learning process.

Establishing Learner-Centered Instruction

Learner-centered instruction means that the focus in the course development and in the technical delivery is on the learners and their ability to retain and apply information. Learner-centered instruction aims to teach the actual performance factors of a technology, rather than the mechanics of the technology. This means that the technical trainer understands how the people in the class will use the technology in their lives—and then focuses on that utilization. This type of education is called performance-based learning.

Performance-based learning actually begins with the design of the course. In the analysis and design of the course, the instructional designers should examine how the technology will be utilized and then design the course content to meet that objective. You can imagine how unsuccessful a technical class might be if the people in the class needed to know a specific aspect of the technology, but there were all sorts of additional content that didn't apply to them. Performance-based learning focuses on how the learner will apply the information in the classroom in their lives and in their roles.

Even with commercial off-the-shelf training solutions, a good instructor will need to established learner-centered instruction. By communicating with the class participants, learning about their roles and responsibilities, and having a full understanding of the technology, the technical trainer can correlate the learning objectives to the practical application of the class participants. By taking the time to learn about the participants you can more effectively teach the materials and the participants can more effectively learn—and then apply their newly gained knowledge. Technical trainers and training departments must gather expectations and learning requirements and then measure the results of training for the actual educational benefits the training has created.

Delivering Performance-Based Training

Assume that an organization will develop and deliver training internally rather than through a third party, such as a training center. When a training request is made to the learning department, one of the first pieces of information that needs to be determined is simply why the request is being made. The learning department needs to understand from the onset why the training is needed and what the expected outcomes of the training are to be. By establishing this first, the organization is more apt to develop and deliver training that is performance-based to meet the defined requirements.

Now for those organizations that provide standardized training classes—the commercial training centers—it would behoove them to understand the customer need, too. Many commercial training centers still sell their training classes like tickets to the movie theater. It's all about filling up the classroom with enough people to make certain the class can happen—and to make a profit. These businesses would do better if they just discovered a bit more information as to why the class is needed. This information can help the center sell additional classes and help the instructor spotlight some specific topics for the clients, but more importantly, it'll help the learners meet their educational goals.

Too often training departments receive a request to develop technical training and they'll immediately go to a subject matter expert for analysis of the technology. The correct approach is to go to the requestor and complete an analysis of how the technology will be utilized and by whom. By first understanding how the technology will be used you'll have definite direction in the development of the course objectives to satisfy the utilization of the technology. Next you'll define the audience for the course and define the following:

- Experience with the technology
- Work and education background
- Audience size for the training
- Attitude toward the technology
- Attitude toward the learning experience
- Preferred learning methods and course expectations
- Constraints and assumptions about the delivery of the training
- Expectations for the course outcomes and take-away deliverables

Organizations should define and communicate these characteristics as early as possible in the requirements gathering and analysis portion of instructional design. By identifying these elements and establishing agreement among the learning stakeholders, organizations are better equipped to create performance-based education than when subject matter experts dissect the technology into beginning, intermediate, and advanced courses. So many technical courses follow the approach of beginning to advanced classes that they miss the opportunity to directly address the learning need that may be scattered across all three courses.

Part of preparing for performance-based training is to confirm that the objectives of the course are in synchronization with the objectives of actually using the technology. Organizations can improve their training development by experimenting with how the technology is actually implemented in production and ensuring that the classroom environment mirrors what users will see in their roles. When there's a difference between the classroom technology and the actual implemented technology, you can anticipate discomfort.

I've consulted in organizations where the development of the software was slightly different in the classroom than in the actual work environment. You can probably guess what happened: Users panicked when they saw the difference between what they experienced in training and what they saw in the live version. Even if the difference is slight, people won't appreciate the difference between what they thought they'd already mastered and what they're expected to utilize in their jobs. There's enough anxiety attached to learning a new technology that differences between the training environment and actual implementations can be magnified to class participants.

Instructors should focus on what people will be able to do after the technical training class. Training doesn't exist to explore every tiny facet and option in the technology—especially if these aren't things the participants will need to know to do their jobs. Technical training must focus on the expected outcomes of the training—with the confirmation, not an assumption, that the outcomes are what are actually needed to satisfy the training request. Job-relevant training keeps learners interested because they can see the link between what you're teaching and what they'll be expected to do with the technology. Job-relevant training focuses on task analysis for the participants. Awareness training aims to make learners aware of the components of the technology —even if the components are part of the performance the learners will actually need in their jobs.

Analyzing Learner Tasks

As part of a learner-centered environment, you should complete learner task analysis. Task analysis is basically immersing yourself into the role of the learner and experiencing how they do their work and how the training will affect that work. For example, imagine a group of learners that are editing photos in older, clunky image manipulation software. The organization wants to move to a recent version of Adobe Photoshop, but they need to focus on the specific goals for the desired outcome of their images.

In learner task analysis you'd first need to understand how the organization is editing the current images, what the end result of the images is, and what their goals for Photoshop may be. By understanding the current state of the process, the actual tasks to create the current deliverables, you'll be better equipped to develop and teach Photoshop for this organization. You'll understand how the learners complete their current assignments and know what the end result of their work should create. In your class you can use relative knowledge to compare and contrast how their processes are completed currently and how the processes will be completed in the new software.

To do task analysis properly, you'll need to first identify who'll be the best person to observe in the analysis. A subject matter expert (SME) is someone who's well versed in the current technology, is experienced in the existing processes, and can clearly state what the desired outcomes of the process should be. In task analysis with the SME you'll be completing the observation in one of two approaches:

- **Passive observation**   With this approach you'll only observe the process, ask no questions, and just take notes. Your goal is to not interrupt the process at all; just watch and learn how the SME completes the work.

- **Active observation**   This approach allows you to interact with the SME, ask lots of questions, and in some cases, even participate in the activity. Active observation is more involved, but can be more time-consuming.

A best practice is to first just perform passive observation—soak up the workflow. Then, once you have a general understanding from the passive observation you'll move into active observation. This approach to task analysis uses the logical flow of the task—

from the beginning to the end result—and it's a fine way to document the current set of actions to get to the final, expected result.

> **NOTE** The process of learner task analysis may not be completed by you the technical trainer or even an instructional designer. A business analyst may be the individual who completes and documents the process and then hands the discoveries over to you. This isn't necessarily a bad approach, but it adds another layer of complexity to the training model. Ideally, the person doing and developing the training should be the person completing the learner task analysis.

In either passive or active observation your goal is to learn how the process currently works so you can explain to learners how the technology will affect their current workflow. In your observations your goal is to understand what the learner is expected to do as a result of your training. Another approach to better understand learner outcomes is to create a hierarchical decomposition of the task. This approach requires you to start with the end result and work backward to identify all of the components and actions that must be evident to get to the end result. For example, two different Photoshop gurus could take two different approaches to create the same end result of a printed, edited photo.

In the hierarchical approach to task analysis you'd identify the components that are evident to get to the end result while acknowledging the multiple processes that may be available to create the same outcome. By thinking about the end result, you can think backward through each of the steps to determine what actions have to occur to arrive at this specific result. Each preceding event leads to the current result, and each current result has a successor event, until you finally arrive at the desired end result for the process. Figure 8-1 shows an example of a hierarchical approach to task analysis by examining predecessor and successor events in the process.

Figure 8-1
The hierarchical approach examines all steps to complete the task.

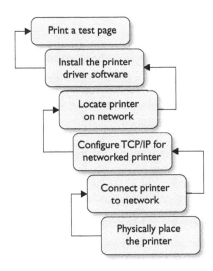

While the primary reason to do learner task analysis is to identify the necessary steps to achieve the desired outcome, there is a valuable by-product: You don't waste training. Training time, seat time, and budgets are wasted when topics are included in the learning objectives that don't contribute to the tasks that learners will actually use in their roles and responsibilities. If you're teaching Microsoft Word and your class spends an hour on creating indexes, this hour is only valuable if the people in the class will actually use the technology to create indexes. You can do the math: If you have a dozen people in class, that's 13 hours wasted every time the instructor teaches indexes (the 12 participants and the instructor). Learner task analysis removes these non-value-added objectives and focuses on what needs to be taught for the benefit of the organization.

NOTE To actually do hierarchical analysis you define what the learner must know in order to do a given task. Each action necessary to achieve the end result is identified in a hierarchy.

Exploring Bloom's Taxonomy

Benjamin Bloom was an educational psychologist at the University of Chicago. His claim to fame is that he led a group of educators to develop a classification of learning goals for people. The actual taxonomy was developed by this group of educators but was named after Bloom, as he led the effort and edited the corresponding work *Taxonomy of Educational Goals*. The taxonomy has evolved since its release in 1956, with a significant update in 2000, but for the most part, stays true to its original concept: Define the objectives educators have for learners.

Traditionally Bloom's Taxonomy focused on pedagogical theories, though it's now a common theme in adult education. The taxonomy divides the learning objectives into three different domains: cognitive, affective, and psychomotor. Like much of adult education theory, Bloom's Taxonomy subscribes to the theory that to learn at a higher level of understanding you must first master the lower-level domains. This doesn't mean that educators should teach just to one domain at a time, but rather, they should embrace all three domains by teaching and structuring classes to allow participants to discover learning through experience and information transfer.

Originally, the *Taxonomy of Educational Goals* just focused on the cognitive domain. Over time, as mentioned, it evolved to include the affective and psychomotor domains. Within each domain there is a related taxonomy of terms that describe the actions within it. People are stronger in different domains based on their experience, maturity, education, and natural leanings. While in this book, and for your CompTIA CTT+ examination, you won't need to learn about the finer details of the taxonomy, you should be familiar with each domain and how it may affect you as a technical trainer.

VIDEO See the video *Learning Bloom's Taxonomy*.

Reviewing the Psychomotor Domain

The psychomotor domain describes the learning and application of physical tools and abilities—like installing a hard drive or punching down a network cable. Technically, the psychomotor domain describes the individual tasks, like using a screwdriver, opening the computer cover, removing the old hard drive, and so on. The psychomotor domain consists of the individual activities of the task that are mastered in order to achieve the end result.

The psychomotor domain describes the learners' skills, motor skills, manipulation of technology, ability to follow instructions, and eventually mastery of the physical activity through repetition. There are seven levels of performance within the psychomotor domain:

- **Perception** This attribute relies on the individual using the senses to determine what physical activity should happen. For example, a technician could smell wire burning and know how to respond while working on the computer; or a person could see a computer fan not spinning and test the power connectivity.

- **Set** Describes the readiness to respond to predictable situations. It's almost like an evolved mindset based on experience with a task. For example, a person could hear a noise in a printer that usually means a paper jam, and then the person could follow a checklist or directions to pull out the bottom tray, flip open the printer cover, reset the toner, and then shove the tray back in place to fix the problem.

- **Guided response** The learner can follow the instructor's directions to perform a motor skills task. For example, as an instructor you might coach a person through the process of installing a piece of hardware or completing a series of steps in a software program to reach a specific result. Once you've guided the learner through the process the learner will then become more efficient, and eventually master, the process through your continued guidance and repetition.

- **Mechanism** The guided responses are learned through repetition, and the participant understands each step of the guided responses and develops a mindset to completing the task. The mechanism is a slightly advanced combination of the set and the guided responses, where the learner can perceive the problem, operate with proficiency, and understand the correct responses to create the expected, predictable end result.

- **Complex overt response** With a bit more complexity than the previous mechanism the learner can complete a complex task based on their understanding and control of their motor skills. For example, a learner could use the mouse and keyboard in combination with a computer program to open, manipulate, edit the printer settings, and print a document. Several perceptions, sets, learned responses, and mechanisms are required to put all the individual tasks together into a hesitant-free execution of the desired result.

PART IV

- **Adaptation**   When a learner has mastered a specific skill, such as operating a printer, they can adapt their existing knowledge and apply it to new conditions and circumstances. For example, the learner could manipulate a different printer based on their existing knowledge of the current printer. A learner might also change the type of paper, the colors to be printed, the draft mode of the printer, and other settings based on their existing proficiency with a similar print device.

- **Origination**   This attribute happens when the learner takes their experience and expertise with existing knowledge and creates a new method, new skill, and expected outcome. For example, an individual could experiment in their photo-editing software to create new filters, new brushes, and effects and print to a new printer to produce a specific type of artwork.

In technology training you might make some assumptions that the people in your class have certain motor skills to complete the needed tasks. You might assume or observe that participants can handle a screwdriver, have the dexterity to open and close computer cases, and use the mouse and keyboard in combination. If you're teaching a beginning course, however, these assumptions may prove to be false. People who have never used the mouse before, installed any hardware, or created a network cable may find the motor skills difficult to master to get the expected results. Of course you'll be patient, coach the learners along, and allow them plenty of time to practice. Encourage your participants to keep trying, to keep experimenting when they're struggling with a complex task—with repetition they'll master the movements.

Reviewing the Affective Domain

Technology can be overwhelming to some people. I've taught classes, and perhaps you have too, where people have gotten teary in frustration with the technology. I've coached employees who have been so engrained with their current processes that the idea of moving from a paper-based workflow to an electronic workflow for data management has been so terrifying they've resigned. I've also worked with learners who have been so excited to embrace a new technology they rushed through exercises, worked through lunch hours, and didn't want to leave the classroom at the end of the day.

The affective domain describes, as in the preceding scenarios, the emotional values and feelings people attach to the technology they're learning. The affective domain is part of an individual's ability to learn, but it's also a significant part of the emotional health that allows a person to empathize with others, consider how a technical implementation may affect employees, and understand the frustration or excitement that others may attach to the technology. As a technical instructor you'll often be using the affective domain to recognize your learners' emotions and feelings toward the technology. The learners in your classes will often reveal their affective domains by expressing, sometimes with great emotion, how they love, hate, or despise the technology they're supposed to be learning.

NOTE I've taught classes, and I'm sure you have to, in organizations that are changing from one technology to a competing technology. In these instances you can clearly see the affective domain at work in the resistance to learning the new technology, as many people are emotionally attached to what they've already mastered.

Within the affective domain there are five stages that learners progress through as they react to the technical training. Figure 8-2 shows the five stages of learning in the affective domain, and you can follow along with this list:

- **Receiving** This first stage of learning in the affective domain requires that the learner at least receive the information you're offering. The participant must, at a minimum, be passively involved in the learning process by being open to learning. If participants come to class with a predetermined decision to refuse to learn, then they've not even started the receiving process to accept the information.

- **Responding** Once a learner has passed through the receiving stage the individual will naturally enter the responding stage by *responding* to what's being presented to them in the learning environment. In responding, the individual participates in the learning process. This stage is evident when a person is asking questions, participating in discussions, completing exercises, and contributing to the course.

- **Valuing** Some components of your teaching will interest a learner more than other topics. When a person becomes really interested in what you're teaching, or they're excited or anxious about a topic, they're attaching value to the information you're teaching. For example, a person may really be excited to learn about configuring an e-mail server because it's what they'll do in their job. That same person, however, may be bored with the configuration of a printer server because they'll never likely do that work or they've already mastered that topic.

Figure 8-2
There are five stages to learning through the affective domain.

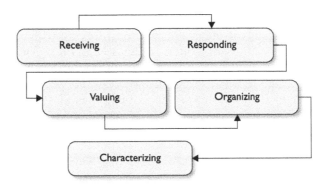

- **Organizing** As a person becomes more confident and experienced in a technology in your class, they'll begin to organize their thoughts, beliefs, and understanding to formulate their own ideas and expectations on outcomes. For example, a learner in a networking class may have an understanding of how a network operates, so they'll test their understanding by connecting and removing network cables to PCs and testing the outcomes to prove or disprove their beliefs and hypotheses about what may happen.

- **Characterizing** When an individual has learned information, they'll apply the information and change their behavior. The learner now has a value and an organized belief that directly affects how they behave and how they'll learn new and relevant information. For example, a person in a Microsoft Word class could have a goal to create formatting styles. They value this topic, as it directly affects their day-to-day work; they've organized their understanding based on what you've taught them, and now they'll continue to refine and experiment with formatting styles to become more proficient in applying this information to meet their particular needs as they fulfill their role.

The affective domain, in some theorists' opinion, is a filter to learning. If the individual has negative emotions about the subject matter they are to learn, then there may be a predetermined refusal to learn. Other theorists believe that people don't really dip into the affective domain until they've processed the information and made a determination about the effect of the learning topic, the technology in your case, and how the subject matter may alter a person's life. As a technical trainer, it's valuable to acknowledge the affective domain, as how people feel affect how they learn. If you can engage learners, which you will as part of a learner-centered environment, people will be more likely to accept the technology, be less intimidated by the material, and feel more comfortable learning something new.

Reviewing the Cognitive Domain

The final domain in Bloom's Taxonomy is the cognitive domain. The cognitive domain is often believed to be end result of the affective and psychomotor domains. As a technical trainer you'll often lecture on and demonstrate technology, with the goal of the learner absorbing the material and leaving the class with the necessary knowledge. Evidence of the cognitive domain is usually seen in the behavioral change a person exhibits based on their complete understanding and acceptance of the value of the education. For example, if you teach a class on how to create and administer a database, the people in the class will show evidence of the cognitive domain by applying their understanding in the workplace because they understand why the database should be administered and the plan to complete its administration.

The application of knowledge, however, isn't always a correct reflection of the cognitive domain. A person could still not understand how to operate with a given technology, but they can be intelligent enough to follow step-by-step instructions. The cognitive domain goes beyond the ability to just follow directions—it's the understanding and the application of the understanding to bring about a specific result. Through experience, practice, and repetition individuals show evidence of the depth of understanding and knowledge.

Here are the components of the cognitive domain, starting at the bottom of the hierarchy:

- **Knowledge**   The fundamental element of the cognitive domain is knowledge, sometimes also referred to as remembering. This element is evident when a person can recall specific information, technical terms and concepts, and answer questions about the technology. For example, a person could explain how a computer connects to the Internet. Many facts, concepts, and ideas have to be expressed with this task analysis.

- **Comprehension**   The second element is comprehension of the technical topic, sometimes referred to as understanding. Certainly there's a difference between just recalling facts and concepts and expressing an understanding of the technical information. This cognitive element is evident when a person can take a learned concept and then explain the concept in their own language. For example, a person would be able to explain the benefits of a wired network versus a wireless network.

- **Application**   The application of knowledge is done by taking existing comprehension and applying it to new scenarios and problems. This is basically building on existing knowledge to discover new knowledge. For example, a person could complete a Network+ course and then troubleshoot a network problem based on what they've learned already. Imagine the person serving as a technician and going to a client's site where they've never worked before. By observing the problem, looking for causal factors, and then applying what they've learned, they can resolve the network connectivity issue.

- **Analysis**   Analysis, in the cognitive domain, is demonstrated by examining a problem or scenario and thinking through the problem's root causes and causal factors. The participant can define what the problem is, describe the relationship between the causal factors and the problem to be solved, and break down the problem into an organized description. For example, a user may not be able to print to a network printer. The learner could break down the problem into three logical components: user's computer, the network, and the remote printer. Then, within each component, they analyze the conditions to determine where the actual problem, or related problems, may exist.

PART IV

Finally, the learner could draw a conclusion as to why the user can't print and how the problem can be resolved.

- **Synthesis** This component of the cognitive domain is sometimes referred to as create because the learner is creating a new solution based on what they've already learned. For example, by understanding how to program and work with Hypertext Markup Language (HTML) an individual can create many different websites. Obviously not all websites look the same, as it's the creativity, or the synthesis of knowledge, that allows people to create and customize webpages. In order to do this well, however, there must be knowledge, understanding, and application of information to put it all together and create a new webpage. Furthermore, several designers could be challenged to create a specific look and feel of a website, but each designer could take their own approach to create the same end result.

- **Evaluation** The final component in the cognitive domain is evaluation. This component is evident when a person can explain their logic and reasoning behind how they use the technology to solve a problem. Consider how two network engineers may have differing, and passionate, opinions on the best network operating system, the best hardware, and the best configurations for their clients. Both engineers may have reliable, usable results, but their beliefs and opinions have been shaped by their knowledge, understanding, and past application (experience). This is evident when they evaluate a problem or opportunity and present a solution that they believe is the preferred method of implementation.

Within the cognitive domain key action verbs are associated with each element. These verbs describe the type of action that demonstrates the element. As a technical trainer you can assess a participant's level of cognitive application by seeing evidence of these verbs in each element. If you're creating exercises and exams, you can choose a category and associated verb to test the learner's depth of comprehension in a given element. For example, a trainer may offer an exercise where the learner is to break down a network infrastructure and then categorize the types of network components. This exercise would test the learner's depth of cognitive application and synthesis. Table 8-1 is a summary of the cognitive elements and the associated verbs.

The cognitive domain is best described as the person's ability to understand and apply information. The depth of understanding and the accuracy of applying knowledge are often based on the experience and maturity of the person doing the application. As you might expect, a person who's new to technology and is taking a hardware configuration course may feel more overwhelmed with the terminology and concepts than a person who's worked in the technology arena for the past 20 years.

Knowledge	Comprehension	Application	Analysis	Synthesis	Evaluation
Arrange	Classify	Apply	Analyze	Arrange	Appraise
Define	Convert	Change	Appraise	Assemble	Argue
Describe	Defend	Choose	Break down	Categorize	Assess
Duplicate	Describe	Compute	Calculate	Collect	Attach
Identify	Discuss	Demonstrate	Categorize	Combine	Choose
Label	Distinguish	Discover	Compare	Comply	Compare
List	Estimate	Dramatize	Contrast	Compose	Conclude
Match	Explain	Employ	Criticize	Construct	Contrast
Memorize	Express	Illustrate	Diagram	Create	Defend
Name	Extend	Interpret	Differentiate	Design	Describe
Order	Generalized	Manipulate	Discriminate	Develop	Discriminate
Outline	Give example(s)	Modify	Distinguish	Devise	Estimate
Recall	Identify	Operate	Examine	Explain	Evaluate
Recognize	Indicate	Practice	Experiment	Formulate	Explain
Relate	Infer	Predict	Identify	Generate	Interpret
Repeat	Locate	Prepare	Illustrate	Plan	Judge
Reproduce	Paraphrase	Produce	Infer	Prepare	Justify
Select	Predict	Relate	Model	Rearrange	Predict
State	Recognize	Schedule	Outline	Reconstruct	Rate
	Review	Show	Point out	Relate	Relate
	Rewrite	Sketch	Question	Reorganize	Select
	Select	Solve	Relate	Revise	Summarize
	Summarize	Use	Select	Rewrite	Support
	Translate	Write	Separate	Set up	Value
			Subdivide	Summarize	
			Test	Synthesize	
				Tell	
				Write	

Table 8-1 The Cognitive Domain Includes Action Verbs for Each Cognitive Element

Chapter Summary

In adult education, and particularly in technical training, the focus is on the learners' ability to comprehend and apply the information you're offering. This concept of moving the focus from the trainer to the participants' needs is the heart of learner-centered instruction. Learner-centered instruction examines the needs of the participants, beginning with the course development, and is carried through to the instructor's delivery of the technical content. The intent is to help learners retain the technical knowledge and apply this information in their roles within the organization. This concept is also known as performance-based learning, because the people in your classes are learning how to change their behavior and perform at higher standards based on the correct information you've offered.

PART IV

Adult learners must see the connection between what you're teaching and how it will affect their lives and job performance. If there's no inquiry into how the learners will apply the information in their lives and jobs, then there's a less realistic chance of creating learner-centered instruction. Commercial trainer centers and in-house training departments alike should examine what the learner needs to know in order to maximize performance in their roles. It's a waste of organizational money and time to teach topics that won't be utilized or applied by the individual. This is why the instructor's wealth of observation, experience, and conversations with learners are all needed to fully capture and understand how the class can be structured, and sometimes modified, to best support the learners' post-class behavior.

In some cases the instructor must play the role of business analyst and instructional designer to fully capture the learners' needs. Analyzing learner tasks, ideally before class begins, gives the instructor insight into the processes, procedures, and expected outcomes of activities learners do in their roles. Shadowing the learners through active and passive observations helps the instructor experience and understand the work that learners will complete. Just understanding how a software program can work isn't enough for an instructor to understand how the learners will actually use the software. For example, an instructor can understand the functionality of Microsoft Excel, but learners can apply the functionality of Microsoft Excel for financial, calendar, and even data usage.

Associated with performance-based training is Bloom's *Taxonomy of Educational Goals*. This philosophy of education and knowledge retention helps define the objectives educators have for learners. Within the taxonomy there are three escalating domains of comprehension and mastery. First, the psychomotor domain defines the motor skills, eye-hand coordination, and manipulation of the technology, such as using a mouse and keyboard. Next is the affective domain that describes the emotional values learners attach to concepts, and sometimes technology, and how it affects their abilities to learn. The cognitive domain is the most robust of the three, as it describes the actual comprehension, application of information, and change in behavior based on what people have learned in your technical classes.

Key Terms

active observation   Part of learner task analysis where the observer is actively involved in the task, asks questions for clarity, and may even participate in the actual work to better understand the tasks the learners will need to be able to complete with the technology.

adaptation   A component of the psychomotor domain in Bloom's Taxonomy that happens when a learner has mastered a specific skill and can adapt their existing knowledge and apply it to new conditions and circumstances.

affective domain   The emotional values and feelings people attach to learning; part of an individual's ability to learn, but it's also a significant part of the emotional health that allows a person to empathize with others.

analysis   A component of the cognitive domain in Bloom's Taxonomy. Analysis in the cognitive domain is demonstrated by examining a problem or scenario and thinking through its root causes and causal factors.

application   A component of the cognitive domain in Bloom's Taxonomy. Application of knowledge is expressed by taking existing comprehension and applying it to new scenarios and problems.

Benjamin Bloom   Education psychologist at the University of Chicago; developed, along with a group of educators, the Taxonomy of Educational Goals to help define the objectives educators have for learners.

characterizing   Part of the affective domain in Bloom's Taxonomy. When an individual has learned information they'll apply the information and change their behavior. The learner now has a value and an organized belief that directly affects how they behave and how they'll learn new and relevant information.

cognitive domain   In Bloom's Taxonomy, the cognitive domain defines the actual knowledge gained and ability to act on understanding as a result of learning.

complex overt response   Component of the psychomotor domain in Bloom's Taxonomy that happens when the learner can complete a complex task based on their understanding and control of their motor skills.

comprehension   A component of the cognitive domain in Bloom's Taxonomy. Comprehension is sometimes referred to as understanding, and is expressed through an understanding of the technical information and the ability of the learner to explain this understanding.

evaluation   A component of the cognitive domain in Bloom's Taxonomy. It is evident when a person can explain their logic and reasoning behind how they use the technology to solve a problem.

guided response   Component of the psychomotor domain in Bloom's Taxonomy where the learner can follow the instructor's directions to perform a motor skills task.

hierarchical approach   Breaks down tasks into a hierarchy of events, sometimes called subtasks, that contribute to the final result of the task or assignment.

knowledge   A component of the cognitive domain in Bloom's Taxonomy. This element is evident when a person can recall specific information, technical terms, and concepts, and answer questions about the technology.

learner-centered environment   The instructor puts the focus of the class on the learners and their need to change their behavior by applying the information gained.

mechanism   Component of the psychomotor domain in Bloom's Taxonomy. The mechanism is a slightly advanced combination of the set and the guided responses, where the learner can perceive the problem, operate with proficiency, and understand the correct responses to create the expected, predictable end result.

organizing   Part of the affective domain in Bloom's Taxonomy. As a person becomes more confident and experienced in a technology in your class, they'll begin to organize their thoughts, beliefs, and understanding to formulate their own ideas and expectations on outcomes.

origination   Component of the psychomotor domain in Bloom's Taxonomy that happens when the learner takes their experience and expertise with existing knowledge and creates a new method, new skill, and expected outcome.

passive observation   Part of learner task analysis where the observer passively watches the tasks from start to completion without interrupting the process.

perception   Component of the psychomotor domain in Bloom's Taxonomy. This attribute relies on the individual using the senses to determine what physical activity should happen.

performance-based training   The priority of the seminar is to help learners perform better in their lives and roles by teaching exactly what they need to know to perform more efficiently.

psychomotor domain   Part of Bloom's Taxonomy that describes the learning and application of physical tools and abilities, motor skills, and individual activities to complete a task.

receiving   Part of the affective domain in Bloom's Taxonomy. This first stage of learning requires that the learner at least be passively involved in the learning process by being open to learning.

responding   Part of the affective domain in Bloom's Taxonomy. In this stage the individual participates in the learning process. This stage is evident when a person is asking questions, participating in discussions, completing exercises, and contributing.

set   Component of the psychomotor domain in Bloom's Taxonomy that describes the readiness to respond to predictable situations.

subject matter expert (SME)   An individual who is well versed in the technology, tasks, and application of the technology to help guide the task analysis and course design and development.

synthesis   A component of the cognitive domain in Bloom's Taxonomy. This component of the cognitive domain is sometimes referred to as create because the learning is creating a new solution based on what the participant has learned.

task analysis   An observation of the actual tasks and subtasks that people do to complete their responsibilities with a given technology.

Taxonomy of Educational Goals   A categorization of education objectives, domains, descriptions, and actions that educators have for learners.

valuing   Part of the affective domain in Bloom's Taxonomy. When a person becomes really interested in what you're teaching, or they're excited or anxious about a topic, they're attaching a value to the information you're teaching.

Questions

1. Your organization subscribes to the learning-centered education philosophy. In this type of environment, the focus of the training is on the learners and their ability to do what with the technology you're teaching?

    A. Make the company more profitable

    B. Use as many features as possible

    C. Use the technology as part of their performance

    D. Use the technology in a fun and engaging way

2. Can an instructor create a learner-centered environment when the organization is using commercially available off-the-shelf training materials?

    A. The instructor cannot unless the materials are designed for the specific learners.

    B. The instructor can if the contents of the materials match exactly what the learners need.

    C. The instructor can if she has the authority to change the class materials.

    D. The instructor can if she communicates with the participants and adapts the course to their needs.

3. What's the first thing a training department must determine when a training request is initiated?

    A. Why the training is needed

    B. When the training is needed

    C. What the training should include

    D. Who the audience for the training will be

4. Complete this statement: Trainers should focus on _____.

    A. What the people will learn in the class

    B. What the people will be able to do after the class

    C. How the training will explore the learning objectives

    D. What the people will be required to experience in class

5. Martha is performing learner task analysis to better understand how Herman does his job. Martha is watching Herman install a new printer server and several pieces of hardware in preparation to teach a technical class. Martha is not asking questions or interrupting Herman; she's just observing his work. What term best describes what Martha is doing in this scenario?

    A. Active observation

    B. Shadowing

    C. On-the-job training

    D. Passive observation

6. Why should an instructor complete learner task analysis? Choose the best answer.

A. To understand how learners do their work

B. To understand what the learner is expected to do as a result of your training

C. To understand the workflow and processes of the learner so that you can best teach the new material

D. To understand how the learner operates and how these operations may affect the learner's ability to receive new information

7. What term is assigned to the learner task analysis approach that often works backwards to understand the preceding tasks that must be completed in order to contribute to the final outcome of the learning process?

A. Project network diagram

B. Passive observation

C. Reverse shadowing

D. Hierarchical approach

8. Which one of the following domains is not part of Bloom's Taxonomy?

A. Cognitive

B. Affective

C. Pedagogical

D. Psychomotor

9. You are teaching a technical class in which participants will learn how install a new piece of equipment in your organization. In this class participants will need to be able to use a special tool as part of the installation. Which component of Bloom's Taxonomy is being addressed when using the tool?

A. Motor skills

B. Psychomotor

C. Affective

D. Cognitive

10. Within the psychomotor domain there are seven levels of performance. Which one of the following is best described as a learner using keyboard shortcuts, the mouse, and eye-hand coordination to work efficiently and hesitation free in a software program?

A. Adaptation

B. Mechanism

C. Complex overt response

D. Set

11. What component of the psychomotor domain in Bloom's Taxonomy is best described as a person using their senses to help determine what physical action should happen next?

    A. Perception

    B. Set

    C. Mechanism

    D. Adaptation

12. Which one of the following statements best describes the affective domain in Bloom's Taxonomy?

    A. The affective domain describes the emotional values and feelings people attach to the technology they're learning.

    B. The affective domain describes the emotional values and feelings people create based on what the technology will bring them.

    C. The affective domain describes the analysis of the technology and training and what the outcomes of the class may bring the learner.

    D. The affective domain describes the desire of the participant to learn.

13. All of the following components are part of the affective domain in Bloom's Taxonomy except for which one?

    A. Receiving

    B. Origination

    C. Responding

    D. Valuing

14. What component of the affective domain in Bloom's Taxonomy is demonstrated by the level of interest an individual has in what you're teaching?

    A. Valuing

    B. Perceiving

    C. Energy

    D. Personalization

15. You've taught a technical class in your organization. Six weeks after the class your training manager reports that errors have been reduced significantly as a result of what you've taught. What component of the affective domain is represented in this scenario?

    A. Valuing

    B. Responding

    C. Characterizing

    D. Applying

16. Which component of the cognitive domain is often considered the basis for all other elements within the domain?

    A. Brain

    B. Knowledge

    C. Comprehension

    D. Application

17. You've taught a technical class on how to use Microsoft Word, including some keyboard shortcuts. Based on the shortcuts you've taught the group, Beth decides to experiment with the key combinations to see what will happen in the software. Which component of the cognitive domain is demonstrated in this scenario?

    A. Beth is using the knowledge component.

    B. Beth is using the analysis component.

    C. Beth is using the synthesis component.

    D. Beth is using the application component.

18. Which one of the following is not a component of the cognitive domain?

    A. Application

    B. Synthesis

    C. Comprehension

    D. Reflection

19. Which component of the cognitive domain in Bloom's Taxonomy would a person be experiencing when they can explain their logic and reasoning behind how they'd configure a web server based on the technology learned in a class about web servers?

    A. Evaluation

    B. Analysis

    C. Application

    D. Comprehension

20. Within the cognitive domain, key action verbs are associated with each element. These verbs describe the type of action that demonstrates the element. How do these action verbs help an instructor?

    A. The action verbs allow an instructor to assess the depth of the cognitive domain in each participant by seeing evidence of the cognitive components through the key words that describe them.

    B. The action verbs allow an instructor to test the learners by asking what the action verbs do for the respective technology.

    C. The action verbs are for instructional designers, not instructors.

D. The action verbs allow an instructor to edit the depth of the cognitive domain in each participant by adding exercises and scenarios for the cognitive components through the key words that describe them.

Questions and Answers

1. Your organization subscribes to the learning-centered education philosophy. In this type of environment the focus of the training is on the learners and their ability to do what with the technology you're teaching?

   A. Make the company more profitable

   B. Use as many features as possible

   C. Use the technology as part of their performance

   D. Use the technology in a fun and engaging way

   C. The best answer is that the focus is on how the learners will use the technology in their performance of their roles and responsibilities. A is incorrect; while there is some belief that using the technology will make the company more profitable, that's not the focus of learner-centered education. B is incorrect, as using many features doesn't help the learner if the learner doesn't need to use all of the features in their jobs. D is incorrect; while training and learning can be fun and engaging, it's not the focus of a learner-centered environment.

2. Can an instructor create a learner-centered environment when the organization is using commercially available off-the-shelf training materials?

   A. The instructor cannot unless the materials are designed for the specific learners.

   B. The instructor can if the contents of the materials match exactly what the learners need.

   C. The instructor can if she has the authority to change the class materials.

   D. The instructor can if she communicates with the participants and adapts the course to their needs.

   D. Communication is the key to creating a learner-centered environment when utilizing commercial materials in a training environment. Choices A, B, and C are incorrect, as these solutions don't address the learners' needs as choice D does. The instructor can assess what the learners need and adapt the course accordingly.

3. What's the first thing a training department must determine when a training request is initiated?

   A. Why the training is needed

   B. When the training is needed

   C. What the training should include

   D. Who the audience for the training will be

A. Of all the choices, this is the best answer because it helps define the reasoning behind the training, sets expectations for the training, and helps the trainers predict what the outcome of the training should be. Choices B, C, and D are important elements to identify, but knowing when the training is needed, what the training will include, and who the audience will be does not define the supporting detail and expectations of the training.

4. Complete this statement: Trainers should focus on _____.

   A. What the people will learn in the class

   B. What the people will be able to do after the class

   C. How the training will explore the learning objectives

   D. What the people will be required to experience in class

B. Training should focus on what the people will be able to do after the class. An instructor's focus should always be on the results of training—how the participants' behaviors will change as a result of the learning. A and D are similar choices, but these examine the actions within the class, not the expected outcomes and results of the education. Choice C isn't a valid answer, as training doesn't explore the learning objectives; the learning objectives help define the content of the training activity.

5. Martha is performing learner task analysis to better understand how Herman does his job. Martha is watching Herman install a new printer server and several pieces of hardware in preparation to teach a technical class. Martha is not asking questions or interrupting Herman; she's just observing his work. What term best describes what Martha is doing in this scenario?

   A. Active observation

   B. Shadowing

   C. On-the-job training

   D. Passive observation

D. This is an example of passive observation, as Martha is not involved in the tasks or stopping Herman from completing his tasks in a normal workflow. A is incorrect, as active observation happens when Martha interrupts the workflow, asks questions, and may even be involved in the analysis. B is incorrect, as shadowing is slang for active or passive observation, not just passive as in this scenario. C is incorrect, as Martha is watching the tasks to prepare for a training session she'll teach, not to complete them as part of her role in the company.

6. Why should an instructor complete learner task analysis? Choose the best answer.

   A. To understand how learners do their work

   B. To understand what the learner is expected to do as a result of your training

C. To understand the workflow and processes of the learner so that you can best teach the new material

D. To understand how the learner operates and how these operations may affect the learner's ability to receive new information

> B. The ultimate goal of learner task analysis is not to understand how learners do their tasks, but to understand what learners are to do as a result of your training. Choices A, C, and D focus on the actual mechanics of the class and the learner's workflow, not the results of training. Performance-based learning focuses on the learners' outcomes of the training class.

7. What term is assigned to the learner task analysis approach that often works backwards to understand the preceding tasks that must be completed in order to contribute to the final outcome of the learning process?

A. Project network diagram

B. Passive observation

C. Reverse shadowing

D. Hierarchical approach

> D. The hierarchical approach describes the analysis process starting with the end result of a workflow and breaking down the outcomes and examining the preceding activities to reach the final result. A is incorrect, as the project network diagram is a visual flow of the work. B is incorrect, as passive observation describes the silent shadowing and observation of a workflow. C, reverse shadowing, isn't a valid analysis term.

8. Which one of the following domains is not part of Bloom's Taxonomy?

A. Cognitive

B. Affective

C. Pedagogical

D. Psychomotor

> C. Pedagogical, the education of children, is not part of Bloom's Taxonomy. Choices A, B, and D are incorrect because cognitive, affective, and psychomotor are all domains of Bloom's Taxonomy.

9. You are teaching a technical class in which participants learn how to install a new piece of equipment in your organization. In this class participants will need to be able to use a special tool as part of the installation. Which component of Bloom's Taxonomy is being addressed when using the tool?

A. Motor skills

B. Psychomotor

C. Affective

D. Cognitive

B. The best answer is psychomotor. A, motor skills, describes the actions being completed in psychomotor, but it's not the best answer, as it's not part of Bloom's Taxonomy. C is incorrect, as affective describes the emotional value people assign to topics and learning. D is incorrect, as cognitive describes the mental understanding, analysis, and behavior of the learners in the training and as a result of the training.

10. Within the psychomotor domain there are seven levels of performance. Which one of the following is best described as a learner using keyboard shortcuts, the mouse, and eye-hand coordination to work efficiently and hesitant free in a software program?

    A. Adaptation

    B. Mechanism

    C. Complex overt response

    D. Set

C. The complex overt response is best demonstrated when the learner can complete a complex task based on their understanding and control of their motor skills. A is incorrect; adaptation happens when a learner has mastered a specific skill, such as operating a printer; they can adapt their existing knowledge; and they can apply it to new conditions and circumstances. B, mechanism, happens when the participant understands each step of the guided responses and develops a mindset to completing the task. The mechanism is a slightly advanced combination of the set and the guided responses where the learner can perceive the problem, operate with proficiency, and understand the correct responses to create the expected, predictable end result. D, the set, is incorrect; the set describes the readiness to respond to predictable situations; the set is almost like an evolved mindset based on experience with a task.

11. What component of the psychomotor domain in Bloom's Taxonomy is best described as a person using their senses to help determine what physical action should happen next?

    A. Perception

    B. Set

    C. Mechanism

    D. Adaptation

A. Perception is the correct answer, as it is the ability of a person to use their senses, such as smell, sight, or sound, to help determine what physical action should happen next. B, set, is incorrect, as set describes the readiness to respond to predictable situations. It's almost like an evolved mindset based on experience with a task. C is also incorrect; mechanism is a slightly advanced combination of the set and the guided responses where the learner can perceive the problem, operate with proficiency, and understand the correct responses to create the expected, predictable end result. D, adaptation, is a component of the psychomotor component that happens when the learner, having mastered a specific skill, such as operating a printer, can adapt their existing knowledge and apply it to new conditions and circumstances.

12. Which one of the following statements best describes the affective domain in Bloom's Taxonomy?

   A. The affective domain describes the emotional values and feelings people attach to the technology they're learning.

   B. The affective domain describes the emotional values and feelings people create based on what the technology will bring them.

   C. The affective domain describes the analysis of the technology and training and what the outcomes of the class may bring the learner.

   D. The affective domain describes the desire of the participant to learn.

   A. In Bloom's Taxonomy the affective domain describes the feelings and emotions that people attach to the technology and the learning process. Choices B, C, and D are incorrect choices, as these statements do not describe the affective domain.

13. All of the following components are part of the affective domain in Bloom's Taxonomy except for which one?

   A. Receiving

   B. Origination

   C. Responding

   D. Valuing

   B. Origination is not part of the affective domain, but is part of the psychomotor domain. Origination happens when the learner takes their experience and expertise with existing knowledge and creates a new method, new skill, and expected outcome. There are five components within the affective domain that you should be familiar with: receiving, responding, valuing, organizing, and characterizing.

14. What component of the affective domain in Bloom's Taxonomy is demonstrated by the level of interest an individual has in what you're teaching?

   A. Valuing

   B. Perceiving

   C. Energy

   D. Personalization

   A. Valuing is the correct answer, as this is the affective term that describes the level of interest a person has in the information you're teaching. Based on what the topic is the level of interest will vary, because people may see the connection between what's being taught in the class and what they'll be doing in their roles and responsibilities within the organization. Choices B, C, and D are all incorrect because these choices are not accurate elements within the affective domain.

15. You've taught a technical class in your organization. Six weeks after the class your training manager reports that errors have been reduced significantly as a result of what you've taught. What component of the affective domain is represented in this scenario?

    A. Valuing

    B. Responding

    C. Characterizing

    D. Applying

C. This is an example of characterizing, as the behavior of the learners has changed as a result of the training. A is incorrect; valuing happens when people value the topic you're teaching because it relates to them personally and they understand the significance of the information. B is not the best choice because responding happens during the training as people respond to the training you've offered. D is incorrect, as applying is not a component within the affective domain.

16. Which component of the cognitive domain is often considered the basis for all other elements within the domain?

    A. Brain

    B. Knowledge

    C. Comprehension

    D. Application

B. Knowledge, sometimes called remembering, is the basis for the other components of the cognitive domain. The other components of the cognitive domain are comprehension, application, analysis, synthesis, and evaluation. A, brain, is not a component of the cognitive domain. C and D are components of the cognitive domain, but these aren't the basis for the cognitive domain.

17. You've taught a technical class on how to use Microsoft Word, including some keyboard shortcuts. Based on the shortcuts you've taught the group, Beth decides to experiment with the key combinations to see what will happen in the software. Which component of the cognitive domain is demonstrated in this scenario?

A. Beth is using the knowledge component.

B. Beth is using the analysis component.

C. Beth is using the synthesis component.

D. Beth is using the application component.

D. In this example Beth is using the application component because she is applying existing comprehension to new scenarios and problems. She's building on existing knowledge to discover new learning. A is incorrect; knowledge is the recall of facts and things learned. B is incorrect, as the analysis phase analyzes how the technology will actually be used in production. C is incorrect; synthesis combines elements learned to create new solutions, such as learning HTML to create many different types of webpages.

18. Which one of the following is not a component of the cognitive domain?

A. Application

B. Synthesis

C. Comprehension

D. Reflection

D. Reflection is not a component of the cognitive domain. The correct components of the cognitive domain are knowledge, comprehension, application, analysis, synthesis, and evaluation. Choices A, B, and C are incorrect, as these are components of the cognitive domain.

19. Which component of the cognitive domain in Bloom's Taxonomy would a person be experiencing when they can explain their logic and reasoning behind how they'd configure a web server based on the technology learned in a class about web servers?

A. Evaluation

B. Analysis

C. Application

D. Comprehension

A. Evaluation is evident when a learner can explain their reasoning and logic behind their decisions based on what they've learned in a technical class. B is incorrect, as analysis is demonstrated by studying a problem and reviewing the root causes and causal factors of the scenario. C, application, isn't the correct answer, as this component is demonstrated when information is applied to new scenarios and problems. D is also incorrect; comprehension is the understanding of a technical concept that a person can express and explain in their own language.

20. Within the cognitive domain key action verbs are associated with each element. These verbs describe the type of action that demonstrates the element. How do these action verbs help an instructor?

A. The action verbs allow an instructor to assess the depth of the cognitive domain in each participant by seeing evidence of the cognitive components through the key words that describe them.

B. The action verbs allow an instructor to test the learners by asking what the action verbs do for the respective technology.

C. The action verbs are for instructional designers, not instructors.

D. The action verbs allow an instructor to edit the depth of the cognitive domain in each participant by adding exercises and scenarios for the cognitive components through the key words that describe them.

A. When an instructor wants to assess the depth of the cognitive domain for each participant, he can examine the evidence of the action verbs in the activities, quizzes, and conversations with the learners. Choices B, C, and D are incorrect. The instructor doesn't need to ask the learners what the action verbs do, but rather just look for evidence of the verbs in the actions the learners take. While instructional designers do use the action verbs to create learning exercises and opportunities, these verbs are also for the instructors.

Promoting Learner Engagement

In this chapter you will:

- Follow the communication model
- Utilize active listening to comprehend what learners are saying
- Rely on effective listening to discover the learners' intent
- Create good quizzes to test learner comprehension
- Implement the social learning theory
- Create games and activities to engage learners

Public speaking can be pretty scary even when you have a class that's excited about the technology and eager to hear what you have to say. But speaking in front of a group can be even more daunting when the group isn't sure why the training is needed, what the objectives for the class are, and how you'll help them do their work better. It's not a pleasant day when you begin your class and you can feel that people aren't interested in what you have to say, you can sense the negative energy in the classroom, and people's body language is telling you all the wrong things. You'll need to assess learner needs, feelings, and perceived threats to turn this group around.

Of course, I'm painting one of the worst-case scenarios for you—most classes are just the opposite: people are excited to be in the classroom, they're eager to hear what you have to share, and they already see the link between the training and their day-to-day work. As your class moves on, however, some of the positive energy this group has presented may begin to wane. It's hard for anyone to sustain a positive mindset and energy when learning new technologies. Learning is hard work, mentally taxing, and can drain the energy from anyone. It's your role, as a technical trainer, to keep people excited about the technology and the learning. It's your role to keep people motivated, involved, and interested in learning the materials.

In order to keep people motivated and interested in the class, you'll need to keep your energy level up, share your excitement, and be interesting so that your participants are interested. You'll monitor your participants for their body language, feedback, and energy levels to find opportunities to bring them back into the course agenda and keep them interested in the technology. As a technical trainer, virtual or in the classroom, how you act and feel will become a mirror for how learners also act and feel. If you're sluggish, bored, or tired, chances are your learners are too. You must constantly monitor your energy and interest—and see how the class is responding—to keep the material fresh and interesting. In this chapter you'll explore some ideas and concepts to keep learners engaged in the materials.

Engaging Technical Learners

Sometimes technical training can be really boring to adult learners. When a technical trainer is lecturing on how Transmission Control Protocol/Internet Protocol (TCP/IP) addresses are broken down into binary numbers, or how to design and model a database, or how to develop software using a waterfall approach, or how—well, you get the idea. Sometimes the information you're teaching is very important, you're a great instructor, but the subject matter is really dry and esoteric. Unless your learners are enthralled by the minutiae of the technology, and some people may be, you'll likely discover that people may nod off and become bored with your class.

Of course, as you've already learned, the first step to teaching a great class is to link the information to how the learners will apply it in their lives and jobs. Learners need to see the importance of the information and how it relates to them. If you fail to link the subject matter to the individual then you'll have a tougher challenge teaching the topic. But some topics, even when you've made the connection, can still just be tough to teach and to learn. These topics, these dry, stuffy topics, require a bit more engagement than the more exciting activities. Learners will perk up when they can see the link between the course content and their lives, but sometimes their energy may be low, they may be tired, or they feel exhausted from learning. In these moments you'll need to work a touch harder to keep these people involved.

To engage a learner means that you interact with them. You'll use activities, questions, conversations, and demonstrations to bring the learners into the learning. The goal is to get the learner involved, listen to their questions, create questions for them, and converse with them. By speaking with the learners in your room you're interacting and engaging them—but how you engage their minds, what you discuss, and the paths to learning discovery are the key elements of being a great technical trainer. You want to help people be interested in the technical topic, you want to create challenges to help learners grow, and you want to pique their interest with good questions and activities. Learners appreciate this, not only because it makes your class more interesting, but it also helps them retain information.

Teaching Through Listening

Often when people think of trainers they think of people who like to talk, and talk, and talk. That might be true for some trainers, but not the great instructors. Great instructors know that a large slice of training time is actually listening to what the people in the class say. Listening to body language, feedback, and questions that participants offer are clues into the comprehension, confusion, and points that likely need clarification in the classroom. Participants appreciate an instructor who will listen, ponder, and then respond to their questions. The instructor's response is only as good as the instructor's comprehension of the participant's questions. No one likes it when a person begins answering a question before they've finished hearing what the question is. To speak over a person's query is rude, and it's also dismissive.

Communication is really what you're doing when you instruct. In Figure 9-1 you're participating in the communication model. The communication model defines all of the components that allow knowledge to be transferred from one person to another. Here are the steps in the model:

- **Sender**   You are the sender as you're sending out the information to your participants.

- **Encoder**   Your message is encoded into a language, series of words, and paralingual aspects that affect the message's meaning. The encoder is whatever component, like your brain or a fax machine, that encodes the message.

- **Medium**   In a classroom environment your voice is the medium; the medium is anything that carries the message between two or more people, like your voice or a network cable.

- **Decoder**   A decoder decodes and interprets the message for the receiver. In your classroom your participant's brain decodes the message so that the individual can understand the information. Another good example of a decoder is a fax machine that accepts an incoming fax.

- **Receiver**   The classroom participant is the receiver of the message.

- **Acknowledgement**   The acknowledgement is a sign from the receiver to the sender that the receiver got the message. Acknowledgements don't necessarily mean that the receiver agrees with the message, or even understands the information, but they got it.

- **Noise**   Anything that interrupts or distorts the message is noise; for example, side conversations, distractions from other participants, or interruptions in the classroom.

- **Barriers**   Barriers are elements that prevent communication from happening, such as network failure in a virtual classroom or people who speak different languages. Note that barriers aren't shown in the figure.

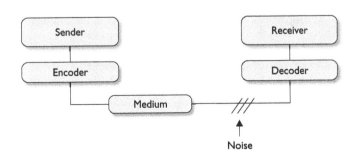

Figure 9-1
The communication model shows the path of a message.

Imagine that you're teaching a class and you send information out to the participants. The model originates with you, and your message is sent to each participant. Now one of the participants has a question. When the participant asks their question they are now the sender and the model is shifted so that you become the receiver. When you answer the question the model shifts again as you're the sender. When multiple people are involved in the conversation the model continues to shift to whomever is the sender and to whomever becomes the receiver.

The receiver in the communication model has an important role, as they must receive the information and offer an acknowledgement in return. As an instructor you're often in the role of the receiver—you have to be involved in the conversation. If you're like me, and I suspect you are, you've been teaching a class, lecturing on a topic you've taught a hundred times before, only to have someone ask you a question on what you just said. And you can't remember what you just said. Your mind was focused on your after-work run, picking up the kids, or your big plans for the weekend. Your body may have been present in the classroom, but your mind was somewhere else. You weren't present in the classroom and the communication model has succumbed to the barrier.

Tied to your role as the receiver in the communication model is how you listen. Active listening happens when you try to understand as clearly as possible what the participant is asking. Active listening in a conversation means that you are paying attention to what the other person is saying and you're actually doing three things:

- **Comprehending** This first component of active listening is simply understanding the words and language the other person is saying. When your mind is elsewhere you can't comprehend the message, so active listening can't happen. Another contingency on active listening is being able to discern the message through the filters—for example, when the sender is using English as a second language and you only speak English, it may be difficult to comprehend the message the sender is offering.

- **Retaining** When the learner sends you a message, you need to retain what the sender is saying in order to react to it. This can be challenging when the learner's question is lengthy, rambling, or lacking logic. Retention of the learner's question, however, helps you process the information and better complete the next step, responding.

- **Responding** When a person is sending you a message, you can offer intermittent feedback, such as nodding your head, crossing your arms, or smiling. These responses can help direct what the other person is saying or help them discover information about their question. This part of active listening offers immediate feedback and lets the sender of the message realize that you're present, involved, and participating in the communication.

Another type of listening is effective listening. Effective listening works along with active listening, but its focus is on understanding the message and its context and meaning. Effective listening aims to truly understand the message that the sender has offered and then to respond appropriately. Your responses in effective listening aren't just verbal, but include eye contact and body language. Effective listening requires that you, the recipient of the message, give the most appropriate feedback to the sender to show that you understand the message and its intent. Effective listening focuses on sending the most appropriate response for the received message.

There are four attributes of responses in effective listening:

- **Probing**   This response asks for more detail without making the sender of the message feel defensive. For example, you might ask the sender to elaborate on their question rather than criticize the question's validity.

- **Reflecting**   This response is actually paraphrasing what the sender has said to confirm your understanding of it. Reflecting isn't just being a parrot of the message; it's actually rephrasing the question to confirm that you and the sender both understand the message.

- **Deflecting**   Sometimes the receiver of the message wants to share a related message to answer the sender's question or comment. This deflection, however, can seem like the recipient isn't acknowledging what the other person said. You can imagine a class where a technical instructor responds to a question with her own story without acknowledging the learner's question. The learner may feel dismissed or feel the instructor is focusing on themselves rather than the class. Deflecting can be useful when the instructor needs to move the course pace along, but deflecting should be used sparingly and with caution.

- **Advising**   This response happens when the instructor gives unsolicited advice to the sender. For example, a student tells the instructor how she won't be allowed to actually configure the server settings in class because of her organization's policies. When the instructor begins offering advice rather than just listening, the instructor is advising, giving unsolicited advice for a problem the learner is experiencing. Instructors must pay attention to what learners are asking versus telling.

Active and effective listening work together. Recall that active listening is about comprehension, retention, and then a response. Effective listening is about understanding the intent and motivation of the message before responding appropriately. In a technical training environment most of the conversation between you and the participants will be direct and focused on the learning objectives. Your goal as a technical trainer is to focus on the learners' needs and meeting the course objectives. Use caution in your responses, as your aim should be to edify the learners, not advise or deflect the conversation to your interests.

Creating Quizzes for Technical Classes

Quizzes can be a great tool to use in technical classes to keep learners involved and to confirm their retention. If you're teaching a multiday event, quizzes first thing in the morning can help learners recall information you've already covered in the class and help them link that knowledge to today's topics. In a single-day or shorter event, quizzes are useful as a review item to keep learners involved with the materials. Quizzes can also keep learners interested in how they're doing in the class—create a little competition, and people can really come alive with answers and accuracy.

Writing good quiz questions, however, takes some time and thought. If you're teaching the same class over and over, you might craft your quizzes to focus on the topics that are the toughest for learners to grasp. You can also create a good, solid quiz, and then use it over and over in your classes. I have a pool of questions I use in my classes that I choose from based on how the class is responding to certain topics. I like to mix up my quizzes with some tough questions, some easy questions, and some tricky questions that really test comprehension. Whatever approach you take to using your quizzes, there are some guidelines you can follow to make the process of creating quizzes easier and more comprehensive for your classes:

- **Multiple-choice questions** Multiple-choice questions are ideal, as they give the learners choices of possible answers and they're fast to grade. When writing multiple-choice quizzes you'll craft a question and then write four to six answers for the learners to choose from. Your answers should be plausible, but not too tricky. You want the learner to be able to discern the choices, but still be tempted by possible wrong answers. The goal isn't to trick the learners, but to really test the learners' comprehension.

- **Fill-in-the-blank questions** These questions require the learner to know the answer based on the statement rather than having an opportunity to guess at a correct answer, as with the multiple-choice questions. When writing these questions terms are a good basis for questions—for example: _____ network cables use twisted-pair wiring to connect computers on an Ethernet network. The learner would have to know that CAT5 cabling uses the twisted-pair wiring to answer the question properly. Your statement needs to provide enough information so that the learner has to provide only one specific term that could answer the question.

- **Essay questions** One of the toughest questions to grade is the essay question. This question asks the learner to provide a narrative for their answer. For example, compare and contrast Microsoft SQL Server and Oracle Server for database management. Now the learner has to share their understanding of each server type and compare the commonalities and differences of both. The technical trainer then has to read the answer and make a judgment on its accuracy and depth. Essay questions may be good choices for longer classes, but can often be energy-draining and too time-consuming for most technical classes.

- **True-or-false questions** These questions ask the learner to read a statement and then determine its accuracy. It's basically a 50/50 chance that the learner is going to get the question correct. These question types are quick and easy to create and grade, but they can be tricky if the learner hasn't comprehended the course material.

A good strategy for creating tests and exams is to display the questions via an overhead projector. Other than the obvious paper-saver, this approach can give you several options as part of your class. You walk the participants through the exam question by question and let each person answer the questions in private and then grade the quiz as a group. You could also divide up the room and create a competition out of answering the test questions, or you could create a competition among all of the participants for each question. Finally, displaying the questions via an overhead projector can also serve as an avenue to create a group discussion about the course topics.

Utilizing Social Learning Theory

The social learning theory posits that people learn from one another by observing, modeling, adapting, and emulating the behavioral models of others. In a technical class, especially a class where people will work on hardware in a lab environment, there's a social aspect to the learning, as the participants will interact with one another, see each other work with the technology, and often coach one another on how the technology has worked for them. If you've ever taught a hardware class, such as the CompTIA A+ course, you've likely experienced the social learning theory.

In the social learning theory the instructor encourages people to work together and have conversations about their immediate experiences completing a task and allows ad hoc demonstrations among the participants. This approach allows people to observe activities so that they can discover learning, but also helps build confidence among the participants, as they may teach topics to the other participants by demonstrating how the technology has worked for them. You can imagine Jane showing Bob how she was able to change some code to get a different result in her software programming. Bob then learns from Jane rather than from the instructor; Jane also has reinforced her learning discovery by teaching Bob how to work with the software.

 VIDEO   See the video *Utilizing Social Learning Theory*.

Dr. Albert Bandura is one of the leading proponents of the social learning theory. Bandura's theory is geared more toward adolescents, but there's much in the theory that can be applied to adult education. In particular, the idea that adults model and emulate what others do is evident in many technology courses. There are four primary elements to the social learning theory that apply to adult education:

- **Attention**   Adults must invest their time and attention to what's being demonstrated and taught if they are to learn the behavior. If people are bored, nodding off, surfing the Web, or texting, they are dividing their attention and the odds of actually learning are diminished.

- **Retention**   The ability to retain what's been taught. If you're teaching or demonstrating a complex topic, you'll likely adjust your teaching approach to appeal to visual, auditory, and kinesthetic learners so that there is ample opportunity for the learners to retain what you're instructing.

- **Reproduction** Adults need an opportunity to practice what they've learned. If you're teaching how to install a second hard drive in a server but don't let people practice what they've seen, the odds of actually reproducing the behavior when it matters become unlikely. Like any new skill, the more often the learner gets to practice the knowledge, the easier the task will become.

- **Motivation** Adult learners want to know why a topic is important in order for them to want to learn. If the learner doesn't make the connection between the classroom topic and how it applies to their life, they will be less likely to give their attention, retain the information, and reproduce the knowledge when it matters most.

Bandura's theory of social learning stresses the concept of learning from others, but it's also important to remember that people need to learn the correct behavior from others. You've probably experienced classes where learners have modeled the wrong behavior from other people based on poor assumptions. A joke I like to tell on social theory deals with two little boys. Mom asks what the boys want for breakfast. The first boy says, "I'll have some damn pancakes." Of course, the mother is shocked and sends the boy to time out. She then asks her second son what he wants for breakfast; this boy responds, "Well, I don't want any damned pancakes!" Learning the right lesson, like swearing or choosing pancakes, requires explanation and some coaching from the technical instructor.

Training with Group Participation

Group participation is an excellent method to get people involved in your class and to encourage social learning. When you introduce group participation, you shift the class from being a pure instructor-led environment to a learner-based environment. Group participation activities draw the learners into the material, and it creates some social responsibility within the classroom, as learners are now dependent on one another's contributions. Group participation gets people's attention and helps them retain the knowledge because they're practicing what they've learned, and you're giving people motivation, as they're now involved with other people's learning.

When creating a group participation event, you'll want to choose an activity that will be complex enough for two people to do together, rather than take a single-person activity and try to shape it to two people. For example, if you were teaching a class on Microsoft Word, an activity to format a document wouldn't be a realistic activity for two or more people to do together in a group activity. The reason why, of course, is because employees don't format documents as a group. Your exercises should be structured to emulate a group event out in the real world so participants make the connection and experience something that is more realistic in an actual production environment.

A good example of a group participation activity, sticking with the Microsoft Word document, could be to utilize formatting and track changes in a document. In this approach, a learner could create a new document and save it to a classroom server, and then a second user could edit the original document using Microsoft Word's track changes features. In this simple exercise two or more people could interact with one another, use the software, and then compare the changes to the document to experience a very real-world scenario. To create a group activity in a technical class, just imagine how people will actually use the technology in their day-to-day jobs and then re-create the scenario in the classroom.

A poorly designed group activity can hinder learning, cause confusion, and lose people's interest in your class. Think through the group activity and how you want the participants to interact with one another and what you expect the end result of the activity to be. When you launch a group activity, explain the steps of the activity to the learners so your participants understand what they're doing in the class and what your expectations of the event are. If the people in your class don't know one another or you're working in a virtual classroom environment, I strongly encourage you to define who will be working with whom in the exercise. I've observed some trainers who leave the group creation process up to the learners only to see people leave the room because they're confused, shy about working with other people, or don't want to work with a stranger in the room. Take charge: explain the activity, assign partners, and then coach people through the activity.

Communication from you, the technical trainer, is key to creating a group exercise that'll work. Explain the roles and responsibilities of the people in the groups; ideally, the division of labor is fair among the group so everyone can contribute and experience the technology. The group activity should feel natural and with clearly defined outcomes and expectations. If people don't understand what they're supposed to be experiencing, then they'll become frustrated and the retention and learning from the experience is diminished. Just like quizzes, I like to display the group activity directions on an overhead projector so everyone knows the expectations for the activity.

Offering Learning Games and Activities

Here's something blunt and honest: Some technology classes can be really dry, stuffy, and boring. Some technical trainers and highbrow educators won't like that comment, but if you face facts, you might be in love with the technology you're teaching, as you should be, but that doesn't mean your participants are going to love the technology too. While you may have made the link between the technical topics and the application of the topics to participants' day-to-day duties, it doesn't necessarily make the learning more enjoyable. Even if learners fully agree that the learning is needed to help them in their careers, it doesn't mean that they'll necessarily retain the information through lectures, demonstrations, and labs.

Games and activities can be introduced into the classroom to mix things up and keep people happily involved in the topic you're teaching. Games can energize your class, engage learners in the activity, and create some competition among the learners in the technical topic. Games also can help learners retain information that might be ignored otherwise. All technical trainers should strive to motivate and engage the people in their classes, and games and challenges are great methods to do this. And games allow learners to—gasp!— actually have some fun while learning.

If you're using quizzes as a method to review material, you may want to consider implementing games occasionally instead. While quizzes are good approaches to reviewing what you're already taught, games can alleviate the stress and anxiety that's often associated with exams. Games are fun and light, while quizzes can seem daunting and more official. You can still use the same questions as the quizzes—just make up a simple game and keep score to get your learners thinking about the competition and not about the idea of being tested on what you've taught. Like a quiz, a game can help you determine how well people are retaining what you've taught and they can give you feedback on retention and comprehension into the class.

Not all games have to be directly tied to the technology you're teaching. Early in the class schedule, games are better served as an ice breaker to learn about people in your class. I've never been fond of the rote introductions that many trainers utilize—sorry, if that's you—but people don't pay attention to the "stand and deliver" quick introductions. If I'm teaching a longer class, I like to use some ice breakers to get people involved, but also to create a fun environment in the classroom. Here are some of my favorite games that I've used to get people learning about each other and to kick off the class:

- **Candy intros** Learners reach into a paper bag and choose one piece of candy. Depending on what color of candy they draw determines what they'll share with the class. For example, a yellow piece of candy might be what their hobby is, a red piece of candy might be a vacation, or a green piece of candy is to describe their job. I'll use this game several times in a multiday event for fun and to keep people learning about each other. I've also used this approach where the color of candy determines a type of question you'll answer as part of the game.

- **Tell a yarn** This is a good game to use if the people in the class are already familiar with one another. To use this game you'll take a ball of yarn and cut it into strings of 12 inches to several feet in length. Then you'll bunch the yarn together into one big pile. You'll instruct learners to choose a string, slowly pull it from the pile, and wind it around their finger as they introduce themselves to the group; the learner should be finished with their introduction by the time they reach the end of the string. The funny part is that some of the ends of yarn are long and some are short, causing learners to quickly adapt their introduction to the group.

- **Speak in questions** This simple game requires learners end every sentence in a question. Divide your class into groups of three or four and instruct them to have a conversation among themselves, but each statement has to be a question. If a person fails to answer in a question then they're eliminated from the game. When each group has been narrowed down to one person, you'll repeat the process with just these remaining people until you get down to just one person. This is a fun exercise and helps people get comfortable speaking with each other in the class. Of course, give a prize to the last remaining interrogator.

Games and activities are a fun way to break away from the usual approach to the class time, but you'll want to balance the amount of fun from the games with the need to cover all of the course objectives. The audience, subject matter, and time constraints should all be considered when playing games in a learning environment. You don't want people to feel like they're rushed for time in the learning because you've spent too much time playing games. You also don't want people to feel bored or stifled in the classroom and ignore their need to mix up the learning with some fun as well.

Chapter Summary

To create a learner-centered training environment for the face-to-face instructor or for the virtual trainer means that the focus is off the instructor and onto the learner. Communicating with the learners equates to speaking with, not speaking to, the participants in the classroom. The communication model calls for a sender and receiver, a coder and decoder, and a medium to transport the message. Active and effective listening, not just talking, are big portions of the communications model to transfer knowledge from the instructor to the learners. Recall that active listening means that the instructor is trying to understand the learners' messages as clearly as possible. Effective listening means that the instructor is trying to understand the meaning behind the learners' messages.

Throughout the training session instructors can rely on quizzes to test learners' comprehension and understanding and to gain feedback on the course content. When creating quizzes the technical trainer should strive for questions that are challenging, that make the learners think about the technical content, and that test the learners' comprehension of the content. The goal isn't to trick the learners, but to create a challenge for the learners to think through the problem presented and to give the best possible answer. Quizzes can test learner comprehension, but they can also be a good method to create some fun competition, group discussion, and interactions among the learners.

Social learning theory posits that people can learn from one another by emulating behavior, interacting with other learners, and watching people complete tasks in an effort to replicate the activity. Social learning theory is a good method to help learners in a technical lab environment—for example, you could partner a more advanced learner with a relatively inexperienced learner. Social learning theory relies on four values: attention, retention, reproduction, and motivation. To have effective social learning, the participants must be interested in the technology that's being taught. The method of teaching the subject matter must be presented to the different types of learners with variety—not just lecture and demonstration. Once learners have been introduced to the technology, they'll need an opportunity to practice what they've learned. Finally, learners need to understand how the learning topic relates to their roles and responsibilities.

Training does not, and should not, be boring. Group participation and games in the classroom can create interest and motivation for learners to get involved in the course. If learners are bored, they are not paying attention and are less likely to retain information, and the effectiveness of your training is lost. Group discussions, exercises with multiple participants, and some friendly competition can all be used to keep learners motivated and interested in the course content. Games and contests can also be used as a reinforcement to the learning. Dividing the class into smaller groups and creating competition among the groups can be a fun way to review material and foster feedback on what you've taught in the class.

Key Terms

acknowledgement   In the communication model, an acknowledgement is a sign from the receiver to the sender that the receiver got the message. Acknowledgements don't necessarily mean that the receiver agrees with the message or even understands the information, only that the receiver has received the message.

active listening   The instructor tries to understand the message as clearly as possible without looking for subtext and hidden agendas in the message. The instructor only listens to the message that is being sent from the learner.

advising   Part of effective listening; this response happens when the instructor gives unsolicited advice to the sender.

attention   Part of the social learning theory; adults must invest their time and attention to what's being demonstrated and taught if they are to learn the behavior.

barriers   Part of the communications model that prevents communication from happening, such as network failure in a virtual classroom or people who speak different languages.

communications model   Defines how communication happens between the sender and receiver and considers barriers to communication and interference with communication.

comprehending   The first part of active listening is understanding the words and language the other person is using.

decoder   The element of the communication model that decodes and interprets the message for the receiver. In a classroom, the participant's brain decodes the message so that the individual can understand the information.

deflecting   Part of effective listening; sometimes the receiver of the message wants to share a related message to answer the sender's question or comment. This deflection, however, can sometimes seem like the recipient isn't acknowledging what the other person said. Deflecting can be useful when the instructor needs to move the course pace along, but deflecting should be used sparingly and with caution.

effective listening   Focuses on understanding the message and the sender's context and meaning. Effective listening aims to truly understand the message that the sender has offered and then to respond appropriately.

encoder   The element of the communication model that encodes the message into the formatting of the medium, such as analog or digital, to be sent through the medium between the sender and receiver.

essay questions   Questions for review that test the learner's comprehension. These questions can be among the toughest to grade. This question type asks the learner to provide a narrative for their answer.

fill-in-the-blank questions   These questions require the learner to know the answer based on the statement rather than having an opportunity to guess at a correct answer, as with the multiple-choice questions.

medium   The element between the encoder and decoder that carries the communication message. In a classroom environment, the instructor's voice is the medium; the medium is anything that carries the message between two or more people, such as a network cable.

motivation   Part of social learning theory; adult learners want to know why a topic is important in order for them to want to learn. If the learner doesn't make the connection between the classroom topic and how it applies to their life, they will be less likely to give their attention, retain the information, and reproduce the knowledge when it matters most.

multiple-choice questions   Questions for review, testing comprehension, and gaining feedback from learners. These questions are ideal, as they give learners choices of possible answers and they're fast to grade.

noise   A component in the communication model that interrupts or distorts the message; for example, side conversations, distractions from other participants, or interruptions in the classroom.

probing   Part of effective listening; this response asks for more detail without making the sender of the message feel defensive.

receiver   The recipient of the message; a classroom participant is the receiver of the message that the technical trainer has sent.

reflecting   Part of effective listening; the receiver paraphrases what the sender has said to confirm understanding of the message.

reproduction   Part of social learning theory; learners need an opportunity to practice what they've learned.

responding   Part of active listening; when a person sends the instructor a message, the instructor can offer intermittent feedback, such as nodding, crossing arms, or smiling. These nonverbal responses can help direct what the other person is saying or help them discover information about their question. This part of active listening offers immediate feedback and lets the sender of the message realize that the receiver is present, involved, and participating in the communication.

retaining   Part of active listening; the learner sends a message that the instructor must retain in order to understand and react to the message.

retention   Part of social learning theory; this is the ability to retain what's been taught. Technical trainers should adjust the teaching approach to appeal to visual, auditory, and kinesthetic learners so that there is ample opportunity for the learners to retain the information.

sender   The originator of the message to be transmitted through the communications model.

social learning theory   People learn from one another by observing, modeling, adapting, and emulating the behavior and actions of other learners.

PART IV

true-or-false questions Quick, simple questions in which the learner reads a statement and then determines its accuracy. While these question types are quick and easy to create and grade, they can be tricky if the learner hasn't comprehended the course material.

Questions

1. You're teaching a class for your organization on a new technology. Marcy, a learner in your class, asks you a question about how the technology saves data to the network servers. You think you understand Marcy's question, but to be certain, you paraphrase the question back to her. What type of listening is this?

   A. Active listening

   B. Effective listening

   C. Parroting

   D. Communications model

2. What component of the communications model is described as the transport of the message?

   A. Decoder

   B. Auditory

   C. Medium

   D. Transporter service

3. You're teaching a virtual class on a new technology for an organization. In the class you've sent a private chat to a participant about their exercises. If you were to examine the communications model, what component would the chat software be?

   A. Encoder

   B. Medium

   C. Decoder

   D. Receiver

4. A participant in your class asks a question about the software you're teaching. The question, you believe, has implications that criticize the decision to implement the software in the organization. You don't want to judge the learner, so you ask some follow-up questions to better understand the meaning and implications of the question. What type of listening is this?

   A. Effective

   B. Active

   C. Evaluative

   D. Consideration

5. You are teaching a class and there are people chatting outside of your classroom door. The chatter is a distraction to the learners in the class. If you were to examine the communications model, what component would the chatter be considered?

   A. Barrier

   B. Message

   C. Distracter

   D. Noise

6. In the active listening model what component is best described as simply understanding the words and language sent in the message?

   A. Comprehending

   B. Understanding

   C. Decoding

   D. Retaining

7. In the active listening model, one component is responding. Which one of the following best describes responding in active listening?

   A. Nonverbal responses

   B. Pauses when speaking

   C. Reversed communications model

   D. Transference

8. A learner asks a question in your technical class, and you want to fully understand the meaning and intent of the question. So, as part of effective listening, you ask follow-up questions for more details. What component of effective listening is this?

   A. Reflecting

   B. Deflecting

   C. Querying

   D. Probing

9. A learner in Beth's class asks a question that centers on the learner's dislike for the software implementation in the organization. Beth responds to the question by offering some advice on how best to manage the software and the feelings toward the implementation. What type of response is this in the effective listening model?

   A. Advising

   B. Reflecting

   C. Deflecting

   D. Probing

10. What's the primary purpose of a quiz in a classroom?

   A. To test the learners

   B. To test the learners' comprehension

   C. To review the material

   D. To see who is following along

11. What question type requires a learner to choose from four to six possible answers?

   A. Multiple-choice questions

   B. Fill-in-the-blank questions

   C. True-or-false questions

   D. Essay questions

12. Which one of the following question types is the hardest to grade?

   A. Multiple-choice questions

   B. Essay questions

   C. Fill-in-the-blank questions

   D. True-or-false questions

13. What theory states that learners can learn by observing, modeling, and emulating what other people do?

   A. Social aspect theory

   B. Social learning theory

   C. Adult learning theory

   D. Community learning theory

14. In social learning theory, what must be present for adults to begin the learning process?

   A. Instructor

   B. Attention

   C. Opportunity

   D. Need

15. Eric is an instructor in your organization and he's changing his teaching style periodically to give participants that learn through auditory, visual, and kinesthetic approaches an opportunity to learn the information. This is an example of what aspect of social learning theory?

   A. Attention

   B. Retention

C. Reporting

D. Reproduction

16. In a technical class Mary watches her friend Bob install a hard drive into a computer. Based on what Bob has done, Mary follows the same steps to complete the installation. What is this process called in social learning theory?

   A. Reproduction

   B. Replication

   C. Transference

   D. Retention

17. Who is the primary proponent of social learning theory?

   A. Frederick Herzberg

   B. Albert Bandura

   C. W. Edwards Deming

   D. Abraham Maslow

18. In social learning theory, what aspect is best described as adults need to know why something is important before they'll learn it?

   A. Reasoning

   B. Confidence

   C. Purpose

   D. Motivation

19. You are teaching a technical class in your organization and you've created several quizzes for your learners. You believe, however, that some of the participants in the group have test anxiety and are not performing well on the quizzes. What other solution could you offer instead of the quizzes that would still test the learners' comprehension?

   A. Quizzes are the best comprehension of learner performance.

   B. Create games using the quiz questions.

   C. Create fill-in-the blank questions.

   D. Offer a verbal exam instead of the written exam.

20. What term describes the initial activity to get learners to know one another in a classroom setting?

   A. Forming

   B. Norming

   C. Ice breaker

   D. Grouping

Questions and Answers

1. You're teaching a class for your organization on a new technology. Marcy, a learner in your class, asks you a question about how the technology saves data to the network servers. You think you understand Marcy's question, but to be certain you paraphrase the question back to her. What type of listening is this?

   A. Active listening

   B. Effective listening

   C. Parroting

   D. Communications model

   A. Active listening means that the listener participates in the listening by trying to clearly and accurately understand the message that is being sent. B, effective listening, is incorrect, as effective listening tries to understand the meaning of the message that is being sent. C is incorrect, as parroting isn't a listening type and is slang for simply repeating a statement without actually trying to understand what the sender is saying. D, the communications model, isn't an appropriate answer for this question.

2. What component of the communications model is described as the transport of the message?

   A. Decoder

   B. Auditory

   C. Medium

   D. Transporter service

   C. The medium is the intermediary component between the sender and receiver, and is responsible for moving the message between the two communicators. A is incorrect; the decoder takes the coded message and puts it back into useable format for the receiver. B is incorrect, as auditory isn't part of the communications model. D is incorrect, as transporter service isn't part of the communications model.

3. You're teaching a virtual class on a new technology for an organization. In the class you've sent a private chat to a participant about their exercises. If you were to examine the communications model, what component would the chat software be?

   A. Encoder

   B. Medium

   C. Decoder

   D. Receiver

B. The chat software is the medium between the sender and receiver. A and C are incorrect choices, as the software isn't the actual encoder or the decoder. You could argue that the software is both the encoder and the decoder in the communications model, but by choosing either A or C you eliminate the other component of the model. D, the receiver, isn't the best answer because the receiver is the student that receives your message. When the student responds you'll become the receiver in the model.

4. A participant in your class asks a question about the software you're teaching. The question, you believe, has implications that criticize the decision to implement the software in the organization. You don't want to judge the learner, so you ask some follow-up questions to better understand the meaning and implications of the question. What type of listening is this?

   A. Effective

   B. Active

   C. Evaluative

   D. Consideration

A. This is an example of effective listening. Effective listening happens when the instructor tries to understand the intent and meaning of the message the learner is offering. B, active listening, is incorrect; active listening aims to just understand and comprehend the actual question without interpreting what the question may actually mean. Choices C and D are not correct, as evaluative and consideration are not examples of listening.

5. You are teaching a class and there are people chatting outside of your classroom door. The chatter is a distraction to the learners in the class. If you were to examine the communications model, what component would the chatter be considered?

   A. Barrier

   B. Message

   C. Distracter

   D. Noise

D. Noise describes any element that may distract from the communication, such as chatter and side conversations in the classroom. A, a barrier, isn't the best choice, as this component prevents communication from happening at all. B is incorrect, as the message is the component of what's actually being communicated. C is incorrect, as a distracter isn't part of the communications model.

PART IV

6. In the active listening model, what component is best described as simply understanding the words and language sent in the message?

   A. Comprehending

   B. Understanding

   C. Decoding

   D. Retaining

   A. Comprehending is the first component in active listening, and it means to just understand the words and messages that have been sent to you. B, understanding, isn't a valid component of the communications model. C, decoding, is also incorrect, as it's not part of the active listening model. D, retaining, is part of the active listening model, but doesn't describe the understanding portion of active listening.

7. In the active listening model, one component is responding. Which one of the following best describes responding in active listening?

   A. Nonverbal responses

   B. Pauses when speaking

   C. Reversed communications model

   D. Transference

   A. Of all the choices, only the nonverbal responses are part of responding. Responding means intermittent responses, nonverbal clues, and verbal responses to the message sent. Choices B, C, and D are incorrect, as these choices do not describe responding in active listening.

8. A learner asks a question in your technical class, and you want to fully understand the meaning and intent of the question that's been asked. So, as part of effective listening, you ask follow-up questions for more details. What component of effective listening is this?

   A. Reflecting

   B. Deflecting

   C. Querying

   D. Probing

   D. This is an example of probing; probing aims to fully understand the question without making the learner feel defensive. A, reflecting, isn't the best choice, as this response is actually paraphrasing what the sender has said to confirm your understanding of the message. B is incorrect, as deflecting means the receiver of the message wants to share a related message to answer the sender's question or comment. C is incorrect, as querying isn't part of effective listening.

9. A learner in Beth's class asks a question that centers on the learner's dislike for the software implementation in the organization. Beth responds to the question by offering some advice on how best to manage the software and

the feelings toward the implementation. What type of response is this in the effective listening model?

A. Advising

B. Reflecting

C. Deflecting

D. Probing

A. This is an example of advising. This response can be useful, but Beth must make certain to not offer unsolicited advice to the learner rather than just advising the learner on the question's intent and meaning. This doesn't mean that the instructor should not anticipate issues or other questions, but rather that the instructor should keep opinions and questionable advice outside of the classroom. B, reflecting, is best demonstrated when Beth paraphrases the content of the learner's question. C, deflecting, means the receiver of the message wants to share a related message to answer the sender's question or comment. D, probing, isn't the best answer, as this is demonstrated when Beth asks additional questions about the learner's concerns.

10. What's the primary purpose of a quiz in a classroom?

A. To test the learners

B. To test the learners' comprehension

C. To review the material

D. To see who is following along

B. Quizzes are used to test the learners' comprehension of the material that's been covered in the class. A is incorrect; to test the learners isn't a complete answer for why the quiz exists. Reviewing the material, C is sometimes correct, but it is not the primary reason for offering a quiz. D, to see who is following along, isn't the best answer for this question.

11. What question type requires a learner to choose from four to six possible answers?

A. Multiple-choice questions

B. Fill-in-the-blank questions

C. True-or-false questions

D. Essay questions

A. Of course, the correct answer is the multiple-choice question. These question types, like the ones in this quiz, challenge the learner by requiring them to choose one of many possible answers. B, fill-in-the-blank questions, require the learner to provide the missing word to complete a statement. C, true-or-false questions, are relatively easy questions; learners must just decide if the statement is true or false. D, essay questions, require the learners to write a narrative about a question or topic.

12. Which one of the following question types is the hardest to grade?

    A. Multiple-choice questions

    B. Essay questions

    C. Fill-in-the-blank questions

    D. True-or-false questions

    B. Essay questions require the learner to write a narrative about a topic, but they also require the instructor to grade the question. Choices A, C, and D are incorrect, as these question types are not difficult to grade.

13. What theory states that learners can learn by observing, modeling, and emulating what other people do?

    A. Social aspect theory

    B. Social learning theory

    C. Adult learning theory

    D. Community learning theory

    B. Social learning theory posits that people learn from one another by observing, modeling, adapting, and emulating the behavioral models of others. Choices A, C, and D are incorrect choices, as these answers do not reflect the actual learning theory.

14. In social learning theory, what must be present for adults to begin the learning process?

    A. Instructor

    B. Attention

    C. Opportunity

    D. Need

    B. Adult learners must give their attention in order to begin the learning process. A, an instructor, is actually not needed in the purest sense of the learning theory, as people can learn by emulating what others do, not what an instructor says. C, opportunity, and D, need, aren't part of the social learning theory, so these choices are incorrect.

15. Eric is an instructor in your organization and he's changing his teaching style periodically to give participants that learn through auditory, visual, and kinesthetic approaches an opportunity to learn the information. This is an example of what aspect of social learning theory?

    A. Attention

    B. Retention

    C. Reporting

    D. Reproduction

B. This is an example of retention, as adult learners must have the opportunity to learn and retain what they've learned to be effective learners. Attention is needed to begin the learning process, so A isn't the best answer for this question. C, reporting, isn't part of social learning theory, so this choice is incorrect. D, reproduction, is the practicing of what's been demonstrated and learned.

16. In a technical class Mary watches her friend Bob install a hard drive into a computer. Based on what Bob has done, Mary follows the same steps to complete the installation. What is this process called in social learning theory?

    A. Reproduction

    B. Replication

    C. Transference

    D. Retention

    A. This is reproduction, as Mary is reproducing the steps that Bob has taken to complete the hard drive installation. B, replication, is incorrect, as this is not part of social learning theory. C, transference is also incorrect because this isn't part of social learning theory. D, retention, describes the ability to retain what was learned, not reproduce the actions.

17. Who is the primary proponent of social learning theory?

    A. Frederick Herzberg

    B. Albert Bandura

    C. W. Edwards Deming

    D. Abraham Maslow

    B. Albert Bandura is the primary proponent of social learning theory. Herzberg is best known for his theory of motivation. Deming was a leader in quality assurance. Maslow is best known for his hierarchy of needs.

18. In social learning theory, what aspect is best described as adults need to know why something is important before they'll learn it?

    A. Reasoning

    B. Confidence

    C. Purpose

    D. Motivation

    D. Adult learners want to know why something is important to them and how they'll apply it to their roles and responsibilities. A, B, and C may be relevant, but reasoning, confidence, and purpose are not part of social learning theory.

19. You are teaching a technical class in your organization and you've created several quizzes for your learners. You believe, however, that some of the participants in the group have test anxiety and are not performing well on the quizzes. What other solution could you offer instead of the quizzes that would still test the learners' comprehension?

A. Quizzes are the best comprehension of learner performance.

B. Create games using the quiz questions.

C. Create fill-in-the blank questions.

D. Offer a verbal exam instead of the written exam.

> **B.** Games and activities are often good substitutes for quizzes when learners are anxious about completing the quiz. A isn't the best choice, as sometimes activities and labs can better capture learner comprehension than exams can. C isn't the best choice, as fill-in-the blank questions can also be seen as a quiz and not alleviate learner anxiety. D may help create a group discussion, but it's not the best choice presented.

20. What term describes the initial activity to get learners to know one another in a classroom setting?

A. Forming

B. Norming

C. Ice breaker

D. Grouping

> **C.** An ice breaker is the initial activity that can bring learners together and help them learn about one another in the classroom. Ice breakers are fun, quick activities to help the group learn about each other and facilitate their comfort level in the classroom. A, B, and D are not valid choices for this question.

Motivating Adult Learners

In this chapter you will:
- Understand how adults learn new things
- Make training relevant for learners
- Maintain a learner-centered environment
- Help adults achieve learning goals
- Identify learning motivation for adults
- Explore competency and confidence

If I told you to pat your head three times and then snap your fingers twice, you'd probably want to know why before you acted. But if I said if you pat your head three times and then snap your fingers I'll give you 20 dollars, you might go right ahead and try the experiment. You were motivated to do the silly actions not because the actions interested you, but because you wanted the reward that was promised to you. You were motivated by the 20-dollar reward—not the experience of patting your head and snapping your fingers. Once you understood what the event was going to bring, you became willing to participate. Adults generally don't enjoy trying new things without understanding why the thing, action, or, in this book, learning is needed in the first place.

In adult education, the motivation to do something must be synchronized with what excites the learner. If, in the head-patting example, you thought the head patting would embarrass you or you didn't want the 20 dollars, then you probably wouldn't be motivated to do the activity. Consider how your motivation might change if you were told to pat your head and snap your fingers or you'll have to pay me 20 dollars. There's incentive for the positive, where I pay you 20 dollars, or there's incentive to avoid the negative, where you'll have to pay me 20 dollars. In adult education, learners are often treated the same way. If the learner isn't excited or interested in the perceived reward, they won't take action in the learning. If there's no consequence of not learning, learners may also not take action.

Motivating adults to learn is more than just a "carrot or the stick" mentality. Motivating adults to learn involves helping adults discover the learning, understand why the learning is practical, and see how the information will help them in their job. Adults want to see why the learning is needed and what's in it for them, but they also want the learning to be relevant and enjoyable. Learning is hard work, but when adults have emotional value attached to learning, they're more likely to be personally invested and willing to learn. It's the willingness that's tied to the motivation. Part of your job as a technical trainer is to help adults find their willingness to get involved, to learn, and then to change their behavior as a result of what they've learned in your class.

Understanding Adult Learners

As an adult you probably don't like to be told what to do. You also probably don't like it when supervisors or even trainers answer the why question with "because I said so." The same is true with adult learners in your classes. The people who come to your classes aren't children and don't want to be treated like children. Adults don't like to be talked down to, patronized, or treated like idiots. Adults like to understand why they're asked to do something, why a topic is important, and how the objective is going to help them succeed. Adults often come to your class with a goal in mind of what they expect from the training—your job is to help them achieve that goal, assuming the goal is realistic, by teaching the functions of the technology, but also by defining how the functions support the goal of the learner.

As a technical trainer you'll introduce each course topic by helping learners see how they'll apply the information in the real world—back in their jobs, usually. You can do this by using an analogy or by simply stating how the objective relates to an activity the learner will be expected to do in their role. Sometimes this will be obvious—like how to connect a printer to their workstation. Other objectives may be more obscure, like how to work in a programming language. Every learner in the class may have a need for the programming language, but how they'll apply the language could be different for each learner. You'll have to use broad enough examples to apply to many different learning goals, but not so esoteric that the examples are irrelevant. In other words, you don't want to be so specific that some learners feel like their learning goals aren't being supported.

If you're wondering how you're supposed to know what the learning goals of the participants are, it's not really a mystery: you'll ask. In your introductions, pre-course conversations, or even as part of an ice breaker exercise you can explore what the goals of the learners are for the technical training. With some courses, the learning goals will be self-explanatory—pass an exam, learn the new technology for operations, or update current skills. The learning goals I'm talking about are the specific aspects of the technology that the learner has an intrinsic interest in: how to configure the paper trays of a printer, how to create style sheets, how to record a macro, and other technology-specific tasks. These specific goals can help you tailor your presentation to engage the learners and keep their interest in the course. All of the information you present in the class may be important to each participant, but it's the specific topics that will keep your learners motivated.

Adapting Adult Learning Characteristics

You've already learned about the adult learning styles of auditory, visual, and kinesthetic, but there are also some characteristics of adult learners you should know to help you teach more effective virtual and face-to-face classes. Many of the adult learning characteristics are based on Malcolm Knowles' study on adult learning—that's the andragogical model. Recall that in this model the focus is on creating a learner-centered environment rather than an instructor-centered environment. This means that the instructor serves more as a facilitator and treats the adults in the room as equals and colleagues in the learning process. Adult education is dependent on the instructor, but the instructor shouldn't assume she's the most important person in the room. Without the learners there'd be no need for the instructor. The instructor's job is to help the learners achieve their goals.

Because adults are goal-oriented, a fundamental approach to teaching is to identify the specific educational goals of each learner and then work toward achieving those goals in the classroom. The technical trainer can also treat each topic, discussion, and exercise as a goal for the learners. I often like to create a challenge for the learners during hands-on exercises, such as a time boundary, a few additional steps in the activity, or by choosing partners to work through the labs together. These challenges aren't to make the course more difficult, but to get the learners to feel the connection between the classroom and the production environment. It's important for the classroom environment to be a safe place to learn and experiment, but trainers also need to help the learners see the practical implementation of the technology.

What I'm really talking about here is that your class needs to be relevant to the learner. No one wants to go to class for a technology that they'll never use—there's no point to it. Adults want to learn topics that are relevant to them. I can recall a specific class where I was teaching how to configure a DNS server and a learner piped up and said this didn't apply to him, as his company wouldn't be using DNS internally. Well, truth be told, he still needed to configure a DNS server as part of the internal configuration in this particular network operating system. The problem wasn't that the learner didn't want to learn; the problem was that I had failed to help the learner see the relevancy of the learning. Until the learner saw and understood how the technology was relevant to his role in his company he was determined not to learn. Relevancy is needed as part of the motivation of learning.

The relevancy of the information you're presenting must be personal to each individual in their role. Adults don't go to class just for fun—usually. Adults go to class to learn a technology with a goal of improving their lives through promotions, opportunities, or financial reward. This means that learning is serious business for most adults and they want the learning topics to directly contribute to their personal goals. Adults aren't looking for gold stars and smiley faces on their exams—they want to see how the outcome of their time invested in your class will help them achieve their personal goals. They must see the correlation between what you're teaching, what they're learning, and the achievement of their personal goals.

NOTE I'll contradict myself in just a moment, as some adults do go to training for fun, but the majority of adult learners have a purpose and goal in mind when they come to a technical training class.

It's not just being practical and relevant that will help learners be engaged and interested in your classes—it's also how you treat the learners. As part of my role as a train-the-trainer consultant I've had to sit through training classes where instructors have taught adults like they were teaching kindergarten. Maybe you've had that experience too—it's painful! Adults want to be treated like an adult, not like a child. Sometimes trainers do this on accident, because they're overenunciating their words and things begin to sound demeaning, but usually it's because trainers don't know better. They've experienced the instructor-centered training their whole life as a learner and the idea of teaching adult-to-adult is foreign to them. I always encourage trainers to be professional, but really to just have a conversation with the people in the room. You're not teaching; you're just talking with people about technology.

The reason why you want to talk *with* adults, and not *to* adults or *at* adults, is because we all have experiences and knowledge that demand respect. Think of all the things you've done and learned as a professional: the different jobs you've held, the contracts you've helped your company win, the scores of people you've trained over the years. These are all elements of your life experiences and contribute to your ability to teach and contribute as a technical trainer. The adults in your class have also done some amazing things that have shaped who they are and how they'll learn. These experiences affect and influence how an adult learns, as it serves as relevant knowledge to build upon. When a trainer dismisses the value of these experiences, it's demeaning and can become a barrier to learning—something no trainer wants to have happen.

In some cases the adult learner may struggle with why the training is needed at all. Consider an organization that's going to shed one technology platform for another. A learner in your class may have mastered everything there is to know about the old platform and can operate smoothly and efficiently with the older technology. Now here comes this new technology, with new ways of achieving things, and with new challenges to reach that same level of efficiency. For the learner, there's some emotional tie to the older way of getting things done and they may be resistant to learning and embracing the new technology—even though it's obvious the learning is needed to help them achieve their goals in the workplace. This learner is experiencing a value adjustment: they need to know why their work requirements will change to new work requirements. Simply stating that this is a management decision is just like saying "because I said so." The learner needs to understand why this change is better for the organization before they'll embrace it.

Facilitating Adult Education

Imagine you're about to teach a four-day technical class that requires 30 percent lecture, 30 percent demonstrations, and 40 percent activities and quizzes. As you might guess, it wouldn't be a good idea to give your lecture in one big chunk, then all of the demonstrations in one big segment, and then turn the class loose to do their activities. Adults learn by hearing you lecture, seeing the demonstration, and then practicing the technology. Wait a minute, that's the three learning styles: auditory, visual, and kinesthetic. While these three learning styles help people absorb the information you're presenting, they're not useful in large, isolated segments, as in my example. People learn best in smaller, digestible chunks of information; these smaller sections make it easier to see the relevancy, experience the new information, and retain it for implementation later.

When you teach technology in smaller sections instead of large chunks of information, learners can see the logical flow of the activities. For example, if you taught the complete process of how to write, format, and print a workbook in a layout and design software package, there would probably be too many steps to remember and later apply. A more practical approach would be to teach the information in smaller steps, like this:

- How to create a document
- How to save the document
- How to define the margins
- How to enter text
- How to format text
- How to create a style
- How to edit styles
- How to print the document

These smaller activities can support the learner's goals, are easy to remember, and are easy to replicate. It's not hard to imagine a trainer teaching a class where she'd explain the importance of saving a document, demonstrating how to save and use the Save As command, and then asking the class to do the same. These tiny steps to learning are incremental and follow a logical workflow, and it's practical to see the relevancy of how each step could be applied in the learner's job. The focus with each step is on the learner, as it's how the learner will create, save, edit, and print the document—not how wonderful the trainer is for knowing all these things that the learner doesn't.

NOTE It's important to keep a positive environment in the classroom. Don't belittle the technology, the course materials, or the learners. I've been in classes where the instructor has ripped apart the software and highlighted its weaknesses. Not good. My company just sunk a bunch of time and money into the software, and we were there to learn—not to have some nerd basically tell us we were idiots for choosing this software. Now the class was aggravated and we were opposed to learning from this schmuck. That's a great example of a trainer-centered, negative classroom, where the focus was on the trainer and not on the learner. A positive classroom encourages learners, keeps opinions private, and coaches learners on the best methods to achieve goals with the technology.

Just as it's important to encourage learners and give positive feedback, it's also important to correct learners when needed. When a learner is failing at completing a task or they explain a concept to you for clarification, you don't want to agree that they're correct if, in fact, they're wrong. You don't want learners to leave the classroom with incorrect information, but you'll need tact to help learners correct their misunderstandings. Of course, you don't want to embarrass the learner in front of their colleagues, but you must help them learn the technology. You can do this several different ways:

- **Be honest.** Simply and politely tell the learner why they're wrong in their understanding and how to actually complete the task or understand the concept. Smile and be friendly when you're taking this approach.

- **Lead the learner.** Through a series of questions and discussions, you can help the learner discover the information. This approach helps the learner make the connections between their misunderstanding and the correct answer and understanding. The instructor should treat the learner with respect and not be demeaning in the question and conversation. The goal is to help the learner, not embarrass the learner.

- **Demonstrate the solution.** Sometimes a learner doesn't understand the correct steps to follow to complete an activity. The instructor can demonstrate the correct steps for the learner on an overhead projector or through the virtual classroom interface. This approach helps the learner see the approach to reach the desired solution, but it's best to then give the learner an opportunity to practice the steps.

- **Create experiments.** When a learner creates a hypothetical situation, they're often actually trying to make the technology relevant to their lives. In these instances you can often help the learner see the relevancy and the solution by creating an experiment for the learner to try in the classroom. This approach is one of the best solutions, as it allows the learner to interact with the technology, but this solution isn't always practical, as configuring the technology for the solution may take more time than the class allows.

When facilitating adult education your goal is to help the learners with their goals. Make the training relevant, interesting, and applicable to the learners' lives and jobs. Learners have experiences, habits, and preferences that affect their ability to learn. The technical trainer needs to understand that learners aren't always going to approach the learning, classroom interactions, and desire to implement the technology with the same gusto the instructor would expect. Adult learners often feel proud of their experiences and preferences and may feel threatened or humbled by having to learn something new. Remember that learning is hard work and adults often feel pressure to perform in a classroom that isn't always realistic, based on the complexity of the technology you're teaching and their experiences before coming to this class. Your job is to diminish their anxiety, make the training relevant, and appeal to their learning styles.

Motivating Adult Learners

Motivation in education is personal for each learner. There's the obvious motivation in which the participant needs to learn the information to maintain their employment, but that's not always the most effective incentive—that's really a fear of consequences. Motivation is more intrinsic for the learner—a desire to know what you know with some personal gain or satisfaction from the learning. Surely you've taken a technology class with the intent to consult or teach in the technology; your desire may have been the financial rewards the knowledge would help you ascertain, but that probably wasn't your only reason for taking the class. There has to be something deeper and more valued in the desire to learn.

For example, I am no fan of database management—I just don't get it, am not interested in it, and it's all I have to think of to nod off to sleep. Database management is the least exciting area of technology to me, so I wouldn't be personally interested in taking a class on that topic (ever again!) and I'm certainly not interested in teaching database management. Imagine, however, if a huge opportunity was presented to me that required me to learn and teach database management. Now I'm stuck: do I seize the opportunity and put up with the pain of learning the technology I don't enjoy, or do I know how awful I'd be if I had to learn, embrace, and work with database management software? The motivation would be the reward of the opportunity, but would the motivation be as deep if I were able to learn a new project management software system and teach something I really enjoy? Probably not.

That's the point I'm getting at—motivation is personal, and external rewards or repercussions aren't as genuine as the internal desire and value associated with the learning. While some external motivation is often needed to get the learner to comply with organizational requirements, the openness to learning is greater when the learner can see the personal value, personal gain, and personal reward of learning the subject. It's difficult to learn anything you despise or that bores you. Learning isn't necessarily easier just because a participant is interested in the topic and sees the personal value the education will bring. The willingness to learn, the dedication to learn, and the tenacity to learn all become more likely for the participant when the proper, personal motivation is present for the learning experience.

 VIDEO   See the video *Motivating Adult Learners.*

Finding Learner Motivation

Adults are motivated to learn for more than just financial rewards. Yes, most technical training is linked to the promises, hopes, and continued financial rewards that mastering a technology will bring, but certainly not all of technology training is based just on the capitalist thought that learning results in money. Some technology is fun—like learning how to work in Adobe Photoshop, or creating a personal website, or creating software applications. People have various reasons why they want to come to your classes and learn what you have to offer.

There are six primary reasons people want to learn:

- **Organization expectations**   For many technical trainers, this is the most common reason for learning. People come to class because they are required to as part of their job. When an organization changes the technology that people use to support the organization, there's a management requirement to help the employees learn the new technology to continue to support the goals of the organization as a whole. If the organization doesn't teach their employees how to use a new technology, the organization is undermining its ability to reach its vision.

- **Career advancement**   If you're teaching a certification course, like any of the CompTIA, Cisco, or Microsoft classes, this is one of the most common motivating factors you'll encounter. People come to these classes to learn a technology to help them pass a certification exam—and advance in their career. Participants want to learn and master a technology to make themselves more attractive to employers, to maintain their competitive edge, and to grow their businesses.

- **Personal interest**   Some participants in your class may not be required to attend your training for any other reason than their own personal interest in the technology. These learners want to learn for the sake of learning, enjoy technology, and have personal motivation to explore and experiment with the technology. While these learners can be good participants, their expectations are vastly different from learners who are there because of organizational requirements and career advancement. The goal of these learners is usually more than to just learn the technology, but to master the technology.

- **Community impact** Some learners seek technical training to help in their community. They see the mastery of a technology as an avenue to volunteer, improve a situation, and participate in a not-for-profit program. They want to learn how to work with the technology and then implement what they've learned for the betterment of their community.

- **Networking opportunities** Some training programs can be fun, social events. Consider lunch meetings where a technical trainer may provide an overview of a technical concept to a group of network administrators. While there may be an interest in the talk the trainer is offering, the primary focus for many of the learners is on socializing and networking with their colleagues and peers.

- **Escapism** It's not uncommon for a technical trainer to encounter a learner who is in class to escape issues in their lives, boredom in their job, or just as a break in their regular routine. These learners can often be in class just to get away from work requirements. Their only motivation may be to dodge responsibility or mild curiosity. You'll have a tough time recognizing these workers and motivating them to learn.

By finding learner motivation, you can adjust your teaching style, conversation, and approach to teaching the class to appeal to each of these motivation types. While your goal is to teach and deliver the course objectives in an effort to change learner behavior, a secondary goal is to engage learners by identifying what's important to them in the classroom. By identifying their motivation and interest in the course, you can introduce topics and analogies that appeal to their motivations, give demonstrations that will help them in their lives, and create opportunities for learners to socialize. Chances are you do this already, but being aware of your actions can help you teach a more appealing class for your learners.

Motivating Adults to Learn

Because most adults come to class with some level of motivation already, you won't have to give big speeches to inspire people to perform in the classroom. You will, however, occasionally have to remind people of the importance of the material and underscore their motivation for learning. The nature of the course, your conversations with the participants, and ice-breaker activities can help you identify what motivates which learners. As a guideline, adults have a desire to be competent in what interests them. Competency, the basis for much of the motivation you'll use in your class, is really gained through application of information and practice. In Figure 10-1, for example, is the spiral of competence and confidence. As people become more confident in a technology, they'll also be willing to take more risks and explore the technology, build on what they've already learned, and then master the technology. Competence results in confidence, which results in more competence.

Figure 10-1
Competence results in confidence, which helps learners have more competence.

Competence

Confidence

Motivated learners will probably already recognize their need to embrace the learning process. This means they'll go right to the activities in class, be engaged in class conversations, and be engaged with you as you teach. It'll be obvious which learners are motivated to learn—they'll be the folks who ask questions, create scenarios of how they'll apply the technology in their lives, and go beyond the requirements of the class to complete their work. Their motivation will help them learn the fundamentals, which gives them confidence to become more engaged, which will result in more confidence—and ultimately they'll have the competence in the technology. Through application and practice, they'll master the technology and be proud of what they've accomplished.

Some learners, however, may be motivated to learn, but it is not very deep, so they need some encouragement from you, the technical trainer. When I talk about motivation, I'm really talking about keeping the learner engaged and involved in the class. The trainer needs to motivate the learner to stay focused, interested, and participating in the course material. The best method to keep a learner involved is to persistently remind the learner why the information is important—give the learner meaning behind what you're teaching. When you can link the meaning of the course content to the learner, you'll elicit involvement. Deep meaning, the passion that fuels the learners' desire to be involved, is usually more intrinsic than external-based, but you can still help learners discover deep meaning for the material you're presenting by reminding them of its importance.

Another approach to maintaining motivation is inclusion in the course delivery. This is really part of the learner-centered environment—keeping the focus on the learners and their goals—but it's also a sense of community and involvement for the whole group of learners. Inclusion is the interdependence that emerges from the shared experience of learning and the connectedness the learners feel as a group. Through group exercises, labs, and discussions, the group of participants can feel a sense of belonging to the class. You'll probably experience inclusion in longer training assignments, such as those events that may last several weeks rather than just a few hours. Inclusion satisfies the social and networking motivation learners often come to class with, but it also helps to keep each learner involved in their contribution to the course.

The technical trainer's attitude and the attitude among the participants directly affect the behavior of the participants. Attitude influences motivation for each learner—for the betterment or detriment of the group. Having the right attitude as the instructor helps you keep learners motivated, interested, and engaged. A poor attitude from the instructor—such as criticizing the technology, belittling participants, or showing frustration during presentations—can cause the motivation of learners to vanish, and consequently your effectiveness as a technical trainer also disappears. Poor attitude from a few participants can also affect the behavior and motivation of other learners. When people have poor attitudes, you'll need to address the issue, as left unchecked the class can derail and learners can become disengaged from the learning experience.

Chapter Summary

Adults like to know why they're being asked to do something and learn something. Adults want to see the link between the stuff you're offering in the classroom and how it'll actually work back in their lives and jobs. When adults come to a technical class, chances are good they already have an idea what the class will help them achieve—and technical trainers usually come prepared with a goal for learners to accomplish in the class. As a technical trainer you'll help adult learners discover knowledge, highlight the link between classroom and application, and help learners achieve their goals.

Because adults are goal-oriented, you should identify the learning goals of each participant so that you can address them, assuming they are relevant, in your class. Goals aren't just for learning objectives, but learners often like to feel challenged with the material and exercises. If the class is too easy, learners can feel like the material is not in-depth enough to really be beneficial to them in their jobs and lives. Learners want the course to be relevant to their goals and to their application of the technology once class is completed. Part of the instructor's role is to show learners how the material is relevant in their lives.

Relevancy can be shown through conversation, lecture, demonstrations, and hands-on activities. Learners want to be led to knowledge, not simply told information. If you can demonstrate the technology or create experiments for the learner, you'll address the kinesthetic learner, visual learner, and auditory learner all at once. By creating different avenues of learning, you're presenting varying opportunities for adults to experience the technology, learn what you're teaching, and see how the technology can be applied in their lives and jobs.

All of this leads you to motivate your learners. To motivate a learner is to keep the learner engaged and interested in what you have to offer in the classroom. While you can contribute to learner motivation, motivation often exists for the learner before class even starts. Learner motivation can stem from organizational requirements, where the training is mandated by the organization, such as when a company moves from one technology to another. Many learners will be motivated by career advancement and expectations the education will bring them. Community involvement opportunity, networking and socializing, and learning for the sake of learning are also possible sources of motivation.

By understanding what motivates a learner the technical trainer can adjust the course content, lecture, and approach in the class to help the learner achieve their goals and maintain interest in the material. Including learners through conversation, synergy, and attitude in the classroom all help them feel engaged and connected in the learning experience. Discussions, activities, and demonstrations help the participants learn the material, interact with other participants, and keep interest level up in the classroom. Ongoing motivation and interest will help the learner gain confidence, which leads to competence. Competence in the technology contributes to more confidence, and so on. Basically, the more motivated a learner is, the more likely the learner will be competent and confident in the technology, and their goals for learning will be achieved.

Key Terms

andragogical model   The focus is on a learner-centered environment where learners discover knowledge through experience.

career advancement motivation   The learner wants to learn and master a technology to make themselves more attractive to employers, to maintain their competitive edge, or to grow their business.

community impact motivation   The learner seeks technical training as an avenue to help their community. The learner sees the mastery of a technology as an avenue to volunteer, improve a situation, and participate in a not-for-profit program.

competence-confidence spiral   As learners become more competent in a technology, they'll become more confident in the technology, which encourages the learner to become even more competent, and the process repeats over and over until mastery of the technology is achieved.

escapism motivation   The learner is in class to escape issues in their lives, boredom in their job, or just as a break in their regular routine.

instructor-centered classroom environment   The instructor becomes the most important person in the classroom, and all learning must come through the instructor at the instructor's pace and discretion.

learner motivation   The reason why the learner is attending the training event.

learner-centered training environment   The classroom environment, instructor focus, and instructor attitude is geared toward helping the learner achieve their learning goals.

learning relevancy   The material in the course must be relevant to the learner's goals, lives, and/or career for the learner to be motivated to learn.

networking opportunities motivation   The participant sees the training program as a fun, social event, such as a networking function or short discussion on a technology.

organization expectations   For many technical trainers, this is the most common reason for learning. People come to class because they are required to as part of their job. When an organization changes the technology that people use to support the organization, there's a management requirement that employees learn the new technology to continue to support the goals of the organization as a whole. If the organization doesn't teach their employees how to use a new technology, the organization is undermining its abilities to reach its vision.

personal interest motivation   The learner attends training based on their personal interest in the technology. These learners want to learn for the sake of learning, enjoy technology, and have personal motivation to explore and experiment with the technology.

Questions

1. What term best describes the concept of the trainer treating the participants as adults in the classroom and as equals rather than as students?

    A. Andragogical model

    B. Instructor-centered model

    C. Colleague learning model

    D. Colleague competency model

2. Martha is attending your class on a new technology your company will use. Martha is not interested in the class, though the other participants are engaged. You ask Martha in confidence what seems to be the problem. Martha reports that she's not going to be using the technology, but her supervisor asked her to attend the class anyway since a colleague cancelled and the cost of the class was already paid for. Which one of the following best describes this situation?

    A. Martha is not engaged.

    B. The training is not relevant to Martha's life.

    C. The instructor hasn't identified Martha's motivation.

    D. The cost of the training is wasted, as Martha isn't motivated to learn.

3. You're observing Mary as she teaches a technical class. In the class Mary is overenunciating her words, is making exaggerated facial expressions, and is speaking in a voice that may be more appropriate for children than adults. What effect do you think this will have on the learners in the class? Choose the best answer.

    A. The learners will leave the class.

    B. The learners will be engaged as long as the learning is relevant.

    C. The learners will not be motivated to learn.

    D. The learners will become angry.

4. Why should you, as a technical trainer, talk *with* adults rather than *to* adults?

    A. Adults demand respect.

    B. Adults like conversations.

    C. Adults learn by lecture.

    D. Adults need your attention.

PART IV

5. An organization is replacing an existing technology with a newer technology that the organization believes is better and more reliable than the older software. Thomas, an employee in the company, is angry about the change and doesn't want the change to happen. In your class he's not motivated to learn, as he's still emotionally attached to the older software and the time he's invested mastering the replaced program. What term describes Thomas's experience?

   A. Self-directed angst

   B. Denial motivation

   C. Value adjustment

   D. Organizational change management

6. What's the advantage of teaching topics in smaller chunks of information appealing to the kinesthetic, auditory, and visual learners?

   A. Adults learn best when information is presented in smaller segments.

   B. Adults learn best when there's variety in the class presentation.

   C. Adults learn in different ways.

   D. Adults learn through different learning styles.

7. You are teaching a class on networking. A learner in your class makes a statement that is blatantly wrong, and you feel the need to correct the statement with the learner and for the class. Which one of the following is the best method to rectify the statement?

   A. Create a demonstration of the situation to prove why the learner's statement is wrong.

   B. Simply say that the learner's statement is wrong.

   C. Explain to the class, without embarrassing the learner, why you're actually correct.

   D. Explain why the learner's statement is wrong.

8. Why do you think learners create hypothetical situations when asking questions in a technical class?

   A. To retain the information

   B. To trick the instructor

   C. To prove how smart they are

   D. To find relevancy

9. When a participant incorrectly answers a question in your class, what's the one thing you should never do in regard to the wrong answer?

   A. Embarrass the learner.

   B. Tell the learner they are wrong.

    C. Ask someone else to help the learner.

    D. Rephrase your question.

10. All of the following are good responses to utilize when a participant in your class makes an incorrect statement except for which one?

    A. Be honest with the learner.

    B. Agree with the learner.

    C. Lead the learner.

    D. Give a demonstration.

11. When it comes to motivation to learn, which one of the following motivators is the best type for adult learners?

    A. External

    B. Intrinsic

    C. Financial

    D. Social

12. A learner has been directed to your class as a part of a requirement for their job in your company. The learner likely has what type of motivation to learn?

    A. Organization expectations

    B. Career advancement

    C. Emotional

    D. Personal interest

13. Which one of the following statements is an example of learning motivation tied to escapism?

    A. I want to learn the technology because it's fun to me.

    B. I want to learn the technology to get a better job.

    C. I want to learn the technology because I'm bored.

    D. I want to learn the technology to meet new friends.

14. Diane is giving a talk at a "lunch and learn" session for her local computer users' chapter. In this hour talk she's keeping the information at a high level and making sure the learners are having fun in the presentation. What type of motivation do you think the majority of the learners have at this function to learn about the technology Diane is teaching?

    A. Personal interest

    B. Escapism

    C. Career advancement

    D. Networking opportunities

15. Complete this statement about learning motivation. Competence results in _____ which results in more _____.

    A. Education, education

    B. Confidence, competence

    C. Confidence, education

    D. Education, confidence

16. Mary is taking classes and studying to pass the CompTIA A+ certification. Mary believes this certification will help her secure a technical job that she'd like to have. What type of motivation does Mary have in this scenario?

    A. External

    B. Career

    C. Financial

    D. Goal

17. An organization has made an upgrade to the software they use as part of their operations. The organization leaders determine that the cost of training is too expensive, so they tell employees to just use the help system instead of the training. Employees complain that the software changes are significant and it's slowing their progress. All of the following statements are true about this issue in this scenario except for which one?

    A. Employees need to know how to do their job.

    B. Employees can learn by experimenting with the software.

    C. Management has a responsibility to give the employees an avenue to learn.

    D. Employees obviously can't utilize the software without training.

18. Thomas is taking a theory of digital design class for his own edification. This is what type of motivation?

    A. Career advancement

    B. Social and networking

    C. Personal interest

    D. Organization requirements

19. Fred is teaching a class on a server operating system. In the class Fred criticizes the software and tells his participants how unreliable the server operating system is. What type of environment has Fred created? Choose the best answer.

    A. Learner-centered

    B. Trainer-centered

    C. Negative

    D. Honest

20. Your organization is replacing current word processing software with a newer version of Microsoft Word. Nancy is very upset by this change, as she's mastered the older software and doesn't like Microsoft Word. Which one of the following words best describes the value judgment Nancy has with Microsoft Word?

   A. Emotional

   B. Logical

   C. Experienced

   D. Personal

Questions and Answers

1. What term best describes the concept of the trainer treating the participants as adults in the classroom and as equals rather than as students?

   A. Andragogical model

   B. Instructor-centered model

   C. Colleague learning model

   D. Colleague competency model

   A. The andragogical model, more commonly known as the learner-centered model, puts the focus on the learners and not the instructor. This adult educational model was popularized by Malcolm Knowles. B, the instructor-centered model, isn't the best choice for the question, as this approach is more geared toward pedagogical approaches than adult education. C and D are both incorrect because these aren't valid terms.

2. Martha is attending your class on a new technology your company will use. Martha is not interested in the class, though the other participants are engaged. You ask Martha in confidence what seems to be the problem. Martha reports that she's not going to be using the technology, but her supervisor asked her to attend the class anyway since a colleague cancelled and the cost of the class was already paid for. Which one of the following best describes this situation?

   A. Martha is not engaged.

   B. The training is not relevant to Martha's life.

   C. The instructor hasn't identified Martha's motivation.

   D. The cost of the training is wasted, as Martha isn't motivated to learn.

   B. The training isn't relevant to Martha's life, so she is not engaged in the learning process. A is incorrect; while this answer could be construed to be correct, it's not the best choice, as it doesn't address the lack of relevancy for Martha. C is incorrect; Martha isn't motivated to learn because the material isn't relevant to her life. D is also incorrect; while the cost of the training could be seen as a waste, the reason the waste exists is because the training is not relevant to Martha. The supervisor should have found a better-suited substitute or delayed the training if possible for the employee.

3. You're observing Mary as she teaches a technical class. In the class Mary is overenunciating her words, is making exaggerated facial expressions, and is speaking in a voice that may be more appropriate for children than adults. What effect do you think this will have on the learners in the class? Choose the best answer.

   A. The learners will leave the class.

   B. The learners will be engaged as long as the learning is relevant.

   C. The learners will not be motivated to learn.

   D. The learners will become angry.

   C. Of all the choices, this is the best choice because Mary is talking down to the learners rather than with the learners. Mary's approach, tone, and speech patterns should be adjusted to speak to the learners as equals and not children. A and D may happen in some cases, but the best answer is C because it's more inclusive than just the learners becoming angry or leaving the class. B is incorrect, as learners will most likely not be engaged by Mary's approach to teaching.

4. Why should you, as a technical trainer, talk *with* adults rather than *to* adults?

   A. Adults demand respect.

   B. Adults like conversations.

   C. Adults learn by lecture.

   D. Adults need your attention.

   A. Adults have experiences and achievements that will contribute to the learning experience. When you talk down to adults, they become disengaged and aren't motivated to learn what you're offering them. While it's true that adults like conversations, can learn through lecture, and often need your attention as the technical trainer, these choices aren't as definitive as A.

5. An organization is replacing an existing technology with a newer technology that the organization believes is better and more reliable than the older software. Thomas, an employee in the company, is angry about the change and doesn't want the change to happen. In your class he's not motivated to learn, as he's still emotionally attached to the older software and the time he's invested mastering the replaced program. What term describes Thomas's experience?

   A. Self-directed angst

   B. Denial motivation

   C. Value adjustment

   D. Organizational change management

C. This is an example of a value adjustment. Thomas has emotional ties to the older technology, and the value of his time and experience may be seen as lost due to the change. Thomas knows he needs to learn the software for his job, but he's still emotionally attached to the older technology. A, B, and D are incorrect, as these terms aren't relevant to the scenario presented in the question.

6. What's the advantage of teaching topics in smaller chunks of information appealing to the kinesthetic, auditory, and visual learners?

   A. Adults learn best when information is presented in smaller segments.

   B. Adults learn best when there's variety in the class presentation.

   C. Adults learn in different ways.

   D. Adults learn through different learning styles.

   A. Large segments of training can affect an adult's ability to learn. When information is presented in smaller, logical segments, adults can learn better by seeing relevant, connected information. B is incorrect; while there may be truth in the statement that adults learn better through a variety of learning styles, the best answer to this question is that adults learn best through smaller segments of information. C and D are incorrect because adults do learn in different ways and learning styles, but smaller segments of training that appeal to a variety of learning styles is the best approach for adults to learn and retain information.

7. You are teaching a class on networking. A learner in your class makes a statement that is blatantly wrong, and you feel the need to correct the statement with the learner and for the class. Which one of the following is the best method to rectify the statement?

   A. Create a demonstration of the situation to prove why the learner's statement is wrong.

   B. Simply state that the learner's statement is wrong.

   C. Explain to the class, without embarrassing the learner, why you're actually correct.

   D. Explain why the learner's statement is wrong.

   D. Of all the choices, the best answer is to simply explain why the learner's statement is wrong. A is incorrect because there's not enough information in the question to determine if a demonstration would be the best approach. The demonstration setup could be a massive amount of work to prove a simple point. B is also incorrect because this answer doesn't explain why the learner is wrong. C is incorrect because this question doesn't indicate that you're correct and the learner is wrong—just that the learner's statement was incorrect.

8. Why do you think learners create hypothetical situations when asking questions in a technical class?

   A. To retain the information

   B. To trick the instructor

   C. To prove how smart they are

   D. To find relevancy

   D. When learners create hypothetical situations, they're often just trying to find relevancy between what you're teaching and how they'll apply the information in their lives. A isn't the best choice; hypothetical situations are more part of the learners' effective listening than an attempt to retain the information. B isn't correct, as hypothetical scenarios are almost always for relevancy than an attempt to trick the instructor. C is incorrect; while there may be an occasional learner that uses a hypothetical scenario to show how smart she may be, the best answer is that learners use hypothetical situations to find relevancy between the information and their lives.

9. When a participant incorrectly answers a question in your class, what's the one thing you should never do in regard to the wrong answer?

   A. Embarrass the learner.

   B. Tell the learner they are wrong.

   C. Ask someone else to help the learner.

   D. Rephrase your question.

   A. You should never embarrass the learner in front of their peers or colleagues. B, C, and D are incorrect, as these are all good examples of things you could do for the learner.

10. All of the following are good responses to utilize when a participant in your class makes an incorrect statement except for which one?

    A. Be honest with the learner.

    B. Agree with the learner.

    C. Lead the learner.

    D. Give a demonstration.

    B. When a learner makes an incorrect statement, you should not agree with the learner about the accuracy of their statement. The learner's incorrect statement and your agreement with it could cause confusion among the other participants in the class. Always, as in choices A, C, and D, correct the learner with tact. By correcting the learner, you're ensuring that all participants leave the class with good information.

11. When it comes to motivation to learn, which one of the following motivators is the best type for adult learners?

    A. External

    B. Intrinsic

    C. Financial

    D. Social

    B. Of all the choices, intrinsic is the best answer because there is an emotional value associated with the desire to learn. A, external motivation, such as threats or rewards, isn't as valuable for learning as pure intrinsic learning. C, financial, is an example of an external motivator and isn't the best type of motivation. D, social, can be an intrinsic motivator, but not always, so this choice isn't the best answer.

12. A learner has been directed to your class as a part of a requirement for their job in your company. The learner likely has what type of motivation to learn?

    A. Organization expectations

    B. Career advancement

    C. Emotional

    D. Personal interest

    A. This is an example of organization expectations, as the training is a requirement for his job. B, career advancement, is a tempting choice, but there's no mention that the training will help the learner move forward in his career. C is incorrect; emotional isn't a type of learning motivation—though intrinsic motivation can have emotional value tied to the decision to learn. D, personal interest, happens when the person wants to learn for the sake of learning.

13. Which one of the following statements is an example of learning motivation tied to escapism?

    A. I want to learn the technology because it's fun to me.

    B. I want to learn the technology to get a better job.

    C. I want to learn the technology because I'm bored.

    D. I want to learn the technology to meet new friends.

    C. Motivation based on escapism describes learners that enroll in a class just to "escape" from their lives or jobs. A is an example of the personal interest motivation. B is incorrect, as this is an example of the career advancement motivation. D is an example of the social motivation.

14. Diane is giving a talk at a "lunch and learn" session for her local computer users' chapter. In this hour talk she's keeping the information at a high level and making sure the learners are having fun in the presentation. What type of motivation do you think the majority of the learners have at this function to learn about the technology Diane is teaching?

   A. Personal interest

   B. Escapism

   C. Career advancement

   D. Networking opportunities

   D. This is an example of networking opportunities, as the "lunch and learn" sessions are good opportunities to meet new colleagues at a social event. A is incorrect; some learners may have a deep interest in the technology, but at this function the information is at a high level and fun. B is incorrect; escapism happens when a learner wants to escape from their jobs or lives and learns just as a distraction from other elements in their life. C is incorrect; career advancement is learning with hopes that the education will bring about new career opportunities.

15. Complete this statement about learning motivation. Competence results in _____ which results in more _____.

   A. Education, education

   B. Confidence, competence

   C. Confidence, education

   D. Education, confidence

   B. The spiral of competence and confidence describes the process of competence resulting in confidence, which helps to create more competence. A, C, and D are incorrect options.

16. Mary is taking classes and studying to pass the CompTIA A+ certification. Mary believes this certification will help her secure a technical job that she'd like to have. What type of motivation does Mary have in this scenario?

   A. External

   B. Career

   C. Financial

   D. Goal

B. The best choice is career, as Mary believes the education and certification will help her advance in her career. A is incorrect; external isn't typically a category of motivation, as organization expectation, social, and even escapism can all be part of external motivation. C is incorrect; financial isn't a classification of motivation. D is also incorrect; Mary's goal is to get the new job, but the category of motivation demonstrated is career advancement.

17. An organization has made an upgrade to the software they use as part of their operations. The organization leaders determine that the cost of training is too expensive, so they tell employees to just use the help system instead of the training. Employees complain that the software changes are significant and it's slowing their progress. All of the following statements are true about this issue in this scenario except for which one?

    A. Employees need to know how to do their job.

    B. Employees can learn by experimenting with the software.

    C. Management has a responsibility to give the employees an avenue to learn.

    D. Employees obviously can't utilize the software without training.

D. All of the statements about this issue are true except for D. Employees can utilize the software without training, but the learning curve for the software may be longer without proper training for the employees. A, B, and C are incorrect choices, as these statements are true given the issue in this scenario.

18. Thomas is taking a theory of digital design class for his own edification. This is what type of motivation?

    A. Career advancement

    B. Social and networking

    C. Personal interest

    D. Organization requirements

C. This is an example of a personal interest motivation. Thomas wants to take the class just to learn more about a topic that interests him. A, career advancement, isn't the best choice, as there's no allusion to Thomas advancing in his career by taking the course. B, social and networking, is generally associated with more fun, high-level events or with the learner taking the class to meet other people. D isn't the best choice, as Thomas isn't required to take the class by his organization.

19. Fred is teaching a class on a server operating system. In the class Fred criticizes the software and tells his participants how unreliable the server operating system is. What type of environment has Fred created? Choose the best answer.

    A. Learner-centered

    B. Trainer-centered

    C. Negative

    D. Honest

    B. This is the best example because Fred is putting his opinions about the server operating system into the official class content. The people in the class may be offended or angry at the comments, as they are investing their time and money into the class—and likely into the technology that Fred is belittling. A is incorrect; a learner-centered environment keeps the focus on the learners. C is incorrect. If there were, for example, problems with the server operating system, Fred could create a learner-centered and honest environment by alerting the users to the problems and offer solutions without criticizing the server operating system.

20. Your organization is replacing current word processing software with a newer version of Microsoft Word. Nancy is very upset by this change, as she's mastered the older software and doesn't like Microsoft Word. Which one of the following words best describes the value judgment Nancy has with Microsoft Word?

    A. Emotional

    B. Logical

    C. Experienced

    D. Personal

    A. Value judgments are the emotional ties a person has to a technical solution. Change is often hardest for people who have mastered a technology and they don't see the opportunities and improvements the newer technology may bring for the entire organization. B, C, and D are not correct terms to describe the emotional attachment Nancy has to the technology.

PART V

Evaluating the Training Event

■ **Chapter 11**   Evaluating Learner Competencies
■ **Chapter 12**   Evaluating Instructor and Course Performance

CHAPTER

Evaluating Learner Competencies

In this chapter you will:
- Measure learning objective retention
- Develop course examinations
- Utilize embedded assessment for ongoing assessment
- Assess learner competencies and information retention
- Implement authentic learning assessments in technical courses
- Create and deliver on technical training learning goals

The goal of technical training is to get learners to change their behaviors based on what they learn in a technical training class. While you motivate people to change behavior in the classroom, you may not have the opportunity to see the actual change of behavior once they've left your training room and have returned to their jobs. As part of your training, you can measure the learners' retention and understanding of the materials to confirm that they understand the processes you've taught.

Determining Learner Competence

The primary goal of teaching a technical class is to help the learners change their behavior. A change of behavior doesn't mean being naughty one day and then good the next—but rather the learner embraces what you've taught and they can apply the information in their lives. While this high-level goal is applicable to any type of training you do, there are obviously more granular, technology-specific, and organization-specific goals that you may have to tailor your seminar to achieve. For example, you want learners to apply the technology, but the organization wants learners to become more efficient in their utilization of the software. You can achieve both goals in a technical training class, but you may have to instruct with the specific goals of the organization in mind to become more efficient with the software.

Learner competence is an assessment of what you've taught and how well the learners have retained the information and can apply it in their lives and employment. Learner competence tests not just retention, but also practical application of the information you've offered. Assessments should test the depth of competency the learner has in relation to the goals of learner behavior and the primary goals of the organization. In other words, you can't just throw a quick quiz together and see what people know. Learner competence assessments, like all parts of training, require specific goals and objectives that you'll need to plan. You may be tasked with creating the assessments, or the instructional designer may create these assessment activities—or a combination of both.

Just as you have learning goals in the course you're teaching, you should also have assessment goals. If you're an instructor in a training company where people come to your class from many different organizations, it may be nearly impossible to create an organization-specific assessment. Consider a class where you have people from ten different companies—all with a common goal to learn the technology, but each company may have differing learning objectives and behaviors the employees are expected to achieve. If, however, you're teaching a technical class for a group of people from one specific organization, then the assessment may be more direct and to the point. In either case you'll want to test learner competence to the extent that you can without creating anxiety or unrealistic expectations.

Creating a Course Examination

One of the most common methods to test learner comprehension is a final exam. A final exam, especially in technical courses that have lasted many days, is a fine method to test learner retention and comprehension for all that the course has covered. Final exams are an example of an outcome assessment; an outcome assessment is a method to judge the effectiveness of the course design and delivery to help the learner retain the course content and achieve the learning goals. Final exams should be comprehensive, including the beginning of the course to the final topics you've covered in class. This approach isn't designed to be mean, though your participants may think so; but it's an approach to test retention and understanding of the technology. You can imagine a 12-week college-level course and how a final exam could test each topic as an inclusive look at retention and application of what's been taught in the class.

The most common type of examination is a "show exam" where learners show what they've learned by answering questions to prove their mastery of the topic you've taught. A show final, while tough and challenging, is a great method to expose weaknesses and strengths of what the participant has learned. A show examination might also be the final step a learner must achieve before moving on to the next level of education—the learner must pass the current course before they can move on to the next. With this approach, the show final serves not only as a review of what the learner was supposed to retain, but also as a sort of prerequisite for more advanced courses.

Show final examinations are a good method to test retention of terms, syntax, and understanding of the technology you've taught. These types of final exams should be fundamental and reflective of the course objectives—you don't want to create questions that extend beyond the defined boundaries of the course. Having said that, you do want a variety of questions that test fundamental topics while also creating varying levels of complexities to test the extent of learner retention and subject mastery. If all the questions are "easy" on the show final and the learner isn't challenged, then you're not really testing mastery of the topic, but just the recollection of terms and high-level concepts.

Another type of final examination is a "usage final" where users demonstrate their knowledge and retention by using the technology. A usage final is an opportunity for the learner to complete the examination by actually using the technology to create an end product or offer a technical solution. Consider a technical course on networking. A usage final may present a scenario such as the following:

> You are a network administrator for your organization. Your company has offices in New York, Chicago, Atlanta, Dallas, and San Francisco. You need to create a WAN solution to allow users from each city to save and access data from a central server, regardless of the location where the user is operating. Assuming that the central server is Chicago, what type of solution would you offer? Your answer should define the WAN needs, security needs, and data reliability needs.

In this usage question the participant doesn't actually have to create a WAN, but they do have explain their approach to solving the problem. The question gives the user enough direction that the learner can define their approach based on what's been taught in the course. In this expository approach the learner needs to understand the concepts of the WAN, how networks are connected, the security needs, and the data reliability. The user has been asked to define a comprehensive solution, but the question also frames the requirements of what the learner must recall and address in their essay. You could even allow the user to draw the solution to show application of the information without having to write their answers in detail. Usage assessment could, if the technology allowed, require the learner to complete a hands-on exercise to prove their mastery of the technology.

 NOTE Your organization may require a specific type of final examination or course assessment exam, so always follow the policies of where you're employed. I'm speaking, of course, to you college professors who must adhere to a standardized testing approach. For you technical trainers and instructional designers who are providing corporate training, you can create an examination that's comprehensive, tough, and pretty much whatever you want. Be warned, however: Make an exam that's too tough, or too easy, and learners will get discouraged.

The type of examination you offer in your classes should reflect not only the content of the course, but the level of learning that was offered in the course. In other words, if your course focused on hands-on activities and technical labs, it's not a good idea to give a multiple-choice examination that tests learners on the nitty-gritty of the technology and doesn't offer access to the actual technology. If your course was entirely theory and lecture-driven, then your exam should reflect that type of training and learning. Be fair to your learners and give exams that are reflective of your teaching style and course content, and that map to the learning objectives of the class.

Final exams should also include an opportunity to continue learning. Maybe you've experienced a class where you complete the final exam, receive your grade, and that's that. A good final exam includes an opportunity to review the questions on the exam, why the questions are right or wrong, and to discuss the logic and validity of the question. No one likes to be wrong, especially when they've prepped, studied, and believe that their answers are correct. If you're teaching a class for technical certification, then it's paramount to include an opportunity to explain the reasoning behind the correctness of the question. That's what I've been trying to do, to the extent that I can, in each chapter's review quiz in the question and answers section. Learners need an opportunity to understand the question's answer—not just if the answer is right or wrong.

Utilizing Embedded Assessments

An embedded assessment tracks learner progress throughout the entire course rather than in an examination at the end of the course. This approach, sometimes called a formative assessment, allows the trainer to measure and track learner participation, engagement, and contribution to the seminar. Embedded assessments are more performance-driven than the final examination approach, and may be better utilized in a technical course because learners can interact with the technology throughout the course—not just at the end of the session. The great thing about embedded assessments is that learners aren't always tested on the material, like a final exam, but their assessment is done as part of the course participation—not as an event aside from the experience of the course.

A fundamental rule of using the embedded assessment approach is to clearly communicate the learning objectives for each module in your technical seminar. This communication not only sets expectations for the learners, but also gives learners an opportunity to self-monitor their progress in the learning. You can imagine the frustration a learner might have if you dive into a technical topic and don't set the boundaries and expectations of the assessment of the learner. The learner may be focused on the lecture portions of the topic and less on the lab experience only to learn that the hands-on activities were of more importance in your grading and assessment. You'll need to define what you're assessing and what the learner should be doing in the module, and then reinforce those expectations with clear directions for the learner to be engaged, participate, and contribute.

Another approach to using the embedded assessment is to require learners to write a lessons-learned summation in their workbook or electronic file. This self-assessment approach allows the participant to encapsulate what's been taught and what they took from the training, and may prompt the learner to ask for clarity on certain topics. The lessons-learned document is actually a learning statement from the participant's point of view. This document can capture not only what the learner has retained, but also provide insight into how the learner may apply this information in their employment and lives. This approach, I believe, is especially effective for longer seminars where learners can review their learning statements as a refresher exercise from class-to-class.

Embedded assessments require the trainer to also be involved in the assessment—correct errors and misstatements, and provide clear instructions for the learners. It's not fair, or beneficial, to allow learners to leave the class with misconceptions about the technology—it's the instructor's job to clarify and correct mistakes without embarrassing the learners. Instructor involvement isn't just for corrections, but for ongoing communication and feedback on learner participation. You'll watch your learners work with the technology and offer encouragement, praise, and more detailed instructions and help when it's warranted. Learners don't need you to hover over their shoulder (usually) while they work, but you should be available and talk with your learners about their progress in the course.

Communication between the learners and the instructor allows you to gauge learner retention, interest, and contribution to the course. You can ask an open-ended question, for example, and then watch who contributes to the dialogue, what's discussed, how participants react to one another, and who is not contributing. You'll need to engage those learners who haven't contributed to the discussion by asking for their thoughts and inputs—and you'll need to control the learners who try to take over and lead the conversation too much. In order to do an effective assessment through the group dialogue, you need to give all learners a chance to contribute.

 VIDEO See the video *Comparing Assessment Types*.

Exploring Authentic Assessment

Often in adult education, trainers like to use the line that people learn by doing. It's true—you can talk about creating a program, installing a hard drive, or configuring software, but until you actually do the activity, it's all theory. You might as well be talking about flying an airplane—it's the doing part that really cements the learning. Adult learners need an opportunity to actually experience the technology, experience what you're teaching, in order to grasp the concepts. Sure, there are the visual and auditory learning styles, but it's often the kinesthetic style, the labs and exercises, that gets adults to the learning.

So, you might correctly reason, if adults often learn best by doing, by experiencing, then adults should also be assessed on their learning through an experience. That is the concept of the authentic assessment: adult learners are tasked with an exercise that includes the summation of the learning and retention. For example, if you were teaching a class on a server operating system, you might have a final assessment of installing and configuring the server operating system, adding users, and testing access and security settings. Your assessment would be a challenge for learners to complete—and you could score their performance based on time to completion, accuracy, methods to complete the task, or any number of performance objects that were in alignment with the learning objectives.

An authentic assessment is much different from a traditional course assessment, like a final exam. In order to complete the authentic assessment, the learner has to demonstrate their retention and ability to apply the information learned. Traditional assessments, like a multiple-choice exam, are fine methods of testing learners' understanding, but they're forced-choice opportunities: the learner can guess, compare answers and questions, and be "book smart" without proving practical application of the information.

Meeting Learning Goals

In order to offer an authentic assessment, the experience of the assessment must be in alignment with the learning goals. Throughout the course you'll explain the learning goals, how each topic supports the learning goals, and help learners link the concept from the course to their lives. This learner-centered approach, something I've discussed throughout this book, aligns with the concept of the authentic assessment. A learner-centered environment helps the learner discover information, rather than the instructor just dictating information. Recall that a learner-centered environment puts the focus on the learner rather than on the instructor. It's more important for participants to learn than it is for the instructor to teach in this environment.

When you're assessing learning competency with an authentic assessment, you want to make certain that your assessment maps to the learning goals. A well-rounded assessment would require the learner to demonstrate all of the requirements of the learning goals for the entire course. For example, learning goals for an organization teaching a Microsoft Word seminar could be for the learner to be able to navigate through Microsoft Word, enter and edit text, format text, and design a document. The instructional designer, using these high-level goals, would create the familiar course outline provided here:

- Unit 1: Getting Started with Microsoft Word
  - Defining the Microsoft Word interface
  - Entering text
  - Accessing menus and buttons
  - Saving, printing, and accessing documents
- Unit 2: Editing Text in Microsoft Word
  - Selecting text
  - Copying, cutting, pasting, and moving text
  - Finding and replacing text
  - Accessing the dictionary and autocorrect options
- Unit 3: Formatting Text
  - Changing fonts and styles
  - Formatting pages, columns, and borders
  - Applying predefined paragraph styles
  - Creating and saving paragraph styles
- Unit 4: Designing Documents
  - Working with headers and footers
  - Inserting tables and graphics
  - Adding sections and page breaks
  - Creating a table of contents

Now the assessment to test the validity of the learning goals would address each of these topics to measure the learners' competency. So an assignment example could be as follows:

Use Microsoft Word to open the document titled "Shakespeare Sonnets" on the classroom server. From this document copy and paste four of your favorite sonnets into a new document and save the file as your name in your home folder. Create three paragraph styles and use them to format your sonnets. Next, choose a piece of clip art that matches the topic of each poem, and insert and format the picture into your file. You may add a page border on every other page of your document. Edit the header and footer to include your name, page numbers, and today's date—but be certain to make the first page of your document without a header. Finally, create a table of contents for your document so readers can quickly find each poem in your document by the page number.

This exercise challenges the participant to complete a task related to each unit in the course. The assessment maps to the learning goals of the class, presents a challenge for the learner to recall the instruction you've offered, and doesn't tell the user how to do the activities, but does require the learner to complete the activities in the assessment. Learners will be challenged, and may need your help to prompt their recall, but they should be able to complete the assignment quickly and accurately if they've mastered the learning goals of the class.

Changing Learner Behavior

If the ultimate goal of training is to change learner behavior, then you need assessments to see if the learning goals were achieved. If an organization is rolling out new calendaring software, for example, and there are 20,000 users to be trained on how to use this new software, there'd be some expectations for user performance. The organization would define the learning goals and create a course outline, and you'd teach a class that supported those learning goals. The users, however, need to retain and apply the information you've offered. The users need to actually use the calendaring software with a defined degree of efficiency and accuracy.

You can imagine the initial disappointment in the organization if an instructor has trained a few hundred people, but the users are confused how to use the software, how to schedule meetings, or how to find resources. The disappointment may quickly grow into anger if management learns that the instructor isn't teaching to the course outline that supports the learning goals. If the instructor is teaching a different approach to scheduling, teaching topics that may be interesting but not relevant to employee performance, or just not teaching the course accurately, then it's a huge waste of time and cost. It's not a subtle point: in order to have the behavior of the learners change, the learners must be taught accurately and to the defined learning goals.

The concept of changing learner behavior has some assumptions tied to it. There's an assumption that learner behavior is going to change for the betterment of the organization. The fundamental assumption is that the learner will learn a new skill, become more proficient, and complete their role in the organization with higher accuracy than before the training took place. This assumption, however, is fundamentally flawed on three points:

- **Learning curve** Training an employee doesn't automatically make them more proficient. It often takes time for the learner to master the topics of the training to achieve the expected level of performance. This is the learning curve in action. The learner often has to go backward in efficiency to reach the higher levels of efficiency achieved over time and experience with the technology.

- **Incorrect learning objectives** The learning objectives must be in alignment with the actual performance of the learners. If the actual needs of the learners are different from the learning goals of the organization, then there'll be a disconnect in the achievement of the learning goals. By completing an accurate pre-course analysis of learner needs, the organization can more accurately capture true task analysis, expected outcomes, and realistic goals for learning. When the organization excludes learners from the course development, the organization may have expectations for the learners that aren't necessarily realistic.

- **Current state assessment** Organizations that have expectations for a future state of performance must first capture the current state of performance. It's nearly impossible to see a change in learner behavior that's not anecdotal without first capturing what the current state of efficiency, accuracy, or other performance indicator the training should map to. Organizations need to determine what specific behaviors should change as a result of the training in relation to what present behavior is acceptable in the organization.

While organizations may want learners to change their behavior, the organization must define what behavior is to change, define the extent of the behavioral change, and provide an avenue for the change to happen. It's unrealistic to set expectations, such as zero defects, without providing the accurate training and allowing experience to achieve the desired level of efficiency. The depth of the training must be in relation to the desired behavioral change. Management may sometimes see the actual cost of training and question the wisdom of the associated cost of labor to learn a new technology. I've seen organizations that reduce the amount of time invested in training—for example, a six-hour class reduced to four hours—but they weren't willing to adjust their expectations of learning outcome as well. Learning is hard work, change is hard work, and when organizations expect change without providing education they're creating unrealistic expectations. Goals for learner outcomes demand appropriate levels of training to be pragmatic.

Chapter Summary

Learner assessments measure how much a learner has retained from their time in your class. While you may be the most wonderful instructor in the world, your participants must be interested in what you're teaching. If you're teaching a class to a group of adult learners who aren't interested in the technology, don't believe the information is relevant to their lives, or don't care about the outcome of the class, their retention will obviously be low. To have retention of information, you must first have attention to information.

Course assessments that measure learner retention must reflect the content of the course and the learning goals of the organization. One of the most common forms of assessments, and sometimes the most dreaded type, is the final exam. This assessment usually consists of multiple-choice questions that quiz the learner on the entire span of the course content. Final exams are an example of a show assessment—the learner shows their retention by achieving a passing score on the exam. A usage final, sometimes called a practical final, challenges the learner to practically use the technology and demonstrate their retention of the information through an expository answer.

An embedded assessment doesn't wait until the end of the course to test learner retention. An embedded assessment utilizes many different elements throughout the course timeline to measure learner competency: quizzes, exercises, group activities, and discussions. To use an embedded assessment, however, the instructor must clearly define the course objectives and how the learner is being graded. It's not fair to the learner to not explain how the assessment is happening—keeping the assessment a secret leads to wrong assumptions on the learner's part, and possibly a skewed performance grading as a result.

An authentic assessment is one of the purest forms of assessment, as it calls for the adult learner to actually use the technology as part of the assessment. The authentic assessment creates a scenario for the adult learners to consider and then use the technology to complete the assessment. The authentic assessment is designed to be in alignment with the course objectives, and gives learners an opportunity to be tested on all areas of the learning goals. Recall that learning goals are the expected outcomes of the training event—ultimately, the change in learner behavior. In order to have learner behavior actually change, the expected change must be defined and be in synch with the capabilities of the technology, training, and capacity of the learners. Learner behavior can change as a result of training, but the depth of the training must be adequate to provide the mechanisms to achieve the desired change and performance improvement.

PART V

Key Terms

authentic assessment   An actual exercise that requires the learner to demonstrate their understanding and application of the learning goals of the technical seminar.

embedded assessment   An assessment approach that tracks learner progress throughout the entire course rather than in an examination at the end of the course.

forced-choice opportunities   The learner is forced to choose an answer in the assessment.

lessons-learned summation   An example of an embedded assessment where the learners summarize what they have learned throughout the course.

outcome assessment   A method to judge the effectiveness of the course design and delivery to help the learner retain the course content and achieve the learning goals.

show exam   Learners show what they have learned in the course, often through a final examination.

usage final   An assessment where users use their retention and understanding of the course material to create a solution.

Questions

1. You are a technical trainer for your organization. You are coaching Beth, a new technical trainer, on the various goals your company has for training. What is the fundamental goal of all technical training?

    A. To help learners change their behavior

    B. To maximize profits

    C. To educate people to do their jobs better

    D. To maximize a return on investment

2. Which one of the following statements best describes a basic learner assessment of competence?

    A. A learner assessment is a review of how well the trainer has taught the material.

    B. A learner assessment is a review of how the learners have changed their behavior.

    C. A learner assessment determines how well the learners have retained the course information.

    D. A learner assessment determines the cost effectiveness of the course.

3. If you're tasked with creating a learner assessment, what must your assessment plan include?

   A. Scope of what's to be assessed based on the learning goals

   B. Cost of what's to be assessed based on investment

   C. Schedule for assessing the learner behavior

   D. Audience to be assessed

4. Mark is designing a technical training class for his public training company. What challenges will Mark have when creating an assessment of learner competence for this type of training event, considering his company type?

   A. There shouldn't be any challenges, as all learners will have the same learning goals.

   B. Learners from different organizations will likely have different learning goals.

   C. Each organization will need to review Mark's learning assessment.

   D. Learners won't learn the same, as each learner may come from a different organization.

5. Which one of the following is an example of an outcome assessment?

   A. Learner evaluation

   B. Learner evaluation throughout the course

   C. Final examination

   D. Instructor performance review

6. What term refers to an exam where learners show or prove their retention by answering in-depth questions?

   A. Show exam

   B. Proof exam

   C. Final exam

   D. Learning exam

7. You are a technical trainer for your organization. At the end of your hardware technology course you require the participants to complete an exercise that utilizes all of the topics you've taught in the course. The final exercise tests the learners' mastery of the topics and their ability to use the information you've taught in a simulated environment. What type of assessment is this?

   A. Mastery

   B. Show

   C. Usage

   D. Demonstration

PART V

8. Mary is creating an assessment for her learners in a technical course. Which one of the following statements best describes the type of assessment Mary should create for her technical class?

   A. The assessment should reflect the content of the course.

   B. The assessment should reflect the content of the course and the level of expected learning.

   C. The assessment should reflect the level of expected learning and the level of actual learning.

   D. The assessment should reflect the learning objectives.

9. Martha is teaching a technical class on how to create a LAN network. The course is primarily designed for advanced technical users and has many hands-on exercises to help learners discover knowledge. Based on this information, which one of the following is the best type of learner assessments Martha should use?

   A. Paper-based final exam

   B. Computer-based adaptive questions

   C. Usage exam

   D. Show exam

10. Mark has created a final exam for his database management course. What should Mark include as part of his final exam?

    A. Explanations for why the questions are correct or incorrect

    B. References for learners based on the answers they've selected

    C. Opportunities for learners to retake the examination

    D. Study sessions and objectives for learners to prepare to pass the examination

11. Mary is teaching a technical class for her organization. In the class she's tracking learner progress throughout the course as part of learner assessment rather than utilizing a final exam at the end of the course. What type of assessment is Mary utilizing?

    A. Embedded assessment

    B. Formalized assessment

    C. Classroom assessment

    D. Learner-progression assessment

12. What is another term for a formative assessment?

    A. Learner-progression assessment

    B. Embedded assessment

    C. Hyper-assessment

    D. Progressive assessment

13. Gary is a technical trainer for his organization, and he's elected to use embedded assessments in his technical classes. With this assessment type what must Gary do to ensure that learners understand the importance of the assessment approach?

    A. Communicate how the final exam will support the goals of the learning.

    B. Communicate the learning objectives for each module in the technical seminar.

    C. Communicate the exam objectives for each module examination.

    D. Communicate the learning milestones and the expectations of the organization.

14. Wendy is teaching a 16-week college course on computer hardware. As part of her course she's requiring participants to keep a lessons-learned summation of each topic the course covered. This summation will accomplish all of the following except for which one?

    A. Helps participants encapsulate what's been taught

    B. Serves as an embedded assessment for the course

    C. Helps the participants formulate questions based on what they've learned

    D. Helps Wendy determine who is paying attention in class

15. You are a technical trainer for your organization and you're using a lessons-learned approach to assess learning knowledge. You notice one of your learners has some incorrect information in their lessons-learned documentation. What's the best approach to take in this scenario?

    A. Count the incorrect statement as a negative score.

    B. Count the incorrect statement as a negative score relative to the amount of correct information.

    C. Correct the mistake without embarrassing the learner.

    D. Advise the learner to correct the mistake.

16. What type of assessment actually requires the learners to complete an activity to prove their understanding of the training?

    A. Authentic assessment

    B. Skills-based assessment

    C. Practicum

    D. Hands-on exercises

17. What must a technical trainer do to ensure that the desired learner behavior change actually happens?

    A. Teach to the behavioral outcomes the instructor feels need to be changed.

    B. Teach the defined course outline.

    C. Teach to the defined learning goals.

    D. Teach based on learner participation and behavior.

18. Complete this statement as it pertains to the learning curve: Training an employee _____ make them more proficient.

    A. Doesn't automatically

    B. Doesn't usually

    C. Will usually

    D. Will rarely

19. A company wants to improve their overall proficiency with an inventory management software program. In order for the organization to become more proficient as a result of training, what must exist first in the organization?

    A. Understanding of task analysis

    B. Current-state assessment

    C. Post-classroom assessment

    D. Process improvement plan

20. Before instructors can teach a class to help change learner behavior, what must first be determined?

    A. What behavior the organization wants the learners to change

    B. What learning outcomes of the course are needed

    C. How the actual training assessments will occur

    D. How the learners will apply the information in their lives

Questions and Answers

1. You are a technical trainer for your organization. You are coaching Beth, a new technical trainer, on the various goals your company has for training. What is the fundamental goal of all technical training?

   A. To help learners change their behavior

   B. To maximize profits

   C. To educate people to do their jobs better

   D. To maximize a return on investment

   A. While all of the choices may have merit, the fundamental goal for all technical training is to change the behavior of learners. What you and Beth teach should result in a change of learner behavior. B and D are valid from a financial point of view if the organization is a for-profit training center, but these aren't the fundamental goals of training. C is incorrect, as not all technical training is to educate people to do their jobs better; some training may be for personal usage, not just an employment scenario. Consider a technical training on photo manipulation software; the training could change the behavior of the people in the training, but the people in the seminar could be using the software for personal, not professional use.

2. Which one of the following statements best describes a basic learner assessment of competence?

   A. A learner assessment is a review of how well the trainer has taught the material.

   B. A learner assessment is a review of how the learners have changed their behavior.

   C. A learner assessment determines how well the learners have retained the course information.

   D. A learner assessment determines the cost effectiveness of the course.

   C. Learner assessments are a learner-focused determination of how well the learners have retained the information taught in the course. A is incorrect; a learner assessment focuses on learner retention, not instructor performance. B is incorrect, as behavior change can be an assessment of learner performance, but the best choice is the retention of information. D is incorrect, as the cost effectiveness of the course can be part of the organization's long-term analysis of the course, but learner assessment is a straightforward determination of learner retention.

3. If you're tasked with creating a learner assessment, what must your assessment plan include?

   A. Scope of what's to be assessed based on the learning goals

   B. Cost of what's to be assessed based on investment

   C. Schedule for assessing the learner behavior

   D. Audience to be assessed

   A. In order to create an effective learner assessment of competence, your assessment plan should include a scope of what you'll be assessing. Just as your training should have learning goals, the assessment should also have goals for determining course effectiveness. B, C, and D are incorrect; while your assessment may include a cost analysis, a schedule for assessment, and the determination of the audience, the best answer is to determine the scope of what you'll be assessing, first and foremost.

4. Mark is designing a technical training class for his public training company. What challenges will Mark have when creating an assessment of learner competence for this type of training event, considering his company type?

   A. There shouldn't be any challenges, as all learners will have the same learning goals.

   B. Learners from different organizations will likely have different learning goals.

   C. Each organization will need to review Mark's learning assessment.

   D. Learners won't learn the same, as each learner may come from a different organization.

   B. In a public training company where learners can come to the training event from many different organizations, each learner may have different learning goals for the event. This makes creating a learning assessment difficult, as each learner's organizational goals and educational goals may vary. A is incorrect, as learners likely won't have the same learning goals to be assessed. C is incorrect; each organization that will be sending employees to the class may want to review the assessment, but it's not likely to affect the overall assessment of the entire organization. D is incorrect, as the organization that employees come from likely won't affect the learning style of each course participant.

5. Which one of the following is an example of an outcome assessment?

   A. Learner evaluation

   B. Learner evaluation throughout the course

   C. Final examination

   D. Instructor performance review

   C. A final examination is the best example of an outcome assessment. Recall that an outcome assessment is a method to judge the effectiveness of the course design and delivery to help the learner retain the course content and achieve the learning goals. A and B are not good answers, as these are too vague to be considered a good example of outcome assessments. D, instructor performance reviews, reviews the instructor's performance in the course, not the retention of learner information.

6. What term refers to an exam where learners show or prove their retention by answering in-depth questions?

   A. Show exam

   B. Proof exam

   C. Final exam

   D. Learning exam

A. A show exam simply means that the learner shows their retention by answering in-depth questions. The exam questions would require the learner to demonstrate their knowledge of concepts in their answers. B, C, and D are not accurate answers, as these exam types may not require the learner to actually show their retention and mastery of the topic.

7. You are a technical trainer for your organization. At the end of your hardware technology course you require the participants to complete an exercise that utilizes all of the topics you've taught. The final exercise tests the learners' mastery of the topics and their ability to use the information you've taught in a simulated environment. What type of assessment is this?

   A. Mastery

   B. Show

   C. Usage

   D. Demonstration

   C. This is an example of a usage assessment. The learners must use the technology and the information you've taught them to complete the assessment and prove their retention and understanding. Mastery and demonstration, choices A and D, are not valid answers, as these are not assessment types. B, show, is an assessment type, but show assessments require learners to demonstrate their knowledge by answering in-depth questions, not actually using the technology.

8. Mary is creating an assessment for her learners in a technical course. Which one of the following statements best describes the type of assessment Mary should create for her technical class?

   A. The assessment should reflect the content of the course.

   B. The assessment should reflect the content of the course and the level of expected learning.

   C. The assessment should reflect the level of expected learning and the level of actual learning.

   D. The assessment should reflect the learning objectives.

   B. Of all the choices, this is the best answer because the assessment should reflect the course content, such as the learning objectives, but also reflect the depth of the learning that should have occurred. A is close to correct, but doesn't include the level of expected training as B does. C and D are incorrect, as these answers do not reflect the depth of learning, only the course content.

9. Martha is teaching a technical class on how to create a LAN network. The course is primarily designed for advanced technical users and has many hands-on exercises to help learners discover knowledge. Based on this information, which one of the following is the best type of learner assessments Martha should use?

A. Paper-based final exam

B. Computer-based adaptive questions

C. Usage exam

D. Show exam

C. Because this course utilizes many hands-on exercises, Martha should create an assessment that reflects that approach and that also utilizes hands-on usage of the technology. A and B are incorrect, as these assessment types don't reflect the usage that the course content focused on. D, show exam, is not the best choice. While a show exam does allow learners to showcase their retention and understanding, the course utilized many hands-on activities, so a usage exam makes the most sense.

10. Mark has created a final exam for his database management course. What should Mark include as part of his final exam?

A. Explanations for why the questions are correct or incorrect

B. References for learners based on the answers they've selected

C. Opportunities for learners to retake the examination

D. Study sessions and objectives for learners to prepare to pass the examination

A. Mark should include explanations for why the exam questions are correct or incorrect. This provides learners an opportunity to continue to learn. B, C, and D are incorrect because Mark doesn't need to provide references for each learner. Mark also doesn't need to provide retake opportunities or study sessions for learners.

11. Mary is teaching a technical class for her organization. In the class she's tracking learner progress throughout the course as part of learner assessment rather than utilizing a final exam at the end of the course. What type of assessment is Mary utilizing?

A. Embedded assessment

B. Formalized assessment

C. Classroom assessment

D. Learner-progression assessment

A. This is an example of an embedded assessment where learner progress is measured throughout the course, not just at the end. B, C, and D are all incorrect, as these aren't valid assessment types.

12. What is another term for a formative assessment?

    A. Learner-progression assessment

    B. Embedded assessment

    C. Hyper-assessment

    D. Progressive assessment

    B. A formative assessment is another name for an embedded assessment. This assessment type tracks learner progress throughout the course, not just at the end. A, C, and D are incorrect choices, as these answers are not valid assessment types.

13. Gary is a technical trainer for his organization, and he's elected to use embedded assessments in his technical classes. With this assessment type, what must Gary do to ensure that learners understand the importance of the assessment approach?

    A. Communicate how the final exam will support the goals of the learning.

    B. Communicate the learning objectives for each module in the technical seminar.

    C. Communicate the exam objectives for each module examination.

    D. Communicate the learning milestones and the expectations of the organization.

    B. Using an embedded assessment means that an ongoing assessment will happen throughout the course, not just at the end of the training. With this approach, the technical trainer must communicate the learning objectives for each module of the course to ensure that learners understand what's expected of them in the training segments. A, C, and D are incorrect choices, as these communications do not reflect the needs and approach Gary should utilize when offering an embedded assessment.

14. Wendy is teaching a 16-week college course on computer hardware. As part of her course she's requiring participants to keep a lessons-learned summation of each topic the course covered. This summation will accomplish all of the following except for which one?

    A. Helps participants encapsulate what's been taught

    B. Serves as an embedded assessment for the course

    C. Helps the participants formulate questions based on what they've learned

    D. Helps Wendy determine who is paying attention in class

    D. The lessons-learned summation is not a tool to determine which learner is paying attention in class. The tool is a summation of what learners have been taught, serves as an embedded assessment, and helps participants formulate questions on what they've learned in the class.

15. You are a technical trainer for your organization and you're using a lessons-learned approach to assessing learning knowledge. You notice one of your learners has some incorrect information in their lessons-learned documentation. What's the best approach to take in this scenario?

A. Count the incorrect statement as a negative score.

B. Count the incorrect statement as a negative score relative to the amount of correct information.

C. Correct the mistake without embarrassing the learner.

D. Advise the learner to correct the mistake.

C. The best approach is to ensure that the learner understands the information. You should correct the problem without embarrassing the learner. A and B are incorrect, as the lessons-learned documentation is not a scoring approach, but an assurance that the information is retained. D is incorrect, as this answer doesn't ensure that the learner has the correct information and isn't embarrassed by the mistake they've made.

16. What type of assessment actually requires the learners to complete an activity to prove their understanding of the training?

A. Authentic assessment

B. Skills-based assessment

C. Practicum

D. Hands-on exercises

A. The authentic assessment requires the learner to complete their assessment by performing an exercise or hands-on activity that proves they have grasped the concepts and information provided in the course. B, C, and D are all good thoughts, but these answers do not reflect the actual, technical name of the authentic assessment.

17. What must a technical trainer do to ensure that the desired learner behavior change actually happens?

A. Teach to the behavioral outcomes the instructor feels need to be changed.

B. Teach the defined course outline.

C. Teach to the defined learning goals.

D. Teach based on learner participation and behavior.

C. The best response is that the trainer must teach the content of the course to the defined learning goals of the organization. These are assumed to be well thought out, designed, and agreed upon. Achieving the learning goals will ensure that the desired learning behavior will actually happen. A is incorrect, as the behavioral outcomes are not based on the instructor's feelings, but on the defined learning goals. B is incorrect, as the course outline may be a good choice, but it's not the best choice, given that the learning goals are a better answer. D is also incorrect because the instructor should teach to the learning goals, not learner participation and classroom behavior.

18. Complete this statement as it pertains to the learning curve: Training an employee _____ make them more proficient.

   A. Doesn't automatically

   B. Doesn't usually

   C. Will usually

   D. Will rarely

A. The best response is that training an employee doesn't automatically make them more proficient. The trained employee needs time to embrace, process, and practice with the content of the training in order to become proficient. B, C, and D are not the best choices, as training may make an employee more proficient if certain other conditions are true, such as practice time and desire.

19. A company wants to improve their overall proficiency with an inventory management software program. In order for the organization to become more proficient as a result of training, what must exist first in the organization?

   A. Understanding of task analysis

   B. Current-state assessment

   C. Post-classroom assessment

   D. Process improvement plan

B. In order to determine the level of performance goals, the organization must first create a current-state assessment. The current-state assessment evaluates the current level of performance, helps to create learning goals, and defines objectives for behavioral change. A is incorrect; an understanding of task analysis is important, but it's the current-state assessment that will help an organization create goals for efficiency. C is incorrect; post-classroom assessments don't help the organization determine what needs to be changed. D, a process improvement plan, is applicable to the goals of proficiency in regard to training.

20. Before instructors can teach a class to help change learner behavior, what must first be determined?

A. What behavior the organization wants the learners to change

B. What learning outcomes of the course are needed

C. How the actual training assessments will occur

D. How the léarners will apply the information in their lives

A. The organization must define what behavior they want the learners to change so that the course may be designed and taught toward the learning behavior objectives. B is incorrect because the assessment procedures are not directly related to the actual learning behavior. C is incorrect; how the training will occur is important, but first the organization must define what learner behaviors are to change. D is incorrect; how the learners will apply the information is a tempting choice, but it's not as correct as the more direct answer of what behavior the organization wants to see the learners change.

Evaluating Instructor and Course Performance

In this chapter you will:
- Understand summative evaluations
- Develop formative evaluations
- Explore the Kirkpatrick model for evaluations
- Utilize evaluations for instructor performance improvement
- Implement e-based evaluation methods

Instructors, all instructors, can continue to improve their delivery, facilitation, and performance in the classroom. Instructor evaluations help organizations determine the level of learner satisfaction, but also give insight to how the instructor may improve. Class evaluations measure the immediate depth of effectiveness of the class design and how the class can be improved for future learners.

Understanding Trainer Evaluations

Organizations need learners to evaluate the performance of the trainer to determine trainer effectiveness. The organization may have other reasons for evaluating the trainer's performance, but the chief reason is to determine if the trainer is performing to a level that's commensurate with the organizational goals. After all, no one, not even you, wants to sit through hours of technical instruction that may not be effective, may be boring, or may be led by an incompetent trainer. That's a waste of time and money.

So while the first goal of trainer evaluations, from the organization's perspective, is cost-driven, there is a more subtle reason for all trainers to be evaluated by the learner: improvement. All of us trainers can always improve. I know that may be hard to believe—it was for me for a long time because I knew I was such a great speaker, but the truth is there are always opportunities to become a better, more effective trainer. While you may be an excellent speaker, technical trainer, and classroom facilitator, there are likely ways to refine this and become a more effective, more knowledgeable, and more confident technical trainer.

Evaluating the technical trainer also gives learners an opportunity to provide feedback. If learners are expected to attend a technical training course, they should also have the permission to communicate what did, and did not, go smoothly in it. The learners can influence future classes, the ongoing role of the instructor, and the instructor's future performance. Learners can be brutally honest in their instructor evaluation—both good and bad. Learners can share what they've enjoyed, despised, and everything in between with just a few checks of their pen. You, the technical trainer, want and need this feedback to help you become a better, more polished, expert trainer. The goal in evaluations isn't in the scoring of your performance, but how you take that information and apply it to future classes.

Utilizing a Summative Evaluation

The most common type of course evaluation is a summative evaluation. A summative evaluation happens at the end of the training course and allows learners to grade their experience in the classroom. Summative evaluations should be anonymous so that the students may answer honestly and with candor, without fear of retribution for their remarks and comments. Ideally, summative evaluations should be required for every course an organization offers and give the participants the opportunity to rank their experience with the instructor on all of the following topics:

- Clearly stated course objectives
- Presentation of the material
- Ability to engage participants in the material
- Classroom time management
- Instructor's technical expertise
- Ability to answer learner questions
- Interaction and availability during hands-on labs and exercises

Summative evaluations include details on more than just the instructor's performance, such as course content, facility review, and the course materials selected. It's important to not include too many sections for the learner to evaluate, however, as people may rush through the evaluation and not offer a genuine evaluation of any of the topics. It's frustrating for an instructor to receive an evaluation where respondents have simply checked the highest possible score for all categories in a rushed effort to complete the evaluation. Summative evaluations should also include opportunities for learners to add comments and suggestions for the course.

Most summative evaluations use a Likert scale approach for the grading of the course and instructor performance. The Likert scale, named after its inventor, psychologist Renis Likert, uses a high-to-low rating of a topic. Technically, the Likert scale is the sum of the scores of all of the items on the evaluation. An evaluation line item, called a Likert item, is just one statement by which learners judge the accuracy of the statement based on their experience. Here's an example of a Likert item:

The instructor clearly met all of the course objectives.

1. Strongly agree
2. Moderately agree
3. Neither agree nor disagree

4. Moderately disagree

5. Strongly disagree

The summative evaluation would have multiple statements rather than questions, and the learner would rank how closely they agree or disagree with the statement. Some Likert scale evaluations only include four possible answers, so the learner cannot choose the neutral "neither agree nor disagree" option. This is called a forced answer, as it requires the learner to agree or disagree to some extent.

The summative evaluation process should be straightforward and simple. The instructor should ask a learner to distribute the evaluations. The instructor should tell participants to complete their evaluation and then put the evaluation into a folder or envelope. The trainer should then leave the classroom while the participants complete the process. This keeps the process anonymous, which does promote more accurate and honest assessments. I'll discuss later in this chapter the value of using electronic evaluations over paper-based assessments, which can also promote more accurate assessments of the course and the instructor's performance.

 VIDEO   See the video *Comparing Summative and Formative Assessments.*

Offering Formative Assessment

Imagine you're taking a week-long technical class, and while you're really enjoying the labs and the instructor's lectures, there are a few things that are really distracting you from learning. A few other participants are chatting during the lectures. The instructor is jingling some coins in his pocket. The overhead lights are flickering. These are all things that could be fixed easily, if only you could tell the instructor without seeming like a whiner.

A formative assessment is an opportunity to tell the instructor what is and what is not working in the classroom while this class is still happening. A formative assessment doesn't happen at the end of the training, but often at the end of each day or in the middle of the class schedule. This allows the trainer to remedy any distractions or ineffective teaching approaches, and change the teaching process for the balance of the course to accommodate learning needs. Formative assessments don't have to be a formal evaluation like the summative evaluation. A formative assessment can ask three or four questions and allow the learners to offer feedback through a written statement rather than a Likert scale. A formative assessment might ask the following:

- What distractions or issues in the classroom should be addressed?
- How do you feel about the pace of the course?
- How do you feel about the balance of lecture to labs?
- What changes should the instructor implement to improve the remainder of the course?

These are just example questions that an instructor can use in order to change the course progression and overall improvement of the course. A formative assessment allows the instructor to react to situations in the classroom that are impeding the training and the education of the participants. It's an easy process to do—you don't even need to have a printout to use this midcourse assessment. An approach I've used is to prepare my formative assessment questions in a PowerPoint slide and present the questions on the projector for the class. I then distribute index cards for the class to answer the questions anonymously for me to review. I'm always cautious to have someone in the class gather the assessment rather than me to keep the input anonymous.

A formative assessment helps you offer immediate feedback and rectification of problems. It's one of the best in-class activities to ensure an improved classroom performance and boost the morale of the students. A formative assessment can ensure that you're keeping your training learner-focused—and it will most likely boost your summative evaluation because you'll manage the classroom better to the comments and suggestions you receive on the formative evaluation. In other words, you don't offer a formative evaluation and then not address the input the learners have offered.

Applying Effective Instructor Evaluations

Instructor evaluations are only effective if you actually review the information that's been offered and then apply it. One way of looking at evaluations is like advice from a doctor—the information is valid, but until you actually do what's being recommended, the advice isn't worth much. It's the action that will make the difference in your training. Pay attention to the evaluations, and consider their value in making you a better technical trainer.

Effective instructor evaluations measure how you did as an instructor, not how you are as a person. It's sometimes difficult to see the evaluation a person in your class offers as genuine advice rather than an attack. Certainly it is easy to understand how some trainers can be offended and hurt by comments and scores participants offer on evaluations. Public speaking is scary, and teaching can be challenging work. Instructors often see themselves as a performer in front of the audience rather than as an instructor in front of colleagues. This isn't necessarily a bad perspective, but the distinction should be made that the reviews are of an instructor, not an artist.

When evaluations are completed, the instructor and the coordinator or supervisor of the instructor should review the evaluations. This process ensures that the supervisor and the instructor both see the scores, comments, and input from the class. This is, I believe, something that many training organizations fail to do. Often the instructor only hears about the negative reviews and not the positive reviews that learners offer. By reviewing the course evaluations with the supervisor, all comments and marks are reviewed—good and bad. This approach also gives the supervisor an opportunity to make recommendations or provide coaching should there be a training performance issue to address.

Reviewing the Kirkpatrick Evaluation Model

The Kirkpatrick Evaluation Model, created by Donald Kirkpatrick, aims to capture how effective the training was in regard to the learning goals for the participants and for the organization. As a recap, there are four levels of evaluation in the Kirkpatrick Model:

- **Level One: Learner Reaction** This level is what most instructors think of when they think of the instructor evaluation. It's the end-of-class evaluation of what the participants thought of the training and the instructor's performance. The instructor is concerned with the immediate feedback of the training and how the learners thought the training transpired.

- **Level Two: Learning Achievement**   This level of evaluation determines the actual increase in learner knowledge. The learning achievement evaluation may be shown through a test, an exercise, or some other assessment to show how the learner has gained knowledge from the start of the course to its completion. The instructor is concerned with the actual knowledge gained as a result of teaching. No technical trainer wants to teach a class and then realize that the learners have not comprehended the information.

- **Level Three: Behavioral Change**   Behavioral change is demonstrated by the learner actually using the knowledge that was gained in the course. Behavioral change can be shown in how efficient the user is in the technology that was taught and whether they perform their work more accurately and efficiently. Instructors are concerned with learners actually applying the technology in their roles and responsibilities in the workplace. This level also assumes that the learners will actually have an opportunity to demonstrate that their behavior has changed.

- **Level Four: Business Results**   Business results link the profitability, cost savings, reduction in errors, and other qualifiers of the organization to the training that the instructor offered. A common Level Four business result is that the training cost X amount of dollars to offer, but Y equates to a return on investment for the training. For example, if the training results in learners being more efficient, then there may be fewer errors and that's a cost savings for the organization. Instructors want to see the value of their training actually implemented in the workforce to show their contribution to the organization's success.

While the Kirkpatrick Evaluation Model aims to assess the success of the training and the instructor, only the Level One evaluation provides immediate feedback on the instructor. To properly conduct a Kirkpatrick Evaluation requires that the organization commit to planning and consistency. The learning goals of the technical course must be considered to measure the success of the trainer and the training content. For example, consider a short, one-hour technical class on how to install new network printers. The Kirkpatrick Levels One, Two, and Three could be simple to capture the class satisfaction, the learning achievement, and the behavioral change if the learners were immediately leaving the class to install the printers. The fourth level, the business results, may take time to quantify the actual value of the course.

Considering E-based Evaluations

There's an assumption in business that computer-based and web-based forms will garner better results than paper-based forms. E-based evaluations—an instructor evaluation that is completed by the learning participants via a website—have garnered some favor in learning institutions over the past few years. From an administrative perspective, e-based evaluations are a blessing: data captured directly from the participants. With this data the organization can track instructor performance, see progress, compare ratings among classes, and even compare instructors. This approach can also track learners; for example, it's possible to see that one learner always gives critical reviews of an instructor, regardless of the actual performance of the course.

E-based evaluations can be configured to capture all sorts of data for a class: instructor performance, strengths on different topics, course materials, classroom management and configuration, and many more topics. This is one of the drawbacks of e-based evaluations, however—too many questions and the learner may get frustrated and bored with the evaluation. There must be a balance between the ease of creating the evaluation and actually completing it. It's a good heuristic to capture the same amount of information electronically that an organization would capture with a paper-based evaluation.

E-based evaluations should be administered directly in the classroom, just as you would with the paper-based evaluations. In my experience, when a learner has the opportunity to complete the evaluation later, back at their desk or home computer, the evaluation goes uncompleted. It's too easy for a learner to promise to complete the electronic evaluation and then get caught in the busyness of life and forget or ignore the evaluation. A learning management system can help track and remind learners of the importance of completing the evaluation in order to consider the class actually completed.

One of the best features of e-based evaluations is the opportunity for open-ended questions. The evaluation can be created to allow students to add more comments and specific examples from the classroom. As a trainer, I prefer the commentary that learners add rather than the quick rating offered on most evaluations. I want to hear what learners thought about the course and what things they enjoyed—or didn't enjoy—as part of the evaluation. Through the electronic-based evaluation, this is a snap to create, and learners are generally more willing to share their thoughts when they can type their comments rather than write out their reviews on paper.

Chapter Summary

Instructor evaluations are needed to help instructors perform better. The goal of an instructor evaluation isn't to judge the instructor, though some may see it as such, but to help the instructor become a better trainer. Instructor evaluations are needed to determine how effective the instructor was in her teaching, her classroom management, and in her abilities to achieve the learning objectives. Evaluations help the organization make decisions about future training, identify opportunities for improvement, and confirm the quality of education the instructor is offering.

The end-of-course evaluation, called the summative evaluation, captures details on the trainer's overall performance. Ideally, the summative evaluation allows the learners to grade the instructor's training anonymously without fear of retribution. These evaluations capture information on the instructor's delivery style, time management, availability, classroom management, and how well the instructor engaged participants in the materials. In most technical classes the evaluation will also offer learners an opportunity to review how technically competent the instructor was in the technology being taught.

Throughout the course the instructor may offer a formative evaluation. This evaluation helps the instructor formulate the remainder of the course based on learner input. For example, this evaluation can tell the instructor to quit pacing, speak more clearly, or not to move the mouse so quickly during demonstrations. Formative evaluations are also good opportunities for the learners to offer input on the classroom setting: temperature, lighting, noise, and other distractions. The formative evaluation allows the instructor to quickly resolve issues to help participants learn and enjoy the remainder of the class.

Formative and summative evaluations alike can use a Likert scale to rank the performance and categories of the instruction. Recall that a Likert scale uses a scoring approach to gauge how much the participant agrees with a statement. For example: "The classroom temperature is appropriate." The learner could rank their agreeability with the statement from one to five, where one is strongly disagree and five is strongly agree. Each item that is being ranked in a Likert scale is technically called a Likert item.

Many organizations subscribe to the Kirkpatrick Evaluation Model to assess not only instructor performance but also the overall effectiveness of the training. There are four levels of evaluation in the Kirkpatrick Model: Level One is learner reaction, Level Two is learner achievement, Level Three is behavioral change, and Level Four is business results. The instructor evaluation is generally associated with just Level One, but the effectiveness of the instructor is actually considered through all four levels.

Finally in this chapter I discussed the merits of using e-based evaluations. These evaluations, completed through an electronic computer-based service, capture the same information as traditional paper-based assessments. E-based evaluations offer data compilation, tracking, reporting, and opportunities for more in-depth reviews of the training. E-based evaluations should not, however, be too exhaustive, as learners may become frustrated with the amount of information the organization is trying to capture.

Key Terms

e-based evaluations   An electronic version of the class evaluation completed by the learning participants through a website or learning management system.

forced answer   A strategy in the Likert scale that forces the learner to agree or disagree to some extent by removing the option of neutral ratings.

formative assessment   Intermittent evaluations completed by the participants to communicate what is and what is not working in the classroom while this class is still happening. A formative assessment doesn't happen at the end of the training, but often at the end of each day or in the middle of the class schedule.

PART V

Kirkpatrick Evaluation Model A learning evaluation model created by Donald Kirkpatrick that aims to capture how effective the training was in regard to the learning goals for the participants and for the organization.

Kirkpatrick Evaluation Model, Level Four This level measures the business results as a result of the training. Business results link the profitability, cost savings, reduction in errors, and other qualifiers of the organization to the training that the instructor offered

Kirkpatrick Evaluation Model, Level One This is the learner reaction to the course and instructor performance. This level is what most instructors think of when they think of the instructor evaluation. It's the end-of-class evaluation of what the participants thought of the training and the instructor's performance.

Kirkpatrick Evaluation Model, Level Three This measures the actual behavioral change in the participants as a result of the training. Behavioral change is demonstrated by the learner actually using the knowledge that was gained in the course.

Kirkpatrick Evaluation Model, Level Two This is the assessment of learning achievement. This level of evaluation determines the actual increase in learner knowledge.

Likert item A statement that learners judge the accuracy of based on their experience in the classroom.

Likert scale Named after its inventor and psychologist, Renis Likert, this is the summation of Likert items. Likert items utilize a high-to-low rating of a topic by allowing the participant to rank their level of agreeability with a statement. The Likert scale is the sum of the scoring for all of the items on the evaluation

summative evaluation Usually an anonymous evaluation of the instructor's performance and overall class success. This evaluation is completed by learners at the end of the training course.

Questions

1. You are the technical trainer for your organization, and you're working with your supervisor on a better method to collect participant evaluations. You'd like the method to be quick, easy to compile, anonymous, and consistent across all classes. Which method would you recommend to your supervisor?

   A. Paper-based evaluations will work the best.

   B. E-based evaluations will work the best, as learners can complete them from anywhere.

   C. E-based evaluations will work the best, but learners must complete them as part of the class.

   D. A blended approach of paper and electronic evaluations is the best approach.

2. You are creating an evaluation form using the Likert scale. In your scale you want participants to choose a positive or negative answer, so you're removing all neutral options. This is called what type of answer?

    A. Forced

    B. Optional

    C. Zero sum

    D. Opt out

3. Beth is teaching a technical class for her organization. This class will last five days, and she has 12 participants in the class. At the end of the second day Beth distributes an evaluation to the participants to gauge their opinion and experience of the class so far. What type of an evaluation is Beth using?

    A. Summative

    B. Intermittent

    C. Formative

    D. Likert

4. What type of evaluation is offered at the end of most technical classes?

    A. E-based evaluation

    B. Formative

    C. Summative

    D. Comprehensive

5. Your organization would like to use the Kirkpatrick Evaluation Model. In this model there are four levels of evaluation. Which one of the following is not a level of evaluation?

    A. Business results

    B. Learner reaction

    C. Technical utilization

    D. Behavioral change

6. Which level of the Kirkpatrick Evaluation Model would include the cost savings as a result of training?

    A. Level One

    B. Level Two

    C. Level Three

    D. Level Four

PART V

7. Which level of the Kirkpatrick Evaluation Model would include the learner's immediate reaction to the trainer's expertise and performance?

   A. Level One

   B. Level Two

   C. Level Three

   D. Level Four

8. Your organization wants to see the participants actually use properly the technology you've taught. Which level of the Kirkpatrick Evaluation Model would include learners' behavioral change?

   A. Level One

   B. Level Two

   C. Level Three

   D. Level Four

9. Robert has finished teaching a technical class for a new client. He has distributed an instructor evaluation for the participants in his class. What type of evaluation has Robert distributed?

   A. Formative

   B. Summative

   C. Conclusive

   D. Comprehensive

10. Frances has just finished her technical class and has distributed an evaluation for the class to complete. Frances tells the participants to write their name in the upper-left corner and to complete the evaluation in pencil. Frances then tells the class that she'll wait in the hallway outside the classroom and the participants should hand her their evaluation as they leave. All of the following are mistakes that Frances has made in the evaluation process except for which one?

    A. Names on the evaluation

    B. Writing in pencil

    C. Leaving the classroom

    D. Handing the evaluation back to her

11. All of the following are reasons why instructor evaluations should be anonymous except for which one?

    A. So that the learners may be frank and honest with their answers

    B. So that the learners can answer the survey without fear of retribution

    C. So that the learners are encouraged to highlight the negative events of the classroom

    D. So that the instructor doesn't know which learner made which remark

12. What is the danger of having a large number of questions on the end-of-class evaluation?

    A. Learners may get confused as to which sections are important.

    B. Learners may get distracted from the learning objectives.

    C. Learners may choose which sections to answer and ignore others.

    D. Learners may rush through the evaluation without giving honest answers.

13. What term is given to each line-item statement in a Likert scale evaluation?

    A. Likert item

    B. Query item

    C. Interrogative item

    D. Question item

14. Ted is reviewing his end-of-class evaluations for a class he recently finished. One of the participants made the comment that the class was enjoyable, but the instructor paced too much, stood in front of the presentation, and the room was too cool for comfort. What type of evaluation could Ted have used to prevent these problems in the classroom?

    A. Summative

    B. Formative

    C. Intermittent

    D. Comfort

15. At the end of a class what two learning stakeholders should review the instructor evaluations?

    A. The instructor and the instructor's supervisor

    B. The instructor and the learners

    C. The learners and the instructor's supervisor

    D. The learners and their supervisors

16. All of the following statements regarding e-based evaluations are accurate except for which one?

    A. E-based evaluations allow organizations to capture data directly from classroom participants.

    B. E-based evaluations ensure better quantitative scores than paper-based evaluations.

    C. E-based evaluations help organizations track instructor performance.

    D. E-based evaluations can allow organizations to track learner evaluations among classes.

17. Beth is allowing learners to complete the e-based evaluation for her classroom performance as an instructor outside of the classroom. What risk does this present?

    A. The learners may forget how well the class actually went.

    B. The learners may forget to complete or forgo completing the e-based evaluation.

    C. The learners may ask someone else to complete the evaluation for them.

    D. The learners may rush through the evaluation rather than completing it thoughtfully.

18. An instructor and her manager are discussing the benefits of using e-based evaluations over paper-based evaluations. Which one of the following is the most compelling reason to use e-based evaluations?

    A. Learners are not anonymous with e-based evaluations.

    B. Trainer reviews are generally more favorable with e-based evaluations than with paper-based evaluations.

    C. Trainer reviews are generally less favorable with e-based evaluations than with paper-based evaluations.

    D. Learners are more inclined to add comments and narratives about their classroom experience with e-based evaluations than paper-based evaluations.

19. What is the goal of using instructor evaluations at the end of a class?

    A. To help the instructor become better

    B. To review the success of the class

    C. To determine the cost effectiveness of the training

    D. To help other trainers learn from the instructor's mistakes

20. You are teaching a technical class for your organization. During the class one of the participants hands you a note that informs you another participant in the class is making noises that are distracting the learners. Which one of the following methods would be the best approach to assess the problem for the class?

    A. Assessment evaluation

    B. Formative evaluation

    C. Summative evaluation

    D. Comprehensive evaluation

Questions and Answers

1. You are the technical trainer for your organization, and you're working with your supervisor on a better method to collect participant evaluations. You'd like the method to be quick, easy to compile, anonymous, and consistent across all classes. Which method would you recommend to your supervisor?

   A. Paper-based evaluations will work the best.

   B. E-based evaluations will work the best, as learners can complete them from anywhere.

   C. E-based evaluations will work the best, but learners must complete them as part of the class.

   D. A blended approach of paper and electronic evaluations is the best approach.

   C. E-based evaluations will give learners the opportunity to expound on their thoughts, but also capture their experience of the classroom and the trainer's performance. The evaluations should, however, be completed as part of the training, not for learners to complete on their own time. A is incorrect, as paper-based evaluations don't allow for quick data compilation. B is incorrect, as electronic evaluations should be completed as part of the class or learners may neglect to complete the evaluation. D is incorrect, as a blended approach doesn't address the need for quick compilation of data.

2. You are creating an evaluation form using the Likert scale. In your scale you want participants to choose a positive or negative answer, so you're removing all neutral options. This is called what type of answer?

   A. Forced

   B. Optional

   C. Zero sum

   D. Opt out

   A. This is an example of a forced answer because the participants must choose a positive or negative answer based on their agreement with the statement. B, C, and D are not valid options or terms associated with a Likert scale.

3. Beth is teaching a technical class for her organization. This class will last five days, and she has 12 participants in the class. At the end of the second day Beth distributes an evaluation to the participants to gauge their opinion and experience of the class so far. What type of an evaluation is Beth using?

   A. Summative

   B. Intermittent

   C. Formative

   D. Likert

   C. This is an example of a formative assessment, as the class is still in progress. This assessment type helps Beth determine what issues she should address to ensure the remainder of the class is a positive experience for the users. A is incorrect, as a summative evaluation is the comprehensive, end-of-course assessment. B is incorrect, as there is not an evaluation called intermittent. D is also incorrect, as Likert is a rating scale used on evaluations, not an evaluation type.

4. What type of evaluation is offered at the end of most technical classes?

   A. E-based evaluation

   B. Formative

   C. Summative

   D. Comprehensive

   C. A summative evaluation is offered at the end of the training course. A is incorrect, as e-based evaluations can be formative or summative, not just one or the other. B is incorrect, as a formative evaluation is offered throughout the course to determine what elements could be rectified to ensure that the remainder of the course is more successful. D is incorrect, as there is not an evaluation called comprehensive.

5. Your organization would like to use the Kirkpatrick Evaluation Model. In this model there are four levels of evaluation. Which one of the following is not a level of evaluation?

   A. Business results

   B. Learner reaction

   C. Technical utilization

   D. Behavioral change

   C. There is not a level of the Kirkpatrick Model that measures technical utilization. A, B and C are incorrect because the business result, learner reaction, and behavioral change are three of the four levels of the Kirkpatrick Evaluation Model.

6. Which level of the Kirkpatrick Evaluation Model would include the cost savings as a result of training?

   A. Level One

   B. Level Two

   C. Level Three

   D. Level Four

   D. Level Four, business results, would track the profitability, cost savings, reduction in errors, and other business-related metrics as part of the evaluation. A is incorrect, as Level One is the learner reaction to the course. B is incorrect, as Level Two describes the assessment of learning achievement from the course. C is incorrect, as Level Three aims to measure the actual behavioral change as a result of the training.

7. Which level of the Kirkpatrick Evaluation Model would include the learner's immediate reaction to the trainer's expertise and performance?

   A. Level One

   B. Level Two

   C. Level Three

   D. Level Four

   A. The first level of the evaluation is the learner reaction to the course and the instructor's overall performance. B is incorrect, as Level Two describes the assessment of learning achievement from the course. C is incorrect, as Level Three aims to measure the actual behavioral change as a result of the training. D is incorrect, as Level Four measures the business results, such as tracking the profitability, cost savings, reduction in errors, and other business-related metrics, as part of the evaluation.

8. Your organization wants to see participants actually use properly the technology you've taught. Which level of the Kirkpatrick Evaluation Model would include learners' behavioral change?

   A. Level One

   B. Level Two

   C. Level Three

   D. Level Four

   C. Behavioral change is the goal of the Level Three evaluations. A is incorrect, as the first level of the evaluation is the learner reaction to the course and the instructor's overall performance. B is incorrect, as Level Two describes the assessment of learning achievement from the course. D is incorrect, as Level Four measures the business results, such as tracking the profitability, cost savings, reduction in errors, and other business-related metrics, as part of the evaluation.

PART V

9. Robert has finished teaching a technical class for a new client. He has distributed an instructor evaluation for the participants in his class. What type of evaluation has Robert distributed?

   A. Formative

   B. Summative

   C. Conclusive

   D. Comprehensive

   B. This is a summative evaluation. Recall that the summative evaluation is distributed at the end of the course and is an evaluation of the instructor's performance and usually the class design. A is incorrect, as a formative evaluation is distributed throughout the course as an intermittent review of the instructor's performance so that the instructor may make corrections during the course. C and D are incorrect, as conclusive and comprehensive are not valid evaluation types.

10. Frances has just finished her technical class and has distributed an evaluation for the class to complete. Frances tells the participants to write their name in the upper-left corner and to complete the evaluation in pencil. Frances then tells the class that she'll wait in the hallway outside the classroom and the participants should hand her their evaluation as they leave. All of the following are mistakes that Frances has made in the evaluation process except for which one?

    A. Names on the evaluation

    B. Writing in pencil

    C. Leaving the classroom

    D. Handing the evaluation back to her

    C. The only valid thing that Frances did in this scenario was to leave the classroom. A, B, and D are incorrect, as Frances should not require the learners to use a pencil, include their names, or return the evaluation directly to her.

11. All of the following are reasons why instructor evaluations should be anonymous except for which one?

    A. So that the learners may be frank and honest with their answers

    B. So that the learners can answer the survey without fear of retribution

    C. So that the learners are encouraged to highlight the negative events of the classroom

    D. So that the instructor doesn't know which learner made which remark

    C. The goal of anonymous evaluations isn't to highlight the negative events, but to ensure honesty in the evaluation. A, B, and D are incorrect choices, as the learners should be able to give honest answers without fear of retribution. Instructors should not know which learners made which remarks on the evaluations.

12. What is the danger of having a large number of questions on the end-of-class evaluation?

A. Learners may get confused as to which sections are important.

B. Learners may get distracted from the learning objectives.

C. Learners may choose which sections to answer and ignore others.

D. Learners may rush through the evaluation without giving honest answers.

D. When the summative evaluation has a large number of questions, the learners may feel overwhelmed and rush through the evaluation. It's important to determine which questions are most important for the class, the instructor by way of review, and the goals of the organization. A, B, and C are not good answers for this question, as the primary risk is that learners will rush through the evaluation.

13. What term is given to each line-item statement in a Likert scale evaluation?

A. Likert item

B. Query item

C. Interrogative item

D. Question item

A. Each line-item statement in a Likert scale evaluation is simply called a Likert item. B, C, and D are incorrect, as query, interrogative, and question are not applicable terms to the Likert scale evaluation technique.

14. Ted is reviewing his end-of-class evaluations for a class he recently finished. One of the participants made the comment that the class was enjoyable, but the instructor paced too much, stood in front of the presentation, and the room was too cool for comfort. What type of evaluation could Ted have used to prevent these problems in the classroom?

A. Summative

B. Formative

C. Intermittent

D. Comfort

B. Ted should have used a formative evaluation in the course to give the learner an opportunity to bring any comfort or learning issue to light. The formative evaluation helps the instructor adjust the course and issues to keep the remainder of the class successful. A is incorrect, as a summative evaluation, like a summary, is the end-of-class evaluation. C and D are incorrect, as these are not valid evaluation types.

15. At the end of a class what two learning stakeholders should review the instructor evaluations?

    A. The instructor and the instructor's supervisor

    B. The instructor and the learners

    C. The learners and the instructor's supervisor

    D. The learners and their supervisors

    A. The instructor and the instructor's supervisor should review the evaluations to ensure that the instructor's performance is accurately reviewed and discussed. This is valid for good and poor evaluations. B, C, and D are not valid choices because the instructor should not review the evaluations with the participants, nor should the participants be obligated to review the evaluations with the trainer's supervisor.

16. All of the following statements regarding e-based evaluations are accurate except for which one?

    A. E-based evaluations allow organizations to capture data directly from classroom participants.

    B. E-based evaluations ensure better quantitative scores than paper-based evaluations.

    C. E-based evaluations help organizations track instructor performance.

    D. E-based evaluations can allow organizations to track learner evaluations among classes.

    B. Just because an organization decides to use e-based evaluations for instructor performance, this does not necessarily mean that the evaluations will have better quantitative scores than paper-based evaluations. The scores for the instructor performance should not change simply because a different type of evaluation process is being utilized. A, C, and D are incorrect because these statements are true in regard to instructor evaluations.

17. Beth is allowing learners to complete the e-based evaluation for her classroom performance as an instructor outside of the classroom. What risk does this present?

    A. The learners may forget how well the class actually went.

    B. The learners may forget to complete or forgo completing the e-based evaluation.

    C. The learners may ask someone else to complete the evaluation for them.

    D. The learners may rush through the evaluation rather than completing it thoughtfully.

B. When learners are not required to complete the e-based evaluation as part of the classroom experience, there's a risk that they will forget or forgo the evaluation. A is incorrect, as learners likely won't forget how well the class went, but may forget to complete the evaluation. C is incorrect; it's doubtful that learners may ask someone else to complete the evaluation. D is also incorrect, as this is a risk even if the learners complete the evaluation in the classroom.

18. An instructor and her manager are discussing the benefits of using e-based evaluations over paper-based evaluations. Which one of the following is the most compelling reason to use e-based evaluations?

    A. Learners are not anonymous with e-based evaluations.

    B. Trainer reviews are generally more favorable with e-based evaluations than with paper-based evaluations.

    C. Trainer reviews are generally less favorable with e-based evaluations than with paper-based evaluations.

    D. Learners are more inclined to add comments and narratives about their classroom experience with e-based evaluations than paper-based evaluations.

D. E-based evaluations make it easier for learners to write comments and narratives than do paper-based evaluations. A is incorrect, as learners can still be anonymous with e-based evaluations. B and C are incorrect, as there's no evidence that trainer reviews are better or worse simply by using an e-based evaluation.

19. What is the goal of using instructor evaluations at the end of a class?

    A. To help the instructor become better

    B. To review the success of the class

    C. To determine the cost effectiveness of the training

    D. To help other trainers learn from the instructor's mistakes

A. The goal of using instructor evaluations at the end of the class is to help the instructor become better. B is incorrect, as the goal of evaluations is to help the instructor improve, not judge, the success of the class. Evaluations may include this information, but it's not the primary goal of the evaluation. C is incorrect; the evaluation likely will not determine the cost effectiveness of the training. D is a tempting choice, but the primary goal is to help the instructor become better in future classes.

20. You are teaching a technical class for your organization. During the class one of the participants hands you a note that informs you another participant in the class is making noises that are distracting the learners. Which one of the following methods would be the best approach to assess the problem for the class?

A. Assessment evaluation

B. Formative evaluation

C. Summative evaluation

D. Comprehensive evaluation

B. A formative evaluation is a great method to determine what distractions in the classroom should be addressed. The evaluation can be straightforward by asking what distractions, if any, should be addressed by the instructor. A is incorrect, as there is not an evaluation called an assessment evaluation. C is incorrect, as the summative evaluation is the end-of-course evaluation for the course and instructor. D is incorrect, as there is not a comprehensive evaluation.

PART VI

Appendices

- Appendix A   Certified Technical Trainer+ Exam Objectives
- Appendix B   About the CD

Certified Technical Trainer+ Exam Objectives

If you're like most technical trainers, you feel confident in your ability to deliver an effective and successful technical class. You're confident in your abilities to stand before adult learners and explain technical concepts in a manner that's easy for participants to understand and apply. Or you're confident in your approach for teaching remote learners through a virtual classroom space. You know how to engage learners, ask questions, and lead people to learning through discovery rather than through constant lecturing. You might be nervous to speak before learners, but you're not afraid to do so.

Passing a written exam, however, might be another story. There's something a little scary about sitting before a computer and taking a test about what you do for a living. Test anxiety isn't anything new—everyone has some level of anxiety for any test they're paying to take. No CTT+ candidate wants to invest hours of their life, pay for the examination, and then fail the actual test. Test anxiety can be managed with some relaxation techniques, breathing exercises, and time management during the actual exam. The greatest method to beat test anxiety, however, is to understand exactly what the CTT+ examination will test you about.

This appendix defines each of the exam objectives in detail and offers some advice on what you should know to pass your CompTIA CTT+ examination. These objectives are published by CompTIA and are accurate as of this writing. You should, as part of your exam preparedness, visit www.comptia.org and confirm the accuracy of these exam objectives. CompTIA can, at their discretion, modify the exam objectives, so it's a good idea to confirm that these objectives are still valid for the exam you're about to pass.

Notice how I said this is the exam you're about to pass. That's the mindset I've tried to subtly use throughout this book—a positive attitude about your ability as a trainer and your confidence to pass this exam. Confidence comes through experience and preparation—something you should be armed with by the time you've reached this point in the book. My hope for you is that you'll pass the exam on your first attempt, but also that you'll become a better trainer.

Planning Prior to the Course

The exam objectives in this domain will test your understanding of the time and effort required to prepare to teach an excellent class. You'll be tested on your understanding of organizational needs and goals for training and how that affects your preparation for the technical class. You'll also need to understand the work you'll do to prepare the physical and virtual classroom space. You'll be tested on the logistics required to teach a class, such as prepping the classroom, configuring software, and ensuring course materials are available prior to the start of the course.

Review of Organizational Needs and Learners' Backgrounds in Relationship to Course Objectives

You'll be tested on your ability to satisfy the organizational needs as part of your training. This means helping learners achievable actionable items, maintain retention, and anticipate parts of the course content where learners may struggle with the material. Keep in mind that these exam objectives happen before the actual course, so this is part of your preparation for the material you'll be teaching. For example, one of the principles in this objective is to adapt the materials to teach things not in the course content but desired by the client. This means you'll need to communicate with the client about the course content, the importance of the objectives, and what's expected of you as part of the class.

This objective will also test your understanding of adapting, customizing, and creating course content for the class. This is where your understanding of the ADDIE principles of instructional design will be beneficial. Recall that ADDIE describes the five phases of instructional design: analysis, design, development, implementation, and evaluation. Not only will you adapt and create learning materials, but you'll also need to adapt and adjust your teaching style and course content to promote learning.

The exam objective requires your knowledge of these technical training principles:

- Key content points likely to cause learner questions
- Points in the content where learner resistance may occur
- Objectives and information not specified in the materials but desired by the client or learner
- Types of needs assessments, such as surveys or interviews with trainees' supervisors
- Situations in which it is appropriate to modify learning materials and delivery tools based on commonly accepted practice or theory
- Techniques used to adjust instructional activities to meet the needs of the group and the situation
- Learning objectives to ensure that content and design retain their original integrity
- Content, audience, and/or situation requirements that are learner centered, rather than instructor centered

- Techniques to ensure that an adequate range of learner characteristics have been addressed
- Instructional design techniques to create customized training
- Available instructional resources and delivery tools in the classroom or virtual session room

You'll be tested on your ability to perform these skills:

- Research additional content information to address potential points of confusion or resistance.
- Assess learners' current skill level and compare results with course prerequisites.
- Assess organizational needs for additional learning outcomes.
- Analyze results of needs assessment of the learner in relation to learning objectives.
- Modify learning materials to meet specific needs of organization, learner, situation, or delivery tools without compromising original course design.

Instructional Environment in Relationship to Learning Objectives

This exam objective requires that you prepare the physical and virtual classroom space for optimal training. Some of the basics are covered, such as confirming the training dates, course materials, and configuration of the software and hardware. You'll also be tested on configuring classroom space for virtual training and stand-up instructor-led training sessions. You'll need to prepare the learning environment so the class is ready to begin without any distractions or delays to the learners. This planning objective considers your approach to addressing problems that need to be corrected before the course begins—the goal is to prepare for a smooth training event with no distractions.

You'll be tested on addressing

- Logistical needs prior to the instructional session (for example, dates of the offering; how materials will be provided (ship to learner or site, send instructions and link to download, space arrangements); adequacy of the facility; equipment; materials; learner registrations; pre-course assignments). For the virtual trainer, this would include creating a session room, sending login instructions to users, setting user privileges, loading and testing session materials, and testing all equipment.
- Logistical needs after the instructional session (for example, equipment and materials are returned, discarded, or made available for their next use; facilities are left in an acceptable condition; problems with the facility, equipment, furniture, or materials are communicated to appropriate authorities). For the virtual trainer, this includes stopping recording, saving files, closing session rooms, running attendance reports, updating learner status, documenting sessions, and following up on technical problems.

- Optimal seating arrangements to provide a viable learning environment consistent with the instructional design.

- Optimal virtual arrangements to provide a viable learning environment consistent with the instructional design (for example, network connection, tool capability to handle audience size, system check).

- Optimal organization of learner supplies, references, and materials (for example, neatly organized and located at each learner's seat or at a convenient central location). For the virtual trainer, consolidate e-mails and files sent to participants.

- Equipment setup techniques that ensure a safe environment (for example, computer terminals, video monitors, power cords, and learner emotional safety, such as the appropriateness of chat).

- Physical environmental needs to maximize learner comfort and safety (for example, ventilation; temperature; lighting; sound; noise; cleanliness; location of restrooms, telephones; rules for smoking; dress and conduct requirements).

- Virtual environmental needs to maximize learner comfort and safety (for example, distractions, pop-up windows, background noise, mute rules, quiet work zone, use do not disturb sign).

- Corrective actions that should be communicated to appropriate authorities (for example, assessment of environmental problems that need to be corrected).

You need to possess these skills as part of this exam objective:

- Review pre-course communications with learners (for example, course announcement, confirmation, description or agenda, prerequisites and pre-course assignments, system check activity, support/helpdesk information, download instructions for materials).

- Alter recommended physical or virtual classroom setup according to specific learner and organizational needs.

- Confirm timings and logistics for course (for example, scheduled breaks, meal arrangements, labs, and activities outside of classroom, time zones for virtual training, materials receipt).

- Ensure that learning-related tools and equipment are properly set up and working, and verify that all learner exercises can be completed as intended (for example, hands-on practice, online tool use).

- Establish a safe learning environment (for example, physical, auditory, chat, agreements, proprietary client information).

- Confirm with learners that the learning environment, both physical and virtual, is comfortable (for example, lighting, sound, conference call or VoIP audio, online tool is functioning well).

- Prepare contingency plans for unique class events (for example, fire drill in classroom, loss of connection, some users not able to view materials).

Utilizing Methods and Media for Instructional Delivery

There are lots of different approaches to teaching technical content. You can demonstrate the technical concepts, draw illustrations on whiteboards, lecture on complex topics, and help learners complete lab exercises as part of the class. The course designers may, or may not, include you as a subject matter expert when they create the course. You'll need to take what the designers have created and treat their course design as the boundaries and expectations for what the learners and the organization expect from the class.

This domain objective also addresses your abilities to effectively present the material to the learners using different presentation tools and media. This can be the typical instructor-led techniques, but also the management of virtual classroom software to facilitate a class to remote learners. You'll also be tested on introducing media, such as animations, related course videos, and sounds, into your classroom space—and the pros and cons of each of these media types.

Selection and Implementation of Instructional Methods

Assuming that you were not involved in the creation of the course materials, you will have to become familiar with the content of the course material, how the designers anticipated the course to flow, and how the exercises within the course should be completed. This domain objective is where you'll be tested on the adult-learning theory of Malcolm Knowles. Knowles developed the concept of andragogy into the Theory of Adult Education—how adults learn. You'll be tested on the recognition and exploration of these adult learning styles, such as auditory, kinesthetic, and visual approaches. In this objective you'll need to adapt your teaching style and promote the learning style of participants to reflect the learning environment, such as classroom environment as opposed to a computer lab.

You'll be tested on these topics:

- Instructional methods as described by course designers
- Pros and cons of each instructional method
- Learning styles associated with adult-learning theory (Malcolm Knowles)
- Learning styles such as auditory, kinesthetic, visual
- Various learning styles for technical learners
- Various learning methods for nontechnical content
- Techniques for delivering instruction in a classroom environment
- Techniques for delivering instruction in a technology-delivered environment (computer-lab)
- Techniques for delivering instruction in a virtual environment

PART VI

You'll need these skills to be a successful technical trainer:

- Use delivery methods as intended by the course designers.
- Adapt delivery methods to meet a variety of learning styles.
- Engage learners through multiple delivery techniques as appropriate to the material, the learners, and the situation.
- Organize and introduce content in a variety of ways (for example, compare and contrast, steps in a process, advantages and disadvantages).
- Identify and implement learning activities that are relevant to the course objectives.
- Monitor learner comfort level during the use of participatory activities.
- Stimulate interest and enhance learner understanding through appropriate examples, demonstrations, media clips, slides, anecdotes, stories, analogies, and humor.
- Use activities that allow learners to contribute to the discussion and review and apply content at appropriate intervals.

Use of Presentation and Instructional Media

When you're teaching a technical class, the participants expect you to control the learning environment and resolve problems that may happen with the technology you're teaching. This exam objective will test your ability to use and manage the media your course relies on for the course content. In traditional classroom training you may have overhead projectors, handouts, and graphics to illustrate the concepts you're teaching. In a virtual classroom you may have shared computer applications, specific features of your virtual classroom software, and audio features. In either learning environment the instructor must control the learning and effectively utilize the presentation and instructional media that will support the learning of the participants.

You will be tested on these topics:

- Types of media that can be used to support and enhance instructional delivery (for example, a graphic display; text display; handouts; shared computer applications; graphics files supported by the specific virtual classroom software)
- Types of media that support and enhance content needs
- Pros and cons of each media type
- Technology limitations associated with e-learning (for example, use of video where low bandwidth slows delivery and access to websites that are blocked for some organizations)

You'll need these instructional skills to

- Use a variety of media/tools to support learning objectives and meet learner needs

- Handle minor problems associated with each particular medium
- Enhance, substitute, or create media as appropriate to support the learning objectives

Maintaining Instructor Credibility and Communications

The participants in your technical classes expect you, the instructor, to be credible, approachable, and an expert in the technology you're teaching and in the management of the classroom. First impressions can affect your credibility with the learners. A neat, well-groomed, and appropriately dressed instructor not only can impress your clients and learners, but also sends a message that you're a professional instructor and prepared to deliver the course. How you behave in the classroom should also reflect your professionalism. Instructors must treat participants with respect, never embarrass the learners, and manage the classroom to promote a positive environment.

The exam objective will also test your ability to effectively communicate with the learners in the class. This means your voice, your speech patterns, and your body language all affect the success of the class. Being an expert in the topic you're teaching will help you have the confidence to deliver effectively in the class, but you'll also need to control your speech and breathing, and eliminate any distractions from your speech and body language. A person can be an expert in the technology, but also be rude, mumble, pace, or exhibit other unacceptable communications. You'll be tested on your ability to teach, which includes your speech and nonverbal communications.

Instructor Delivery Competence and Content Expertise

This exam objective will test your ability to deliver with confidence and expertise in the classroom environment. You'll need to present yourself to clients and learners as a professional—this means timeliness, dress, humor, and teaching style. You'll also be tested on your ability to address problems in the classroom and engage learners. As a professional instructor you'll be able to adapt the course material to engage the learners in conversations of how they'll actually use the technology in their roles in the organization.

You'll be tested on these topics related to this exam objective:

- Personal conduct acceptable to clients and learners (for example, timeliness, clothing, grooming, appropriate use of humor and/or language to the learners and situation)
- Acceptable manners and behaviors for learners
- Consistency of values and actions is demonstrated; responsibility is accepted where appropriate without blaming or belittling others, the learning materials, or management (acceptable self-disclosure techniques)
- Instructional content (course material)
- How learners use course content post-training (analysis of the business needs)

You should have the ability to demonstrate these skills:

- Maintain consistent behavior with all learners.
- Demonstrate confidence with and mastery of subject matter.
- Provide and elicit from learners practical examples of how knowledge and skills will transfer to their workplaces.
- Handle relevant learner inquiries on topics for which the instructor has limited expertise.
- Maintain positive atmosphere and avoid criticizing other members of the training team, the training materials, or the tools.

Instructor Communication and Presentation Skills

Instructors are, to some extent, public speakers. As a public speaker you need to be able to speak clearly and precisely to your audience. In a technical class it's easy to overuse jargon, so the instructor must make certain the participants understand the message through feedback and active listening. It's often how you say something, not just what you're saying, that affects the message. Instructors must be aware of their tone, inflection, pitch, and tempo and how it may alter the meaning of the message. The instructor must also monitor her speech for phrases and vocalizations that can be distracting and annoying in the classroom.

You'll be tested on these topics:

- Grammar and syntax (for example, logical arrangement of words and sentences; proper use of vocabulary)
- Colloquialisms, technical terms, acronyms, and organizational jargon used for clarification at the appropriate level for the content and the group
- Use of voice (for example, tempo, rhythm, volume, inflection, rate of speech, use of audio optimization options)
- Vocalization (for example, avoidance of distracting expressions and utterances)
- Nonverbal communication (for example, eye contact, gestures, silence/pauses, body movement, and facial nuances are used to emphasize and clarify content points)
- Technical nonverbal tools such as emoticons

You'll need to possess these skills as a technical instructor:

- Pronounce words correctly at appropriate tempo and use suitable grammar and syntax, recognizing potential for an international audience.
- Explain and clarify content points through inflection, emphasis, and pauses.
- Ensure verbal and nonverbal communication is free of bias (for example, sexual, racial, religious, cultural, and age).

- Employ purposeful pointers, body language, and/or vocal intonation to enhance learning and call attention to critical points.

- Minimize distracting trainer behaviors (for example, playing with object in hand, making noise with change in a pocket, or nervously rocking or pacing; excessive mouse movement; background noise on audio; keyboard noise).

- For the classroom trainer, use body language and other nonverbal techniques to minimize or eliminate learner disruptions. For the virtual trainer, use private chat and group agreements to mitigate disruptions.

- Use course overviews, advanced organizers, and session summaries at appropriate times to orientate learners and link key learning points.

Facilitating Adult Education

There's a difference, of course, between teaching a class and leading a class of adult learners to the information they need for their roles and lives. Technical trainers do teach, but the process is more than just lecturing—it's the management of the classroom, the guidance of all the adult learners in the classroom, and the effective presentation of the material. Trainers must keep the learners organized and working toward the common goals of the course—without letting more advanced learners feel bored and the learners with not as much experience feel left behind. Much of group facilitation focuses on learners knowing what to expect in the course—and it's up to the instructor to communicate the plan.

Engaging learners is done through communication: lecture, body language, demonstrations, and lots of questions. Questions must be formulated to be effective and engage the learner in recall, application, discussion, or other feedback. Communication isn't just questions, but also interaction with adult learners—engaging them in the course through conversations, social learning, and group exercises. Exercises and quizzes are also effective tools for engaging adult learners—and you'll be tested on these on your CTT+ certification exam. Quizzes and exercises help learners judge their retention, refresh their memory on the course content, and can create fun competition as part of your training.

Establishment and Management of a Learner-Centered Environment

When groups come together for learning and work, they'll often move through phases, such as Tuckman's forming, storming, norming, and performing, to reach collaboration. For your CTT+ examination you should also be familiar with the concept of Cog's Ladder, which describes the group development phases as the polite stage, why we're here stage, power stage, cooperation stage, and the final collaborative phase called the esprit stage. Both of these theories are evident in adult education when learners come together. The adult educator should be aware of these phases and how they may affect the training and the learning.

You will be tested on

- Group dynamics
- Group development phases
- Group facilitation techniques
- Techniques to engage learners

You should demonstrate these skills as a technical trainer:

- Open a training session in a positive way.
- Communicate the course plan to the learners.
- Communicate learner performance objectives as indicated by course design. Obtain input from the learners about their personal objectives and expectations.
- Reconcile any discrepancies between learning objectives and learner expectations.
- Establish an environment that supports learning and maintains focus on meeting stated learning objectives.
- Establish a learning environment free of bias, favoritism, and criticism that optimizes the productive participation of all the learners.
- Manage course flow and pace activities based on learner needs while ensuring that all learning objectives are met.
- Provide opportunities and assistance for learners to identify and achieve initial, intermediate, and terminal objectives.
- Facilitate group dynamics in a positive way, including encouraging interactions that are respectful of the rights of individual learners and redirecting unproductive digressions.
- Create opportunities for learners to work with and learn from each other to attain the learning objectives while building individual learner confidence.
- Handle learner disruptions as discreetly as possible.
- Use virtual class tools like chat and polling to optimize learner contribution.
- Use virtual class tools to achieve learning objectives.

Promotion of Learner Engagement and Participation

Learners expect trainers to lead them toward the discovery of new information. Trainers can do this by asking questions, engaging the learners, and active listening. You'll need to ask open-ended questions to create conversations and closed questions to test recall of information. Throughout the class you'll balance the lecture, demonstrations, conversations, and hands-on exercises to appeal to the different types of learners, but also to keep the learning experience active. Recall that social learning is the process of learners learning from each other, so trainers should promote group exercises and conversations in the classroom.

In this exam objective you'll be tested on

- Active listening techniques
- Types and uses of questions
- Pros and cons of each type of question
- Cognitive levels
- Frequency of elicitation and interactions
- The value of social learning

You will need to demonstrate these skills:

- Use active listening techniques to acknowledge and understand learner contributions.
- Use a variety of types and levels of questions to challenge learners, involve them, and monitor their progress.
- Use questions that lead learners from recall to application of content.
- Direct questions appropriately.
- Create opportunities for learners to contribute to the discussion.
- Employ activities to encourage learners to ask and answer questions themselves.

Assessment of Learners' Needs for Additional Explanation and Encouragement

When learners aren't grasping content, it is the responsibility of the instructor to help them learn the material without impeding on the learning of other participants in the classroom.

The instructor must watch the learners' body language for signs of confusion or questions regarding the course content. This is especially important on complex topics, as learners may feel intimidated or embarrassed to ask questions. In a virtual classroom environment the instructor should encourage the use of private chats, surveys, and emoticons to gauge learner retention and understanding. Whenever answering a question in the class the trainer should not embarrass the learner, but promote learning and comfort with asking additional questions.

You will be tested on

- Tools and techniques for determining learners' need for clarification (e.g., body language, learner questions or comments, asking learner to perform the application, emoticons, polling/surveying/quizzing, private chat)
- Techniques for providing positive and negative feedback

You should demonstrate these skills:

- Interpret and confirm learners' verbal and nonverbal communication to identify those who need clarification and feedback.
- Determine how and when to respond to learners' needs for clarification and/or feedback.
- Provide feedback that is specific to learners' needs.
- Elicit learner feedback on the adequacy of trainer responses.

Motivation and Positive Reinforcement of Learners

To motivate and reinforce learners the technical trainer needs to be aware of the learning goals of the learner, the organization, and the expected outcomes for the training. To motivate learners the trainer should help learners see the connection between the course content and how they'll apply the course information in their lives. In this objective you'll also be tested on how learners learn, the different learning styles, and different techniques you can use to motivate and challenge learners to help them discover the learning.

You'll be tested on these topics:

- Theories of learner motivation (for example, goal orientation, activity orientation, learning orientation)
- Personality and different learning styles of learners
- Relevance of learning to job requirements
- Techniques for motivating learners (for example, praise, rewards, access to the application)

You should be able to demonstrate these skills:

- Encourage and match learner achievement to learner and organizational needs and goals.
- Determine and apply appropriate motivational strategies for individual learners.
- Plan and use a variety of reinforcement techniques during training.
- Engage and invite relevant participation throughout the session.

Evaluating the Training Event

There are multiple reasons why the training event should be evaluated by the organization—and there are different types and approaches to evaluation that you should be familiar with. First, the instructor should evaluate the learners as the course is in motion to determine their understanding and retention of the material. This gives the instructor the opportunity to clarify concepts, help learners learn, and make adjustments in the learning approach to better serve the participants. Assessments during the course can be conversations, exercises, or quizzes and exams to determine learner retention.

Organizations also want to determine the effectiveness of the training event and the trainer's level of performance in the classroom. It's only logical that a training event is designed to ascertain certain education goals, so it's also logical to measure the outcome of the training to determine if the learning goals have been achieved. The instructor evaluation is used to determine the effectiveness of the training materials, classroom space, and the instructor's performance. The evaluation of these items is not necessarily to judge or grade, but to help the organization and the instructor perform better in the future.

Evaluation of Learner Performance During and at Close of Instruction

Instructors don't just lecture, but they engage the learner in the classroom. Part of the learner engagement is to assess how well the participants are learning, retaining, and interacting with the technology the class focuses on. Throughout the training event the instructor must observe and assess each participant for their performance and involvement in the class. This exam objective will test your abilities to determine learner performance and make rectifications to your training approach to better support learner goals. Once class is over there is also a need for post-training support. This information and plan should be communicated to the learners as part of the classroom delivery.

You will be tested on your knowledge of

- Performance assessment methodology
- Need for multiple observations and evaluations of each learner
- Need for the same evaluation standards across learners
- Evaluation techniques, including both formative and summative
- Post-course support methods to communicate with learners

You should have the skills to

- Monitor learner progress during training.
- Develop, select, and administer appropriate assessments that are in compliance with recognized and accepted measurement principles.
- Gather objective and subjective information that demonstrates learner knowledge acquisition and skill transfer.
- Compare learner achievements with learning objectives.
- Suggest additional training or resources to reinforce learning objectives.

PART VI

Evaluation of Instructor and Course

The point of evaluating the instructor is to determine how the instructor can improve her performance before the training event. Instructor evaluations help the organization determine the overall effectiveness of the instructor. You'll be tested on your understanding of Kirkpatrick's levels of evaluation and how an organization can apply this information to improve training. Evaluations are also useful for an organization to determine how effective the course design is. Based on instructor and participant feedback, instructional designers can revisit the course material and make updates and corrections for better delivery in future classes.

You will be tested on

- Methods to evaluate instructional delivery
- Types of evaluation (e.g., Kirkpatrick's levels of evaluation)
- Legal requirements associated with preparing reports on learners
- Organizational requirements for end-of-course reports
- Required record-keeping of individual learner activity and behavior, such as attendance

You should be able to demonstrate these skills:

- Evaluate the success of the course design, including modifications made during delivery.
- Critique one's own preparation for and delivery of a training event.
- Evaluate impact of external influences on the training event.
- Evaluate the effectiveness of the training to meet the learning objectives.
- Use evaluation results to adjust and improve one's own performance in the next training event.
- Prepare a report documenting end-of-course information.
- Report recommended revisions and changes to existing materials and suggestions for new programs and activities, as appropriate.
- Report information about learning in both physical and virtual environments.
- Submit reports to customers in accordance with contractual agreements or requests.

About the CD

The CD-ROM included with this book comes complete with MasterExam practice exam software, video training from the author, a CompTIA CTT+ Exam Objectives List as available from CompTIA at the time of publication, a score tracker spreadsheet, and a PDF copy of the book. The software is easy to install on any Windows 2000/XP/Vista/ Windows 7 computer and must be installed to access the MasterExam feature. You may, however, browse the PDF copy of the book and the videos directly from the CD without installation. To register for the bonus MasterExam, simply click the Bonus MasterExam link on the main launch page and follow the directions to the free online registration.

System Requirements

Software requires Windows 2000 or higher and Internet Explorer 6.0 or above and 20MB of hard disk space for full installation. Flash Trainer requires a 500 MHz or higher processor, 256MB of RAM or higher, 1024 × 768 or higher-resolution monitor, and Microsoft .NET 2.0 Framework. The PDF copy of the book requires Adobe Acrobat Reader.

Installing and Running MasterExam

If your computer's CD-ROM drive is configured to auto-run, the CD-ROM will automatically start up upon inserting the disk. From the opening screen you may install MasterExam by clicking the MasterExam link. This will begin the installation process and create a program group named LearnKey. To run MasterExam use Start | All Programs | LearnKey | MasterExam. If the auto-run feature did not launch your CD, browse to the CD and click the LaunchTraining.exe icon.

MasterExam

MasterExam provides you with a simulation of the actual exam. The number of questions, the type of questions, and the time allowed are intended to be an accurate representation of the exam environment. You have the option to take an open-book exam, including hints, references, and answers; a closed-book exam; or the timed MasterExam simulation.

When you launch MasterExam, a digital clock display will appear in the bottom-right corner of your screen. The clock will continue to count down to zero unless you choose to end the exam before the time expires.

Video Training

Video clips from the author provide detailed examples of key certification topics in audio-visual format. You can access the videos directly from the CD's table of contents by clicking the Videos link on the main launch page. If you're having trouble viewing the videos, check to see that QuickTime is installed on your system. QuickTime can be downloaded free of charge from the Apple website.

PDF Copy of the Book

The entire contents of the Exam Guide are provided in PDF. Adobe's Acrobat Reader has been included on the CD.

Help

A help file is provided through the help button on the main page in the lower-left corner. An individual help feature is also available through MasterExam.

Removing Installations

MasterExam is installed to your hard drive. For best results removing the MasterExam software, use Start | All Programs | LearnKey | Uninstall. To remove the Flash Trainer program, use Start | Control Panel | Add Or Remove Programs.

Technical Support

For questions regarding the content of the PDF copy of the book, MasterExam, or videos, please visit www.mhprofessional.com or e-mail customer.service@mcgraw-hill.com. For customers outside the United States, e-mail: international_cs@mcgraw-hill.com.

LearnKey Technical Support

For technical problems with the CD and MasterExam software (installation, operation, removing installations), please visit www.learnkey.com, e-mail techsupport@learnkey .com, or call toll-free at 1-800-482-8244.

accommodators   These learners are similar to the convergers, but they're more inclined to experiment with the technology, create "what-if" scenarios, and combine knowledge to see the result. These learners like a loosely structured training event that allows them time to test their theories and understanding of a technology. These people are sometimes referred to as concrete-active.

acknowledgement   In the communication model, an acknowledgement is a sign from the receiver to the sender that the receiver got the message. Acknowledgements don't necessarily mean that the receiver agrees with the message, or even understands the information; only that the receiver has received the message.

active learning   The learner is actively involved in the technology and topic through exercises, practice, hands-on activities, and interactions with the instructor and other participants. Active learning comes from hands-on involvement with the technology you're teaching.

active listening   The instructor tries to understand the message as clearly as possible without looking for subtext and hidden agendas in the message. The instructor only listens to the message that is being sent from the learner.

active observation   Part of learner task analysis where the observer is actively involved in the task, asks questions for clarity, and may even participate in the actual work to better understand the tasks the learners will need to be able to complete with the technology.

adaptation   A component of the psychomotor domain in Bloom's Taxonomy that happens when a learner has mastered a specific skill and can adapt their existing knowledge and apply it to new conditions and circumstances.

ADDIE model   An instructional design model that uses the phases of analysis, design, development, implementation, and evaluation to describe the five cyclic stages of instructional design and development.

advising   Part of effective listening; this response happens when the instructor gives unsolicited advice to the sender.

affective domain   The emotional values and feelings people attach to learning; part of an individual's ability to learn, but it's also a significant part of the emotional health that allows a person to empathize with others.

analysis   A component of the cognitive domain in Bloom's Taxonomy. Analysis, in the cognitive domain, is demonstrated by examining a problem or scenario and thinking through its root causes and causal factors.

analysis The first phase of the ADDIE model. This phase determines the learning needs, why the training is needed, and the learning objectives and goals for the training.

andragogical model The focus is on a learner-centered environment where learners discover knowledge through experience.

andragogy Used to describe the science and applications used to teach adults. In Greek, andragogy means man-leading, which is most commonly associated with leading adults. It was developed into the Theory of Adult Education by Malcolm Knowles.

application A component of the cognitive domain in Bloom's Taxonomy. Application of knowledge is expressed by taking existing comprehension and applying it to new scenarios and problems.

articulation Speaking with clarity and distinction to increase the likelihood of the message being understood by the class participants.

assessing performance One of nine categories of learning as defined by Gagné. The instructor may test the learners' knowledge through an assessment exam, exercises without coaching, or other methods for the learner to show understanding of the material.

assessment exams Often given as a course prerequisite to determine the depth of knowledge and experience a participant has on a given technology.

Assessment of Learners' Needs for Additional Explanation and Encouragement Exam objective that judges the trainer's ability to quickly assess learners' needs, anticipate and answer questions, and offer encouragement to participants.

assimilators These learners want to know the specific directions to reach a desired result. They want to understand the exact step-by-step instructions to apply the technology in their work and lives. These learners are sometimes called abstract-reflective learners.

attention Part of the social learning theory; adults must invest their time and attention to what's being demonstrated and taught if they are to learn the behavior.

attitude Part of Gagné's Conditions of Learning. The learners' attitude toward the training, the instructor, the technology, and themselves affects their abilities to learn. The instructor can reward and recognize proper behavior to promote good learning.

auditory/verbal learners These learners like to listen to an instructor explain technical concepts. These types of learners may like a good lecture, but they also like to interact with the instructor and other people in the classroom. Group conversations and opportunities to discuss questions appeal to these people.

authentic assessment   An actual exercise that requires the learner to demonstrate their understanding and application of the learning goals of the technical seminar.

barriers   Part of the communications model that prevents communication from happening, such as network failure in a virtual classroom or people who speak different languages.

behavior evaluation   The third level of Kirkpatrick's Evaluation Model measures the change in learners' behavior as a result of the course. The behavior measurement is the determination of actual usage and implementation of what's been taught in the technical training.

Benjamin Bloom   Education psychologist at the University of Chicago; developed, along with a group of educators, the Taxonomy of Educational Goals to help define the objectives educators have for learners.

career advancement motivation   The learner wants to learn and master a technology to make themselves more attractive to employers, to maintain their competitive edge, or to grow their business.

characterizing   Part of the affective domain in Bloom's Taxonomy. When an individual has learned information, they'll apply the information and change their behavior. The learner now has a value and an organized belief that directly affects how they behave and how they'll learn new and relevant information.

chat   Some area of the web-based software where the instructor and the users can type messages directly to one another, to everyone in the group, or to just a few participants.

classroom checklist   A checklist of the required configurations of a classroom to confirm that the training environment has been properly prepared so that the training may begin.

classroom lighting   The consideration of the type of lighting in the classroom, such as track lighting, recessed lighting, fluorescent lighting, or natural light, and how the lighting can be manipulated to best support the learning objectives.

classroom seating configuration   The typical classroom configuration where the tables, chairs, and computers are all aligned the same and facing the front of the room, where the instructor will present.

classroom-based training   The instructor and the participants are in the same physical space for the learning. The trainer and learners can see one another and interact with verbal and nonverbal communications, and the instructor can quickly assess who's on target with the learning and which learners need encouragement and support.

cognitive domain In Bloom's Taxonomy, the cognitive domain defines the actual knowledge gained and ability to act on understanding as a result of learning.

Cognitive Learning Theory A theory that focuses on how people process and retain information. This theory is less concerned with the behavior the learning brings about than with how the learning happens internally within each participant. The Cognitive Learning Theory begins with the instructional design and its effect on learning.

cognitive strategies Part of Gagné's Conditions of Learning. The learners will internally process what the instructor is teaching by using their learning strategies.

communications model Defines how communication happens between the sender and receiver, and considers barriers to communication and interference with communication.

community impact motivation The learner seeks technical training as an avenue to help their community. The learner sees the mastery of a technology as an avenue to volunteer, improve a situation, and participate in a not-for-profit program.

competence-confidence spiral As learners become more competent in a technology, they'll become more confident in the technology, which encourages the learner to become even more competent, and the process repeats over and over until mastery of the technology is achieved.

complex overt response Component of the psychomotor domain in Bloom's Taxonomy that happens when the learner can complete a complex task based on their understanding and control of their motor skills.

comprehending The first part of active listening is understanding the words and language the other person is using.

comprehension A component of the cognitive domain in Bloom's Taxonomy. Comprehension is sometimes referred to as understanding, and is expressed through an understanding of the technical information and the ability of the learner to explain this understanding.

CompTIA CTT+ Certified Technical Trainer An individual who has shown competency and skill in teaching technical courses. The CTT+ requires the individual to pass the CompTIA CTT+ Essentials examination and a performance-based examination showcasing the trainer in the classroom environment or in a virtual classroom environment.

Constructivist Learning Theory A theory that believes the learners' cognitive development is based on their experiences. The outcome of a learning opportunity, whether in the class or through self-led discovery, is that the learners make sense of the experience based on the outcomes of the current and previous learning experiences.

convergers These people thrive on detailed, hands-on activities with the technology in order to learn how the technology works. They prefer to be active in labs and testing rather than in lecture-driven training. These learners are sometimes called abstract-active learners.

cordless presentation tool A device, like a cordless mouse, that will allow the instructor to roam around the room and still click through the presentation. Some devices have features to navigate forwards and backwards, and may include a laser pointer.

course logistics All of the coordination of materials, software, hardware, classroom equipment, security information, access to data, refreshments, travel, communications, and any related aspects of preparing and managing the classroom environment.

course prerequisites A determination of the existing knowledge that the learner must have, either through prior training or experience, to enroll in a technical training course.

CTT+ performance-based exam The recording of a training professional and corresponding paperwork that will be judged by CompTIA as to the ability of the instructor in the recording to satisfy the requirements of the classroom-based instructor exam or the virtual-based instructor exam. The recorded presentation should be formatted as MPEG, MPEG4, or FLV and should be between 17 and 22 minutes in duration.

CTT+ TK0-201 The CompTIA CTT+ Essentials computer-based examination. A passing score is 655 on a scale of 100 to 900.

CTT+ TK0-202 The CompTIA CTT+ Classroom Trainer performance-based examination.

CTT+ TK0-203 The CompTIA CTT+ Virtual Classroom Trainer performance-based examination.

decoder The element of the communication model that decodes and interprets the message for the receiver. In a classroom, the participant's brain decodes the message so that the individual can understand the information.

decorative visuals Clip art and pictures that are used more for decorations than as teaching elements; decorative visuals can be a learning distraction if they don't support the learning environment.

deflecting Part of effective listening; sometimes the receiver of the message wants to share a related message to answer the sender's question or comment. This deflection, however, can sometimes seem like the recipient isn't acknowledging what the other person said. Deflecting can be useful when the instructor needs to move the course pace along, but deflecting should be used sparingly and with caution.

demonstration area Some virtual classroom software allows the instructor to share their desktop so that the users can see the instructor interact with the technology.

design The second phase of the ADDIE model defines the direction and content of the technical training.

development The third phase of the ADDIE model is the actual creation of the course content and material.

diaphragm A respiratory muscle that helps to bring air into and out of the lungs. The diaphragm helps with voice projection in public speaking.

divergers These people utilize the concrete experience and reflection to best learn. The learners want to experience the technology you're teaching, but they must understand how the information will be applied in their jobs and lives. These learners are sometimes referred to as concrete-reflective.

Domain 1: Planning Prior to the Course The actions the trainer should take to prepare for a successful training session. This domain accounts for 13 percent of the CompTIA CTT+ Essentials examination.

Domain 2: Methods and Media for Instructional Delivery This exam domain tests your understanding of utilizing different methods, technology, demonstrations, lecture, handouts, and other media to instruct. This domain accounts for 14 percent of the CompTIA CTT+ Essentials examination.

Domain 3: Instructor Credibility and Communications This exam domain tests your ability to instruct, to communicate, and to interact with participants. First impressions, speech patterns, organization, and command of the classroom all affect instructor credibility. This domain accounts for 14 percent of the CompTIA CTT+ Essentials examination.

Domain 4: Group Facilitation This exam domain tests the core skills that an instructor must have to teach, understand learning styles, approach learning, and manage the classroom. This domain accounts for 45 percent of the CompTIA CTT+ Essentials examination.

Domain 5: Evaluate the Training Event This domain tests your knowledge of course and instructor evaluations, expectations for the instructor, and how final reports for the course are prepared and delivered to the organization. This exam domain accounts for 18 percent of the CompTIA CTT+ Essentials examination.

e-based evaluations An electronic version of the class evaluation completed by the learning participants through a website or learning management system.

education   In the adult domain, education is defined as the broad goals of transferring knowledge from one individual to another with the intent to direct and influence the course of an individual's life.

effective listening   Focuses on understanding the message and the sender's context and meaning. Effective listening aims to truly understand the message that the sender has offered and then to respond appropriately.

eliciting performance   One of nine categories of learning as defined by Gagné. The instructor offers time for the learner to practice the new information through exercises, additional demonstrations, and confirmation of understanding.

embedded assessment   An assessment approach that tracks learner progress throughout the entire course rather than in an examination at the end of the course.

encoder   The element of the communication model that encodes the message into the formatting of the medium, such as analog or digital, to be sent through the medium between the sender and receiver.

enhance retention and transfer   One of nine categories of learning as defined by Gagné. The instructor makes a determination of skills learned by the participants; the participants apply the skills and are able to retain and retrieve the information at will.

escapism motivation   The learner is in class to escape issues in their lives, boredom in their job, or just as a break in their regular routine.

essay questions   Questions for review that test the learner's comprehension. These questions can be among the toughest to grade. This question type asks the learner to provide a narrative for their answer.

Establishment and Management of a Learner-Centered Environment   Exam objective that judges how well the instructor encourages learners, shifts the focus from the trainer to the learner, and promotes learning in the classroom environment.

evaluation   A component of the cognitive domain in Bloom's Taxonomy. It is evident when a person can explain their logic and reasoning behind how they use the technology to solve a problem.

evaluation   The fifth and final phase of the ADDIE model is the review of the course's ability to satisfy the learning objectives and instructional goals.

Evaluation of Instructor and Course   Exam objective that measures the instructor's understanding of course evaluations and instructor evaluations. The instructor must also review the course, define successes and failures, and report outcomes to the organization as needed.

Evaluation of Learner Performance During and at Close of Instruction Exam objective that tests the trainer's ability to examine, observe, and anticipate learner progress. Instructors can demonstrate their expertise in this exam objective by using different methods to gauge learner comprehension, such as changing the instruction, offering demonstrations, and assigning hands-on activities to engage the learner.

fill-in-the-blank questions These questions require the learner to know the answer based on the statement rather than having an opportunity to guess at a correct answer, as with the multiple-choice questions.

first-time, first-use penalty The first time an endeavor is attempted by a person or organization, there are likely to be additional cost and time requirements for the implementation of the technology or training.

forced answer A strategy in the Likert scale that forces the learner to agree or disagree to some extent by removing the option of neutral ratings.

forced-choice opportunities The learner is forced to choose an answer in the assessment.

formative assessment Intermittent evaluations completed by the participants to communicate what is and what is not working in the classroom while this class is still happening. A formative assessment doesn't happen at the end of the training, but often at the end of each day or in the middle of the class schedule.

gain attention One of nine categories of learning as defined by Gagné. The instructor must get the participant's attention by linking the subject matter to the participant's life and making the topic interesting.

guided response Component of the psychomotor domain in Bloom's Taxonomy where the learner can follow the instructor's directions to perform a motor skills task.

hierarchical approach Breaks down tasks into a hierarchy of events, sometimes called subtasks, that contribute to the final result of the task or assignment.

ice breakers Activities, stories, or introductions to "break the ice" in a classroom environment to make people feel comfortable with one another and the instructor.

implementation The fourth phase of the ADDIE model is the trainer's delivery of what's been developed for the course content.

inflection The variation and pitch in voice that affects the meaning of the message.

inform objectives One of nine categories of learning as defined by Gagné. Learners need to know what the instructor is going to teach, and the objectives help the learner anticipate and set expectations for the class.

Instructional Environment in Relationship to Learning Objectives Exam objective that tests how the instructor will convey the details of the classroom to the participants; how the classroom is configured; and how the participants may interact with the technology, the instructor, and colleagues in the room.

instructional goal An instructional goal is a statement that defines the high-level objectives for the course. It's a statement that communicates the broad learning objectives and expected outcomes of the course.

Instructor Communication and Presentation Skills Exam objective that judges the ability of the CompTIA CTT+ candidate to clearly speak to, present to, and train the participants in the room.

Instructor Delivery Competence and Content Expertise Exam objective that tests and judges the instructor's classroom presence and ability to manage learners, address individual needs, adapt the instruction for learners, and link class materials to organizational needs.

instructor-centered classroom environment The instructor becomes the most important person in the classroom, and all learning must come through the instructor at the instructor's pace and discretion.

intellectual skills Part of Gagné's Conditions of Learning. Learners will use prerequisite skills and knowledge to process new, relative knowledge; to experiment with the technology to solve a problem for deeper understanding; and to apply new information to current problems.

Kirkpatrick Evaluation Model A learning evaluation model created by Donald Kirkpatrick that aims to capture how effective the training was in regard to the learning goals for the participants and for the organization.

Kirkpatrick Evaluation Model, Level Four This level measures the business results as a result of the training. Business results link the profitability, cost savings, reduction in errors, and other qualifiers of the organization to the training that the instructor offered.

Kirkpatrick Evaluation Model, Level One This is the learner reaction to the course and instructor performance. This level is what most instructors think of when they think of the instructor evaluation. It's the end-of-class evaluation of what the participants thought of the training and the instructor's performance.

Kirkpatrick Evaluation Model, Level Three This measures the actual behavioral change in the participants as a result of the training. Behavioral change is demonstrated by the learner actually using the knowledge that was gained in the course.

Kirkpatrick Evaluation Model, Level Two   This is the assessment of learning achievement. This level of evaluation determines the actual increase in learner knowledge.

Kirkpatrick's Four Levels Evaluation Model   Don Kirkpatrick developed four levels of training evaluation: reaction, learning, behavior, and results. Each level of evaluation becomes more involved and generally takes longer to implement, do well in, and see actual measurements.

KISS rule   A heuristic for designing slides, handouts, or instructional tools that means you'll Keep It Simply Simple.

knowledge   A component of the cognitive domain in Bloom's Taxonomy. This element is evident when a person can recall specific information, technical terms, and concepts and answer questions about the technology.

knowledge application   The evidence that knowledge transfer has actually occurred. Knowledge application is evident in the application of the skills, the fulfillment of the course expectations, and the return on the training investment.

knowledge transfer   In a technical training environment, knowledge transfer happens when accurate information is transferred from the instructor to the learner.

Kolb's Learning Cycle   David Kolb defined four elements that create a cycle of learning and understanding. Adult learning can begin at any of the elements, as the cycle is like an ongoing spiral based on experience and current understanding. The four elements are concrete experience, observation and reflection, forming abstract concepts, and testing knowledge in new situations.

learner motivation   The reason why the learner is attending the training event.

learner-centered environment   The focus of the training should be encouraging and engaging, and should motivate the participants to learn the material being presented. The instructor puts the focus of the class on the learners and their need to change their behavior by applying the information gained.

learner-centered training environment   The classroom environment, instructor focus, and instructor attitude are geared toward helping the learner achieve their learning goals.

learning curve   The negative curve of productivity tracking that happens when learning a new technology, process, or approach. The learning curve is often described as a short-term backward trend in productivity to move to long-term trends in efficiency.

learning environment   The classroom space where learning through technical training is expected to happen.

learning evaluation   The second level of Kirkpatrick's Evaluation Model attempts to assess the knowledge gained as a result of the training session. This level may use a pre- and post-course assessment to measure competence.

learning handouts   Additional information for the learners that is distributed to help support the learning objectives. Handouts may be called job aids, learner assistants, cheat sheets, or reference cards.

learning need   Describes what the learner needs to know to operate within the organization, complete a specific task or role, or manage a given technology.

learning objectives   Define the increased knowledge that learners will have as a result of the specifics of the training. Learning objectives are the specific goals of the specific content of the training course. They define the exact application of the knowledge, not how the knowledge will be transferred from the instructor to the participants. Learning objectives are the end product of the breakdown of the instructional goal, the topical units, and the learning outcomes. They clearly define the behavior that participants will possess as a result of the technical training.

learning outcome   A statement that describes what a topical unit will accomplish. Learning outcomes communicate the purpose of each component in a topical unit.

learning relevancy   The material in the course must be relevant to the learner's goals, lives, and/or career for the learner to be motivated to learn.

lessons-learned summation   An example of an embedded assessment where the learners summarize what they have learned throughout the course.

Likert item   A statement that learners judge the accuracy of based on their experience in the classroom.

Likert scale   Named after its inventor and psychologist, Renis Likert, this is the summation of Likert items. Likert items utilize a high-to-low rating of a topic by allowing the participant to rank their level of agreeability with a statement. The Likert scale is the sum of the scoring for all of the items on the evaluation.

make-or-buy decision   The process an organization completes to determine the value proposition of making the course materials internally or purchasing standardized materials from a vendor.

mechanism   Component of the psychomotor domain in Bloom's Taxonomy. The mechanism is a slightly advanced combination of the set and the guided responses, where the learner can perceive the problem, operate with proficiency, and understand the correct responses to create the expected, predictable end result.

medium   The element between the encoder and decoder that carries the communication message. In a classroom environment, the instructor's voice is the medium; the medium is anything that carries the message between two or more people, such as a network cable.

mnemonic visual   A visual and a mnemonic device to help people remember key facts and information.

motivation   Part of social learning theory; adult learners want to know why a topic is important in order for them to want to learn. If the learner doesn't make the connection between the classroom topic and how it applies to their life, they will be less likely to give their attention, retain the information, and reproduce the knowledge when it matters most.

Motivation and Positive Reinforcement of Learners   Exam objective that judges the trainer's encouragement to participants during interactions, motivation of the learners by linking course material to roles and responsibilities, and promotion of a learner-focused environment.

motor skills   Part of Gagné's Conditions of Learning. The learner will complete a physical movement by first learning the correct movement from the instructor, practicing the correct movement over and over, and then refining the movement based on feedback and the outcomes of the movement.

multiple-choice questions   Questions for review, testing comprehension, and gaining feedback from learners. These questions are ideal, as they give learners choices of possible answers and they're fast to grade.

networking opportunities motivation   The participant sees the training program as a fun, social event, such as a networking function or short discussion on a technology.

noise   A component in the communication model that interrupts or distorts the message; for example, side conversations, distractions from other participants, or interruptions in the classroom.

nonverbal communication   The body language, eye contact, posture, and gestures that affect the verbal communication and messages sent between people. The posture, facial expressions, and body language that affect the message of the instructor. Fifty-five percent of all communication is nonverbal.

organization expectations   For many technical trainers, this is the most common reason for learning. People come to class because they are required to as part of their job. When an organization changes the technology that people use to support the organization, there's a management requirement that employees learn the new technology to continue to support the goals of the organization as a whole. If the organization doesn't teach their employees how to use a new technology, the organization is undermining its abilities to reach its vision.

organizational visuals   Artwork that is used to organize concepts, group similar topics, and demonstrate logical grouping of things.

organizing   Part of the affective domain in Bloom's Taxonomy. As a person becomes more confident and experienced in a technology in your class, they'll begin to organize their thoughts, beliefs, and understanding to formulate their own ideas and expectations on outcomes.

origination   Component of the psychomotor domain in Bloom's Taxonomy that happens when the learner takes their experience and expertise with existing knowledge and creates a new method, new skill, and expected outcome.

outcome assessment   A method to judge the effectiveness of the course design and delivery to help the learner retain the course content and achieve the learning goals.

pace   The speed and tempo of spoken communication that may affect the ability of learners to comprehend what's being shared.

paralingual   The meaning beyond the spoken word—characterized by tone and inflection that affects the meaning of the message.

Pareto's Law   Eighty percent of the effects come from just 20 percent of the causes. In technical training, this is relevant to participant management, as you'll discover 80 percent of the classroom disruptions come from just 20 percent of the participants.

Parkinson's Law   Work expands to fill the time allotted to it.

passive learning   The learner absorbs information through listening, reading, and reason. The participant accepts what the instructor says and then applies the information on exams, feedback, and in the workplace.

passive observation   Part of learner task analysis where the observer passively watches the tasks from start to completion without interrupting the process.

pedagogy   Used to describe the process of teaching; it's the vocation and strategies for teaching. Pedagogy is more closely related to teaching children than adults. Pedagogy is Greek, and it means to lead the child.

perception   Component of the psychomotor domain in Bloom's Taxonomy. This attribute relies on the individual using the senses to determine what physical activity should happen.

performance-based training   The priority of the seminar is to help learners perform better in their lives and roles by teaching exactly what they need to know to perform more efficiently.

personal interest motivation   The learner attends training based on their personal interest in the technology. These learners want to learn for the sake of learning, enjoy technology, and have a personal motivation to explore and experiment with the technology.

present stimulus material   One of nine categories of learning as defined by Gagné. The instructor teaches the objectives in an interesting, engaging way.

probing   Part of effective listening; this response asks for more detail without making the sender of the message feel defensive.

projection   The ability to speak with enough clarity and volume so that the participants can hear the message.

Promotion of Learner Engagement and Participation   Exam objective that judges the trainer's ability to ask questions of the participants, present challenges, and give exercises that promote learning and classroom engagement.

providing feedback   One of nine categories of learning as defined by Gagné. The learners need feedback on their performance and understanding; this can mean corrections and reinforcement or confirmation of understanding.

providing learning guidance   The instructor helps the learner understand the new material through demonstration, repetition, and applied examples such as case studies.

psychomotor domain   Part of Bloom's Taxonomy that describes the learning and application of physical tools and abilities, motor skills, and individual activities to complete a task.

public speaking   The act of an individual standing before a group of peers, colleagues, and strangers and speaking on a concept.

question parking lot   A section of the classroom whiteboard or flipchart that's dedicated for questions that aren't necessarily relevant to the class topic, but the instructor will answer later in the course or after the class.

reaction evaluation   The first of the four levels of Kirkpatrick's Evaluation Model. The reaction evaluation is the immediate, end-of-course evaluation, sometimes called "smile sheets," to measure the participant's overall satisfaction with the course. These are called smile sheets to quickly measure how "smiley" participants are. Some evaluations can even use a scale of sad faces, neutral face, to a happy face to measure learner reactions.

receiver   The recipient of the message; a classroom participant is the receiver of the message that the technical trainer has sent.

receiving   Part of the affective domain in Bloom's Taxonomy. This first stage of learning requires that the learner at least be passively involved in the learning process by being open to learning.

reflecting   Part of effective listening; the receiver paraphrases what the sender has said to confirm understanding of the message.

relational visuals   Graphics that show relationships among data; for example, bar charts and pie charts are relational graphics.

representational visuals   Artwork that represents the actual technology, line drawings of concepts, and screen captures or photographs from the technology. This type of artwork shows the learners how the concept is applied.

reproduction   Part of social learning theory; learners need an opportunity to practice what they've learned.

responding   Part of active listening; when a person sends the instructor a message, the instructor can offer intermittent feedback, such as nodding, crossing arms, or smiling. These nonverbal responses can help direct what the other person is saying or help them discover information about their question. This part of active listening offers immediate feedback and lets the sender of the message realize that the receiver is present, involved, and participating in the communication.

responding   Part of the affective domain in Bloom's Taxonomy. In this stage, the individual participates in the learning process. This stage is evident when a person is asking questions, participating in discussions, completing exercises, and contributing.

results evaluation   The fourth and final level of Kirkpatrick's Evaluation Model measures the overall results of the training on the organization as a whole. This evaluation can measure key performance indicators, such as profitability, efficiency, or the reliability of technology, as direct outcomes from the training session.

retaining   Part of active listening; the learner sends a message that the instructor must retain in order to understand and react to the message.

retention Part of social learning theory; this is the ability to retain what's been taught. Technical trainers should adjust the teaching approach to appeal to visual, auditory, and kinesthetic learners so that there is ample opportunity for the learners to retain the information.

review Periodic refreshers of what has been taught in the course to help learners remember and recall key information.

Review of Organizational Needs and Learners' Backgrounds in Relationship to Course Objectives Exam objective to test the trainer's preparation for the course, how the learner will use the information to be taught, and how the participants are confirmed for course prerequisites.

Robert Gagné's Conditions of Learning This theory states that the expected outcomes of education require specific training in consideration of the types of learners in the education process. The trainer must recognize and accommodate the learning style for each participant.

role configuration In the virtual classroom environment, roles are usually moderator, instructor, host, student, or something similar. The instructor may be able to change the roles so that a participant can do the demonstration for the class.

room color Color does have an effect on the learners' brain activity. Red, orange, and yellow stimulate brain activity, while green, blue, and violet promote relaxation.

Selection and Implementation of Instructional Methods Exam objective that will test the trainer's ability to move from topic to topic, select appropriate classroom materials, and adjust the course delivery to promote learner participation.

sender The originator of the message to be transmitted through the communications model.

set Component of the psychomotor domain in Bloom's Taxonomy that describes the readiness to respond to predictable situations.

show exam Learners show what they have learned in the course, often through a final examination.

social learning theory People learn from one another by observing, modeling, adapting, and emulating the behavior and actions of other learners.

stage fright The dread and anxiety a person feels before and during public speaking; stage fright can hinder the technical trainer from delivering a successful training session.

stage presence The confidence, speaking abilities, and ownership of the technology, training space, and leadership of the classroom by the technical trainer.

stage presence The presence the instructor has when presenting to learners; it's the ability to appear comfortable while commanding the audience's attention and being in charge in the classroom.

standard operating procedures The rules for instructional designers to define the expectations and procedures for the content of the course development.

stimulate recall of prior knowledge One of nine categories of learning as defined by Gagné. Based on past experiences or previous training, the instructor builds new information on working memories of the participant.

storyboard A series of drawings to visualize a process, event, or workflow; storyboards help course designers see how a task should be completed to better teach a technical concept.

student monitoring An area of the web-based training interface where users can "raise their hand"; change a status indicator like green, yellow, or red; or participate in polling for group questions.

style manual Defines the language, grammar practices, and generally accepted approach for writing the course content.

subject matter expert (SME) An individual who is well versed in the technology, tasks, and application of the technology to help guide the task analysis and course design and development.

summaries End-of-course summations of what's been taught; the focus is on the learning objectives and most important elements of the technical training. Summaries may also happen at the end of learning modules or topics.

summative evaluation Usually an anonymous evaluation of the instructor's performance and overall class success. This evaluation is completed by learners at the end of the training course.

synthesis A component of the cognitive domain in Bloom's Taxonomy. This component of the cognitive domain is sometimes referred to as create because the learning is creating a new solution based on what the participant has learned.

tactile/kinesthetic learners These learners remember by doing. Any hands-on exercises or lab components are usually appealing to the tactile/kinesthetic learner.

task analysis An observation of the actual tasks and subtasks that people do to complete their responsibilities with a given technology.

Taxonomy of Educational Goals A categorization of education objectives, domains, descriptions, and actions that educators have for learners.

Toastmasters International   A nonprofit organization established to help people be better public speakers.

topical units   An outline topology of what the technical training will include. Topical units are based on the course learning objectives.

trainer confidence   The self-assurance and belief that a trainer has to teach, control, and manage the technical classroom.

training   Focuses on the skills, tools, and competencies to help people complete their roles in an organization.

transformational artwork   A visual aid that shows how change has happened over time.

transitions   The process of moving from one technical concept to another in a smooth, seamless manner so that participants will learn new information based on what they've already learned.

true-or-false questions   Quick, simple questions in which the learner reads a statement and then determines its accuracy. While these question types are quick and easy to create and grade, they can be tricky if the learner hasn't comprehended the course material.

usage final   An assessment where users use their retention and understanding of the course material to create a solution.

Use of Presentation and Instructional Media   This exam objective will judge how the trainer utilizes all of the available media in their presentation. The trainer should use the most appropriate media type to engage the learners and to promote different learning styles.

U-seating configuration   The classroom chairs and tables create a U-shape, often along the perimeter of the room, where the attendees will pivot from looking at the instructor to the materials and equipment on their desks.

VAK Model   This model describes the visual, auditory, and kinesthetic learning styles. Some learners learn better by watching and observing, such as through your demonstrations. Auditory learners prefer you to lecture and explain concepts to them, as they learn best through auditory signals. The kinesthetic learner must touch, experience, and interact with the subject matter in order to learn the technology.

valuing   Part of the affective domain in Bloom's Taxonomy. When a person becomes really interested in what you're teaching, or they're excited or anxious about a topic, they're attaching a value to the information you're teaching.

verbal information   Part of Gagné's Conditions of Learning. The learner needs the instructor to teach the information in logical segments, provide enough information so that the learner can comprehend and process the concepts, and link the topic to the learners' roles and lives.

virtual classroom-based training   The instructor and the learners are not in one location, but are utilizing software to meet via a network and to participate in a remote training session. The users and instructor operate through a software interface to convey learning, involve participants, ask questions, chat, share control of desktops, lecture, and complete exercises.

visual aids   Anything that you use, such as a prop, the whiteboards, or a flipchart, to visually demonstrate the concepts of the class to the learners.

visual/nonverbal   These learners like to see demonstrations, videos, illustrations, and charts. They learn best by watching an instructor interact with the technology or demonstrate esoteric concepts by walking them through a figure or workflow.

visual/verbal   These learners like to listen to you talk, but also like it when you write down key notes on a whiteboard or through a PowerPoint presentation. A good technical lecture that includes a slide deck, demonstrations, and notes jotted on a whiteboard will appeal to these learners.

visualization   The mental process of imagining a successful activity, such as a sporting event, but for the technical trainer, it's the vision of teaching a technical topic.

vocalizations   The filler words and phrases, such as "uhs," "ums," and "like," that distract from the value of the spoken message.

whiteboard   The area in a virtual classroom software environment where slides appear, where the instructor can share multimedia files, and where the instructor can draw figures and illustrations.

INDEX

A

abrasive behavior, 188–189
accommodators, 121, 130
acknowledgement
    in communication model,
        263–264, 272
    of mistakes, 212
action verbs, for cognitive elements,
    244–245
active learning, 117–118, 131
active listening, 264, 272
active observation, in task analysis, 236–
    237, 246
activities
    engaging learners with, 128, 213,
        269–271
    for reviewing concepts, 215
adaptation component, of psychomotor
    domain, 240, 246
ADDIE model
    analysis phase, 57
    defined, 66
    design phase, 57–59
    development phase, 59–60
    evaluation phase, 62–64
    implementation phase, 60–62
    overview of, 56
Adobe Photoshop seminar goals, 46
adult learners, motivating
    adapting adult learning
        characteristics, 287–288
    answers to review questions,
        301–308
    defined, 296
    facilitating learning, 289–291
    key terms, 296–297

locating, 292–293
maintaining, 211–212, 293–295
overview of, 285–286
personal aspect of, 291
review questions, 297–301
summary, 295–296
testing on, 8–9, 20, 26, 366
advising response, in effective listening,
    265, 272
affective domain, stages of learning in,
    240–242, 246
analysis element, of cognitive domain,
    243–244, 245, 247
analysis phase, ADDIE model, 57, 66
andragogical model
    defined, 113, 131, 296
    motivation and, 287
    in technical training, 114
animations, in slideshow presentations, 91
appealing training, 58
application element, of cognitive domain,
    243, 245, 247
application, knowledge, 44, 67
articulation, in instructor delivery,
    206–207, 217
assessment
    authentic, 315–318, 320
    current state, 318
    e-based, 337–338
    formative, 62, 314–315, 335–336, 339
    learner competencies. *See* learner
        competence assessment
    learners' needs. *See* learners' needs
        evaluation
    performance, 21, 26–27, 123, 131
    summative, 62, 334–335, 340

assessment exams
creating, 312–314
for evaluation, 63, 66
pre-course, 54–55
assimilators, 120, 131
assumptions, in design strategy
document, 59
attention element, in social learning
theory, 267, 272
attitude
condition of learning, 122, 131
maintaining motivation and,
294–295
audience. *See also* learner(s)
connecting to, 205–206,
209–210, 214
listening to, 212–213
understanding, 179–180, 235
auditory/verbal learners, 119, 131
authentic assessment, 315–318, 320

B

backups, of recorded presentations, 15
Bandura, Dr. Albert, 267
barriers, in communication model,
263–264, 272
behavior, learner
changing, 64, 66, 317–318, 337
disruptive, 188–189
Bloom, Benjamin, 238, 247
Bloom's Taxonomy
affective domain, 240–242
cognitive domain, 242–245
overview of, 238
psychomotor domain,
239–240
boorish behavior, 188–189
breath control, 207
building upon existing knowledge, in
Cognitive Learning Theory, 124
business analyst, 237
business results evaluation,
64, 67, 337

C

Candy Intros game, 270
career advancement motivation, 292, 296
Cartoon font, in learning handouts, 93
Certified Technical Trainer+ certification,
3–4, 28
change, behavioral, 64, 66, 317–318, 337
characterizing stage, in Bloom's Taxonomy,
241, 242, 247
charm, in instructor delivery, 212–214
chats, 156, 160
clarity, in instructor delivery, 206–207
classroom-based training, 28
classroom checklist, 179, 190
classroom management
adding presentation software, 90–92
answers to review questions,
102–110
creating learning handouts, 93–94
key terms, 97–98
managing environment, 89–90
overview of, 81–82
planning course logistics, 86–88
preparing environment, 83–86
review questions, 98–102
room color support of, 94–95
summary, 96–97
testing on, 5–6, 17, 357–358
utilizing music in, 95–96
Classroom Trainer exam. *See* CTT+ TKO-
202 (CTT+ Classroom Trainer
performance-based exam)
clip art, in slideshow presentations,
92, 157
Cognitive Apprenticeship, 126
cognitive domain, Bloom's Taxonomy
defined, 247
elements of, 242–244
key action verbs for, 244–245
Cognitive Learning Theory, 124–125, 131
cognitive strategies, 122, 131
color, in learning environment, 94–95, 98
commercial training centers, 234–235

communication
    assessment exams and, 55, 314–315
    in creating group exercises, 269
    identifying learners' needs and, 44
    in learning handouts, 93
    managing learners, 184
    model, 263–264, 272
    need for pre-training, 153
    nonverbal, 85, 98, 183–184, 190
    skills, testing of, 7, 18–19, 24
    training in. *See* public speaking
community impact motivation, 293, 296
competence-confidence spiral,
    293–294, 296
competencies, assessing learner
    answers to review questions, 324–
        332
    assessment exams, 54–55
    authentic assessment in, 315–318
    behavioral change in, 317–318
    creating course exam, 312–314
    creating course prerequisites, 53–54
    embedded assessments for,
        314–315
    key terms, 320
    learning goals in, 316–317
    overview of, 52–55, 311–312
    review questions, 320–324
    summary, 319
    testing on, 9–10, 21
complex overt response component,
    239, 247
comprehending component, of active
    listening, 264, 272
comprehension element, of cognitive
    domain, 243, 245, 247
CompTIA Network+ seminar, 45
concrete experience, in Kolb's Learning
    Cycle, 120
confidence-competence spiral, 293–294
confidence, instructor
    answers to review questions,
        195–203

defined, 190
    involving learners, 183–186
    key terms, 190
    learner behavior and, 186–189
    overview of, 177–178
    positive environment and,
        181–182
    preparing to train, 179–181
    review questions, 190–195
    summary, 189–190
    testing on, 7–8, 18–19, 24,
        361–362
configuration, classroom, 83–86, 97
constraints
    design strategy document, 59
    organizational, 57
Constructivist Learning Theory,
    125–126, 131
contact management system, 153
convergers, 121, 131
cordless presentation tools, 92, 97
course content
    expertise in, 7, 18, 24
    relating to learner's background,
        17, 22
    reviewing/summarizing, 214–216
course context, 59
course evaluation
    answers to review questions,
        345–352
    applying, 336–338
    e-based, 337–338
    formative assessment, 335–336
    key terms, 339–340
    Kirkpatrick's model and,
        336–337
    overview of, 333–334
    review questions, 340–344
    summary, 338–339
    summative evaluation, 334–335
    testing on, 9–10, 21, 27, 368
course logistics, 86–88, 97
course manual, 149–150

course materials
  answers to review questions,
    166–173
  designing effective training, 152–153
  ensuring quality design, 153–155
  financial impact of, 148–150
  internal solutions for creating,
    150–151
  key terms, 160–161
  make-or-buy decision, 148–151
  managing. *See* instructional materials
  overview of, 59–60, 147
  review questions, 162–165
  selecting media visuals, 157–159
  summary, 159–160
  testing on, 6, 18, 23, 360–361
  virtual classroom challenges,
    155–157
course planning. *See also* classroom
  management; learners' needs evaluation
    environment and, 22–23
    organizational needs and, 17, 22
    testing on, 5–6, 29, 356–357
course prerequisites
  creating, 53–54
  defined, 66
  enforcing/exam questions and, 54
course structure, 59
credibility, instructor. *See* instructor
  confidence
CTT+ (Certified Technical Trainer+)
  certification, 3–4, 28
CTT+ TKO-201 (CTT+ Essentials computer-
  based exam)
    course evaluation domain, 9–10
    course planning domain, 5–6
    defined, 29
    group facilitation domain, 8–9
    instructor credibility domain, 7–8
    methods/media domain, 6
    overview of, 4–5
    study strategy to pass, 10–12

CTT+ TKO-202 (CTT+ Classroom Trainer
  performance-based exam)
    defined, 28–29
    objectives specific to, 17–22
    overview of, 13
    recording presentation, 14–16
    scoring of, 16–17
CTT+ TKO-203 (CCT+ Virtual Classroom
  Trainer performance-based exam)
    defined, 28–29
    objectives specific to, 22–27
    scoring of, 21–22
current state assessment, 318

D

decoder, in communication model, 263–
  264, 272
decorative visuals, 157, 160
deflecting response, in effective listening,
  265, 272
delivery, instructor
  answers to review questions,
    222–229
  charm in, 212–214
  clarity in, 206–207
  connecting to audience, 209–210
  key terms, 217
  maintaining learner interest, 211–212
  overview of, 205–206
  review questions, 218–221
  reviewing/summarizing content,
    214–216
  summary, 216–217
demonstration(s)
  area, in virtual classrooms, 157, 160
  facilitating learning with, 290
  guidelines for, 128–129
design phase, ADDIE model, 57–59, 66
design strategy document, 59
designing technical training, 151–155
desk arrangement, in classroom
  management, 84–86

determining what needs to be learned, in
    Cognitive Learning Theory, 124
development phase, ADDIE model,
    59–60, 66
diaphragm, in voice projection, 207, 217
didactic approach, to teaching, 114
disinterest, signs of, 211–212
disruptive behavior, 186–189
divergers, 120, 131
domain 1 (course planning)
    evaluating learners' needs. *See*
        learners' needs evaluation
    managing technical classrooms.
        See classroom management
    testing on, 5–6, 17, 22–23, 356–358
domain 2 (methods/media)
    instructional materials. *See*
        instructional materials
    instructional methods. *See*
        instructional methods
    testing on, 6, 17–18, 23, 359–361
domain 3 (credibility/communications)
    instructing with confidence. *See*
        instructor confidence
    successful leadership. *See* instructor
        delivery
    testing on, 7–8, 18–19, 24, 361–363
domain 4 (group facilitation)
    engaging learners. *See* learner
        engagement
    learner-centered instruction. *See*
        performance-based learning
    motivating learners. *See* motivating
        adult learners
    testing on, 8–9, 19–20, 24–26,
        363–366
domain 5: training evaluation
    assessing learners. *See* learner
        competence assessment
    assessing trainer/course. *See* instructor
        evaluations
    testing on, 9–10, 21, 26–27, 366–368
driving through, by class participant, 26

E

e-based evaluations, 337–338, 339
editing, of recorded presentation, 15
editor, of course material, 149
education, 45, 66
effective learning, 58
effective listening, 264–265, 272
efficient training, 58
eliciting performance, instructional event,
    123, 132
embedded assessments, 62, 314–315, 320,
    335–336, 339
embouchure, in speech, 207
employees, organizations and, 152–153
encoder, 263–264, 272
encouragement. *See* motivating adult
    learners
engaging learners
    answers to review questions,
        278–284
    creating quizzes, 265–267
    embedded assessments and, 314–315
    games/activities for, 269–271
    group participation and, 268–269
    instructional methods for. *See*
        instructional methods
    key terms, 272–274
    overview of, 261–262
    review questions, 274–277
    social learning theory in, 267–268
    summary, 271
    testing on, 8–9, 19–20, 25, 364–365
    through listening, 262–265
enhancing retention/transfer, 123, 132
entertainment, in instructor delivery, 213
environment, learning. *See also* classroom
    management
    configuration of, 179
    defined, 97
    familiarity with, 180
    learner-centered, 19, 24–25, 29
    learning objectives relating to, 17,
        22–23, 30

environment, learning *(continued)*
  managing, 89–90
  positive, 181–182, 290
  preparing, 61, 82–88
escapism motivation, 293, 296
essay questions, 266, 272
Essentials computer-based exam, 4–10, 29
ethernet networking, 91
evaluation element, of cognitive domain, 244, 247
evaluation phase, ADDIE model, 62–64, 66
evaluations
  e-based, 337–338
  formative, 62, 314–315, 335–336, 339
  of instructor/course. *See* instructor evaluations
  of learner performance. *See* learner competence assessment
  of learners' needs. *See* learners' needs evaluation
  summative, 62, 334–335, 340
exam preparation
  answers to review questions, 34–41
  five knowledge domains, 4–10
  key terms, 28–30
  overview of, 3–4
  for performance-based exams. *See* CTT+ TKO-202 (CTT+ Classroom Trainer performance-based exam)
  review questions, 31–34
  study strategies for, 10–12
  summary, 27–28
  for virtual classroom exams, 21–27
expectations, organizational, 292, 296
experiments, facilitating learning with, 290
expertise, in course content
  delivery and. *See* instructor delivery
  developing. *See* instructor confidence
  testing on, 7, 18, 24, 361–363
explanation, additional, 20, 25–26, 365–366

F
facilitation. *See also* learner engagement
  of adult learning, 289–291
  of technical classes, 115–116
  testing on, 8–9, 19–20, 25–26, 363–366
  using Constructivist Learning Theory, 125–126
facts, interesting, 210
feedback, 123, 132, 333–334, 336
fill-in-the-blank questions, 266, 272
fillers, in public speaking, 208–209
final examinations, 312–314
financial impact, of course materials, 148–150
first-time, first-use penalty, 149, 161
flashcards, 11
fonts, 90, 93
forced answers, 335, 339
forced-choice opportunities, 315, 320
formative assessments, 62, 314–315, 335–336, 339
forming abstract concepts, 120
Four Levels Evaluation Model, Kirkpatrick, 63–64
four-step approach, to teaching, 126–127

G
Gagné, Robert, 122
Gagné's Conditions of Learning, 122–124, 132–133
gaining attention, instructional event, 123, 132
games, 128, 213, 215, 269–271
Goal-Based Learning, 126
goals, exam. *See* exam preparation
goals, learning
  achieving, 316–317
  defining, 44–46, 50, 66, 67
  developing, 46–50
  incorrect, 318
  learning environment and, 17, 22–23

motivation and, 286, 287
writing out, 50–52
grooming, personal, 180
group
    development phases, 8–9
    exercises, 127
    facilitation. *See* facilitation
    participation, 268–269
guidance, learning, 123, 132
guided response component, of
    psychomotor domain, 239, 247

H

handouts, learning, 93–94, 98
hardware configuration, 87
hierarchical approach, to task analysis,
    237, 238, 247
honesty, facilitating learning with, 290
human resources department, 51
humor, starting presentations with, 209

I

ice breakers, 213–214, 217, 270
implementation phase, ADDIE model,
    60–62, 66
in-house development, of training
    materials, 148–151
inclusion, motivation and, 294
independent answers, in assessment
    exams, 55
inflection, voice, 207, 217
informing objectives, instructional event,
    123, 132
instructing with confidence. *See* instructor
    confidence
instructional analysis, 57
instructional designer, 149
instructional environment
    configuration of, 179
    defined, 97
    familiarity with, 180
    learner-centered, 19, 24–25, 29

learning objectives relating to, 17,
    22–23, 30
managing, 89–90
positive, 181–182, 290
preparing, 61, 82–88
instructional events, Gagné's, 123–124
instructional goals
    defining, 44–46, 50, 66, 67
    developing, 46–50
    learning environment and, 17, 22–23
    motivation and, 286, 287
    writing out, 50–52
instructional materials
    answers to review questions,
        166–173
    designing effective training, 152–153
    for engaging learners. *See*
        instructional methods
    ensuring quality design, 153–155
    financial impact of, 148–150
    internal solutions for creating,
        150–151
    key terms, 160–161
    make-or-buy decision, 148–151
    overview of, 147
    review questions, 162–165
    selecting media visuals, 157–159
    summary, 159–160
    testing on, 6, 18, 23, 360–361
    virtual classroom challenges,
        155–157
instructional methods. *See also* technical
  training
    answers to review questions,
        138–145
    Cognitive Learning Theory and,
        124–125
    Constructivist Learning Theory and,
        125–126
    creating group exercises, 127
    demonstrations, 128–129
    different learning styles and, 116–121
    facilitating technical classes, 115–116

instructional methods *(continued)*
    four-step approach, 126–127
    Gagné's theory of instruction and, 122–124
    key terms, 130–133
    overview of, 113–114
    review questions, 133–137
    summary, 129–130
    testing on, 6, 17–18, 23, 359–360
    utilizing games/simulations, 128
instructional systems development (ISD) model, 56
instructor-centered classroom environment, 288, 296
instructor confidence
    answers to review questions, 195–203
    defined, 190
    involving learners, 183–186
    key terms, 190
    learner behavior and, 186–189
    overview of, 177–178
    positive environment and, 181–182
    preparing to train, 179–181
    review questions, 190–195
    summary, 189–190
    testing on, 7–8, 18–19, 24, 361–362
instructor delivery
    answers to review questions, 222–229
    charm in, 212–214
    clarity in, 206–207
    connecting to audience, 209–210
    key terms, 217
    maintaining learner interest, 211–212
    overview of, 205–206
    review questions, 218–221
    reviewing/summarizing content, 214–216
    summary, 216–217
    testing on, 7–8, 18–19, 24, 362–363
    utilizing voice in, 208–209
instructor evaluations
    answers to review questions, 345–352
    applying, 336–338
    e-based, 337–338
    formative assessment, 335–336
    key terms, 339–340
    Kirkpatrick's model and, 336–337
    overview of, 333–334
    review questions, 340–344
    summary, 338–339
    summative evaluation, 334–335
    testing on, 9–10, 21, 27, 368
integrating new knowledge, in Cognitive Learning Theory, 124
intellectual skills, 122, 132
interest, maintaining, 211–212. *See also* motivating adult learners
interesting facts, starting presentations with, 209
internal development solutions, 150–151
introductions, 213–214, 270
ISD (instructional systems development) model, 56

K

key terms
    classroom management, 97–98
    confident instruction, 190
    exam preparation, 28–30
    instructional methods, 130–133
    instructor delivery, 217
    instructor evaluations, 339–340
    learner competence assessment, 320
    learner engagement, 272–274
    learners' needs evaluation, 66–67
    motivating adult learners, 296–297
    performance-based learning, 246–248
kinesthetic learners, 119
Kirkpatrick, Donald, 63, 336
Kirkpatrick's Four Levels Evaluation Model, 63–64, 66, 336–337, 340
KISS rule, 90, 97
knowledge application, 44, 67
knowledge, Cognitive Learning Theory and, 124–125

knowledge element, of cognitive domain, 243, 245, 247
knowledge transfer, 44, 67
Knowles, Malcolm, 113, 287
Kolb, David, 120
Kolb's Learning Cycle, 120–121, 132

L

lead role, in facilitating learning, 290
leading with confidence. *See* instructor confidence
learner behavior
    changing, 64, 66, 317–318, 337
    disruptive, 188–189
learner-centered environment
    achieving learning goals, 316–317
    defined, 30, 247, 296
    establishment/management of, 19, 24–25, 29
    motivation and, 287, 294
    testing on, 8–9, 19, 24–25, 363–364
learner-centered instruction. *See* performance-based learning
learner competence assessment
    answers to review questions, 324–332
    assessment exams, 54–55
    authentic assessment in, 315–318
    behavioral change in, 317–318
    creating course exam, 312–314
    creating course prerequisites, 53–54
    embedded assessments for, 314–315
    key terms, 320
    learning goals in, 316–317
    overview of, 52–53, 311–312
    review questions, 320–324
    summary, 319
    testing on, 9–10, 21, 26–27, 367
learner engagement
    answers to review questions, 278–284
    creating quizzes, 265–267
    embedded assessments and, 314–315

games/activities for, 269–271
group participation and, 268–269
instructional methods for. *See* instructional methods
key terms, 272–274
overview of, 261–262
review questions, 274–277
social learning theory in, 267–268
summary, 271
testing on, 8–9, 19–20, 25, 364–365
through listening, 262–265
learner reaction evaluation, 63, 67, 336–337
learner(s)
    backgrounds of. *See* learners' needs evaluation
    behavior, 64, 66, 186–189, 317–318, 337
    involving, 183–186
    motivating. *See* motivating adult learners
    performance. *See* learner competence assessment
    task analysis, 236–238
    types of, 119–121
learners' needs evaluation
    ADDIE model overview, 56
    analyzing learning need, 57
    answers to review questions, 72–79
    defined, 28, 67
    designing training, 57–59
    developing course, 59–60
    evaluating course, 62–64
    identifying topical units, 46–47
    implementing course, 60–62
    instructional goals and, 44–46
    key terms, 66–67
    learning outcomes and, 47–50
    overview of, 43–44
    review questions, 68–72
    summary, 64–65
    testing on, 5–6, 17, 22, 356–357
    writing learning objectives, 50–52

learning activities, 269–271, 289
learning curve, 149, 161, 318
learning environment. *See also* classroom
    management
        configuration of, 179
        defined, 97
        familiarity with, 180
        learner-centered, 19, 24–25, 29
        learning objectives relating to, 17,
            22–23, 30
        managing, 89–90
        positive, 181–182, 290
        preparing, 61, 82–88
learning evaluation, Kirkpatrick's model,
    63, 67, 337. *See also* learner competence
    assessment
learning guidance, providing, 123, 132
learning handouts, 93–94, 98
learning objectives
    achieving, 316–317
    defining, 44–46, 50, 66, 67
    developing, 46–50
    incorrect, 318
    instructional environment and, 17,
        22–23
    motivation and, 286, 287
    writing out, 50–52
learning outcomes
    assessing, 312–314
    defining, 47–50, 67
    focusing on, 234–236
learning relevancy, 287, 296
learning stakeholders, 51
learning styles
    teaching for different, 18, 23,
        116–121
    VAK Model, 119
learning theories
    Cognitive Learning Theory, 124–125
    Constructivist Learning Theory,
        125–126
    four-step approach, 126–127
    Gagné's Conditions of Learning,
        122–124

lecture approach, 115
lessons-learned summations, 314, 320
lighting, 14, 84, 90, 97
Likert item, 334, 339, 340
Likert, Renis, 334
Likert scale, 334–335, 339, 340
listening
    active, 264
    to audience, 212–213
    effective, 264–265
    engaging learners and, 262–265
logistics, course, 86–88, 97

M

make-or-buy decision, 148–151, 161
management, classroom
    adding presentation software, 90–92
    answers to review questions, 102–110
    creating learning handouts, 93–94
    key terms, 97–98
    managing environment, 89–90
    overview of, 81–82
    planning course logistics, 86–88
    preparing environment, 83–86
    review questions, 98–102
    room color support of, 94–95
    summary, 96–97
    testing on, 5–6, 17, 357–358
    utilizing music in, 95–96
measurement, of learner competencies.
    See learner competence assessment
mechanism component, of psychomotor
    domain, 239, 247
media, instructional
    answers to review questions,
        166–173
    designing effective training, 152–153
    for engaging learners. *See*
        instructional methods
    ensuring quality design, 153–155
    financial impact of, 148–150
    internal solutions for creating,
        150–151

key terms, 160–161
make-or-buy decision, 148–151
overview of, 147
review questions, 162–165
selecting media visuals, 157–159
summary, 159–160
testing on, 6, 18, 23, 360–361
virtual classroom challenges, 155–157
medium, in communication model, 263–264, 273
memory maps, 94
methods, instructional. *See also* technical training
answers to review questions, 138–145
Cognitive Learning Theory and, 124–125
Constructivist Learning Theory and, 125–126
creating group exercises, 127
demonstrations, 128–129
different learning styles and, 116–121
facilitating technical classes, 115–116
four-step approach, 126–127
Gagné's theory of instruction and, 122–124
key terms, 130–133
overview of, 113–114
review questions, 133–137
summary, 129–130
testing on, 6, 17–18, 23, 359–360
utilizing games/simulations, 128
Microsoft Word fundamental seminar
course goals of, 45
defining learning outcomes, 48–50
identifying topical units, 47
writing learning objectives, 51–52
mistakes, acknowledging, 212
mnemonic visuals, 159, 161
motivating adult learners
adapting adult learning characteristics, 287–288
answers to review questions, 301–308
defined, 296
facilitating learning, 289–291
key terms, 296–297
locating, 292–293
maintaining, 211–212, 293–295
overview of, 285–286
personal aspect of, 291
review questions, 297–301
summary, 295–296
testing on, 8–9, 20, 26, 366
motivation element, in social learning theory, 268, 273
motor skills, 122, 132
mouse pointer, 157
movement, in instructor delivery, 214
multiple-choice questions, 54–55, 266, 273
music, 95–96

N

neatness, in handouts, 93–94
needs
analysis, in course design, 153
evaluating learners'. *See* learners' needs evaluation
organizational, 17, 22
networking opportunities motivation, 293, 296
noise, in communication model, 263–264, 273
nonverbal communication, 85, 98, 183–184, 190

O

objectives
exam. *See* exam preparation
learning. *See* learning objectives
observation and reflection, in Kolb's Learning Cycle, 120
open-ended questions, 115, 338
optimal performance, 57

organization
    constraints of, 57
    employees and, 152–153
    expectations of, 292, 296
    learning objectives for, 51
    needs of, 17, 22, 30
organizational visuals, 158, 161
organizing stage, in affective domain, 241,
    242, 248
origination component, of psychomotor
    domain, 240, 248
outcomes
    assessment, 312–314, 320
    of learning, 47–50, 67, 234–236
overhead projectors, 87, 266–267, 269

P

pace, in spoken communication, 208,
    216, 217
paralingual attributes, of questions,
    211, 217
Pareto's Law, 186, 190
Parkinson's Law, 152, 161
participants' learning objectives. See
    learning objectives
participation, learner. See learner
    engagement
passive learning, 117–118, 132
passive observation, in task analysis,
    236–237, 248
pedagogy, 113, 132
perception component, of psychomotor
    domain, 239, 248
perfect class, 88
performance
    analysis, 57
    eliciting, 123, 132
    in instructor delivery, 213
    of learners. See learner competence
        assessment
    optimal, 57
performance-based exams. See CTT+ TKO-
    202 (CTT+ Classroom Trainer
    performance-based exam); CTT+ TKO-

203 (CCT+ Virtual Classroom Trainer
    performance-based exam)
performance-based learning
    achieving learning goals, 316–317
    affective domain in, 240–242
    answers to review questions,
        253–260
    Bloom's Taxonomy and, 238
    cognitive domain in, 242–245
    defined, 248
    delivering, 234–236
    key terms, 246–248
    learner task analysis, 236–238
    overview of, 233–234
    psychomotor domain in, 239–240
    review questions, 249–253
    summary, 245–246
    testing on, 8–9, 19, 24–25, 363–364
Performance-Based Training, 126
personal grooming, 180
personal group therapy, 188
personal interest motivation, 292, 296
phones, turning off, 182
Piaget, Jean, 125
planning, course. See also classroom
    management; learners' needs evaluation
    environment and, 22–23
    organizational needs and, 17, 22
    testing on, 5–6, 29, 356–357
positive learning environment,
    181–182, 290
positive reinforcement, 9, 20, 26, 30, 366.
    See also motivating adult learners
posture, of instructor, 207
PowerPoint slideshows, 90–92, 95, 96
pre-training communication, 153
preparation, exam
    answers to review questions, 34–41
    five knowledge domains, 4–10
    key terms, 28–30
    overview of, 3–4
    for performance-based exams. See
        CTT+ TKO-202 (CTT+ Classroom
        Trainer performance-based exam)

review questions, 31–34
study strategies for, 10–12
summary, 27–28
for virtual classroom exams, 21–27
prerequisites, course, 53–54
present stimulus material, instructional
event, 123, 132
presentation recording, 14–16
presentation skills
developing confidence in. *See*
instructor confidence
testing on, 7–8, 18–19, 24
presentation software, 90–92
probing response, in effective listening,
265, 273
Problem-Based Learning, 126
project manager, 148
project planning, 150
projection, in spoken communication,
207, 217
proofreader, 149
providing feedback, 123, 132
providing learning guidance, 123, 132
psychomotor domain, 239–240, 248
public speaking
clarity in, 206–207
defined, 190
effective training and, 178, 181
stage fright and, 206
utilizing voice in, 208–209

Q

quality assurance, 60
quality control, 60
quality course design, 153–155
question parking lot, 182, 185, 190
questions
assessment exam, 54–55
guidelines for, 115–116
for involving learners, 184
from learners, 118–119
managing different types of,
184–186

managing irrelevant, 182
paralingual attributes of, 211, 217
starting presentations with, 210
quizzes, 215, 265–267

R

reaction evaluation, Kirkpatrick's model,
63, 67, 336–337
real-world application, of course content,
7, 17, 20
receiver, in communication model,
263–264, 273
receiving stage, in affective domain,
241, 248
recording presentation, for exam,
14–16
reflecting response, in effective listening,
265, 273
refreshments, course logistics and, 87
reinforcing new knowledge, 124–125
relational visuals, in virtual classroom,
158, 161
relaxation techniques, 181
relevancy of learning, 287, 296
repetition, learning by, 215
representational visuals, in virtual
classroom, 158, 161
reproduction element, in social learning
theory, 268, 273
respect, for learners, 288, 290
responding component, of active listening,
264, 273
responding stage, in affective domain,
241, 248
results evaluation, Kirkpatrick's model, 64,
67, 337
retaining component, of active listening,
264, 273
retention element, in social learning
theory, 267, 273
reviews
of course content, 214–216, 217
of exam questions, 313–314

role configuration, in virtual classrooms, 157, 161
room color, learning environment, 94–95, 98
rules, assessment exam, 54–55

S

Score Tracker file, 11
scoring, of Classroom Trainer exam, 16–21
seating configuration, 84–86, 97
sender, in communication model, 263–264, 273
set component, of psychomotor domain, 239, 248
shading, in handouts, 94
show final examinations, 312, 320
simplicity, in slideshow presentations, 90–92
simulations, 128
slideshow presentations, 90–92, 95, 96
social learning theory
    defined, 273
    elements of, 267–268
    group participation, 268–269
    learning games/activities, 269–271
social time, 187–188
software, 87, 90–92
Speak In Questions game, 270
speaking, public
    clarity in, 206–207
    defined, 190
    effective training and, 178, 181
    stage fright and, 206
    utilizing voice in, 208–209
stage fright, 180–181, 182, 206
stage presence, 84, 98, 177, 190
stakeholders, internal, 150
standard operating procedures, for course design, 154–155, 161
stimulating recall of prior knowledge, 123, 133
storyboards, 154, 161

storytelling
    beginning presentations with, 210
    model, for slideshow presentations, 91
structure, course, 59
structuring knowledge, in Cognitive Learning Theory, 124
student monitoring, in virtual classrooms, 156, 161
study strategy, to pass CTT+ Essentials exam, 10–12
style manual, for course design, 154–155, 161
subject matter expert (SME), 148, 151, 236, 248
submission forms, for Classroom/Virtual Classroom Trainer exams, 15–16
submitting recorded presentation, 15, 217
summaries, for reviewing concepts, 215–216
summative evaluations, 62, 334–335, 340
symbiotic relationship, of employee/ organization, 152–153
synthesis element, of cognitive domain, 244, 245, 248

T

tactile/kinesthetic learners, 119, 133
task analysis, 57, 153, 236–238, 248
Taxonomy of Education Goals (Bloom), 238, 248
teaching vs. facilitation, 115
technical classroom management. See classroom management
technical support, 87
technical training. See also instructional methods
    ADDIE model of. See ADDIE model
    course goals for. See learning objectives
    defined, 67
    didactic approach, 114

four-step approach, 126–127
problems with standardized, 44
scope, in design strategy
document, 59
successful delivery in. *See* instructor
delivery
technology, classroom vs. implemented,
235–236
Tell A Yarn game, 270
temperature, training room, 84
testing knowledge, in Kolb's Learning
Cycle, 120
Theory of Adult Education, andragogy
and, 113
time factor, in developing course materials,
149, 150, 151, 152
time limits, for recording presentations, 13,
14, 15
time management technique, 127
Times New Roman font, in
handouts, 93
topical units, 46–47, 67
trainer confidence. *See* instructor
confidence
trainer evaluations. *See* instructor
evaluations
trainer of technology, in course material
development, 148
training. *See* technical training
training materials, managing. *See*
instructional materials
training room configuration, 83–86
transfer, knowledge, 44, 67
transformational artwork, 159, 161
transitions, 214–215, 217
true-or-false questions, 266, 274

U

U-seating configuration, 84, 86, 98
usage final examinations, 313, 320

V

VAK Model of learning styles, 119, 133
valuing stage, in affective domain, 241, 248
VARK Model of learning styles, 119
verbal/auditory learners, 119, 131
verbal information, 122, 133
verbose learners, 187–188
virtual classroom-based training, 30
Virtual Classroom Trainer exam. *See* CTT+
TKO-203 (CCT+ Virtual Classroom
Trainer performance-based exam)
virtual classrooms
managing course materials in,
155–157
selecting media visuals for, 157–159
visual aids
defined, 98
instructing with, 84, 89–92
virtual classroom, 157–159
visual learners, 119
visual/nonverbal learners, 119, 133
visual/verbal learners, 119, 133
visualization, 180, 190
vocalizations, 208–209, 217

W

whiteboard, 156, 161
workbooks, 149–150
workflow process, 154
writer, in course material development, 149

New Online Resources for IT Professionals!

Certification Shows You Know IT—Now Share IT

Join the IT Pro Community to network and engage with professionals from around the world. You can also post your resume on the CompTIA IT Job Board—an employment website designed for CompTIA certified professionals. Highlight your certification status so you'll come up first when employers search for qualified candidates.

Get Involved. Get Smart.
Get on the Path to Success.